by
Cliff Charpentier

Lerner Publications Company • Minneapolis

The author and publisher believe all information regarding NFL player transactions to be accurate up to May 1, 1990, when this book was set to go to press. For subsequent information, please consult the Fantasy Football Newsletter. An order form is at the back of the book.

Cover photo courtesy of Chuck Cook, *The Times-Picayune.*

Composed in Times Roman and Helvie Light
by Just Your Type Graphic Arts Services Inc.,
Minneapolis, Minnesota

Manufactured in the United States of America

International Standard Book Number: 0-8225-9957-0
1 2 3 4 5 6 7 8 9 10 99 98 97 96 94 93 92 91 90

DEDICATIONS AND ACKNOWLEDGMENTS

Thanks again to everyone who helped to make this book.

First to my wife, Lori, and my children—Kelly, Cliff Jr., and Matthew—for their continued support and consideration.

To my sister, Denise, and my partner and very good friend, Tom Kane, who continue to help make this project a lasting success.

To Cheri Smith, who jumped in to help out under emergency circumstances—we couldn't have done it without you.

To Marty Fleischhacker, my nephew, who continues to help us grow.

To those behind the scenes, whom I've come to appreciate in a big way:

Rex Estby   Don Collyard
Mike Kenow   Bill Gehrman
Chris Friberg

To Denise's crew, who always come through for us.

And to all of you readers—thank you for your support and the best of luck to you in the 1990 season.

To anyone I may have missed, thank you.

CONTENTS

CHAPTER 2: Fantasy Football Basics

THE AUTHOR'S 1989 SEASON

IT'S ALL IN HOW YOU MEASURE SUCCESS

Fantasy Football can be a very fun and exciting game or it can just as easily be a frustrating, humbling experience. Each year we franchise owners use our football knowledge to draft a fantasy team. We hope to win. Sure, many teams' success evolves from intense study of the game, but there are many teams that win without study. I believe one of the most frustrating things for a franchise owner—at least for me—to watch is a casually interested owner realizing success.

It's fairly evident that I do extensive research on the game. Like many involved franchise owners, I believe that deep involvement should be rewarded with success. I guess when looking at my regular-season record, now 75–36 (.676) over the past 10 seasons, I should feel satisfied. But I'm not. Although for four years in a row prior to 1989 I made it to the final four in our 16-team league, I have only one Fantasy Bowl Championship to show for it. Two other owners, who really don't have the hard-core attitude toward the game that I do, have two championships apiece to brag about. Their combined regular-season won-lost records of 95–105 (.475) don't compare to mine, but winning two championships sure makes a difference.

Going into the 1989 season, my annual goals—first, to make the playoffs and second, to win my division—had to be set higher. I wanted to win it all, which (as you'll see) may have caused me to make some hasty moves.

DRAFT PREPARATION

Going into the 1989 season, I wasn't really high on any specific teams that I thought would fare well. I didn't have a real positive feeling that the Bengals would duplicate their offensive production of 1988. I wasn't sure what I thought of Gerald Riggs going to Washington.

I did, however, still like the prospect of having Randall Cunningham. I also liked Neal Anderson of the Bears, but I knew I'd have to place very high in the draft order to get him. Beyond my preference for those two, I was open to selecting any player. I also wasn't really set on a nine-point quarterback-wide receiver combo, unlike in many of my previous years. Each round I was going to choose the best player available.

THE DRAFT

Every year, anticipating who is going to get the #1 draft pick or where each team will fall in the first-round draft order is exciting. In our league, the cards are shuffled, cut, and placed face down on a table. A different set of cards is laid out for determining draft order for every other round. The deck labelled with an "A" represents rounds 1 and 2 and generates the most excitement. Who's going to get the ace of spades? As commissioner, I usually wait until the other 15 franchises have selected their cards before picking up the only one left. I slowly squeezed out my card. It wasn't the ace of spades. It was the six of spades—I'd draft 6th out of 16 franchises in the first round. It also meant I'd select 10th in the second round, because we reverse the order every other round.

During our 10-minute recess before the draft, each franchise owner tries to figure out which players will go before he gets a shot at them. Drafting sixth, I anticipated that the likes of Ickey Woods, (coming off a strong rookie season), Neal Anderson, Eric Dickerson, Jerry Rice, Roger Craig, and perhaps either Dan Marino or Randall Cunningham would go before my pick. I toyed with the thought of choosing Gerald Riggs, who had gone to Washington in the offseason, but I was afraid his knees wouldn't hold up. I sat down and got the draft underway. The first player chosen was no surprise: Ickey Woods, Cincinnati Bengals. Following Woods were Eric Dickerson, Neal Anderson, Roger Craig, and Herschel Walker, leading up to my pick.

I was ecstatic. The choice seemed so obvious, so easy. Although I prefer taking a running back in the first round, I felt I had to take the best player available. With little hesitation, I grabbed **Jerry Rice.** The prospect of having a perennial scorer like Rice had me excited already, especially since I had expected him to be gone already.

Now, going into the second round, I knew most of the primary running backs would be gone. Since I had drafted a wide receiver in the first round, I needed to grab the best running back available in the second round. I took **John Stephens** of New England because, although Stephens had scored only four touchdowns as a rookie in 1988, his 1,168 yards rushing indicated that he would be a main weapon for the Patriots and could easily expand his touchdown production.

Following rounds 1 and 2, my draft order went like this:

Round 3:	16th
Round 4:	1st
Round 5:	13th
Round 6:	4th
Round 7:	8th
Round 8:	9th
Round 9:	2nd
Round 10:	15th
Round 11:	7th
Round 12:	10th

On to round #3. Keeping with my best-player-available philosophy, I grabbed **Al Toon** of the New York Jets. I usually draft my running backs before my receivers, but the chance to have two superb wideouts in Rice and Toon swayed me.

After having to wait for the 16th pick in round #3, I enjoyed having the 1st pick of the fourth round. With Toon and Rice as my receivers, and with most high-quality quarterbacks gone, I went for **Ken O'Brien** of the Jets. Even though O'Brien wasn't one of my top choices, the move could pay off if he found Toon 10 times or so.

By round #5, six of the league's top kickers had gone, so I opted for **Kevin Butler** of the Bears. Butler had had success before and he would be kicking for a good team with a fairly easy schedule. In round #6, I knew it was time to select my second running back. The cream of the crop had been skimmed away, and the best player left was **Freeman McNeil** of the Jets. I wasn't comfortable having three starters from one team, but McNeil was the best player available.

My pick in round #7 was a banged-up **Rueben Mayes** of the New Orleans Saints. I could only hope that he would rid himself of injury and reclaim his rookie magic. In round #8, I felt I got a steal in wide receiver **J. T. Smith** of the Phoenix Cardinals. I already had two excellent wide receivers, but I felt Smith would be either great insurance or great bait. Round #9 was time for a gamble on a rookie—**Daryl Johnston** of the Cowboys. A second-round pick out of Syracuse, he had been used for some close-in goal-line touchdowns in the preseason, which made him a good gamble. In the 10th round I reached even further and selected tight end **Darryl Ingram**, another rookie. Ingram had been used considerably by the Vikings in the preseason (mostly because Steve Jordan was holding out), and at times his play had been very impressive.

For my round-#11 selection, I grabbed quarterback **Steve De Berg**, the probable starter for Kansas City, as my backup for O'Brien. As my last draft choice, I took a shot at another rookie, wide receiver **Shawn Collins** of Atlanta. Collins was a highly touted first-round pick who had fared well in the preseason and might pan out.

REGULAR SEASON

With Jerry Rice and Al Toon as a solid nucleus for my team, I planned early on to make a few transactions to solidify my club. Our draft was two weeks before the NFL regular-season opener, so each franchise owner could evaluate his 12-man roster in two more preseason games and make changes. I took advantage of both weeks. In the first week following our draft I dropped rookie tight end **Darryl Ingram** of the Vikings, because veteran Steve Jordan was still a lock for the job. In Ingram's place I picked up veteran tight end **Ron Heller**, who had been acquired by Atlanta in the offseason and had been racking up preseason receptions. Then, in the week before the NFL season opener, I dropped **Rueben Mayes**, who would be forced to miss the season because of injury, and replaced him with **George Adams** of the New York Giants. The reason I added Adams was that Joe Morris had suffered a season-ending injury in the last preseason game, which caused a mad scramble for the Giants' running backs. With O. J. Anderson and rookie Lewis Tillman already gone, I felt Adams was a good early-season gamble.

So, going into the 1989 season opener my roster looked like this:

Jerry Rice	Wide Receiver	San Francisco 49ers
John Stephens	Running Back	New England Patriots
Ken O'Brien	Quarterback	New York Jets
Al Toon	Wide Receiver	New York Jets
Kevin Butler	Kicker	Chicago Bears
Freeman McNeil	Running Back	New York Jets
Rueben Mayes (dropped)	Running Back	New Orleans Saints
J. T. Smith	Wide Receiver	Phoenix Cardinals
Daryl Johnston	Running Back	Dallas Cowboys
Darryl Ingram (dropped)	Tight End	Minnesota Vikings
Steve De Berg	Quarterback	Kansas City Chiefs
Shawn Collins	Wide Receiver	Atlanta Falcons

Preseason Pickups

Ron Heller	Tight End	Atlanta Falcons
George Adams	Running Back	New York Giants

From these 12 players my initial starting lineup was:

QB	O'Brien	NYJ
RB	Stephens	NE
RB	McNeil	NYJ
WR	Toon	NYJ
WR	Rice	SF
TE	Heller	ATL
K	Butler	CHI

My opponent's starting lineup was:

QB	Simms	NYG
RB	Heard	KC
RB	Heyward	NO
WR	Reed	BUF
WR	W. Davis	CHI
TE	Shuler	NYJ
K	T. Zendejas	HOUS

WEEK #1

Just before game time I took advantage of a player move, taking out Al Toon because of an injury and putting in J. T. Smith. Although I didn't like the thought of starting three Jets, I did it anyway because I knew three key defensive players for the Patriots, whom my guys would be playing, would be out.

By the noon kickoff my anticipation and anxiety were high. I was into it. I had a poor history of season openers, but I felt good about this game. The early games started and I had the good fortune to see my opponent's kicker go up against the defensively strong Minnesota Vikings. My hometown Vikes held Tony Zendejas to one point. I loved it.

Meanwhile, for me, Ken O'Brien threw a couple of touchdown passes, and John Stephens ran for a score, as I jumped out 12–1. My kicker, Kevin Butler, booted five points. After my opponent's running back Craig Heyward got on the board with a touchdown, we had a 17–7 score going into the late games.

I added another TD on a Jerry Rice score, which gave me a 23–7 lead going into Monday night, with my opponent having only his quarterback, Phil Simms, remaining. It looked like a lock, since Simms would have to score 17 points to beat me—very unlikely. It didn't happen. Simms threw for two scores, making the final score 23–13 and giving me a 1–0 record.

TRANSACTION NIGHT

I was happy to be 1–0, but I wasn't yet happy with my roster. First, I dropped **George Adams** when it became apparent he wasn't going to fill in for the injured Joe Morris. In Adams's place I picked up **D. J. Dozier** of the Vikings, just to bolster my set of running backs.

Second, I dropped rookie **Daryl Johnston** and picked up another rookie running back, **Bobby Humphrey**. Humphrey was on our fantasy waiver wire and I had been impressed with his early-season showing with the Broncos.

In a rather hasty third transaction, I dropped **D. J. Dozier**, whom I had just picked up, and replaced him with **Darryl Ingram**, whom I had dropped two weeks earlier. The reason—Viking veteran Steve Jordan had been a contract holdout, and Ingram still had a chance to see some action and prove himself.

WEEK #2

Here are the starting lineups for me and my opponent for week #2 (my team is the French Connection):

French Connection			Mediterranean Meatballs		
QB	O'Brien	NYJ	QB	Elway	DEN
RB	Stephens	NE	RB	Allen	LARd
RB	Humphrey	DEN	RB	Bell	LARm
WR	Rice	SF	WR	Duper	MIA
WR	J. T. Smith	PHOE	WR	A. Carter	MINN
TE	Heller	ATL	TE	Jordan	MINN
K	Butler	CHI	K	Anderson	PITT

I opted to start Bobby Humphrey over Freeman McNeil because Humphrey seemed to be winning Denver's main running-back position. And Al Toon remained out, so I left J. T. Smith in.

My opponent had scored 33 points in his season-opening win and had a very formidable lineup. I thought it was solid. Fortunately, he had an off week. Elway threw one touchdown pass, and the only rushing touchdown was by Greg Bell. Kicker Gary Anderson added 4 points for 13 points total.

For me, O'Brien threw for one score, and I got touchdowns out of Humphrey, Jerry Rice, and J. T. Smith. Add 8 from my kicker, Kevin Butler, and I got a 29–13 win and moved to 2–0. Boy, I love this game! (When I win.)

TRADE NIGHT

Although 2–0, I still wasn't content. On trade night, I again dropped tight end **Darryl Ingram** and grabbed running back **Earl Ferrell** off the waiver wire.

WEEK #3

My week #3 opponent came in with a 1–1 record. I was then leading the league with 80 points over two games. Looking at my opponent's lineup (below), I knew I had to score a ton to win.

French Connection			F-Troop		
QB	O'Brien	NYJ	QB	Wilson	MINN
RB	Humphrey	DEN	RB	N. Anderson	CHI
RB	McNeil	NYJ	RB	O.J. Anderson	NYG
WR	Rice	SF	WR	Blades	SEAT
WR	Toon	NYJ	WR	Ellard	LARm
TE	Heller	ATL	TE	Holman	CIN
K	Butler	CHI	K	Biasucci	IND

My only lineup change was Freeman McNeil for John Stephens, who was questionable for the game because of an ankle injury.

In the early games, Alfred Anderson of the Vikings was ruled down at the one-foot line, and on the very next play my opponent's quarterback, Wade Wilson, rushed for a touchdown. These are the times when you mumble to yourself, "This could only happen to me."

In the Bears-Lions game, my opponent had Neal Anderson, and I had Kevin Butler. I got the best of them, as Butler outscored Anderson, 17–6. In the Colts-Falcons game, Dean Biasucci kicked for seven points, while O. J. Anderson added a touchdown to put me behind 25–17 lead going into the late games.

I still had my quarterback-wide receiver combination, Ken O'Brien and Al Toon, along with Freeman McNeil, Bobby Humphrey, and Jerry Rice. My opponent still had Brian Blades and Henry Ellard, along with Rodney Holman on Monday night.

I love this: NBC cut away from the Denver–LA Raiders game because the Broncos were blowing them out. The game they cut to was the Jets-Dolphins. Al Toon had scored once, and then Ken O'Brien threw another touchdown, his third of the day. On top of that, Mr. Reliable, Jerry Rice, added a pair of scores. With both of my opponent's receivers getting shut down, I carried a 44–25 lead into Monday night, with F-Troop having only tight end Rodney Holman left.

Getting four touchdowns out of a tight end isn't impossible, but it is unlikely, and that's what they needed to beat me. Usually when a touchdown play is called back, and then your opponent's player scores on the very next play, it's a bad omen. That's what happened. An Eddie Brown touchdown was called back, and Holman scored on the next play. In fact, Holman scored twice before the half. Uh-oh! Nevertheless, I hung on and won, 44–37, going to 3–0.

TRADE NIGHT

You'd think that, being 3-0, I'd start to be content with my team, but I wasn't. I still felt I was a good running back away from having a good team. It's hard to get a franchise to part with a good running back, though, so my offer would have to be something special.

The only team willing to deal away any perennial scorer was the previous year's champion, *Boyer's Spoilers*. They hadn't drafted well and they knew it. The *Spoilers* had the likes of Barry Sanders, Keith Byars, and Johnny Hector as their backs and they were willing to part with Hector. Although I didn't like adding another New York Jet to my roster, I went for **Johnny Hector**, thinking that he could be my missing piece if he scored 10 or more touchdowns. To get him, I had to give up John Stephens, Freeman McNeil, and J. T. Smith. Bad move? Maybe. None of these players were my starters, though, so I did it.

Besides the three-for-one deal, I also picked up 49er tight end **Brent Jones** and dropped **Ron Heller**. Jones was seeing plenty of passes on a very successful offensive line. I also added kicker **Paul McFadden** of Atlanta, bringing my roster to 12.

WEEK #4

Going into week #4, I had some new names to play with and I did. I started my newly acquired Hector and Brent Jones. I also put Earl Ferrell in for Bobby Humphrey. The week #4 lineups looked like this:

	French Connection			JMD Warriors	
QB	O'Brien	NYJ	QB	Kosar	CLE
RB	Hector	NYJ	RB	Craig	SF
RB	Ferrell	PHOE	RB	Kinnebrew	BUF
WR	Toon	NYJ	WR	Slaughter	CLE
WR	Rice	SF	WR	A. Miller	SD
TE	Jones	SF	TE	Thornton	CHI
K	Butler	CHI	K	Lansford	LARm

I knew that one of my opponent's running backs, Larry Kinnebrew, had been suspended for one game by the Bills, and my opponent wasn't aware of it. I had the advantage of having one more player, but an advantage doesn't always spell a win.

Such was the case this time. After reeling off three consecutive wins and making a blockbuster trade to solidify my team, I bombed out. There was nothing exciting about this game. I tallied only three points by my kicker, Kevin Butler, and the rest of my team shut down. I got beaten handily, 28–3, and was brought back to reality at 3–1. Still, I maintained a one-game lead in my division.

TRADE NIGHT

Okay, time to settle down a bit. I had already done as much player transacting as I normally do in an entire season. The only move I made on this trade night was to drop **John Stephens** and pick up **Steve Walsh** of the Cowboys. Although Stephens had been part of my three-for-one deal the previous week, I couldn't have let him go then without exceeding our league's limit of three transactions per trade night. So Stephens went to *Boyer's Spoilers*, and Walsh replaced him on my roster.

WEEK #5

In this meeting, I faced Tom Kane, my favorite longtime rival and my partner in Fantasy Sports, Inc. Tom was on a roll, with a record of 4–0. The key was his defense (ha-ha)—he had given up only 45 points through his first four games. I hoped to do something about that. Our lineups looked like this:

French Connection			Lodi's Big Daddys		
QB	O'Brien	NYJ	QB	Montana	SF
RB	Hector	NYJ	RB	Byner	WASH
RB	Ferrell	PHOE	RB	Brooks	CIN
WR	Rice	SF	WR	Givins	HOUS
WR	Toon	NYJ	WR	Green	PHOE
TE	Jones	SF	TE	Novacek	PHOE
K	Butler	CHI	K	M. Bahr	CLE

I had another poor offensive showing in this one, as I got touchdowns only out of Earl Ferrell and Mr. Reliable (Jerry Rice). My kicker, Kevin Butler of the Bears, added 5 for a total of 17 points.

Tom got three touchdown passes out of Montana, two touchdowns from James Brooks, one out of Byner, and 4 points from Matt Bahr for an easy 31–17 win.

My record dropped to 3–2, and I really started to wonder about the trades I had made. J. T. Smith took advantage of an injury to teammate Roy Green and scored three times. John Stephens added a touchdown. Meanwhile, Johnny Hector, my great addition, failed to score. This, I started to think, may have been the worst trade blunder of my career.

TRADE NIGHT

On trade night I elected to make one personnel move. I dropped the inconsistent **Steve De Berg** and replaced him on my roster with **Frank Reich**. Reich would be replacing the injured Jim Kelly at quarterback for the Buffalo Bills. Kelly was expected to be out three to four weeks.

WEEK #6

Fed up with the ineffectiveness of my players from the New York Jets, I benched Ken O'Brien and Johnny Hector. As their replacements, I started Reich and Bobby Humphrey of the Broncos. I also replaced the injured Al Toon with rookie Shawn Collins of Atlanta. The starting lineups looked like this:

French Connection			Treanor's Electric Co.		
QB	Reich	BUF	QB	Tomczak	CHI
RB	Humphrey	DEN	RB	Dickerson	IND
RB	Ferrell	PHOE	RB	Pinkett	HOUS
WR	Rice	SF	WR	Taylor	SF
WR	Collins	ATL	WR	L. Hill	NO
TE	Jones	SF	TE	Jackson	PHIL
K	Butler	CHI	K	Cofer	SF

In the early games, the *Electric Co.* got three touchdown passes out of Tomczak and seven points from their kicker, Mike Cofer. I got touchdowns from both Jerry Rice and Brent Jones, while Kevin Butler added four extra points. The score was 16–16 after the early games.

Then I had to go visit my in-laws for dinner. On the way, I heard the Broncos stop Dickerson three times inside the five, once on fourth down. My opponent got a touchdown out of Lonzell Hill, and I countered with a score of my own by Bobby Humphrey. This latest action re-tied the score, this time at 22. It also assured me of the win, because I was the home team and my first tie breaker, Paul McFadden, had tallied some scores. It didn't go that far, though, because I still had Frank Reich on Monday night. Reich threw for two scores, giving me a 28–22 win and a 4–2 record, along with a share of the division lead with *F-Troop*.

TRADE NIGHT

This was the transaction-deadline night. After this night, the 12 players on each roster were permanent.

I made only one move—I dropped **Paul McFadden** and picked up **Ron Johnson** of the Philadelphia Eagles. Johnson would be the starter in Philadelphia, replacing the injured Mike Quick, who was out for the season.

WEEK #7

For this week's game I had a couple of injuries to keep an eye on. Running back Bobby Humphrey was questionable with bruised ribs, while wide receiver Shawn Collins had had a groin injury. I decided not to take any chances. I replaced Humphrey with Johnny Hector and Collins with Ron Johnson. The starting lineups looked like this:

	French Connection			Armchair Sleepers	
QB	Reich	BUF	QB	Everett	LARm
RB	Ferrell	PHOE	RB	Vick	NYJ
RB	Hector	NYJ	RB	Clack	DALL
WR	Rice	SF	WR	Gault	LARd
WR	Johnson	PHIL	WR	Anderson	LARm
TE	Jones	SF	TE	Johnson	LARm
K	Butler	CHI	K	Karlis	MINN

The team I was up against was not only 2–4 but also the league's lowest-scoring team. Through six games they had scored only 85 points—only 14.1 points per game. These are the teams that scare me. I was ready to explode!

The early games started out interestingly enough. The *Sleepers* got touchdowns out of both Daryl Clack and Willie Gault, while their kicker, Rich Karlis, added 8.

For me, quarterback Frank Reich came through with three touchdown passes, and Earl Ferrell rushed for three scores. The score was 27–20 after the early games.

My opponent still had his guns, though—the passing combo of Jim Everett and either Flipper Anderson or Damone Johnson. I still had Jerry Rice and Brent Jones, and Old Reliable Mr. Rice got me a pair of touchdowns and a 39–20 lead. Then the unthinkable happened. Jim Everett threw for three touchdowns, and when I found out the last two went to Damone Johnson I could have thrown up. I mean, I was sick! This propelled my opponent to a 41–39 lead. But not to panic. I still had my kicker, Kevin Butler, on Monday night. I needed four points to win because my opponent had the tie breaker already won. Let's see . . . just four points. That's a field goal and an extra point or four extra points.

To make what could be a really long story short, I lost. The Bears were held in check all night by the Cleveland Browns' defense. Butler managed only one extra point, and I lost 41–40. Who would have thunk it? How does a team averaging 14 points a game turn that around and score 41? How does a kicker score only one point? Besides those little niceties, do you want to know what really fried me? I had benched Bobby Humphrey because of his sore ribs, and Humphrey had scored. Had I played him, I would have won 46–41. But I didn't. I now fell to 4–3 but so did the team I was tied with. They had an insurmountable point lead on me, however, which is our league's first tie breaker.

TRANSACTION NIGHT

With our transaction deadline passed, we entered the first week of our league's player-addition draft. Each team is allowed to add two players to its roster, one of whom has to be added this week, the first week after the trade deadline. The other can be added any week prior to the end of our 12-week regular season.

I elected to make one of my player additions. I grabbed **Doug Williams**, quarterback of the Washington Redskins, who was just being activated from an early-season injury. I was thinking that I wouldn't have Frank Reich to use much longer, expecting Jim Kelly to return, so Williams's addition would be timely.

WEEK #8

After scoring 40 points the previous week, I elected to make only one lineup change, one that I wish I had made the previous week. I inserted Bobby Humphrey for Johnny Hector. The starting lineups then looked like this:

French Connection			The Jayhawks		
QB	Reich	BUF	QB	Marino	MIA
RB	Ferrell	PHOE	RB	Highsmith	HOUS
RB	Humphrey	DEN	RB	Ball	CIN
WR	Rice	SF	WR	Johnson	DEN
WR	Johnson	PHIL	WR	Martin	DALL
TE	Jones	SF	TE	Awalt	PHOE
K	Butler	CHI	K	Lowery	KC

Going into this game, I figured the key was Dan Marino. I always fear playing Marino. Fortunately, the Dolphins were playing the very tough Buffalo defense. Marino was held to just one touchdown pass. In fact, that may have been the difference. The *Jayhawks* also got touchdowns out of Eric Ball and Vance Johnson. Their kicker, Nick Lowery, added 5 points, to give the *Jayhawks* a total of 20.

For me, Frank Reich threw for a score, while my two 49ers, Jerry Rice and Brent Jones, chipped in with touchdowns. My kicker, Kevin Butler, added 8 very important points for a 23–20 victory.

This was great! Neither team had any players going on Monday night, so I had already locked in the win. This close victory upped my record to 5–3, keeping me tied for the division lead.

TRADE NIGHT

Knowing that I had only one player addition left, I decided to hold onto it, seeing no immediate need to make a move.

Going into this game, I thought things were beginning to play into my hands. Frank Reich was relinquishing his quarterbacking duties to Jim Kelly, but Doug Williams, whom I had picked up in the player-addition draft, was slated to start against the lowly Cowboys on Sunday night. I inserted Williams. The matchup looked like this:

	French Connection			S & M Boys	
QB	Williams	WASH	QB	Hebert	NO
RB	Ferrell	PHOE	RB	Hilliard	NO
RB	Humphrey	DEN	RB	Rozier	HOUS
WR	Rice	SF	WR	Carrier	TB
WR	Johnson	PHIL	WR	Turner	NYG
TE	Jones	SF	TE	Warren	WASH
K	Butler	CHI	K	Igwebuike	TB

Regardless of Sunday's outcome, both teams knew the game would be decided in Monday night's game, which pitted San Francisco against New Orleans. This meant my Jerry Rice and Brent Jones against their Bobby Hebert and Dalton Hilliard. So, the question for Sunday was, "Who would have what kind of lead going into Monday night?"

In Sunday's day games, the *S & M Boys* jumped ahead with a touchdown out of Mike Rozier and seven points from their kicker, Donald Igwebuike. In the early Sunday games I got seven points out of Kevin Butler and then added two touchdowns by Bobby Humphrey in the late games, giving me a 19–13 lead going into Sunday night.

This left me with Doug Williams on Sunday night and two players on Monday night, against their two players Monday night. With a six-point lead, I liked my advantage. That was until a very rusty Doug Williams failed to generate much offense even against the Cowboys. With Williams shut down, my lead stayed at six, with two players for each of us playing on Monday night. The six-point difference was also significant: My opponent was one or two touchdown passes away from not only tying but winning. They were the home team and their first reserve had already scored, giving them the victory in the event of a tie.

On Monday, I tried to avoid thinking about the game, but I thought about it almost constantly. I knew I needed the win to keep pace for the divisional lead with *F-Troop*, who had already locked in a very sleazy 10–9 victory. (Where's the justice? I had just lost 41–40 a short two weeks earlier, and then they win 10–9!)

By game time, my body was going through a series of anxiety attacks. Fortunately, it was only a short time into the game when Jerry Rice scored to put me up by 12. But the *S&Mers* countered with a Hilliard touchdown to draw them back within six. Thank God for Mr. Reliable, as Rice scored again before the half to put my lead back to 12. In the second half I felt fairly comfortable with my 12-point lead, but not with the fact that, although I had to go to the bathroom, I refused to leave the room for fear I might ruin my luck. No, I'm not superstitious. Twice in the third quarter New Orleans crossed into 49er territory but had to settle for field goals. I hung on for a 31–19 victory and a continued share of the division lead at 6–3.

TRADE NIGHT

I decided again to hold onto my second player-addition move.

WEEK #10

It was time to head back within my division for the final three regular-season games. At the season's outset, I had swept the first three divisional games. I didn't think that would happen again this time around.

I was up against the *P D Destroyers*, whom I had slipped by, 23–13, to open the season. The *Destroyers*, at 4–5, were a pretty good team. Here were the matchups:

	French Connection			P D Destroyers	
QB	Williams	WASH	QB	Simms	NYG
RB	Humphrey	DEN	RB	Metcalf	CLE
RB	Ferrell	PHOE	RB	Worley	PITT
WR	Rice	SF	WR	Clayton	MIA
WR	Johnson	PHIL	WR	Reed	BUF
TE	Jones	SF	TE	Dressel	NYJ
K	Butler	CHI	K	T. Zendejas	HOUS

I was afraid of my opponent's receivers, Mark Clayton and Andre Reed, while running back Eric Metcalf could score from anywhere. There would be only one Monday-night player, the *Destroyers'* kicker, Tony Zendejas from the Houston Oilers. I would need a big lead going into Monday night.

In Sunday's early games, the *Destroyers* jumped out with two touchdowns from Andre Reed and another from Mark Clayton for an early 18–8 lead, as I got 8 points out of my kicker, Kevin Butler. My other early-game players, Doug Williams, Bobby Humphrey, and Ron Johnson, got shut down. This left me with Earl Ferrell, Jerry Rice, and Brent Jones, while the *Destroyers* still had Phil Simms and Eric Metcalf, along with Zendejas on Monday night.

Of these late Sunday players, only Mr. Reliable scored. In fact, Jerry Rice scored twice. This propelled me to a very close 20–18 lead, with the *Destroyers* looking forward to having their kicker on Monday night.

My first thought was of a few weeks back, when I needed four points out of my kicker on Monday night, and he got only one. Well, the *Destroyers* needed only three to beat me, and I knew it was highly unlikely that I would pull this one off.

I'm one of those diehard hopefuls. If there's a chance, I believe. By halftime I was really believing, as Cincinnati had held Zendejas to only one point. Could I really pull this off?

My answer came soon and hard in the second half. Zendejas exploded for the *Destroyers,* accounting for a total of 14 points. The final score ended up 32–20, but that wasn't the worst of it. *F-Troop,* the team I was tied with, needed a touchdown from their tight end, Rodney Holman, on Monday night to win. Holman scored in the second half Monday night, capping off a terrible night. My loss and their win put me a game back, with two games to go.

TRADE NIGHT

Again I elected to hold onto my one player-addition move, but this meant I would have to use it the next week, before our league's last regular-season game.

WEEK #11

This week's matchup was against the *Meatballs,* a team I had beaten 29–13 in week #2. The *Meatballs,* at 2–8, looked on paper like they had a much better team than their record indicated. Our lineups looked like this:

French Connection			Mediterranean Meatballs		
QB	O'Brien	NYJ	QB	Elway	DEN
RB	Humphrey	DEN	RB	Bell	LARm
RB	Ferrell	PHOE	RB	Perryman	NE
WR	Rice	SF	WR	Duper	MIA
WR	R. Johnson	PHIL	WR	A. Carter	MINN
TE	Jones	SF	TE	Jordan	MINN
K	Butler	CHI	K	Anderson	PITT

I had made my one player change just prior to kickoff on Sunday, inserting Ken O'Brien for Doug Williams. Williams had been less than effective for the Redskins and was losing his starting job back to Mark Rypien.

In the *Meatballs'* lineup, with players like Elway, Bell, Duper, Carter, and Jordan, there was the potential for a big score. That is not how things turned out, however. In fact, the only points the *Meatballs* were able to muster before the Monday-night game were kicker Gary Anderson's eight points. They failed to get any touchdowns from their six-point players, leaving only quarterback John Elway for Monday night.

I didn't fare much better. I did manage one touchdown from Jerry Rice in Sunday's late games. Combined with 7 points from Kevin Butler, that gave me a 13–8 lead going into Sunday night's game. In that contest I had my quarterback Ken O'Brien. But O'Brien failed to score, so my 13–8 lead was carried into Monday night, when the *Meatballs* would have John Elway and I would have Bobby Humphrey.

Monday night was bizarre. You know how sometimes when you're up against a player going into Monday night and you hope he might turn an ankle on the way to the stadium or catch a stomach virus—nothing serious, just something to keep him out of the game? It happened! I tuned in Frank, Al, and Dan, and they started talking about Elway being detained in the locker room because of a stomach virus. Gary Kubiak would start. "WHAT?" That's right. "Kubiak will start," said one of my buddies who had called, knowing I was up against Elway. Usually I am aware of such happenings but I had just learned about this. So that was it. The game was over. Bobby Humphrey failed to score but Elway had failed to play and I won 13–8. Sleazy, but I'll take it.

That was the good news. My record moved to 7–4. *F-Troop,* the division leader, also won, going to 8–3. Though I played them the next week in the regular-season finale and could tie them if I won, they had built a 55-point lead. With that kind of lead it was virtually impossible to think I could overtake them to win the division. Too bad. All season, *F-Troop*'s owners and I had said that the divisional title would come down to the last game. And it had, except *F-Troop* had almost assured themselves of the divisional title because of their point lead.

TRADE NIGHT

This marked the last transaction night before the end of the regular season. Any team still wanting to make their second player-addition move would have to do it tonight. With my second and last move, I grabbed **Buford Jordan** of the New Orleans Saints. Jordan was seeing plenty of action at fullback for the Saints and had scored two touchdowns the previous week.

WEEK #12

It was a bit disappointing going into this game, knowing I had only a remote chance of winning the division. If I won, I would have beaten *F-Troop* twice, and though we would have identical records, they would more than likely be divisional champs. Their 55-point lead was just too much to overcome. You'd think I'd be kicking myself for being commissioner and making most-points-scored the first tie breaker over head-to-head matchups. But I wasn't. I still believed that *F-Troop,* by scoring more points over 12 games, had had a better season than I. I was just lucky to have been able to come up with big games against them.

All this was running through my mind, and I had not even played the game yet. Here are the starting lineups:

	French Connection			F-Troop	
QB	O'Brien	NYJ	QB	Trudeau	IND
RB	Humphrey	DEN	RB	O.J. Anderson	NJG
RB	Jordan	NO	RB	N. Anderson	CHI
WR	Rice	SF	WR	Blades	SEAT
WR	Toon	NYJ	WR	Ellard	LARm
TE	Jones	SF	TE	Holman	CIN
K	Butler	CHI	K	Breech	CIN

By game time, knowing I had little chance to win the division, I turned my attention to winning to extend my overall regular-season winning dominance. Over 10 years my regular-season record was by far tops in our league. With *F-Troop* being one of the teams near the top with me, I found pleasure in extending my overall lead.

Going into this contest, I was happy to have Al Toon return to my lineup. Toon had been out for weeks with two sprained ankles. I also elected to start my newly acquired Buford Jordan, who was coming off that two-touchdown performance from the week before.

With little chance of winning the division I did not keep as close an eye on the games as I normally do. I was actually visible to my wife and kids. Why not? There was nothing to be decided. By half-watching and listening, I gathered that I was beating *F-Troop* by a decent margin, 17–4 going into Monday night. On Sunday, Ken O'Brien and Al Toon had teamed up for a nine-point play, while Bobby Humphrey added a score and Kevin Butler added two more points. For *F-Troop,* a touchdown pass out of Jack Trudeau and a single extra point from Jim Breech accounted for their scoring.

This left me with Jerry Rice and Brent Jones, while *F-Troop* had O. J. Anderson, all in the San Francisco–New York Giants Monday-night matchup. I ended up dominating the night, as both Rice and Jones scored for me, while Anderson accounted for only one score. This made the final outcome 29–10, giving each team an 8–4 record. But again *F-Troop* won the division, based on their having scored 36 more points. What this really meant was that *F-Troop,* by winning the division, had a bye the next week, while I would have to play an extra playoff game starting next week. At least I had made the playoffs and fared well with an 8–4 record.

PLAYOFFS

TRANSACTION NIGHT

At the outset of the playoffs, each franchise making the playoffs is allowed to make one more roster addition. This is to help ensure that each team can field a full lineup each remaining week. Most teams take this opportunity to pick up a good backup in the event of injury. I picked up Pat Ryan of the New York Jets. Ryan is Ken O'Brien's backup, and with O'Brien's shaky status, Ryan would provide a sort of security.

PLAYOFF WEEK #1

According to our league guidelines, each of the four divisional winners is awarded a bye the first week. The second- and third-place teams then match up in wild-card games. (The fourth-place teams from each division are eliminated.) This meant I would be playing the third-place *P D Destroyers,* a team that I had split with during the season. Our lineups looked like this:

French Connection			P D Destroyers		
QB	O'Brien	NYJ	QB	Simms	NYG
RB	Humphrey	DEN	RB	Metcalf	CLE
RB	Hector	NYJ	RB	Worley	PITT
WR	Rice	SF	WR	Clayton	MIA
WR	Toon	NYJ	WR	Reed	BUF
TE	Jones	SF	TE	Dressel	NYJ
K	Butler	CHI	K	T. Zendejas	HOUS

I was now wondering if (and hoping that) the Jets would put together a couple of good games. They had started scoring since Toon had returned healthy. In fact, Johnny Hector had scored twice the previous week. I was also hoping my blockbuster trade for Hector would finally pay off.

The game started off well for me with an early touchdown by Johnny Hector. The *Destroyers'* quarterback, Phil Simms, was held to only one touchdown pass and his kicker Tony Zendejas to only three points. My kicker, Kevin Butler, kicked for 4 points, giving me a 10–6 lead. But this was to turn into a defensive struggle. I was delighted to see his Eric Metcalf and Tim Worley held scoreless. What hurt me was that my big gun, Jerry Rice, was also held scoreless, as were Al Toon and Brent Jones. So that was it. I held a slim four-point lead, but he still had Mark Clayton and Andre Reed. A little later that afternoon I learned that Clayton had scored, so I then assumed I had lost 12–10. In a replay late that night, though, Johnny Hector's touchdown looked very close to a shuffle pass from Ken O'Brien.

When I got up Monday morning I quickly opened the paper to the box scores, and sure enough, it was officially ruled a pass. This meant Ken O'Brien was credited with three points and gave me a sleazy one-point lead. Now, normally I don't call my opponents to harass them, but I called Pat, the owner of the *Destroyers,* to ask him if he had had time to read the paper yet. He just started chuckling. You see, Pat had welcomed the fun of calling to harass me about his win. And now it was my chance to harass him. I knew he still had Andre Reed left on Monday night, but Reed had to score to beat me.

All day I played with the possibilities of Reed scoring or not scoring. As game time approached, I was very anxious. I decided it was best not to watch the game, choosing to go help my brother-in-law do some sheet-rocking. I arrived at his house before the game, and he asked me if I wanted to listen to the game on the radio. I promptly said, "No!" Upstairs though, I could hear his son watching the game. I could hear about every third play. Finally, he said we should just turn it on, so he dialed it up on his radio. The game was midway through the first quarter and Reed hadn't scored yet. In fact, the Seahawks seemed to be playing inspired football.

Going into the second quarter the Seahawks continued to play well and I started to believe I had a chance. That was until I heard something like "Reed makes the catch over the middle, he gets hit at the 50 [Go down!], but breaks through, he's to the 40, to the 30, they're not going to catch him. Touchdown, Buffalo." OK, come on, there's a flag or something, right? Nope! Reed scores, I lose, my season's over, just like that! Funny; that's the only touchdown the Bills scored that night. This is a funny game, a game where so much is determined by luck. But that's what keeps it interesting. Speaking of interesting, all four of our second-place teams lost to the third-place teams in the first round of our playoffs. Funny game, all right.

ON TO NEXT SEASON

So it's on to next year. I don't feel too bad, though. Four years in a row prior to this season, I had made it to our final four. Sooner or later luck will go against you. Despite probably too many hasty moves, I still managed an 8–4 record, thus keeping intact my margin as the all-time regular-season winningest coach. Over the decade of the 80s, I had posted a record of 75–36 with a winning percentage of .676. Here's how that stood up amongst the rest of our 16-member league (with teams having played five or more seasons):

TWIN CITY METRO FANTASY FOOTBALL LEAGUE
(Career Overall Standings)

NAME	WON	LOST	TIE	PCT.
1. French Connection	75	36	0	.676
2. Lodi's Big Daddys	52	35	0	.598
3. F-Troop	64	47	0	.577
4. JMD Warriors	51	41	0	.554
5. D C Express	30	25	1	.545
6. Boyer's Spoilers	52	49	0	.515
7. Costra Nostra	57	54	0	.514
8. Deciding Factor	56	55	0	.505
9. S & M Boys	28	28	0	.500
10. The Bogarts	28	28	0	.500
11. Farrell's Untouchables	46	53	0	.465
12. Treanor's Electric Co.	43	56	1	.434
13. Armchair Sleepers	46	64	1	.419
14. Mediterranean Meatballs	36	51	0	.414
15. The Jayhawks	45	56	0	.405
16. P D Destroyers	36	45	0	.356

Again, some bragging. Although I've had only one Fantasy Bowl Championship, I've had four final-four performances to be proud of. I guess it boils down to how you measure success. I would have liked a second Fantasy Bowl Championship, but my yearly consistency, proven by my regular-season mark, has demonstrated my success. If I experience near the same success in the 1990s, I will be very content.

PLAYOFF DREAM TEAM

If you read this section in last year's digest, you're well aware of my obsession with extending my Fantasy Football pleasure into the playoffs. My neighbor Mike Kenow and I draft Playoff Dream Teams. The two of us sit down the week before the playoffs begin and, from the 10 playoff teams, draft fantasy teams to pit against each other. The teams are composed of the following:

> 2 Quarterbacks
> 4 Running Backs
> 4 Wide Receivers
> 2 Tight Ends
> 2 Kickers

The scoring is done as during the regular season, six points for rushing or receiving touchdowns and three for passing touchdowns. Kickers are awarded three points for field goals and one for extra points. The strategy, you'll learn, is a little different. As the playoffs continue and the teams drop out, so do our fantasy players who are on those teams. So, pick players from teams that will go furthest in the playoffs.

In last year's contest, Mike had beaten me on the strength of six Jerry Rice touchdowns. This brought our series record to 2–1 in my favor. With Mike now in my regular-season league, things were a little more interesting this year. We had tried to find Mike a franchise opening in our league for three years, but it wasn't until this year that a spot opened up for him. Mike fared well with a league-leading 9–3 regular-season record and third place. I had to keep pressing the point that it's winning over a long period of time that proves fantasy brilliance. So with my decent 8–4 record, I wanted some redemption. Who would own the neighborhood bragging rights?

I won the coin toss and promptly grabbed Jerry Rice as the #1 pick. Mike countered with Buffalo's Thurman Thomas, which I thought was a little early for Thomas. I came right back, selecting Joe Montana to give me a very potent nine-point combination. Mike came back and picked John Taylor of the 49ers to prevent me from monopolizing the entire 49er passing attack. I later grabbed 49er tight end Brent Jones and running back Roger Craig, while Mike snatched up kicker Mike Cofer. Guess which team we both felt would be in the Super Bowl. Following the rest of our picks, our rosters looked like this:

Cliff			Mike		
QB	Montana	SF	QB	Elway	DEN
QB	Everett	LARm	QB	Kelly	BUF
RB	O.J. Anderson	NYG	RB	Thomas	BUF
RB	Craig	SF	RB	Humphrey	DEN
RB	Metcalf	CLE	RB	Bell	LARm
RB	Walker	MINN	RB	Mack	CLE
WR	Rice	SF	WR	Taylor	SF
WR	A. Carter	MINN	WR	C. Carter	PHIL
WR	Ellard	LARm	WR	Slaughter	CLE
WR	Reed	BUF	WR	Hill	HOUS
TE	Jones	SF	TE	Johnson	LARm
TE	Jackson	PHIL	TE	Jordan	MINN
K	Karlis	MINN	K	Cofer	SF
K	Treadwell	DEN	K	T. Zendejas	HOUS

SCORING BREAKDOWN

(X) Did not participate   (-) Indicates player's team eliminated from playoffs

Cliff		Wild Card Wk #1	Wk #2	Wk #3	Super Bowl Wk #4	TOTAL
QB Montana	(SF)	X	12	6	15	33
QB Everett	(LARm)	6	6	0	-	12
RB O.J. Anderson	(NYG)	X	6	-	-	6
RB Craig	(SF)	X	6	6	6	18
RB Metcalf	(CLE)	X	6	0	-	6
RB Walker	(MINN)	X	0	-	-	0
WR Rice	(SF)	X	12	0	18	30
WR A. Carter	(MINN)	X	0	-	-	0
WR Ellard	(LARm)	6	0	0	-	6
WR Reed	(BUF)	X	6	-	-	6
TE Jones	(SF)	X	6	6	6	18
TE Jackson	(PHIL)	0	-	-	-	0
K Karlis	(MINN)	X	7	-	-	7
K Treadwell	(DEN)	X	6	13	4	23
		12	73	31	49	165

Mike		Wild Card Wk #1	Wk #2	Wk #3	Super Bowl Wk #4	TOTAL
QB Elway	(DEN)	X	3	9	6	18
QB Kelly	(BUF)	X	12	-	-	12
RB Thomas	(BUF)	X	12	-	-	12
RB Humphrey	(DEN)	X	0	0	0	0
RB Bell	(LARm)	6	0	0	-	6
RB Mack	(CLE)	X	0	0	-	0
WR Taylor	(SF)	X	6	6	6	18
WR C. Carter	(PHIL)	0	-	-	-	0
WR Slaughter	(CLE)	X	12	0	-	12
WR Hill	(HOUS)	0	-	-	-	0
TE Johnson	(LARm)	6	0	0	-	6
TE Jordan	(MINN)	X	0	-	-	0
K Cofer	(SF)	X	5	12	7	24
K T. Zendejas	(HOUS)	11	-	-	-	11
		23	50	27	19	119

As you can see by the scoring breakdown, Mike hasn't stuck his head outside his house since Super Bowl Sunday. I really tried not to rub it in—not too bad, anyway. But, with a 16-point lead going into the Super Bowl game and seeing my Montana-Rice combo score first and then Montana find Brent Jones shortly thereafter, I was tempted to call. Still, being the sportsman that I am, I waited until after the game and called to ask Mike if he had watched the game. He had a few choice sentences in reply. Beating him by such a big margin was all it was cracked up to be. I had neighborhood bragging rights for the year. The series went to 3–1 in my favor and Mike has to live with that for one entire year. I wonder how he's going to feel when it goes to 4–1. Mike? (He's going to hate reading this.)

Is there someone out there with whom you'd enjoy a little competitive one-on-one (fantasy) dream-team football? Try it, you'll like it. (If you win!)

CHAPTER 1

PLANNING YOUR 1990 FANTASY FOOTBALL DRAFT

I
INITIAL CONSIDERATIONS

How did your 1989 season go? Were you a Fantasy Football success? Did your preseason hunches pan out? If so, you probably latched onto the likes of Dalton Hilliard, Sterling Sharpe, or Don Majkowski. These three were probably not at the top of most preseason fantasy draft lists in 1989—but will be this year.

Did you have the misfortune to draft someone like Joe Morris, Mike Quick, Ickey Woods, or Gary Anderson? If so, you were in trouble early on. Morris, Quick, and Woods were lost for the season with injuries, while Gary Anderson of the Chargers held out the entire season over contract matters. Losing a player of this caliber can really set a fantasy team back. It takes some tough maneuvering to recover from the loss of a first-round choice like one of these, but good fantasy owners can meet the challenge.

Of the 1989 rookies, did you have the foresight to grab Barry Sanders of the Detroit Lions? Sanders had plenty of promise, but many felt that he wouldn't be a productive fantasy player, especially in his first season, because he was going to play for the hapless Detroit Lions. He proved them wrong. Eric Metcalf of Cleveland also fared well in his rookie campaign. One of the biggest surprises was seventh-round selection Marion Butts of the San Diego Chargers. Butts stepped in for contract holdout Gary Anderson and rushed for nine scores. Another good rookie in 1989 was Bobby Humphrey, a supplemental draft pick of the Denver Broncos. Humphrey rushed for over 1,100 yards and scored eight touchdowns. Having any one of these rookies could easily have made your 1989 season a success.

Besides surprise players, 1989 also had predictable fantasy producers. Jerry Rice put together another 17-touchdown season. Neal Anderson and Greg Bell produced big rushing stats and 15 touchdowns apiece. Quarterbacks Joe Montana, Jim Everett, Jim Kelly, and Dan Marino all produced seasons of 25-plus touchdowns.

Why don't all of our preseason picks pan out? An injury may be less serious than those that ended the season for Joe Morris, Mike Quick, and Ickey Woods, but it can nonetheless keep a player out of the lineup for weeks. Players like Anthony Carter, Eric Dickerson, J. T. Smith, and many others were slowed by injuries that greatly affected their play and stats.

Remember, too, that the replacement for an injured player usually benefits statistically. This can be misleading when you examine the stats to rate players for the next season. Be sure to keep this in mind. The injury to Ickey Woods certainly benefited running mate James Brooks statistically. The injury to Joe Morris boosted the year-end stats of O. J. Anderson. How will the healthy return of these players affect statistics in 1990?

Another aspect to consider when looking at 1989 is which teams and players may be on the upswing and which may be on the downswing. The Green Bay Packers are definitely on the upswing. Led by quarterback Don Majkowski and wide receiver Sterling Sharpe, the Pack has a bright future. Other teams that may be making a move for the better are the Detroit Lions led by Barry Sanders and the Kansas City Chiefs led by Christian Okoye and a strong defense. And a young, improving Pittsburgh Steeler team looks to be on the upswing. On the downswing are the Chicago Bears, who need to regroup quickly. The Dallas Cowboys still have to look years into the future to see anything like a winning season. The New England Patriots are in dire need of a good young signal-caller. The Phoenix Cardinals also need a quarterback, and their entire cast is getting on in years.

All of these factors account for some interesting changes in the rankings of the top players from year to year. To illustrate, let's compare 1988's leaders to 1989's at each position and for both the Basic and Performance Point scoring methods. Because of ties in fantasy-point totals, some categories below include more than 10 players.

BASIC SCORING METHOD—RUNNING BACKS

1988

NAME	TEAM	TDs	FANTASY POINTS
1. G. Bell	LARm	18	108
2. Woods	CIN	15	90
3. Dickerson	IND	15	90
4. Riddick	BUF	14	84
5. Brooks	CIN	14	84
6. N. Anderson	CHI	12	72
7. Warner	SEAT	12	72
8. Hampton	MIA	12	72
9. Rozier	HOUS	11	66
10. Craig	SF	10	60

1989

NAME	TEAM	TDs	FANTASY POINTS
1. Hilliard	NO	18	108
2. N. Anderson	CHI	15	90
3. Bell	LARm	15	90
4. Sanders	DET	14	84
5. O.J. Anderson	NYG	14	84
6. Thomas	BUF	12	72
7. Okoye	KC	12	72
8. Metcalf	CLE	10	60
9. Walker	MINN	10	60
10. Brooks	CIN	9	54

BASIC SCORING METHOD—WIDE RECEIVERS

1988

NAME	TEAM	TDs	FANTASY POINTS
1. Clayton	MIA	14	84
2. Sanders	WASH	12	72
3. Dr. Hill	HOUS	10	60
4. Ellard	LARm	10	60
5. Rice	SF	10	60
6. E. Brown	CIN	9	54
7. B. Hill	TB	9	54
8. Langhorne	CLE	8	48
9. Paige	KC	8	48
10. Blades	SEAT	8	48

1989

NAME	TEAM	TDs	FANTASY POINTS
1. Rice	SF	17	102
2. Sharpe	GB	13	78
3. C. Carter	PHIL	11	66
4. Miller	SD	11	66
5. Taylor	SF	10	60
6. Reed	BUF	9	54
7. Fernandez	LARd	9	54
8. Clayton	MIA	9	54
9. Carrier	TB	9	54
10. G. Clark	WASH	9	54

BASIC SCORING METHOD—TIGHT ENDS

1988

NAME	TEAM	TDs	FANTASY POINTS
1. Johnson	LARm	6	36
2. Jackson	PHIL	6	36
3. Jordan	MINN	5	30
4. Shuler	NYJ	5	30
5. Kay	DEN	4	24
6. Bavaro	NYG	4	24
7. Awalt	PHOE	4	24
8. Novacek	PHOE	4	24
9. West	GB	3	18
10. Holohan	LARm	3	18

1989

NAME	TEAM	TDs	FANTASY POINTS
1. Holman	CIN	9	54
2. West	GB	5	30
3. Johnson	LARm	5	30
4. Brenner	NO	4	24
5. Jones	SF	4	24
6. Wilkins	ATL	3	18
7. Thornton	CHI	3	18
8. Edmunds	MIA	3	18
9. Jordan	MINN	3	18
10. Bavaro	NYG	3	18

BASIC SCORING METHOD—QUARTERBACKS

1988

NAME	TEAM	PS TDs	RSH TDs	FANTASY POINTS
1. Cunningham	PHIL	24	6	96
2. Everett	LARm	31	0	93
3. Esiason	CIN	28	1	90
4. Marino	MIA	28	0	84
5. Moon	HOUS	17	5	81
6. Montana	SF	18	3	72
7. Brister	PITT	11	6	69
8. Lomax	PHOE	20	1	66
9. Pelluer	DALL	17	2	63
10. Simms	NYG	21	0	63

1989

NAME	TEAM	PS TDs	RSH TDs	FANTASY POINTS
1. Majkowski	GB	27	5	111
2. Montana	SF	26	3	96
3. Moon	HOUS	23	4	93
4. Everett	LARm	29	1	93
5. Kelly	BUF	25	2	87
6. Marino	MIA	25	2	87
7. Cunningham	PHIL	21	4	87
8. Esiason	CIN	28	0	84
9. Elway	DEN	18	3	72
10. Rypien	WASH	22	1	72

BASIC & PERFORMANCE POINT METHODS—KICKERS

1988

NAME	TEAM	FANTASY POINTS
1. Norwood	BUF	129
2. Cofer	SF	121
3. Anderson	PITT	118
4. Lansford	LARm	117
5. T. Zendejas	HOUS	114
6. Biasucci	IND	114
7. Leahy	NYJ	112
8. Andersen	NO	110
9. Nelson	MINN	108
10. Karlis	DEN	105

1989

NAME	TEAM	FANTASY POINTS
1. Cofer	SF	136
2. Lohmiller	WASH	128
3. Treadwell	DEN	120
4. Lansford	LARm	120
5. Karlis	MINN	120
6. Norwood	BUF	115
7. T. Zendejas	HOUS	115
8. Jacke	GB	108
9. Lowery	KC	106
10. Andersen	NO	104

PERFORMANCE POINT METHOD—RUNNING BACKS

1988

NAME	TEAM	YARDS	FANTASY POINTS
1. Dickerson	IND	2,036	189
2. Craig	SF	2,036	189
3. Walker	DALL	2,019	188
4. Settle	ATL	1,594	145
5. J.L. Williams	SEAT	1,528	140
6. N. Anderson	CHI	1,477	135
7. G. Bell	LARm	1,336	124
8. G. Anderson	SD	1,301	121
9. Stephens	NE	1,266	118
10. Woods	CIN	1,265	114

1989

NAME	TEAM	YARDS	FANTASY POINTS
1. Thomas	BUF	1,913	178
2. Hilliard	NO	1,776	165
3. B. Sanders	DET	1,752	163
4. N. Anderson	CHI	1,709	157
5. Dickerson	IND	1,522	143
6. Okoye	KC	1,492	143
7. Brooks	CIN	1,545	141
8. Craig	SF	1,527	141
9. Humphrey	DEN	1,307	121
10. Walker	MINN	1,338	119

PERFORMANCE POINT METHOD—WIDE RECEIVERS

1988

NAME	TEAM	YARDS	FANTASY POINTS
1. Ellard	LARm	1,421	135
2. Rice	SF	1,413	130
3. E. Brown	CIN	1,268	120
4. A. Carter	MINN	1,266	119
5. Sanders	WASH	1,162	108
6. Clayton	MIA	1,133	108
7. Dr. Hill	HOUS	1,141	104
8. Green	PHOE	1,098	103
9. E. Martin	NO	1,095	101
10. Lipps	PITT	1,102	101

1989

NAME	TEAM	YARDS	FANTASY POINTS
1. Rice	SF	1,499	143
2. Carrier	TB	1,412	136
3. Sharpe	GB	1,449	135
4. Ellard	LARm	1,405	134
5. Reed	BUF	1,343	125
6. Miller	SD	1,263	120
7. G. Clark	WASH	1,248	118
8. McGee	CIN	1,247	115
9. Slaughter	CLE	1,236	115
10. Monk	WASH	1,194	111

PERFORMANCE POINT METHOD—TIGHT ENDS

1988

NAME	TEAM	YARDS	FANTASY POINTS
1. Jackson	PHIL	869	81
2. Shuler	NYJ	805	75
3. Jordan	MINN	756	68
4. Bavaro	NYG	672	62
5. Holohan	LARm	640	56
6. Edmunds	MIA	567	52
7. Novacek	PHOE	570	51
8. Hall	TB	555	48
9. Holman	CIN	527	47
10. Metzelaars	BUF	438	38

1989

NAME	TEAM	YARDS	FANTASY POINTS
1. Holman	CIN	736	67
2. Sievers	NE	615	57
3. Jackson	PHIL	648	57
4. Holohan	LARm	510	44
5. Dyal	LARd	499	44
6. Jordan	MINN	506	43
7. Jones	SF	500	42
8. Thornton	CHI	392	34
9. Brenner	NO	398	34
10. Edmunds	MIA	382	33

PERFORMANCE POINT METHOD—QUARTERBACKS

1988

NAME	TEAM	RSH YDs	PS YDs	FANTASY POINTS
1. Cunningham	PHIL	628	3,808	238
2. Marino	MIA	-17	4,434	215
3. Everett	LARm	104	3,964	191
4. Esiason	CIN	238	3,572	188
5. Elway	DEN	234	3,309	177
6. Kelly	BUF	154	3,381	174
7. Pelluer	DALL	319	3,139	174
8. Simms	NYG	152	3,359	172
9. Lomax	PHOE	53	3,395	167
10. Testaverde	TB	138	3,240	166

1989

NAME	TEAM	RSH YDs	PS YDs	FANTASY POINTS
1. Majkowski	GB	358	4,318	234
2. Cunningham	PHIL	631	3,400	221
3. Everett	LARm	31	4,310	210
4. Moon	HOUS	268	3,631	193
5. Marino	MIA	-5	3,997	191
6. Esiason	CIN	278	3,525	189
7. Montana	SF	226	3,521	188
8. Rypien	WASH	56	3,868	184
9. Kosar	CLE	70	3,533	173
10. Krieg	SEAT	161	3,309	167

In the Basic Scoring Method, only 3 of the 10 leading running backs from 1988 returned to the top 10 in 1989. Of the 10 best wide receivers of 1988, only 2 returned to the top 10 in 1989. Of the tight ends, five returned. More than half of the 10 top quarterbacks returned, with 6 nearly duplicating their previous year's performance. From the kicking ranks, five top-10 placers made the same group in 1989.

Here are the Performance Point Method comparisons: Of the running backs, none of the top 3 from 1989 had even been a top-10 finisher in 1988, and only 4 of 1988's top-10 finishers again finished there in 1989. Of the wide receivers, only 2 of the top 10 of 1988 were in that group in 1989. And of the leading quarterbacks of 1988, only 4 returned to the top 10 in 1989.

What does this tell us? Teams change, players change, statistics change. Those Fantasy Franchise owners who draft purely on the basis of the previous year's statistics, with no regard for injury or other happenings, may be in trouble. We saw probably fewer than 50% of the leading players from 1988 reclaim top-10 distinction the following year. If we were to expand that to all players, there would obviously be a big statistical change each year. Successful fantasy owners forecast by combining the helpful facts from the previous year with their feel for the game, including foresight for teams and players on the upswing or downswing.

Successful fantasy owners realize that O. J. Anderson's 1989 success was helped by Joe Morris's injury. The injury to Ickey Woods benefited the year-end production of James Brooks. Marion Butts, a seventh-round draft pick, became a good fantasy player because Gary Anderson sat out the 1989 season over a contract squabble. Injuries, retirements, contract negotiations, drug use, and other factors can all play a part in one player's success and another player's failure. 1989 statistics may not tell us much about 1990 results.

In upcoming sections we'll study last year's player variables, such as injuries, to see how they affected a player's performance, how they may have influenced another player's statistics, and what effect may carry over into the 1990 season. We'll look at how last year's rookies fared and why. We'll also look at offseason roster changes, including significant trades or retirements, and at what effect they may have on the upcoming season. You can combine the information and recommendations in this book with your feel for Fantasy Football to make your 1990 season a success.

II
HELPFUL FACTS from the 1989 SEASON
(Key Injuries, Trades, and Other Happenings
That Affected 1989 Performances)

Many Fantasy Franchise owners preparing for a draft make a big mistake by considering only the previous year's player statistics. Many factors contribute to a player's success or failure, and they should be carefully examined.

We will review the 1989 season to learn some of the underlying reasons why some players were statistically successful and why others were not. We need to know why some of our predictions came true and why others did not. We'll look at injuries, trades, contract holdouts, suspensions, and other events to see how each may have helped one player but hurt another. We'll also review the 1989 rookies to see how their performances were affected by injuries and other players' performances.

Why do this? So we don't overlook any of a player's potential for 1990. We may be able to forecast a "sleeper" better or know which veterans may have a comeback year.

Season-ending injuries suffered by Joe Morris and Ickey Woods boosted the statistics of O. J. Anderson and James Brooks. If Morris and Woods return healthy in 1990, I wouldn't expect Anderson and Brooks to produce big numbers this year. How about less significant injuries like the back and knee problems that plagued Philadelphia tight end Keith Jackson? Surely his 1989 stats suffered. How did the blockbuster Herschel Walker trade to Minnesota affect various players' 1989 stats and, more important, what does it imply for 1990?

There are many situations in which one player's injury, trade, etc., may have boosted another's success. All of these factors from the previous year should be examined carefully before you select your 1990 fantasy team. Don't draft purely on the basis of the previous year's stats. A set of brilliant statistics from 1989 may be merely a once-in-a-career fluke.

Following is a team-by-team discussion of events that may have played a part in a certain player's success or failure in 1989. Following this review is a rundown on the top rookies of 1989.

ATLANTA FALCONS

IR—Alex Higdon (Tight End)
Higdon, who suffered a severe knee injury after scoring in two of the first three games of 1988, was forced to sit out the entire 1989 season.

IR—Paul McFadden (Kicker)
A thigh injury placed McFadden on the injured reserve and forced him to miss the last seven games of 1989. Greg Davis, who kicked for the Falcons in 1988, replaced him. Davis hit only 23 of 34 field-goal attempts (.677), so McFadden could return in 1990.

I—Chris Miller (Quarterback)
Miller suffered cracked ribs early in the 1989 season and was originally projected to miss up to a month of action. He missed only one game, though, which took only a small toll on his year-end stats.

I—Michael Haynes (Wide Receiver)
Haynes missed five games in 1989 with a shoulder injury, but he still managed a decent season—40 receptions for 681 yards and four touchdowns. In his absence, Floyd Dixon filled in and boosted himself statistically.

BUFFALO BILLS

IR—Robb Riddick (Running Back)
Riddick, a perennial short-yardage scorer for the Bills, missed the entire 1989 season with a knee injury. This may have played a big part in the improvement of Thurman Thomas's touchdown production from 2 in 1988 to 12 in 1989.

I—Jim Kelly (Quarterback)
Though Kelly's year-end stats of 3,130 passing yards and 25 touchdown passes were impressive, he would have fared far better had he not missed three games with a separated shoulder.

CHICAGO BEARS

The only significant factor affecting player performances for the Bears in 1989 was the ineffectiveness of Mike Tomczak. Tomczak's inconsistency led the Bears to bring Jim Harbaugh into action occasionally.

CINCINNATI BENGALS

IR—Ickey Woods (Running Back)
A knee injury suffered by Woods in the second game of 1989 knocked him out for the season. The injury gave both rookie Eric Ball and veteran Stanford Jennings more playing time, and James Brooks took advantage of the opportunity to up his stats.

I—Boomer Esiason (Quarterback)
Though Esiason put together some impressive numbers in 1989, he was hobbled for much of the season with an ankle injury.

I—Eric Ball (Running Back)
Given the opportunity to prove himself when Ickey Woods went down, Ball also suffered injuries. Though less significant than the injury to Woods, both ankle and hip injuries slowed Ball's play.

HO—Eddie Brown (Wide Receiver)
Brown held out 48 days into training camp, did not catch a pass in game #1, and had a big deficit in year-end statistics in 1989.

HO—Rodney Holman (Tight End)
Holman's 42-day holdout seems to have had little effect on a stellar 1989 season.

CLEVELAND BROWNS

S—Kevin Mack (Running Back)
After serving a suspension for drug involvement, Mack also spent some time in prison for the same reason. It cost him the first 12 games of the 1989 season.

HO—Lawyer Tillman (Wide Receiver)
Missing 55 days of training camp can really set a rookie back. Tillman's year-end total of only six receptions confirms that.

DALLAS COWBOYS

IR—Michael Irvin (Wide Receiver)
After getting off to a fast start, with 26 receptions for 378 yards through game #6 of 1989, Irvin's potentially big season ended abruptly with a knee injury. His absence benefited a number of players statistically, including James Dixon, Derrick Shepard, and Cornell Burbage.

IR—Kelvin Martin (Wide Receiver)
Martin was another Cowboy receiver well on his way to a very productive season (46 receptions for 644 yards through 11 games) before a knee injury ended his season. His injury benefited the same receivers who profited from Michael Irvin's absence.

I—Troy Aikman (Quarterback)
A fractured index finger sidelined Aikman the better part of six games in 1989. He did return, however, to recapture the starting job from fellow rookie Steve Walsh.

TR—Herschel Walker (Running Back)
Walker's trade to the Vikings opened things up for the likes of Paul Palmer and Daryl Johnston.

DENVER BRONCOS

IR—Tony Dorsett (Running Back)
Dorsett's knee injury ended not only his season but also his career; youth, in the person of Bobby Humphrey, will inherit the position.

IR—Ricky Nattiel (Wide Receiver)
A knee injury kept Nattiel out of the first eight games of 1989 and limited him to only 10 receptions for the entire season.

S—Orson Mobley (Tight End)
As a violator of the NFL's drug rules, Mobley was suspended for 30 days at the outset of 1989 and missed the first three games of the season.

DETROIT LIONS

IR—Chuck Long (Quarterback)
Long's elbow injury kept him from competing for the Lions' quarter-backing job. His absence led the Lions to take a good look at Rodney Peete, who seems to have won the job. With Bob Gagliano becoming a solid backup to Peete, Long may be trade material.

IR—John Ford (Wide Receiver)
Second-round draft choice Ford missed most of his rookie season because of a hamstring injury and saw only minor action late in the year.

I/HO—Barry Sanders (Running Back)
Holding out for 51 days seemed to have little effect on Sanders's rookie-year performance. A hip injury, however, kept him out of game #6 and may have slowed him a bit for part of the season.

I—Rodney Peete (Quarterback)
Peete, who was very impressive when he did play, missed half of the games in 1989 because of strained ligaments in his knee. If he can stay healthy in 1990, he could put together some big numbers.

GREEN BAY PACKERS

I—Brent Fullwood (Running Back)
After a strong start, Fullwood suffered a midseason hamstring injury that greatly reduced his performance in the second half of 1989.

I—Ed West (Tight End)
This steady performer started the season with four touchdowns in the first three games of 1989, but a knee injury greatly hindered his performance from that point on.

HOUSTON OILERS

I/HO—Mike Rozier (Running Back)
Rozier held out 41 days into training camp and subsequently suffered through knee trouble and a very poor 1989 season of only 301 yards rushing.

I/HO—Drew Hill (Wide Receiver)
Though Hill was a 39-day holdout, he got off to a strong start in 1989. He missed games #11 and #12, however, because of a chipped bone in his back.

INDIANAPOLIS COLTS

IR—Chris Chandler (Quarterback)
Chandler, who began the year as the team's starter, missed game #4 and the rest of the season after suffering a knee injury. This allowed Jack Trudeau's emergence as the team's signal caller.

I—Eric Dickerson (Running Back)
Though Dickerson again put together some impressive numbers, he was slowed near midseason by a hamstring injury that kept him out of game #9.

KANSAS CITY CHIEFS

IR—Mike Elkins (Quarterback)
The Chiefs didn't get a chance to look at their second-round choice, Elkins, as he spent the year on injured reserve with a back injury.

IR—Naz Worthen (Wide Receiver)
Worthen, the Chiefs' third-round draft choice, spent much of the year on the injured-reserve list with a rib injury.

I—Christian Okoye (Running Back)
The tough-running Okoye had a standout season but did miss one game with a thigh injury.

HO—Stephone Paige (Wide Receiver)
Paige, late getting into camp, did not catch a pass until the third game of 1989 and ended the year with only 44 receptions and two touchdowns.

RL—Carlos Carson (Wide Receiver)
Carson's poor showing led to his ultimate release (he was later picked up by Philadelphia), which opened opportunities to Emile Harry and veterans Pete Mandley and Clarence Weathers.

LOS ANGELES RAIDERS

IR—Tim Brown (Wide Receiver)
After an excellent rookie season in 1988, when he produced 43 receptions for 725 yards and six touchdowns, Brown went into 1989 as the focus of some high expectations—which evaporated when he suffered a season-ending knee injury in the opening game. His absence may have played a part in the very successful season put in by Mervyn Fernandez.

IR/HO—Marcus Allen (Running Back)
Allen held out for 36 days, which may have contributed to his mediocre performance through the first five games in 1989. Then a knee injury sidelined him for eight weeks, taking a heavy toll on his stats.

LOS ANGELES RAMS

I—Henry Ellard (Wide Receiver)
Though Ellard's total of 70 receptions for 1,382 yards and eight touchdowns was very impressive, he might have fared even better had he not missed a couple of games with a strained calf muscle.

HO—Greg Bell (Running Back)
A 36-day holdout seems to have had little effect on this veteran's stats for the season.

HO—Damone Johnson (Tight End)
Johnson held out 38 days over contract problems, and his stats fell.

HO—Cleveland Gary (Running Back)
As a rookie, holding out 56 days into training camp can put you way behind. In Gary's case, the long holdout kept him from ever getting on track.

MIAMI DOLPHINS

IR/RL—Fuad Reveiz (Kicker)
A groin injury put Reveiz on the injured reserve, giving rookie Pete Stoyanovich a shot at the kicking job. Stoyanovich grabbed the opportunity and Reveiz was ultimately released. He has since signed with the San Diego Chargers as a free agent.

IR—Troy Stradford (Running Back)
Stradford suffered a season-ending knee injury, forcing him to miss the last eight games of 1989.

IR—Lorenzo Hampton (Running Back)
Hampton's year-end stats were greatly affected by a knee injury. He was left unprotected by the Dolphins as a Plan B free agent with Denver.

IR—Scott Schwedes (Wide Receiver)
Schwedes missed the entire first half of the 1989 season with a knee injury.

IR—Ron Davenport (Running Back)
Davenport was used only sparingly; a groin injury also contributed to a very poor showing in 1989.

I—Mark Duper (Wide Receiver)
A total of 49 receptions for 717 yards might be impressive for many receivers but not for Duper. A bothersome knee injury plagued him throughout the year.

HO—Mark Clayton (Wide Receiver)
Clayton was a 47-day training-camp holdout and did not catch a pass in the season opener. He did rebound later, though, for a very productive season.

HO—Sammie Smith (Running Back)
This rookie running back held out 57 days into training camp, which played a big part in his poor early-season showing. A strong second-half performance gave us a better idea of what he's capable of.

MINNESOTA VIKINGS

I/HO—Anthony Carter (Wide Receiver)
After holding out 28 days into training camp, Carter seemed to be plagued by injuries all year long.

I—Wade Wilson (Quarterback)
Wilson missed two games in 1989 because of a fractured knuckle, which was only part of the reason for his very disappointing season in 1989.

TR—Herschel Walker (Running Back)
The trade that brought Walker to Minnesota seems to have been more confusing and detrimental than helpful to the Viking offense. Walker's year-end numbers were decent but not near what we expect from him. If he remains a Viking, perhaps the Vikes will figure out how to use him better.

I/HO—Steve Jordan (Tight End)
Coming in late to training camp may have contributed to a poor showing by this former Pro Bowl man. Slowed by an ankle injury, Jordan managed only 35 receptions in 1989.

NEW ENGLAND PATRIOTS

IR—Stanley Morgan (Wide Receiver)
The aging veteran Morgan spent time on the injured reserve in 1989 because of a fractured fibula. This helped boost playing time and year-end stats for both Cedric Jones and rookie Hart Lee Dykes.

IR—Michael Timpson (Wide Receiver)
This rookie fourth-round selection spent the 1989 season on the injured-reserve list with a hamstring injury.

I/HO—Irving Fryar (Wide Receiver)
Fryar, who held out 44 days into training camp, suffered a sprained knee and hobbled to a statistically very poor season. His misfortunes also contributed to very productive seasons for both Cedric Jones and rookie Hart Lee Dykes.

I—John Stephens (Running Back)
After rushing for over 1,100 yards as a rookie in 1988, Stephens fell well short of that mark in 1989. This could have been largely due to his having missed two complete games in 1989 with an ankle injury.

NEW ORLEANS SAINTS

IR—Floyd Turner (Wide Receiver)
Sixth-round draft choice Floyd Turner was having a decent season, with 22 receptions through game #12, before a broken arm ended his season.

I—Brett Perriman (Wide Receiver)
Because of a knee injury, second-year player Perriman got off to a slow start in 1989. He finished strongly, with 10 receptions for 209 yards over the season's last three games.

I—Buford Jordan (Running Back)
Jordan, plagued by a hamstring injury, started slowly in 1989, rushing for only 37 yards on four carries through the season's first nine games.

NEW YORK GIANTS

IR—Joe Morris (Running Back)
The broken foot that Morris suffered late in the preseason was definitely one of the year's most significant injuries. His absence certainly left some room for veteran O. J. Anderson to show what he can do.

IR—Mark Bavaro (Tight End)
This perennial all-pro missed the last nine games of 1989 because of a knee injury.

IR—Raul Allegre (Kicker)
Allegre had hit 20 of 26 field-goal attempts before a leg injury sidelined him for the last six games of 1989. In his absence, Bjorn Nittmo filled in with an admirable performance, hitting 9 of 12 attempts.

I—Phil Simms (Quarterback)
Phil Simms's year-end stats in 1989 took a dip from his norm, perhaps because he missed almost two entire games with an ankle injury.

NEW YORK JETS

IR/HO—Wesley Walker (Wide Receiver)
After a 44-day holdout, Walker did two stints on the injured-reserve list, once with an ankle injury and once with a neck injury. He was released.

IR—Mickey Shuler (Tight End)
This standout tight end was off to a solid start before suffering a knee injury that kept him out of the entire second half of the '89 season.

I/HO—Al Toon (Wide Receiver)
Toon, a 38-day holdout, produced some impressive numbers (63 receptions, 673 yards) despite missing five games with ankle and shoulder injuries. Imagine what his numbers would have been had he played another third of a season.

HO—Johnny Hector (Running Back)
Following a 56-day holdout, Hector got off to a very slow start, rushing only eight times for 15 yards in the 1989 season's first three games.

PHILADELPHIA EAGLES

IR—Mike Quick (Wide Receiver)
For the second straight year, Quick had his season cut short by injury. This time around, Quick fell victim to a knee injury that sidelined him for the last 10 games of 1989. The slack was taken up by Cris Carter, Keith Jackson, and Quick's replacement, Ron Johnson.

I—Keith Jackson (Tight End)
Jackson had fantastic year-end numbers (63 receptions, 648 yards, three touchdowns), but they could have been even better. He missed three games in 1989 because of knee and back injuries.

PHOENIX CARDINALS

IR—Neil Lomax (Quarterback)
Lomax, suffering from degenerative arthritis in his hips, missed the entire 1989 season and ultimately retired from football.

IR—Stump Mitchell (Running Back)
Mitchell suffered a devastating knee injury that required reconstructive surgery. Mitchell's absence from the last 13 games of 1989 put a heavy burden on Earl Ferrell and may have forced the Cardinals to pass far more often than they would have liked.

IR—J. T. Smith (Wide Receiver)
This solid, aging performer was having another fantastic season, latching onto 62 receptions for 778 yards and five touchdowns, before a fractured fibula ended his season by eliminating him from the last seven games of 1989. Projected out, those pre-injury figures show Smith on his way to a season of 100-plus receptions. His fill-in, Ernie Jones, was the statistical beneficiary of Smith's absence.

I—Roy Green (Wide Receiver)
A fractured collarbone sidelined Green for four weeks of the 1989 season and played a major role in lowering his year-end stats.

I—Earl Ferrell (Running Back)
Having sprained an ankle very early in the 1989 season, Ferrell missed game #2 and got off to a slow start.

I—Gary Hogeboom (Quarterback)
Hogeboom became the starter when Neil Lomax's return was ruled out, and he started off well, throwing for 10 touchdowns in the first four games of 1989. But both an arthritic throwing elbow and a hand injury caused him to miss action and lowered his year-end stats.

PITTSBURGH STEELERS

I—Bubby Brister (Quarterback)
Brister's year-end stats for 1989 were down some from his 1988 showing. He threw for only 2,365 yards and nine touchdowns, having missed two complete games with a knee injury.

HO—Louis Lipps (Wide Receiver)
Despite holding out for 36 days, Lipps had a 50-reception season in 1989, equal to his 1988 output.

SAN DIEGO CHARGERS

IR—Rod Bernstine (Tight End)
Bernstine was off to a fast start in 1989, latching onto 21 receptions in the season's first five games before a knee injury ended his season. If he had played the entire season at that pace, he would have had more than 60 receptions, so he's certainly not a player to overlook for 1990 if he returns healthy.

IR—Billy Joe Tolliver (Quarterback)
Tolliver, who finished up the year as the team's starting signal caller, was sidelined early in the year with a broken collarbone.

IR—Mark Vlasic (Quarterback)
The Chargers once had very high hopes for Vlasic, who continues to be bothered by knee trouble.

IR—Quinn Early (Wide Receiver)
As a rookie in 1988, Early grabbed 29 receptions for 365 yards and four touchdowns. Many thought he would build on that output in 1989, but a knee injury in game #4 knocked him out for the season.

I—Jim McMahon (Quarterback)
A combination of a shoulder injury and inconsistent play benched McMahon in favor of the young Billy Joe Tolliver.

HO—Gary Anderson (Running Back)
Anderson sat out the entire 1989 season because of a contract squabble. His absence certainly was the key to the success of seventh-round pick Marion Butts. What will Anderson do in 1990?

SAN FRANCISCO 49ers

I—Mike Sherrard (Wide Receiver)
The 49ers took a chance on Sherrard, who hadn't seen much action the last couple of years because of a broken leg. Sherrard seems to have recovered now, and the 49ers activated him late in the season. How well can he play now?

SEATTLE SEAHAWKS

IR—Steve Largent (Wide Receiver)
Largent missed six games in 1989 because of a fractured elbow. He has now retired.

IR—Tommy Kane (Wide Receiver)
As a rookie in 1988, Kane spent most of the year on the injured-reserve list with a groin injury. In 1989, Kane again fell victim to injury, this time a knee problem that sidelined him for the last 11 games of the season. With Steve Largent retiring, it would have been nice to get a better feel for Kane's ability.

I—J. L. Williams (Running Back)
Though his receptions and receiving yards were still way up there, Williams had a big dropoff in rushing yards in 1989. Some of that could be attributed to an ankle injury that slowed his play and kept him out of game #12.

I—Robert Tyler (Tight End)
Tyler, who had been the starting tight end, suffered an ankle injury that sidelined him for the second half of the 1989 season.

TAMPA BAY BUCCANEERS

IR—Frank Pillow (Wide Receiver)
This second-year wideout missed the entire 1989 season with a broken foot. As a rookie in 1988, Pillow latched onto 15 receptions for 206 yards.

I—Vinny Testaverde (Quarterback)
A knee injury kept Testaverde out of three games in 1989, definitely limiting his stats.

WASHINGTON REDSKINS

IR—Kelvin Bryant (Running Back)
Bryant suffered a herniated disk in his neck from an auto accident, forcing him to miss the entire 1989 season. His absence opened the way for Earnest Byner's productive season. The questions now presented are: Will he return in 1990? Whose performances will that affect?

I—Gerald Riggs (Running Back)
Riggs, who the Redskins hoped would become their dominant running back, got off to a strong start in 1989, rushing for 658 yards through the first seven games. But an assortment of injuries (chest, knee, ankle, arch) severely limited his play, as he finished the season with only 834 rushing yards total. His potential is obviously great, but his durability is the question mark.

I—Doug Williams (Quarterback)
A significant back injury kept Williams out of action for the first eight weeks of 1989. When he did return, he was very ineffective and was released by the Redskins.

HOW THE 1989 ROOKIES FARED

A rookie doesn't always have an opportunity to prove himself in his first year of NFL action, so it's a good idea to look back and see what events—such as injuries—may have affected a rookie's inaugural season. Keep in mind that many prize rookie prospects, especially contract holdouts, may have missed some action—not because of injury but because they had trouble learning their team's strategies and systems. Still, remember that these are prime blue-chip players, who somehow impressed the scouts while they were in college. Chances are that such rookies have some potential even if it wasn't fully realized in their rookie season.

Here's a look at how the rookies of 1989 performed. First we'll take a look at the players from the first two rounds—the NFL scouts' blue chippers—and then we'll look at potential standouts that came in later rounds.

EARLY PICKS

NFL Round SELECTED	NAME	POS	TEAM DRAFTED BY
1	Troy Aikman	QB	Dallas

COMMENTS: The highly touted Aikman is the Cowboys' quarterback of the future. In his rookie season, he not only had to learn the ropes but also missed five games with a fractured left index finger. If he remains healthy in 1990, he should easily improve on his 1,749-yard, nine-touchdown season of 1989.

1	Barry Sanders	RB	Detroit

COMMENTS: Can't ask for much more out of a rookie. Sanders was 1989's Fantasy Rookie of the Year for good reason. His 1,470 rushing yards and 14 touchdowns were just a sampling of what kind of career lies ahead.

1	Tim Worley	RB	Pittsburgh

COMMENTS: After a slow start (279 rushing yards through the first eight games of 1989), Worley came on in the second half of the season, rushing for 491 yards during the last seven games and scoring four touchdowns in the last three games. This should have fantasy fans excited.

1	Sammie Smith	RB	Miami

COMMENTS: Smith held out 57 days into training camp, greatly diminishing his early-season play in 1989. Smith rushed for only 167 yards through the first seven games of 1989 but gained 492 yards over the last eight games. He also added six touchdowns during that last eight-game stretch.

1	Eric Metcalf	RB	Cleveland

COMMENTS: "Electrifying" best describes Metcalf's style. Although his total of 633 rushing yards wasn't especially impressive, his 54 receptions for another 397 yards demonstrate his versatility.

EARLY PICKS

NFL Round SELECTED	NAME	POS	TEAM DRAFTED BY
1	Hart Lee Dykes	WR	New England

COMMENTS: After a slow start of only 9 receptions through eight games in 1989, Dykes caught fire, with 40 receptions and four 100-yard games over the season's last eight games.

1	Andre Rison	WR	Indianapolis

COMMENTS: Rison put together an outstanding rookie campaign with 52 receptions for 820 yards and four touchdowns—not bad on a team that features Eric Dickerson.

1	Cleveland Gary	RB	Los Angeles Rams

COMMENTS: Waiting 56 days to come to contract terms with the Rams really hurt Gary early on. He didn't make his debut until game #4 and rushed only 37 times for 163 yards in a very disappointing rookie season.

1	Shawn Collins	WR	Atlanta

COMMENTS: The Falcons have to be very pleased with the 58-reception, 862-yard season Collins put together in 1989. As the Falcons mature, Collins will grow right along with them; a bright future is ahead of him.

2	John Ford	WR	Detroit

COMMENTS: Ford spent a good portion of his rookie season on injured reserve with a hamstring injury, limiting him to only five receptions and action in only three games. Healthy in '90, he may be given the chance to show why he was a second-round pick.

2	Lawyer Tillman	WR	Cleveland

COMMENTS: Tillman's 55-day holdout over a contract squabble really limited his 1989 performance. He recorded only six receptions for 70 yards and three touchdowns, including a blocked-punt recovery while playing on specialty teams.

2	Mike Elkins	QB	Kansas City

COMMENTS: A back injury put Elkins on the injured reserve from the outset of 1989.

2	Danny Peebles	WR	Tampa Bay

COMMENTS: Peebles, playing behind Mark Carrier and Bruce Hill, had a disappointing 10-reception rookie season in 1989.

2	Eric Ball	RB	Cincinnati

COMMENTS: Given a real shot at proving himself when an injury ended the season early for Ickey Woods, Ball was far from impressive. He rushed for only 391 yards and three touchdowns on 98 carries. And if Ickey Woods comes back 100% healthy from his injury, Ball would have to improve dramatically to see much playing time in 1990.

EARLY PICKS

NFL Round SELECTED	NAME	POS	TEAM DRAFTED BY
2	Daryl Johnston	RB	Dallas

COMMENTS: After scoring a couple of short-yardage touchdowns in the 1989 preseason, Johnston attracted some real fantasy attention. But even after the trade of Herschel Walker by the Cowboys, Johnston's rookie numbers were disappointing: only 212 yards rushing and only three touchdowns, all through the air.

2	Walter Reeves	TE	Phoenix

COMMENTS: Because he played behind two excellent tight ends, Robert Awalt and Jay Novacek, Reeves's disappointing rookie season, in which he had only one reception, was not much of a surprise. With Jay Novacek now departed to Dallas, Reeves may have more opportunity to prove himself in 1990.

2	Billy Joe Tolliver	QB	San Diego

COMMENTS: Tolliver missed much of the first half of his rookie season in 1989, spending time on the injured-reserve list with a broken collarbone. After recovering, Tolliver started the last four games of 1989 and closed out the season with two 300-yard games.

2	Wesley Walls	TE	San Francisco

COMMENTS: Walls, who played behind Brent Jones, did not make much of an impact as a receiver, latching onto only four receptions. Walls spent much of his rookie season doing work on special teams.

LATER-ROUND PICKS WHO MAY PAN OUT

NFL Round SELECTED	NAME	POS	TEAM DRAFTED BY
3	Derek Hill	WR	Pittsburgh

COMMENTS: Hill did not have a standout rookie campaign, but his 28 receptions placed him third on the team and gave the Steelers hope for the future.

3	Keith Jones	RB	Atlanta

COMMENTS: Though he rushed for only 202 yards, Jones was second on the team to John Settle (690 yards). More impressive was his total of 41 receptions, second this time to the 58 receptions of fellow rookie Shawn Collins.

3	Don Beebe	WR	Buffalo

COMMENTS: Beebe recorded only 17 receptions as a rookie in 1989. However, the two that went for touchdowns (each covering 63 yards) demonstrated his downfield ability.

LATER-ROUND PICKS WHO MAY PAN OUT

NFL Round SELECTED	NAME	POS	TEAM DRAFTED BY
3	Erik Wilhelm	QB	Cincinnati

COMMENTS: Playing behind Boomer Esiason certainly limits your playing time, but Wilhelm played well enough to take the backup job from Turk Schonert. Wilhelm passes from the left, as Esiason does, and in other ways recalls the player he hopes one day to replace.

4	Darryl Ingram	TE	Minnesota

COMMENTS: While veteran Steve Jordan held out in the preseason, Ingram filled in admirably, demonstrating skills that may make him a starter in the near future.

5	Dave Meggett	RB	New York Giants

COMMENTS: Meggett became a receiving specialist for the Giants, scoring four long-range receiving touchdowns in 1989 on plays of 62, 33, 53, and 57 yards. He also added a 76-yard punt return and could be a real find for the future.

6	Rodney Peete	QB	Detroit

COMMENTS: Though Peete struggled through knee problems as a rookie, he proved himself an exciting player as both a passer and a runner, an excellent selection to run the Lions' "run-and-shoot" offense.

6	Chris Jacke	K	Green Bay

COMMENTS: Jacke played a big part in the Packers' 1989 success. After Green Bay went through a slew of kickers in 1988, Jacke's 22 of 28 (.786) on field-goal attempts and 42 of 42 on extra points made him a real find for the Pack.

7	Marion Butts	RB	San Diego

COMMENTS: This seventh-rounder really benefited from the season-long holdout of veteran Gary Anderson. Butts responded with an impressive 683 rushing yards and nine touchdowns.

8	Pete Stoyanovich	K	Miami

COMMENTS: With veteran Fuad Reveiz on injured reserve with a groin injury, Stoyanovich won the kicking job. He hit 19 of 26 field-goal attempts (.731) and 38 of 39 extra points and hopes it was good enough for him to keep his job in 1990.

III
FREE AGENTS:
POTENTIAL 1990 HOLDOUTS or
THOSE HEADED FOR NEW NFL TEAMS

This year the NFL continues its Plan B free-agency system, which was put into effect last year. Each NFL team is allowed to protect 37 players from its roster. The unprotected players become unrestricted free agents on February 1 and are free to sign on with any other team before April 1, with no compensation due to the teams they're leaving. Last year, Gary Hogeboom was left unprotected by Indianapolis and became the starting quarterback for Phoenix.

Other unprotected players who made an impact after signing with new teams were Eric Sievers with New England (left unprotected by the LA Rams), Mike Mularkey with Pittsburgh (left unprotected by Minnesota), Jeff Jaeger with the LA Raiders (left unprotected by Cleveland), Chris Bahr with the San Diego Chargers (left unprotected by the LA Raiders), and Paul McFadden with the Atlanta Falcons (left unprotected by the NY Giants). Some familiar names appear on the unprotected list this year as well and are potential impact players for whomever they end up with. The likes of Joe Morris, Doug Williams, Curt Warner, Wesley Walker, and Sammy Winder were left unprotected.

When thinking of free agents, be sure also to include all rookie draft picks, each of whom must sign a contract before appearing in uniform. Training time missed sets any player back physically and mentally, but for a rookie it is especially harmful because it delays his number-one job, learning the new team's system.

Of the 1989 rookies, such players as Sammie Smith of the Miami Dolphins, Cleveland Gary of the Los Angeles Rams, and Lawyer Tillman of the Cleveland Browns were slow to sign their contracts, came late into training camp, and didn't fare as well as possible.

We must also consider the "protected" veteran players whose contracts have expired. In 1989, Eddie Brown, Rodney Holman, Mark Clayton, Marcus Allen, Irving Fryar, Anthony Carter, Steve Jordan, Johnny Hector, Wesley Walker, Al Toon, Mike Rozier, Drew Hill, Louis Lipps, Mike Quick, Greg Bell, Damone Johnson, and Gary Anderson were among the holdouts. Many of these players were not in proper condition when they went into the season and consequently suffered injuries and had subpar seasons. Gary Anderson was not able to come to terms at all with San Diego and sat out the entire season.

You can see why it's a good idea to keep an eye both on veteran free agents and on early-round draft choices. You can see the importance of keeping up with possible holdouts and those unrestricted free agents who may have already signed with a new team for 1990. The impact grows as the season nears and players miss preseason conditioning and games.

Following are two lists. First is one that shows each veteran player who is "protected" but whose current contract has expired. These players are restricted free agents and may negotiate into the preseason, so they're the ones to keep a close eye on. The second list is of unrestricted free agents. They're the players whom their teams did not protect; if one of them signs with another team, the team he's leaving does not have to be compensated, if he was signed by April 1.

NOTE: This list of free-agent signings for veterans will be updated in our first preseason newsletter, available in early August—a must if you want to be properly prepared for your Fantasy Football draft. Also included will be the updated list of all rookie signings.

PROTECTED FREE AGENTS / POTENTIAL 1990 HOLDOUTS

(Status key: S=Signed, RT=Retired, RL=Released, TR=Traded, Blank=No Status Update Yet)

RUNNING BACKS

NAME	TEAM	STATUS	NAME	TEAM	STATUS
Gene Lang	ATL		Troy Stradford	MIA	
Larry Kinnebrew	BUF		D. J. Dozier	MINN	
Jamie Mueller	BUF		Marvin Allen	NE	
Neal Anderson	CHI	S	Bob Perryman	NE	
Tim Manoa	CLE		Maurice Carthon	NYG	
Barry Redden	CLE		Lee Rouson	NYG	
Herman Fontenot	GB		Johnny Hector	NYJ	
Brent Fullwood	GB		Freeman McNeil	NYJ	
Keith Woodside	GB		Keith Byars	PHIL	
Allen Pinkett	HOUS		Anthony Toney	PHIL	
Mike Rozier	HOUS		Earl Ferrell	PHOE	
Christian Okoye	KC	S	Tony Jordan	PHOE	
Herman Heard	KC		Vai Sikahema	PHOE	
James Saxon	KC		Ron Wolfley	PHOE	
Marcus Allen	LARd		Tim Spencer	SD	
Vance Mueller	LARd		Gerald Riggs	WASH	
Steve Smith	LARd				

WIDE RECEIVERS

NAME	TEAM	STATUS	NAME	TEAM	STATUS
Tim McGee	CIN		Stanley Morgan	NE	
Leonard Harris	HOUS		Lonzell Hill	NO	
James Pruitt	IND		Roy Green	PHOE	
Pete Mandley	KC		Jamie Holland	SD	
Mike Alexander	LARd		Jeff Chadwick	SEAT	
Jim Jensen	MIA		Mark Carrier	TB	
Scott Schwedes	MIA		Bruce Hill	TB	
Anthony Carter	MINN		Frank Pillow	TB	
Jim Gustafson	MINN				

TIGHT ENDS

NAME	TEAM	STATUS	NAME	TEAM	STATUS
Keith McKeller	BUF		Pete Holohan	LARm	
Pete Metzelaars	BUF		Damone Johnson	LARm	
Butch Rolle	BUF		Brian Kinchen	MIA	
Eric Kattus	CIN		Lin Dawson	NE	
Jim Riggs	CIN		Robert Awalt	PHOE	
Ed West	GB		Arthur Cox	SD	
Mike Dyal	LARd		Don Warren	WASH	
Ethan Horton	LARd				

QUARTERBACKS

NAME	TEAM	STATUS	NAME	TEAM	STATUS
Hugh Millen	ATL		Rich Gannon	MINN	
Frank Reich	BUF		Steve Grogan	NE	
Mike Tomczak	CHI		Marc Wilson	NE	
Gary Kubiak	DEN		John Fourcade	NO	S
Bob Gagliano	DET		Bobby Hebert	NO	
Chuck Long	DET		Dave Wilson	NO	
Don Majkowski	GB		Don McPherson	PHIL	
Cody Carlson	HOUS		Jim McMahon	SD	RL
Steve Beuerlein	LARd		Jeff Kemp	SEAT	
Jay Schroeder	LARd		Dave Krieg	SEAT	

KICKERS

NAME	TEAM	STATUS	NAME	TEAM	STATUS
Dean Biasucci	IND		Roger Ruzek	PHIL	
Rich Karlis	MINN		Mike Cofer	SF	
Jason Staurovsky	NE				

UNPROTECTED FREE AGENTS / HEADED FOR A NEW NFL TEAM

(Signed By=NFL team that player has signed to play with in 1990;
RL=Released, not having signed with another team and having since been
released by his current team; RT=Retired; NCO=No Contract Offer)

Please Note: NCO=No Contract Offer. Because of the new free-agency system, unprotected free agents had to be offered at least 100% of their previous year's salary by April 15th or they were free to negotiate with any other team.

RUNNING BACKS

NAME	TEAM	SIGNED BY	NAME	TEAM	SIGNED BY
Andra Johnson	ATL		Jessie Clark	MINN	
James Primus	ATL		Patrick Egu	NE	NYJ
Ronnie Harmon	BUF	SD	Mosi Tatupu	NE	
Robb Riddick	BUF		George Wonsley	NE	
Thomas Sanders	CHI	SD	Paul Frazier	NO	GB
Matt Suhey	CHI		Bobby Morse	NO	
Brian Taylor	CHI		George Adams	NYG	NE
John Holifield	CIN		O. J. Anderson	NYG	
Stanford Jennings	CIN		Joe Morris	NYG	
Keith Jones	CLE	DALL	Brad Baxter	NYJ	
Paul Palmer	DALL	CIN	Mark Konecny	NYJ	
Broderick Sargent	DALL		Mark Higgs	PHIL	MIA
Kevin Scott	DALL		Tony Baker	PHOE	
Curtis Stewart	DALL		Stump Mitchell	PHOE	
Junior Tautalatasi	DALL		Tim Tyrell	PITT	
Ken Bell	DEN		Ray Wallace	PITT	
Tony Dorsett	DEN	RT	Eric Wilkerson	PITT	DET
Sammy Winder	DEN		Harry Sydney	SF	
Tony Paige	DET		Spencer Tillman	SF	
Tracy Johnson	HOUS	ATL	Kevin Harmon	SEAT	
Tommie Agee	KC	DALL	Curt Warner	SEAT	LARm
Kenny Gamble	KC		Don Smith	TB	BUF
Bobby Joe Edmunds	LARd	SEAT	James Wilder	TB	WASH
Kerry Porter	LARd		Reggie Branch	WASH	
Steve Strachan	LARd		Kelvin Bryant	WASH	
Mel Farr	LARm		Reggie Dupard	WASH	
Tom Brown	MIA	WASH	Joe Mickles	WASH	SD
Lorenzo Hampton	MIA	DEN	Jamie Morris	WASH	NE

WIDE RECEIVERS

NAME	TEAM	SIGNED BY	NAME	TEAM	SIGNED BY
Stacey Bailey	ATL		Leo Lewis	MINN	
Darryl Franklin	BUF		Glen Antrum	NE	NYJ
Flip Johnson	BUF	GB	Kitrick Taylor	NE	
John Kolesar	BUF		Rod Harris	NO	DALL
James Lofton	BUF		Mike Jones	NO	
Steve Tasker	BUF		Stacey Robinson	NYG	
Glen Kozlowski	CHI		Phillip Epps	NYJ	RL
Dennis McKinnon	CHI	DALL	Michael Harper	NYJ	RL
Tom Waddle	CHI		Wesley Walker	NYJ	RL
John Garrett	CIN		Anthony Edwards	PHIL	
Ira Hillary	CIN	MINN	Gregg Garrity	PHIL	
Mike Martin	CIN		Ron Johnson	PHIL	
Gerald McNeil	CLE	HOUS	William Osborn	PHIL	
Scott Ankrom	DALL		Mike Barber	PHOE	CIN
Cornell Burbage	DALL	MINN	Don Holmes	PHOE	
Bernard Ford	DALL	HOUS	Andy Schillinger	PHOE	MINN
Keith McDonald	DET		Daryl Usher	PHOE	
Stacey Mobley	DET	GB	Jason Johnson	PITT	DEN
Walter Stanley	DET	WASH	Weegie Thompson	PITT	
Mike Williams	DET	DALL	Phil McConkey	SD	
Erik Affholter	GB		Terry Greer	SF	DET
Carl Bland	GB		Mike Wilson	SF	
Aubrey Matthews	GB	DET	Louis Clark	SEAT	
Kenny Jackson	HOUS		Steve Largent	SEAT	RT
Matt Bouza	IND		Jim Sandusky	SEAT	
Emile Harry	KC		Paul Skansi	SEAT	
Clarence Weathers	KC	GB	Carl Harry	WASH	HOUS
Timmie Ware	LARd	KC	Steve Hobbs	WASH	
Ron Brown	LARm		Joe Howard	WASH	

TIGHT ENDS

NAME	TEAM	SIGNED BY	NAME	TEAM	SIGNED BY
Ron Heller	ATL	SEAT	Chris Dressel	NYJ	
Alex Higdon	ATL		Billy Griggs	NYJ	PITT
Gary Wilkins	ATL		Greg Werner	NYJ	PHIL
Ron Middleton	CLE	WASH	Jimmie Giles	PHIL	
Ozzie Newsome	CLE		David Little	PHIL	DEN
Wilbur Strozier	CLE		Jay Novacek	PHOE	DALL
Clarence Kay	DEN		Terry O'Shea	PITT	
Pat Kelly	DEN	NYJ	Craig McEwen	SD	
Clint Didier	GB		Andy Parker	SD	
John Spagnola	GB		Mark Walczak	SD	
Bob Mrosko	HOUS	NYG	Brent Jones	SF	
Chris Verhulst	HOUS	DEN	Donnie Dee	SEAT	GB
Mark Boyer	IND	NYJ	Rod Jones	SEAT	KC
John Brandes	IND	WASH	Harper LeBel	SEAT	PHIL
Trey Junkin	LARd		William Harris	TB	GB
Bruce Hardy	MIA	RL	Terry Orr	WASH	
Carl Hilton	MINN	RL	Ken Whisenhunt	WASH	
Zeke Mowatt	NYG	NE			

QUARTERBACKS

NAME	TEAM	SIGNED BY	NAME	TEAM	SIGNED BY
Scott Campbell	ATL		Tommy Kramer	MINN	RL
Gale Gilbert	BUF		Doug Flutie	NE	
Turk Schonert	CIN		Jeff Rutledge	NYG	WASH
Babe Laufenberg	DALL		Pat Ryan	NYJ	RL
Blair Kiel	GB		Neil Lomax	PHOE	RT
Tom Ramsey	IND		Todd Blackledge	PITT	
Don Strock	IND		David Archer	SD	
Ron Jaworski	KC		Kerwin Bell	TB	
Mark Herrmann	LARm		Joe Ferguson	TB	
Cliff Stoudt	MIA		Doug Williams	WASH	RL

KICKERS

NAME	TEAM	SIGNED BY	NAME	TEAM	SIGNED BY
Greg Davis	ATL		Bjorn Nittmo	NYG	KC
Paul McFadden	ATL		Al Del Greco	PHOE	
Jim Breech	CIN		Chris Bahr	SD	
Matt Bahr	CLE		John Carney	TB	SD
Mike Lansford	LARm				

IV
OFFSEASON NOTES

SIGNIFICANT INJURY UPDATES

1. Raul Allegre (New York Giants/Kicker)
Allegre, who missed the last six games of the 1989 regular season with a leg injury, is expected to arrive healthy at training camp.

2. Mark Bavaro (New York Giants/Tight End)
Bad news about Mark Bavaro. In April the Giants didn't feel Bavaro would be healthy enough from his knee injury to be ready for training camp. Keep an eye out as the season nears.

3. Rod Bernstine (San Diego Chargers/Tight End)
Bernstine's knee has been rehabilitated after an injury that kept him out of the last 11 games of 1989. The Chargers expect him to be ready for training camp.

4. Tim Brown (Los Angeles Raiders/Wide Receiver)
Brown, who suffered a knee injury that forced him to miss most of the 1989 season, is expected to be ready and in training camp.

5. Kelvin Bryant (Washington Redskins/Running Back)
Bryant, who suffered a herniated disk in his neck in an auto accident before the 1989 season, is not expected to return to football. The Redskins have placed him on the Injured, Unable to Perform list.

6. Chris Chandler (Indianapolis Colts/Quarterback)
Chandler, who missed much of the '89 season with a knee injury, was reported by the Colts to be fully recovered.

7. Quinn Early (San Diego Chargers/Wide Receiver)
Early, who missed the last 12 games of the 1989 season because of a knee injury, has gone through rehabilitation and is expected at training camp.

8. Mike Elkins (Kansas City Chiefs/Quarterback)
Elkins, a second-round selection of the Chiefs a year ago, missed the entire 1989 season with back trouble. The Chiefs say they expect him to be 100% healthy this year.

9. Alex Higdon (Atlanta Falcons/Tight End)
Higdon missed all but two games of the 1988 season and the entire 1989 season due to a knee injury. The Falcons said that he was attending school in late April and they were unsure whether he would return.

10. Michael Irvin (Dallas Cowboys/Wide Receiver)
The Cowboys hope to have Irvin, who missed the last 10 games of the '89 season, ready for the season opener. The team was unsure at press time if he would be ready when training camp starts.

11. Chuck Long (Detroit Lions/Quarterback)
An elbow injury kept Long out of almost the entire 1989 season. The Lions say he is ready to return and they expect him to show up healthy to training camp.

12. Kelvin Martin (Dallas Cowboys/Wide Receiver)
Kelvin Martin missed much of the 1989 season with a knee injury, but is expected to report to training camp at full strength.

13. Rueben Mayes (New Orleans Saints/Running Back)
Mayes missed the entire 1989 season with an achilles tendon injury, but is expected to be healthy for the 1990 season.

14. Paul McFadden (Atlanta Falcons/Kicker)
McFadden's thigh injury, which kept him out of the last seven games of 1989, is a thing of the past, and he is expected to be ready to go.

15. Stump Mitchell (Phoenix Cardinals/Running Back)
The Cardinals say that Mitchell is doing well in his rehabilitation from the knee injury that kept him out of the last 13 games of 1989. He is expected in training camp.

16. Joe Morris (New York Giants/Running Back)
According to the Giants, Morris will be ready for the 1990 season; he missed the entire 1989 campaign because of a preseason injury.

17. Rodney Peete (Detroit Lions/Quarterback)
Peete, who missed action in 1989 due to knee trouble, is expected to be healthy upon his arrival at training camp.

18. Mike Quick (Philadelphia Eagles/Wide Receiver)
When I contacted the Eagles, they had a wait-and-see attitude toward Mike Quick's condition. Quick missed the last 10 games of the 1989 season with knee trouble. We'll keep a close eye on his possible return and comment in the preseason newsletter follow-ups.

19. Robb Riddick (Buffalo Bills/Running Back)
Riddick, who missed the entire 1989 season with a knee injury, is currently undergoing therapy. He is also awaiting doctor approval of his return to play this year.

20. Mickey Shuler (New York Jets/Tight End)
Shuler suffered a knee injury that sidelined him the last eight games of 1989. The Jets say that Shuler is working out, but his status for the 1990 season was uncertain at press time.

21. Vinny Testaverde (Tampa Bay Buccaneers/Quarterback)
Testaverde, bothered by knee trouble late in the '89 season, missed the last two games. The Buccaneers report that he should be 100% okay for 1990.

22. Robert Tyler (Seattle Seahawks/Tight End)
Tyler missed the last eight games of the 1989 season with an ankle injury. The Seahawks expect him back healthy for the 1990 season.

23. Mark Vlasic (San Diego Chargers/Quarterback)
Vlasic, who missed the entire 1989 season with a knee injury, is expected to be ready for training camp and to compete for the Chargers' quarterbacking duties.

24. Ickey Woods (Cincinnati Bengals/Running Back)
Woods, who missed the last 14 games of the 1989 season with a knee injury, was still in rehabilitation when this book went to print. The Bengals said they would not comment on his progress until training camp.

KEY NFL PLAYER TRADES, RELEASES, AND PICKUPS

Plan B free agency has accelerated offseason player transactions. This year's offseason was no exception, with many key players jumping teams. The player transactions that follow involve key players who may have a fantasy impact in 1990.

Gary Anderson (Running Back)
Traded to: Tampa Bay Buccaneers
From: San Diego Chargers
Anderson, who sat out the entire 1989 season because of a contract dispute, has been traded to the Tampa Bay Buccaneers. The Bucs are getting themselves a very versatile back who can catch the ball as well as run with it. In 1988 with the Chargers, Anderson rushed for 1,119 yards and added 182 more on 32 receptions.

Mark Boyer (Tight End)
Unprotected free agent with: Indianapolis Colts
Signed with: New York Jets
Boyer, who saw his role with the Colts diminish to only 11 receptions in 1989, has signed as a Plan B free agent with the New York Jets.

Thornton Chandler (Tight End)
Free agent signed with: New York Giants
Chandler, formerly with the Dallas Cowboys, has signed with the New York Giants. The Giants had lost Mark Bavaro's backup, Zeke Mowatt, to New England through Plan B free agency, so Chandler may fit in as Bavaro's backup.

Phillip Epps (Wide Receiver)
Free agent with: New York Jets
Epps, a former standout with the Green Bay Packers before coming to the Jets in 1989, has been released.

Terrence Flagler (Running Back)
Traded to: Dallas Cowboys
From: San Francisco 49ers
Flagler, who many think has much talent but hasn't been able to show it because he has played behind Roger Craig, may finally get his chance. Flagler has been traded to the young Dallas Cowboys, with whom he should at least get an opportunity to demonstrate his skills.

Lorenzo Hampton (Running Back)
Unprotected free agent with: Miami Dolphins
Signed with: Denver Broncos
Hampton, who scored 12 touchdowns in both 1986 and 1988 for the Dolphins, has signed as a Plan B free agent with the Denver Broncos. Hampton rushed for only 48 yards in 1989 for Miami, but his history indicates an ability to score. With Denver he'll have to battle hard for playing time, because he'll be competing with the likes of Bobby Humphrey and Sammy Winder.

Bruce Hardy (Tight End)
Unprotected free agent with: Miami Dolphins
Hardy, a former starter for the Dolphins, has struggled with injuries in recent years and has been released.

Ronnie Harmon (Running Back)
Unprotected free agent with: Buffalo Bills
Signed with: San Diego Chargers
Harmon was primarily used as a receiver out of the backfield with Buffalo, and latched onto 37 and 29 receptions over the past two seasons, respectively. If he makes the Chargers' roster, I expect to see him in a similar role.

Ron Heller (Tight End)
Unrestricted free agent with: Atlanta Falcons
Signed with: Seattle Seahawks
After a season in which their top tight end had only 14 receptions, the Seahawks went shopping. They grabbed Ron Heller, who had made 33 receptions and one touchdown for the Falcons in 1989.

Tommy Kramer (Quarterback)
Unprotected free agent with: Minnesota Vikings
Kramer, a former all-pro quarterback who has spent his entire pro career with the Vikings, has been released.

Dennis McKinnon (Wide Receiver)
Unprotected free agent with: Chicago Bears
Signed with: Dallas Cowboys
McKinnon's role with the Bears diminished the last couple of years, and he was openly disgruntled. The Bears left him unprotected, and the Cowboys, who struggle to keep their wide receivers healthy, signed him. McKinnon is a fine possession receiver and as a veteran should be able to help stabilize the Cowboys.

Jim McMahon (Quarterback)
Released by: San Diego Chargers
The Chargers, still weary from last year's contract bout with Gary Anderson, didn't want to go through it all again with McMahon. He has been released.

Jamie Morris (Running Back)
Unprotected free agent with: Washington Redskins
Signed with: New England Patriots
Morris, left unprotected by the Redskins, has signed with the New England Patriots. Morris is a quick scatback runner and had one 100-yard game for the Redskins in 1989.

Zeke Mowatt (Tight End)
Unprotected free agent with: New York Giants
Signed with: New England Patriots
Mowatt was of pro-bowl caliber until a knee injury took its toll. Mowatt has since been playing in Mark Bavaro's shadow. In signing with New England, Mowatt perhaps sees a chance to prove himself again.

Bjorn Nittmo (Kicker)
Unprotected free agent with: New York Giants
Signed with: Kansas City Chiefs
Nittmo, who filled in admirably for the injured Raul Allegre in 1990, went unprotected. He has signed with the Kansas City Chiefs, and he'll battle veteran Nick Lowery for kicking duties.

Jay Novacek (Tight End)
Unprotected free agent with: Phoenix Cardinals
Signed with: Dallas Cowboys
In Novacek the Cowboys have signed themselves a quality tight end. And by leaving Phoenix, Novacek will escape the shadow of Robert Awalt and may really come into his own.

Paul Palmer (Running Back)
Unprotected free agent with: Dallas Cowboys
Signed with: Cincinnati Bengals
Palmer, who signed as a Plan B free agent in 1989 with Dallas, has taken the same route in signing with the Cincinnati Bengals. Palmer rushed 434 yards with Dallas in '89, but I don't think he'll get the same opportunity with Cincinnati in 1990.

Fuad Reveiz (Kicker)
Free agent signed with: San Diego Chargers
Reveiz, a former kicker for the Miami Dolphins, was sidelined for the 1989 season with a groin injury. He has now signed with the San Diego Chargers and will try to win their placekicking job.

Andre Rison (Wide Receiver)
Traded to: Atlanta Falcons
From: Indianapolis Colts
Rison, who grabbed 52 passes in an outstanding rookie season in 1989, has been dealt to the Atlanta Falcons. Rison was part of the deal that secured the number-one overall draft pick, quarterback Jeff George, for the Indianapolis Colts.

Pat Ryan (Quarterback)
Unprotected free agent with: New York Jets
Ryan, a sometime starter for the Jets, has been released.

Timmy Smith (Running Back)
Unprotected free agent with: San Diego Chargers
Signed with: Dallas Cowboys
Just three short years ago, Smith rushed for over 200 yards in the Super Bowl. After that he played sparingly for the Redskins in 1988 and didn't make the Chargers' 1989 club. Smith may make his presence felt with the young Cowboys.

Walter Stanley (Wide Receiver)
Unprotected free agent with: Detroit Lions
Signed with: Washington Redskins
Stanley had a couple of productive years with Green Bay before coming to Detroit last season, but with the Lions in 1989 Stanley produced only 24 receptions. Now, in signing with the receiver-deep Redskins, he'll probably be a kick returner.

Wesley Walker (Wide Receiver)
Unprotected free agent with: New York Jets
At 34, this aging star surely knew his days were numbered. He has been given his release by the Jets.

Curt Warner (Running Back)
Unprotected free agent with: Seattle Seahawks
Signed with: Los Angeles Rams
Warner was once one of the league's premier running backs. A knee injury really slowed his play and led the Seahawks to leave him unprotected. Two years ago, after recovering from the knee injury, Warner produced some excellent year-end numbers (1,025 rushing yards and 12 touchdowns), but last year his production really slipped (631 rushing yards and 4 touchdowns). It'll be interesting to see what kind of impact, if any, Warner will have with the Rams in 1990.

James Wilder (Running Back)
Unrestricted free agent with: Tampa Bay Buccaneers
Signed with: Washington Redskins
Joe Gibbs and the Redskins sure like to get their hopes up on aging NFL running backs. Last year they obtained Gerald Riggs and Earnest Byner in the offseason. This time they snapped up veteran James Wilder. Sure, Wilder has had big years, but that was some time ago.

Doug Williams (Quarterback)
Unprotected free agent with: Washington Redskins
It's a funny business! Just three short years ago Williams led the Redskins to a Super Bowl victory; now they've given him his release.

Randy Wright (Quarterback)
Free agent signed with: Pittsburgh Steelers
Wright, a former starter for the Green Bay Packers, did not play with any NFL team in 1990 and has signed with the Pittsburgh Steelers.

RETIREMENTS

Neil Lomax/Phoenix Cardinals (Quarterback)
Lomax, suffering from a degenerative arthritic hip, has finally given in to retirement.

Tony Dorsett/Denver Broncos (Running Back)
Before he became a Denver Bronco, Dorsett was a standout for years with the Dallas Cowboys . He played only one season as a Bronco. A knee injury forced him to miss the entire 1989 season and ended this aging star's career. Recovery is tough, especially for someone who has played as long as Dorsett.

Steve Largent/Seattle Seahawks (Wide Receiver)
This long-time sure-handed receiver has decided it's time to hang it up. Largent will be missed by fans of the Seahawks, Fantasy Football, and football in general.

Earl Ferrell/Phoenix Cardinals (Running Back)
Running back Earl Ferrell announced a surprise retirement. He apparently tested positive on an NFL drug test and was on his way to being banned for the 1990 season. If he can remain drug-free for a year, Ferrell can apply to the NFL for reinstatement.

NEW NFL HEAD COACHES

Atlanta Falcons (Jerry Glanville)
Glanville knows how to stir up controversy. As coach for the Houston Oilers, he was known for hard-hitting—perhaps even cheap-shot—defenses. In Atlanta, they'll welcome his aggressiveness. They want a winner, and it's hard to say whether that will be Glanville. With the Oilers' real talent he was a .500 coach (35–35); in Atlanta he has to coach a young, unproven team.

Houston Oilers (Jack Pardee)
In replacing Jerry Glanville with Jack Pardee, the Oilers gain a coach with plenty of experience. Pardee was coaching the University of Houston and he has eight years of NFL coaching experience. The Oilers know they have talented players. Now they hope they have a head coach who can take them to the promised land—the Super Bowl.

New England Patriots (Rod Rust)
At 61 years of age, Rod Rust gets his shot to run the show. Rust has been an assistant coach in the NFL for 14 years. His last post was in Pittsburgh as defensive coordinator. Rust takes over from Raymond Berry, who had a falling out with general manager Pat Sullivan. Rust gets a team that wound up 5–11 in 1989 and hasn't been playoff-bound in any of the last three seasons.

New York Jets (Bruce Coslet)

Taking over for the departed Joe Walton will be Bruce Coslet. Coslet was an innovative offensive coordinator for the Cincinnati Bengals before he became the Jets' head coach. Coslet has been around the NFL for 10 years, and he's got a creative offensive mind, which should benefit an offense that has really struggled to put it together. Don't expect immediate miracles, but Coslet should help rekindle the Jet offense.

Phoenix Cardinals (Joe Bugel)

Bugel, serving as offensive line coach for the Redskins, comes from a traditional winner. He takes over the tough task of making a winner out of Phoenix. With Neil Lomax's retirement, he'll have to make a decision at quarterback. He has veteran Gary Hogeboom and youngsters Timm Rosenbach and Tom Tupa from whom to choose. At other spots in the offense, he has many aging stars to go with, like Roy Green and J. T. Smith. Once again the Cardinals will field talent, and now it's up to Joe Bugel to guide them to winning ways.

V
1990 ROOKIE CLASS

EARLY-OUT JUNIORS POPULATE THE DRAFT

This year's NFL draft was a little different, as 38 underclassmen made themselves available. The likes of Houston quarterback Andre Ware, Illinois quarterback Jeff George, and running backs Reggie Cobb (Tennessee) and Marcus Wilson (Virginia) were all worthy picks. Eight of these underclassmen, four of them at fantasy positions, were drafted in the first round. Whether juniors or seniors, can any of these newly drafted rookies actually help your Fantasy Football team? Most rookies don't make an impact in their rookie season; some do. Barry Sanders, Eric Metcalf, Andre Rison, and Shawn Collins did well in 1989, and some rookies may excel this year, too.

Who will make a difference? In this section I evaluate 1990's rookies to determine who may be immediately effective and who will be groomed for future stardom. The rookies who may make an immediate difference in 1990 are going to teams with an immediate need at a certain position. The players who may make an impact later are going to teams that are planning for the future.

As background to our evaluation of this year's rookies, we'll first take a look at last year's draftees from the first couple of rounds—the blue chippers. Analyzing both successful and unsuccessful seasons helps us to see how this year's rookies may fare. Then I'll list this year's draft choices from fantasy scoring positions only—QBs, RBs, et al.— and evaluate this year's rookie crop. (For a more extensive look at the 1989 rookies, see Section II in this chapter, "How the 1989 Rookies Fared.")

1989 BLUE CHIPPERS
ROUND #1

OVERALL PICK	NAME	POS	COLLEGE	NFL TEAM
1	Troy Aikman	QB	UCLA	Dallas
3	Barry Sanders	RB	Oklahoma St.	Detroit
7	Tim Worley	RB	Georgia	Pittsburgh
9	Sammie Smith	RB	Florida St.	Miami
13	Eric Metcalf	RB	Texas	Cleveland
16	Hart Lee Dykes	WR	Oklahoma St.	New England
22	Andre Rison	WR	Michigan St.	Indianapolis
26	Cleveland Gary	RB	Miami	LA Rams
27	Shawn Collins	WR	Northern Arizona	Atlanta

ROUND #2

OVERALL PICK	NAME	POS	COLLEGE	NFL TEAM
30	John Ford	WR	Virginia	Detroit
31	Lawyer Tillman	WR	Auburn	Cleveland
32	Mike Elkins	QB	Wake Forest	Kansas City
33	Danny Peebles	WR	N. Carolina St.	Tampa Bay
35	Eric Ball	RB	UCLA	Cincinnati
39	Daryl Johnston	RB	Syracuse	Dallas
40	Walter Reeves	TE	Auburn	Phoenix
51	Billy Joe Tolliver	QB	Texas Tech	San Diego
56	Wesley Walls	TE	Mississippi	San Francisco

Of this group of blue chippers, Barry Sanders, Eric Metcalf, Andre Rison, and Shawn Collins were the most effective. Others showed some signs of promise, though, and shouldn't be overlooked for this year. Still others were injured and did not get to show their stuff.

Looking beyond these first two rounds, we see the likes of Dave Meggett (5th round), Rodney Peete (6th round), Chris Jacke (6th round), Marion Butts (7th round), and Pete Stoyanovich (8th round), all of whom experienced reasonable success. So don't get caught looking only at the highly touted blue chippers.

Let's look at this year's rookies, with an eye to predicting which players can help our fantasy teams in 1990.

1990 ROOKIE CLASS BY ROUND

ROUND #1

OVERALL PICK	NAME	POS	COLLEGE	NFL TEAM
1	Jeff George	QB	Illinois	Indianapolis
2	Blair Thomas	RB	Penn State	NY Jets
7	Andre Ware	QB	Houston	Detroit
17	Emmitt Smith	RB	Florida	Dallas
19	Darrell Thompson	RB	Minnesota	Green Bay
20	Steve Broussard	RB	Washington State	Atlanta
21	Eric Green	TE	Liberty	Pittsburgh
24	Rodney Hampton	RB	Georgia	NY Giants
25	Dexter Carter	RB	Florida State	San Francisco

ROUND #2

OVERALL PICK	NAME	POS	COLLEGE	NFL TEAM
26	Alexander Wright	WR	Auburn	Dallas
28	Reggie Rembert	WR	West Virginia	NY Jets
30	Reggie Cobb	RB	Tennessee	Tampa Bay
31	Anthony Thompson	RB	Indiana	Phoenix
36	Anthony Johnson	RB	Notre Dame	Indianapolis
38	Harold Green	RB	South Carolina	Cincinnati
42	Carwell Gardner	RB	Louisville	Buffalo
45	Leroy Hoard	RB	Michigan	Cleveland
50	Mike Bellamy	WR	Illinois	Philadelphia

ROUND #3

54	Mike Jones	TE	Texas A & M	Minnesota
58	Richard Proehl	WR	Wake Forest	Phoenix
59	Tommy Hodson	QB	Louisiana State	New England
64	Peter Tom Willis	QB	Florida State	Chicago
67	Walter Wilson	WR	East Carolina	San Diego
68	Ron Lewis	WR	Florida State	San Francisco
70	Neil O'Donnell	QB	Maryland	Pittsburgh
77	Fred Barnett	WR	Arkansas State	Philadelphia
78	Latin Berry	RB	Oregon	LA Rams
80	Greg McMurtry	WR	Michigan	New England

ROUND #4

83	Stacey Simmons	WR	Florida	Indianapolis
84	Troy Taylor	QB	California	NY Jets
86	Cary Conklin	QB	Washington	Washington
87	Jesse Anderson	TE	Mississippi	Tampa Bay
88	Tony Moss	WR	Louisiana State	Chicago
90	Chris Warren	RB	Ferrum (VA)	Seattle
93	Scott Mitchell	QB	Utah	Miami
96	Fred Jones	WR	Grambling	Kansas City
97	Chris Calloway	WR	Michigan	Pittsburgh
100	Eddie Fuller	RB	Louisiana State	Buffalo
102	Jackie Harris	TE	N.E. Louisiana	Green Bay

ROUND #5

OVERALL PICK	NAME	POS	COLLEGE	NFL TEAM
115	Larry Centers	RB	Stephen F. Austin	Phoenix
116	Reggie Thornton	WR	Bowling Green	Minnesota
117	Pat Chaffey	RB	Oregon State	Chicago
118	Jeff Campbell	WR	Colorado	Detroit
120	James Gray	RB	Texas Tech	New England
121	Reggie Redding	TE	Fullerton State	Atlanta
123	Lynn James	WR	Arizona State	Cincinnati
125	Charles Arbuckle	TE	UCLA	New Orleans
128	Barry Foster	RB	Arkansas	Pittsburgh
130	Brian Mitchell	RB	S.W. Louisiana	Washington
131	Cedric Smith	RB	Florida	Minnesota
132	Charles Wilson	WR	Memphis State	Green Bay
133	Calvin Williams	WR	Purdue	Philadelphia
135	Craig Kupp	QB	Pacific Lutheran	NY Giants
137	Leroy Holt	RB	USC	Miami

ROUND #6

138	John Friesz	QB	Idaho	San Diego
139	Mike Pringle	RB	Fullerton State	Atlanta
140	Terance Mathis	WR	New Mexico	NY Jets
141	Derrick Douglas	RB	Louisiana Tech	Tampa Bay
142	Tyrone Shavers	WR	Lamar	Phoenix
149	Marcus Wilson	RB	Virginia	LA Raiders
153	Tony Jones	WR	Texas	Houston
155	Ronald Heard	WR	Bowling Green	Pittsburgh
156	Mike Buck	QB	Maine	New Orleans
161	Tim Stallworth	WR	Washington State	LA Rams
163	Derrick Walker	TE	Michigan	San Diego
164	Ronnie Haliburton	TE	Louisiana State	Denver

ROUND #7

169	Johnny Johnson	RB	San Jose State	Phoenix
178	Scott Galbraith	TE	USC	Cleveland
184	Andy Murray	RB	Kentucky	Houston
187	Nathaniel Lewis	WR	Oregon Tech	San Diego
191	Aaron Emanuel	RB	USC	NY Giants
192	Shannon Sharpe	WR	Savannah State	Denver

ROUND #8

OVERALL PICK	NAME	POS	COLLEGE	NFL TEAM
194	Willie Green	WR	Mississippi	Detroit
200	James Rouse	RB	Arkansas	Chicago
201	J. J. Flannigan	RB	Colorado	San Diego
204	Doug Wellsandt	TE	Washington State	Cincinnati
205	Thomas Woods	WR	Tennessee	Miami
206	Ken Clark	RB	Nebraska	Indianapolis
207	Jerry Gdowski	QB	Nebraska	New Orleans
220	Dwight Pickens	WR	Fresno State	San Francisco

ROUND #9

223	Dale Dawkins	WR	Miami	NY Jets
228	Johnny Bailey	RB	Texas A & I	Chicago
230	Leon Perry	RB	Oklahoma	LA Raiders
231	Phil Ross	TE	Oregon State	Miami
232	Darvell Huffman	WR	Boston U.	Indianapolis
233	Broderick Graves	RB	Winston-Salem	New Orleans
235	Michael Owens	RB	Syracuse	Kansas City
237	Pat Coleman	WR	Mississippi	Houston
238	Clarkston Hines	WR	Duke	Buffalo
240	Eugene Rowell	WR	S. Mississippi	Cleveland
241	Terry Allen	RB	Clemson	Minnesota
242	Kirk Baumgartner	QB	Wisc-Stevens Point	Green Bay
245	Tony Lomack	WR	Florida	LA Rams
247	Todd Ellis	QB	South Carolina	Denver

ROUND #10

249	Pat Newman	WR	Utah State	Minnesota
252	Dave Elle	TE	South Dakota	Phoenix
253	Anthony Landry	RB	Stephen F. Austin	New England
254	Mike Busch	TE	Iowa State	Tampa Bay
258	Bill Miller	WR	Illinois State	Detroit
260	Gary Cooper	WR	Clemson	New Orleans
263	Craig Hudson	TE	Wisconsin	Kansas City

ROUND #11

OVERALL PICK	NAME	POS	COLLEGE	NFL TEAM
281	Terry Anthony	WR	Florida State	Tampa Bay
282	Dempsey Norman	WR	St. Francis, IL	Phoenix
283	Tommy Stowers	TE	Missouri	San Diego
285	Reginald Warnsley	RB	S. Mississippi	Detroit
291	Ernest Thompson	RB	Georgia Southern	Kansas City
292	Al Edwards	WR	N.W. State, LA	Buffalo
296	Clemente Gordon	QB	Grambling	Cleveland
299	Harry Jackson	RB	St. Cloud State	Green Bay
300	Tyrone Watson	WR	Tennessee State	Philadelphia
303	Ron Lewis	WR	Jackson State	LA Raiders
304	Myron Jones	RB	Fresno State	LA Raiders

ROUND #12

OVERALL PICK	NAME	POS	COLLEGE	NFL TEAM
307	Todd Hammel	QB	Stephen F. Austin	Tampa Bay
308	Donnie Riley	RB	Central Michigan	Phoenix
311	Gene Benhart	QB	Western Illinois	Indianapolis
312	John Gromos	QB	Vanderbilt	Seattle
313	Robert Clayborn	WR	San Diego State	Detroit
314	Andre Riley	WR	Washington	Cincinnati
317	Major Harris	QB	West Virginia	LA Raiders
318	Tony Jeffery	WR	San Jose State	Kansas City
319	Richard Bell	RB	Nebraska	Pittsburgh
321	Reggie Slack	QB	Auburn	Houston
323	Kerry Simien	WR	Texas A & I	Cleveland
326	Elliot Searcy	WR	Southern U.	San Diego
327	David Lang	RB	Northern Arizona	LA Rams
328	Judd Garrett	RB	Princeton	Philadelphia
329	Matt Stover	K	Louisiana Tech	NY Giants
331	Demetrius Davis	TE	Nevada-Reno	LA Raiders

GOOD ROOKIE FANTASY PROSPECTS FROM THE 1990 DRAFT

How many good fantasy players were there in this year's draft? Only time will tell. Jeff George signed with the Indianapolis Colts for $15 million over six years, but how soon will he make an impact? Many of the newly drafted players could make a significant difference for your fantasy team. Let's take a look at some of these prospects.

RUNNING BACKS

Blair Thomas *(1st round, New York Jets/College: Penn State)*
The Jets may have satisfied a big need at running back in drafting Blair Thomas. Thomas, who has great cutback moves, can run well both inside and out. He may be able to step right in and help the Jet offense, which could really use his firepower. Freeman McNeil, Johnny Hector, and Roger Vick, beware!

Emmitt Smith *(1st round, Dallas Cowboys/College: Florida)*
Smith, a junior, elected to jump into this year's draft. In 1989 he rushed for 1,599 yards and scored 14 touchdowns. With the Cowboys needing to solidify the running back position since the departure of Herschel Walker, Smith may get his shot early on. Although he's going to a young team, Smith should give the Cowboys some real spark.

Darrell Thompson *(1st round, Green Bay Packers/College: Minnesota)*
At just over six feet and just under 220 pounds, Thompson has the size and strength to run inside. He also quickly gets off the mark and through the line. He'll make a great addition to the Packers, who can't be happy with Brent Fullwood's inconsistency. Thompson may be just what the doctor ordered for the Packers.

Steve Broussard *(1st round, Atlanta Falcons/College: Washington State)*
With the departure of Gerald Riggs to Washington in 1989 and John Settle's subpar performance, the Falcons must have felt that they had a need at running back. Broussard gives them a very fast breakaway threat. He stands 5'7", and they may also use him returning kicks, which he did in college. Training camp will give us a clearer picture.

Rodney Hampton *(1st round, New York Giants/College: Georgia)*
The Giants have the uncertainties of Joe Morris's recovery from a season-long injury and O. J. Anderson's age. In grabbing Hampton in the first round, they acquired a player with good size (6'0", 215 pounds) and dependable hands, which could help him make an immediate impact in 1990.

Dexter Carter *(1st round, San Francisco 49ers/College: Florida State)*
With Roger Craig and Tom Rathman in their backfield, the 49ers were in no serious need at running back. In Carter, they got a fast, dangerous open-field runner with sure hands, but his talents may not come into play right away.

Reggie Cobb *(2nd round, Tampa Bay Buccaneers/College: Tennessee)*
The Bucs had already acquired running back Gary Anderson from the San Diego Chargers just before the draft, and their choice of Reggie Cobb was something of a surprise. Cobb has great potential and a history of drug use. Has he beaten the problem?

Anthony Thompson *(2nd round, Phoenix/College: Indiana)*
With Stump Mitchell coming off a season-long knee injury in 1989 and the surprise retirement of Earl Ferrell, the Cardinals were looking to strengthen their running attack, which they did by drafting Thompson. Thompson had a great college career, highlighted by his 1,793-yard, 24-touchdown season in 1989. He could become a solid pro runner, with a chance to prove himself early on.

Anthony Johnson *(2nd round, Indianapolis Colts/College: Notre Dame)*
Johnson is a strong, hard-running fullback, someone the Colts may need if Eric Dickerson follows through on his desire to be traded or retire. Johnson may become very useful in short-yardage, goal-line situations.

Harold Green *(2nd round, Cincinnati Bengals/College: South Carolina)*
With Ickey Woods recovering from a knee injury and Eric Ball not playing as well as the Bengals had hoped, Green was a good choice. In Green, the Bengals have a quick outside runner with good hands; he should fit well into their offense.

Carwell Gardner *(2nd round, Buffalo Bills/College: Louisville)*
At just over six feet and 228 pounds, Gardner has both power and speed. His drawback is that he lacks experience; he used to play defensive end and has yet to become an accomplished back. His impact may not be immediate, but if he works hard his future could be bright.

Leroy Hoard *(2nd round, Cleveland Browns/College: Michigan)*
Hoard is a strong, punishing runner who can also catch. He could complement Eric Metcalf well in the Cleveland backfield.

Latin Berry *(3rd round, Los Angeles Rams/College: Oregon)*
Not only is Berry a breakaway runner, but he can also get tough, inside yards. And he's known as a good receiver. All those skills will help, but he'll have to compete with the likes of Greg Bell, Curt Warner, and Robert Delpino for playing time.

WIDE RECEIVERS

Alexander Wright *(2nd round, Dallas Cowboys/College: Auburn)*
The young Cowboys continue to build for the future. In Wright, they get a fast but unrefined receiver. Wright also returns kicks, which may be his short-term role, unless Michael Irvin and Kelvin Martin (both of whom are coming off season-ending knee injuries in 1989) don't stay healthy.

Reggie Rembert *(2nd round, New York Jets/College: West Virginia)*
At 6'4", Rembert will make a great target. He also possesses the speed to be a game breaker and should complement Al Toon well. He could make a big impact as a rookie, especially since the Jets have released veteran standout Wesley Walker and are needy at this position.

Mike Bellamy *(2nd round, Philadelphia Eagles/College: Illinois)*
Perhaps Mike Quick's knee problems have the Eagles concerned. Bellamy can also be used as a kick returner, and that might be his main duty if Mike Quick returns 100% healthy.

Richard Proehl *(3rd round, Phoenix Cardinals/College: Wake Forest)*
Coming to a team that has two aging wideouts in Roy Green and J. T. Smith, Proehl should get a shot at breaking into the lineup soon. He brings a reputation for good hands and the ability to catch the ball over the middle. He also returns kicks, which is a short-term possibility.

Walter Wilson *(3rd round, San Diego Chargers/College: East Carolina)*
Even though he doesn't have great speed, Wilson can still get open to make catches. The Chargers are a young team searching for young talent, which could give Wilson a shot.

Greg McMurtry *(3rd round, New England Patriots/College: Michigan)*
At 6'2" and 200 pounds, McMurtry makes for a nice-sized target. Although he doesn't have super speed, he can jump well and he runs with very fluid strides. He could help a team looking to replace aging Stanley Morgan.

Stacey Simmons *(4th round, Indianapolis Colts/College: Florida)*
Simmons is still working his way back to health after leg surgery. He has great speed and good hands, and with the departure of Andre Rison to Atlanta in the Jeff George trade, there is a wide-receiver vacancy.

Tony Moss *(4th round, Chicago Bears/College: Louisiana State)*
With the Bears losing veteran Dennis McKinnon to Dallas via Plan B free agency, there's a need at wide receiver. Moss comes to the Bears with a reputation for being an excellent athlete with extremely quick moves and great after-the-catch ability.

Chris Calloway *(4th round, Pittsburgh Steelers/College: Michigan)*
Despite his lack of notable size or speed, many scouts liked Calloway for his quickness and competitiveness. Pittsburgh, where the Steelers are still searching for a receiving mate for Louis Lipps, should provide him opportunity.

TIGHT ENDS

Eric Green *(1st round, Pittsburgh Steelers/College: Liberty)*
His only drawback seems to be his size—over 270 pounds. Not only is he a good blocker, but he also possesses good hands (62 receptions and 10 touchdowns in 1989). The Steelers hadn't even used their tight end actively in their offense, until Mike Mularkey joined the team last season.

Mike Jones *(3rd round, Minnesota Vikings/College: Texas A & M)*
Although the Vikings have Steve Jordan and didn't seem to have a strong need at tight end, Jones seemed too good at this stage of the draft to pass up. The future could be bright for Jones, who can block well, run well, and catch the ball in traffic.

Jesse Anderson *(4th round, Tampa Bay Buccaneers/College: Mississippi)*
Anderson may lack blocking skills, but he is strong in receiving skills, with good hands and the ability to run deep routes.

QUARTERBACKS

Jeff George *(1st round, Indianapolis Colts/College: Illinois)*
The Colts had enough confidence in George's ability to trade last year's rookie standout wide receiver Andre Rison and offensive lineman Chris Hinton to get him. They'll also pay $15 million over six years for his services. George, a junior, took an early out to turn pro. At Illinois he played in a pro-type offense and displayed a strong arm, quick release, and good touch—all skills that the Colts are betting he'll refine to become a great NFL quarterback.

Andre Ware *(1st round, Detroit Lions/College: Houston)*
Getting this year's Heisman Trophy winner gives the Lions two in a row, following Barry Sanders last year. Ware comes to the Lions with all the skills to direct the Lions' run-and-shoot offense; he is the perfect match for this offense. I'm sure he's got the attention of the rest of the NFC Central Division. Ware runs well, has a quick release, and wields a strong arm, all of which should lead this young Lion team to a bright future.

Tommy Hodson *(3rd round, New England Patriots/
College: Louisiana State)*
Hodson has a quick, accurate release. In 1989 he threw for over 2,600 yards and 22 touchdowns. The Patriots are certainly in need of a good young signal caller, and Hodson hopes to fill the bill.

Peter Tom Willis *(3rd round, Chicago Bears/College: Florida State)*
Willis had started only two games prior to the '89 season, when he hit 211 of 346 passes (61.0%) for 3,124 yards and 20 touchdowns. He's known for his toughness and quick delivery. With Chicago, he may not get an immediate shot, but a lack of consistency from Mike Tomczak and Jim Harbaugh may give him his chance sooner than expected.

Gary Conklin *(4th round, Washington Redskins/College: Washington)*
At 6'4" and 215 pounds, Collins is an excellent size for a pro quarterback. He can throw deep, but he lacks consistency. His usefulness would seem to be in the future, with the Redskins relying on Mark Rypien and Stan Humphries for their immediate needs.

KICKERS

Matt Stover *(12th round, New York Giants/College: Louisiana Tech)*
Stover was the only placekicker drafted in this year's draft. With the Giants, he'll have to battle Raul Allegre, who is coming off a leg injury, for the 1990 kicking chores.

VI
RATING THE 1990 NFL TEAM SCHEDULES

This section rates the upcoming year's team schedules. Something to consider when selecting your fantasy team for 1990 is the strength or weakness of your team's 1990 opposition. Obviously, a player facing an easy schedule has a good chance of having a statistically successful, productive year.

First, we'll look at last year's standings and see how each team did. Then we'll look at each team's 1990 schedule and rate its schedule according to how the current year's opposition performed in 1989.

This is not a fail-safe method of selecting players, but it is something important to consider when choosing between two players whom you have rated almost equally.

The following pages show the 1989 final standings, followed by the rankings for each team's 1990 schedule.

1989 AMERICAN CONFERENCE STANDINGS

Eastern Division

TEAM	W	L	T	PCT.	PTS.	OPP.
Buffalo	9	7	0	.563	409	317
Indianapolis	8	8	0	.500	298	301
Miami	8	8	0	.500	331	379
New England	5	11	0	.313	297	391
NY Jets	4	12	0	.250	253	411

Central Division

TEAM	W	L	T	PCT.	PTS.	OPP.
Cleveland	9	6	1	.594	334	254
Houston	9	7	0	.563	365	412
Pittsburgh	9	7	0	.563	265	326
Cincinnati	8	8	0	.500	404	285

Western Division

TEAM	W	L	T	PCT.	PTS.	OPP.
Denver	11	5	0	.688	362	226
Kansas City	8	7	1	.531	318	286
LA Raiders	8	8	0	.500	315	297
Seattle	7	9	0	.438	241	327
San Diego	6	10	0	.375	266	290

1989 NATIONAL CONFERENCE STANDINGS

Eastern Division

TEAM	W	L	T	PCT.	PTS.	OPP.
NY Giants	12	4	0	.750	348	252
Philadelphia	11	5	0	.688	342	274
Washington	10	6	0	.625	386	308
Phoenix	5	11	0	.313	258	377
Dallas	1	15	0	.063	204	393

Central Division

TEAM	W	L	T	PCT.	PTS.	OPP.
Minnesota	10	6	0	.625	351	275
Green Bay	10	6	0	.625	362	356
Detroit	7	9	0	.438	312	364
Chicago	6	10	0	.375	358	377
Tampa Bay	5	11	0	.313	320	419

Western Division

TEAM	W	L	T	PCT.	PTS.	OPP.
San Francisco	14	2	0	.875	442	253
LA Rams	11	5	0	.688	426	344
New Orleans	9	7	0	.563	386	301
Atlanta	3	13	0	.188	279	437

How can this ranking of schedules help us? I recommend that, when you are deciding on a fantasy draft pick, you lean toward players on teams that face the easier schedules. The flip side is obviously that you should note which teams face the tough schedules and recognize that they'll have a hard time having productive seasons.

Let's examine a couple of scenarios. All four NFC Eastern Division teams are in the top 10 of easy schedules, courtesy of facing last year's 1-15 Cowboys. The New York Jets, who struggled through 1989 with injuries to many key players, have the fortune of having the league's easiest schedule. If they can stay healthy and get on track, a number of their players could have productive seasons.

For the Atlanta Falcons, things will be quite different, and times should be tough. The Falcons match up against the Super Bowl Champion San Francisco 49ers (14-2), the Los Angeles Rams (11-5), and the New Orleans Saints (9-7) twice each. Their season should be a long one. The Dallas Cowboys will have trouble improving as they face the league's fourth toughest schedule. This means that players like Troy Aikman, Daryl Johnston, and Paul Palmer will continue to take their licks, so don't look for any big numbers from that group.

This schedule ranking and analysis should provide some feel for the opposition your fantasy players will face in 1990.

The following 1990 rankings are based on the win-loss records of opponents during the 1989 season. Rankings go from the easiest schedule (top) to the most difficult schedule (bottom).

1990 DIFFICULTY RANKINGS of TEAM SCHEDULES
1990 Opponents' Combined 1989 Records

TEAM	WON	LOST	TIED	PCT.
1. NY Jets	113	142	1	.443
2. Tampa Bay	115	141	0	.449
3. San Diego	117	136	3	.463
4. Philadelphia	120	136	0	.469
5. Miami	123	132	1	.482
6. Washington	124	132	0	.484
7. Buffalo	125	130	1	.490
8. NY Giants	126	130	0	.492
9. Phoenix	126	130	0	.492
10. Indianapolis	126	129	1	.494
11. Chicago	127	128	1	.498
12. Denver	126	127	3	.498
13. Kansas City	128	127	1	.502
14. New England	128	127	1	.502
15. San Francisco	129	126	1	.506
16. New Orleans	129	126	1	.506
17. Cincinnati	129	125	2	.508
18. Seattle	129	125	2	.508
19. Detroit	130	125	1	.510
20. Green Bay	131	124	1	.514
21. Pittsburgh	131	123	2	.516
22. LA Raiders	131	123	2	.516
23. Houston	131	122	3	.518
24. LA Rams	132	123	1	.518
25. Dallas	133	123	0	.520
26. Cleveland	135	120	1	.529
27. Minnesota	136	117	1	.541
28. Atlanta	138	117	1	.541

VII
A TEAM-BY-TEAM
1989 REVIEW / 1990 PREVIEW

Here is a team outlook by position, with teams listed alphabetically. **RB** = Running Back, **WR** = Wide Receiver, **TE** = Tight End, **QB** = Quarterback, and **K** = Kicker

ATLANTA FALCONS
Home Stadium: Atlanta-Fulton County Stadium
Playing Surface: Grass

RB: What a terribly disappointing season for John Settle and for fantasy owners who drafted him in 1989! In 1988, Settle rushed for 1,024 yards on 232 carries, added 570 more yards on 68 receptions, and scored eight touchdowns. The Falcons were confident enough in Settle at the start of the 1989 season to trade Gerald Riggs to Washington. Then came Settle's 1989 season of only 690 yards rushing on 179 carries, 316 yards on only 39 receptions, and only five touchdowns. The Falcons have to be hoping for a big rebound from Settle in 1990. If they don't get it, they'll have to look to rookie Steve Broussard out of Washington State, second-year player Keith Jones, or veteran Gene Lang for help.

WR: The Falcons have found themselves quite a wide receiver in last year's first-round draft choice, Shawn Collins. Collins latched onto 58 receptions for 862 yards and three touchdowns as a rookie in 1989. The Falcons also have Michael Haynes, who grabbed 40 receptions for 681 yards in '89, despite missing five games with a shoulder injury. Also contributing was Floyd Dixon, with 25 receptions for 357 yards, while Stacey Bailey had a poor season with only 8 receptions. The Falcons have also added last year's rookie standout Andre Rison from the Indianapolis Colts. Rison could team with Shawn Collins to make quite a young receiving tandem.

TE: At tight end, the Falcons are still waiting for the return of Alex Higdon, who suffered a severe knee injury way back in the second game of 1988. In 1989, however, they got some solid play from unprotected free agent Ron Heller, who came over from San Francisco. Heller had 33 receptions in 1989, leading Falcon tight ends, while another unprotected free agent, Brad Beckman, added 11 receptions. Heller, however, has been lost to the Seattle Seahawks through Plan B free agency. That leaves Beckman, possibly Higdon, and rookie fifth-round selection Reggie Redding for the job.

QB: Chris Miller continues to mature at quarterback. He even stayed healthy for the most part in 1989, missing only one game, and upped his passing yards from 2,133 in 1988 to 3,459 in 1989. The biggest struggle he and his teammates face in 1990 is the league's toughest schedule.

K: Paul McFadden began the 1989 season as the Falcons' placekicker and hit on 15 of 20 (.750) field-goal attempts before falling victim to a thigh injury. He was replaced by Greg Davis, who had kicked for the Falcons in 1988, had gone to New England as an unprotected free agent, and had been released by the Patriots after nine games of the 1989 season. Davis rejoined the Falcons to become their kicker for their last six games, during which he hit only 7 of 11 (.636) on field-goal attempts, seemingly leaving the job wide open for 1990.

BUFFALO BILLS
Home Stadium: Rich Stadium
Playing Surface: AstroTurf

RB: Thurman Thomas improved on his 1988 rookie numbers with a sensational sophomore season of 1,244 yards rushing and another 669 yards on 60 receptions. Thomas also scored 12 touchdowns, 6 on the ground and 6 through the air, as scoring specialist Robb Riddick missed the entire season with a knee injury. The Bills also got 534 rushing yards and six touchdowns out of Larry Kinnebrew. Receiving specialist Ronnie Harmon helped out with 29 receptions for 363 yards and four touchdowns but has since been lost to the San Diego Chargers via Plan B free agency. The main man in 1990 should be Thurman Thomas, unless Riddick returns healthy to share the scoring load or rookie second-round pick Carwell Gardner steps in to make an immediate impact.

WR: Andre Reed gets better and better. Reed followed up a 71-reception, 968-yard, six-touchdown season in 1988 with a sensational 88-reception, 1,312-yard, nine-touchdown season in 1989. Chris Burkett started the year with the Bills but was released and finished the season with the Jets. Flip Johnson chipped in 25 receptions, while veteran James Lofton, who signed on partway into the season, grabbed only 8 receptions, 3 for touchdowns. Speedster Don Beebe added 17 receptions, 2 of which covered 63 yards for touchdowns.

TE: Pete Metzelaars saw his 1989 production drop off, as he latched onto only 18 receptions. Keith McKeller became a pleasant surprise with 20 receptions for 341 yards and two scores. Meanwhile, Butch Rolle caught his fifth reception in three years, all of which have gone for scores.

QB: Despite missing three games with a separated shoulder, Jim Kelly threw for over 3,100 yards and 25 touchdowns in 1989, marks he could easily reach in 1990—if he stays healthy.

K: After leading the league in scoring in 1988, Scott Norwood posted somewhat lower numbers in 1989. Nevertheless, his 23 of 30 (.767) on field-goal attempts and 46 of 48 extra points gave him 115 points in a solid effort.

CHICAGO BEARS
Home Stadium: Soldier Field
Playing Surface: AstroTurf

RB: In running back Neal Anderson, the Bears have one of the best. Anderson rushed for 1,275 yards and added 434 more on 50 receptions, while scoring 15 touchdowns in 1989. Brad Muster took over the bulk of the fullback duties from Matt Suhey and rushed for 327 yards and five touchdowns, adding three more scores through the air. Both Anderson and Muster should be big producers for the Bears again in 1990.

WR: The Bears are not a pass-oriented football team. Dennis Gentry led the club with 39 receptions for 463 yards and only one touchdown. Following Gentry were Ron Morris, Dennis McKinnon, and Wendell Davis—29, 28, and 27 receptions, respectively—who accumulated only seven touchdowns among them. Of this group, Dennis McKinnon was left unprotected through the new Plan B free-agency system and now is a member of the Dallas Cowboys. The Bears also will take a look at fourth-round rookie Tony Moss out of Louisiana State.

TE: Jim Thornton grabbed 24 receptions for 3 touchdowns in 1989, while Cap Boso latched onto 17 receptions, scoring once. Both should continue to battle for playing time in 1990.

QB: With Jim McMahon off to San Diego, Mike Tomczak became the team's full-time starter. At least that's how the 1989 season began. Inconsistency then led to Tomczak's being replaced by Jim Harbaugh, and this battle for the number-one spot should continue in 1990, unless one or the other improves dramatically.

K: Butler hit his first 14 attempts before ending up the season 15 of 19 (.789) on field-goal attempts in 1989. He should return to get his kicks for the Bears in 1990.

CINCINNATI BENGALS
Home Stadium: Riverfront Stadium
Playing Surface: AstroTurf

RB: Ickey Woods, who had such a standout rookie season in 1988, missed almost the entire 1989 season after suffering a knee injury in the second game. James Brooks stepped in to have another fabulous year, rushing for 1,239 yards, adding 306 more through the air on 37 receptions, and scoring nine touchdowns. The Bengals, searching for a replacement for Woods, used rookies Eric Ball and Craig Taylor, along with veteran Stanford Jennings. All were less than impressive, so you can bet the Bengals are praying for Woods's healthy return in 1990. The Bengals have acquired Paul Palmer, a former Dallas Cowboy, via Plan B free agency, and they drafted Harold Green from South Carolina in the second round to help solidify their running attack.

WR: At wide receiver, Tim McGee stepped to the forefront, grabbing 65 receptions for 1,211 yards and eight touchdowns. Eddie Brown, as a contract holdout, was late in reporting. He then got off to a slow start but finished with 52 receptions. Both are outstanding wideouts and should continue their success in 1990.

TE: It may be tough for Rodney Holman to duplicate in 1990 his 1989 "Fantasy Tight End of the Year" numbers—50 receptions for 736 yards and nine touchdowns.

QB: Though hampered by an ankle injury, Boomer Esiason still threw for over 3,500 yards and 28 scores in 1989, stats that have become the norm for him.

K: Veteran Jim Breech was let go at the outset of 1989, giving way to Jim Gallery. Gallery's 2 of 6 (.333) on field-goal attempts brought Breech back for the Bengals' last 12 games of 1989, and Breech wound up hitting 12 of 14 (.847) field-goal attempts. This should give him the edge for Cincinnati's 1990 kicking chores, though he was again left unprotected in Plan B free agency.

CLEVELAND BROWNS
Home Stadium: Cleveland Stadium
Playing Surface: Grass

RB: The Browns were pleased by the performance of rookie first-round pick Eric Metcalf. Metcalf proved elusive while rushing for 633 yards, adding 397 more through the air, and scoring 10 touchdowns. A big disappointment was veteran Kevin Mack's absence most of the year because of suspension and prison time related to drugs. The Browns also got contributions from Tim Manoa, Barry Redden, and Keith Jones, but it's evident that Metcalf and Mack are this team's primary weapons, although second-round rookie Leroy Hoard could grab some playing time.

WR: Webster Slaughter and Reggie Langhorne continue to blossom as standout receivers, grabbing 65 and 60 receptions, respectively, in 1989. Veteran Brian Brennan latched onto only 28 receptions in 1989 and has seen his role continue to diminish. Rookie second-round draft choice Lawyer Tillman, a 55-day training-camp holdout, was quite a disappointment, grabbing only six receptions on the year. I expect Tillman to do better than that in 1990.

TE: Many thought veteran Ozzie Newsome had closed out his career in 1989, but it's not so. He's coming back for another round in 1990.

QB: Bernie Kosar continues to prove that an immobile quarterback can wreak havoc on NFL defenses. He threw for over 3,500 yards in 1989, and in 1990 he should surpass his somewhat low 1989 mark of 18 touchdown passes.

K: Veteran Matt Bahr hit a disapppointing 16 of 24 (.667) field-goal attempts in 1989 and may have left the door open for a challenger in 1990.

DALLAS COWBOYS
Home Stadium: Texas Stadium
Playing Surface: Texas Turf

RB: The blockbuster trade that sent Herschel Walker to the Minnesota Vikings also sent the Cowboys searching for a new identity. The Cowboys picked up Paul Palmer, who became their primary rusher with 434 yards. Rookie Daryl Johnston came on late in the year, when he picked up most of his 212 rushing yards. Neither, though, could replace what Walker used to give the Cowboys, so the search goes on. The Cowboys have lost Palmer via Plan B free agency but have acquired both Terrence Flagler from the 49ers and former Redskin/Charger Timmy Smith, along with Emmitt Smith out of Florida, their number-one draft pick. I expect big things from Emmitt Smith and Flagler.

WR: Both Michael Irvin and Kelvin Martin were off to splendid seasons until both suffered season-ending knee injuries. The Cowboys got some solid relief work from James Dixon, Cornell Burbage, Derrick Shepard, and Bernard Ford, but they hope to have both Irvin and Martin back healthy in 1990. Meanwhile, Burbage was lost via Plan B free agency to Minnesota and Bernard Ford to Houston, but the Cowboys acquired veteran Dennis McKinnon, formerly of the Bears. Dallas also has high expectations for second-round rookie Alexander Wright out of Auburn.

TE: Steve Folsom put together a decent 28-reception performance in 1989, while rookie Keith Jennings came on late in the year with 6 receptions in the season's last two games. The big news may be the acquisition of Jay Novacek. Novacek, a former Cardinal, has had his share of success in the NFL.

QB: The Cowboys seem to have settled on Troy Aikman as their present and future. Although he missed five games with a fractured index finger in 1989, Aikman returned to recapture the starting job from fellow rookie Steve Walsh. Walsh served as Aikman's backup in '89, but he may become trade bait to help bolster this young team at other positions.

K: Roger Ruzek, who began the 1989 season as the Cowboys' kicker, was let go after hitting a dismal 5 of 11 (.454) on field-goal attempts. His replacement, Luis Zendejas (who began the year with Philadelphia), didn't fare much better, hitting on only 5 of 9 (.555) attempts with the Cowboys. This seems to leave the job wide open for 1990.

DENVER BRONCOS
Home Stadium: Denver Mile High Stadium
Playing Surface: Grass

RB: After the season- and career-ending knee injury to Tony Dorsett, the Broncos were delighted with their acquisition of supplemental draft pick Bobby Humphrey. Humphrey rushed for over 1,100 yards and scored eight touchdowns. He appears to have a very bright future. Another rookie, seventh-round pick Mel Bratton, saw his contributions grow towards season's end. Veteran Sammy Winder filled in well but has relinquished his starting role to Humphrey. Receiving specialist Steve Sewell saw his stats slip to only 25 receptions in 1989. The Broncos have also added former Dolphin Lorenzo Hampton, through Plan B free agency, to their stockpile of running-back talent.

WR: Vance Johnson put together his finest season, with 76 receptions for 1,095 yards and seven touchdowns. Meanwhile, the other two "amigos" didn't fare as well. Mark Jackson had a disappointing 28 receptions, and Ricky Nattiel had only 10, partly because he spent much of the year on the injured-reserve list with a knee injury. The clutch catches of Michael Young, who finished the year with 22 receptions, were pleasant surprises, and the Broncos hope to get Jackson's and Nattiel's reception levels back up in 1990.

TE: Orson Mobley served a 30-day drug-alcohol suspension to start off the '89 season and wound up with a disappointing 17 receptions. Clarence Kay was also far from impressive, producing only 21 receptions and two touchdowns. Both hope to redeem themselves in 1990.

QB: The strong-armed John Elway produced over 3,000 passing yards, but he remains a Fantasy Football disappointment with only 18 touchdowns in 1989.

K: The Broncos decided to let veteran Rich Karlis go and settled on David Treadwell. Treadwell came through in grand style, hitting 27 of 33 (.818) field-goal attempts, and should have a lock on Bronco kicking duties for 1990.

DETROIT LIONS
Home Stadium: Pontiac Silverdome
Playing Surface: AstroTurf

RB: The Lions' running attack got quite a boost with the drafting of first-rounder Barry Sanders, who exploded for 1,470 rushing yards and 14 touchdowns as a rookie. He certainly gives another dimension to the Lions' run-and-shoot offense.

WR: The run-and-shoot offense certainly benefited Richard Johnson. Johnson has become the Lions' most productive receiver, compiling a 70-reception, 1,091-yard, eight-touchdown season in 1989. Robert Clark also put together a fine 40-reception season, while rookie Jason Phillips grabbed the spotlight toward season's end with 24 receptions over the last six games, including a 10-reception performance against Tampa Bay. All three could again be in the thick of things for the Lions in 1990.

TE: The Lions' new run-and-shoot offense left no production opportunity for the tight-end position.

QB: In 1989, rookie Rodney Peete ran the offense when he wasn't slowed by the knee injury that hampered him much of the season. Backup Bob Gagliano filled in well and was the Lions' primary signal caller over the last five games—all victories. But the big news for 1990 is the drafting of first-round selection Andre Ware out of Houston. Ware is the perfect man to run the Lions' run-and-shoot offense and may make them immediate contenders in the NFC Central. Ware has all the skills to become one of the league's best offensive stars.

K: Not much has to be said about veteran Eddie Murray's sharpshooting, a league-leading 20 of 21 (.952) on field-goal attempts and a perfect 36 of 36 on extra points in 1989.

GREEN BAY PACKERS
Home Stadium: (Green Bay) Lambeau Field
Playing Surface: Grass
Home Stadium: (Milwaukee) Milwaukee County Stadium
Playing Surface: Grass

RB: Brent Fullwood has been the Packers' main offensive weapon on the ground. He got off to a strong start in 1989, rushing for five touchdowns in the season's first three games, but never scored again after that. He also rushed for 434 yards through the first five games but wound up with only 821 for the season. The Packers hope to get more consistency from him in 1990. Besides Fullwood, Keith Woodside shared some of the rushing load, while Herman Fontenot became the receiving specialist with 40 receptions in 1989. The Packers also have very high expectations for rookie first-round selection Darrell Thompson out of Minnesota. Thompson could step right in and become the running back they need.

WR: Second-year man Sterling Sharpe really came into his own in 1989, producing a 90-reception, 1,423-yard, 12-touchdown season that quickly put him among the league's elite receivers. Perry Kemp added a solid 48-reception performance, while Jeff Query, Aubrey Matthews, and Carl Bland rounded out the receiving crew. Matthews has since signed with the Detroit Lions as a Plan B free agent.

TE: At tight end, steady Ed West was off to a fast start with four touchdowns in the season's first three games, before a knee injury sidelined him for part of the season. The Packers also have veterans John Spagnola and Clint Didier, but if West is healthy he's the man.

QB: There was much question before the 1989 season as to who would be the Packers' signal caller. After a brilliant 4,318-yard, 27-touchdown season by Don Majkowski, there should be no questions going into 1990.

K: After going through five kickers in 1988, the Packers were delighted with the performance of rookie Chris Jacke. Jacke hit 22 of 28 (.786) field-goal attempts and all 42 extra points in 1989.

HOUSTON OILERS
Home Stadium: Astrodome
Playing Surface: AstroTurf

RB: Mike Rozier held out 41 days into training camp, a delay that may have played a part in his dismal 301-yard rushing performance in 1989. His days as an Oiler may be numbered. Meanwhile, Alonzo Highsmith, Allen Pinkett, and Lorenzo White split up the rushing duties, and this division of labor should recur in 1990.

WR: Drew Hill was another contract holdout, but his numbers (66 receptions for 930 yards and eight touchdowns) don't look like those of a holdout who also missed two games with a back injury. Besides Hill, the Oilers also have the very talented Ernest Givins (55 receptions), Haywood Jeffires (47 receptions), and Curtis Duncan (43 receptions). All of them should be back grabbing Warren Moon aerials in 1990.

TE: Tight end for the Oilers is not usually a statistically bountiful position. That remains true. Chris Verhulst and Bob Mrosko caught four and three passes, respectively, in 1989. Mrosko signed with the New York Giants for the 1990 season.

QB: Warren Moon continues to lead the Oilers' attack, throwing for over 3,600 yards and 23 touchdowns in 1989 and rushing for 4 more scores.

K: This was Luis Zendejas's second consecutive poor season. In 1987 he hit 20 of 24 (.833) field-goal attempts, but in 1988 he went only 22 of 34 (.647) and last year 25 of 37 (.676). I wonder if he'll be around another year.

INDIANAPOLIS COLTS
Home Stadium: Hoosier Dome
Playing Surface: AstroTurf

RB: A rushing tally of 1,311 yards is a little dip from the norm for Eric Dickerson, but a hamstring injury slowed his play in 1989. There is some talk of early retirement, but he still has much to give. Regardless, Albert Bentley will continue to be an excellent backup or starter. His 52 receptions in 1989 prove he's not a one-dimensional player. The Colts also went out and added second-round pick Anthony Johnson out of Notre Dame to their roster. Johnson—a big, tough runner—may become a prime goal-line weapon.

WR: Billy Brooks had a another sensational year in 1989 with 63 receptions. Meanwhile, rookie Andre Rison was all the Colts had hoped for and stole the other receiving spot from Matt Bouza, producing 52 receptions. Rison has since been dealt to the Atlanta Falcons for Jeff George. This leaves a vacancy at one of the wideout spots. Speedster Clarence Verdin may be a candidate, or the Colts may turn to rookie fourth-round selection Stacey Simmons out of Florida.

TE: In 1989, Pat Beach and Mark Boyer continued to share tight-end duties for the Colts. Both saw their statistical success drop way off, with only 25 receptions between them. In 1990, Boyer signed as a Plan B free agent with the New York Jets.

QB: A season-ending knee injury knocked Chris Chandler out in the third game of 1989. Jack Trudeau stepped in and played well, but not well enough to be a lock for the job in 1990. Now that the Colts have signed $15 million rookie Jeff George, it should only be a matter of time before George gets the call.

K: Dean Biasucci had another productive year in 1989, hitting 21 of 27 (.778) field-goal attempts, with three of his six misses from more than 50 yards out. He should have little trouble hanging onto his job in 1990.

KANSAS CITY CHIEFS
Home Stadium: Arrowhead Stadium
Playing Surface: AstroTurf

RB: Despite missing one game with a thigh injury, Christian Okoye still managed to lead the league in rushing in 1989 with 1,480 yards. He's fast becoming one of the league's most feared workhorse backs. To occasionally spell Okoye, the Chiefs look to Herman Heard, James Saxon, or Todd McNair.

WR: After some big years, Stephone Paige had a disappointing 44-reception season in 1989 and did not catch a pass until the third game of the season. This was partly due to his coming to training camp late. Veteran Carlos Carson was let go after the season's outset and finished the year with Philadelphia. Veterans Pete Mandley and Emile Harry put together some decent numbers (35 and 33 receptions, respectively). Clarence Weathers, picked up from Indianapolis at midseason, added 17 receptions, while rookie third-round draft pick Naz Worthen spent much of the year on the injured reserve with a rib injury. Weathers was lost via Plan B free agency to Green Bay. The Chiefs drafted Grambling's Fred Jones in the fourth round of this year's draft to help solidify their receiving crew.

TE: Jonathan Hayes, a former top draft pick who grabbed only 18 receptions in 1989, still hasn't produced the numbers once thought to be within his reach. Chris Dressel, who latched onto nine receptions in the first five games, was ultimately let go and picked up by the New York Jets. Alfredo Roberts, another tight end used by the Chiefs, managed only eight receptions in 1989.

QB: This may be a big question mark for the Chiefs in 1990. Veteran Steve De Berg saw most of the action in 1989, playing well enough to lead the Chiefs to respectability. Aging veteran Ron Jaworski also got his shot, probably his last. Steve Pelluer was given an opportunity, too, but failed to seize it. Meanwhile, rookie second-round draft pick Mike Elkins spent the year on injured reserve with a back injury and never got a showing. The bottom line is that for a team on the upswing the quarterbacking assignment in 1990 may be passed around.

K: Though his field-goal performance dipped in 1989 (.727 on 24 of 33 attempts), Nick Lowery has proved over the years that he is one of the league's finest. Nonetheless, the Chiefs signed former New York Giant Bjorn Nittmo to battle for the job.

LOS ANGELES RAIDERS
Home Stadium: Los Angeles Memorial Coliseum
Playing Surface: Grass

RB: Marcus Allen, a contract holdout, got off to a poor start and then suffered a knee injury that forced him to miss eight games of the 1989 season. Steve Smith and Vance Mueller filled in admirably until Bo Jackson arrived. And arrive he did, rushing for 950 yards in only 11 games. Too bad they can't have his services for the entire 16 games. Because Jackson can't show until midseason, they'll have to get more out of Marcus Allen and keep him healthy.

WR: The sophomore jinx hit Tim Brown in 1989, when he was lost for the season after suffering a knee injury in the regular-season opener. Mervyn Fernandez stepped in to have his best season since coming over from the Canadian Football League—57 receptions for 1,069 yards and nine touchdowns. Willie Gault's 28 receptions marked another disappointing year, especially since he got more playing time because of Tim Brown's injury.

TE: Todd Christensen was unable to return from his 1988 knee injury, so the Raiders had to look elsewhere. Mike Dyal has been a nice surprise; in 1989 he grabbed 27 receptions for 499 yards and two scores.

QB: Many felt that another year to ease into the Raider system would help Jay Schroeder, but by season's end his ineffectiveness allowed Steve Beuerlein to take over the starting job. Beuerlein played well, starting the season's last six games.

K: Signing as a Plan B free agent in 1989, Jeff Jaeger hit 23 of 34 (.676) field-goal attempts in 1989, maybe not good enough to lay claim to the job for 1990.

LOS ANGELES RAMS
Home Stadium: Anaheim Stadium
Playing Surface: Grass

RB: Despite only three games of 100-plus yardage, Greg Bell continued to plow ahead for big season-end totals. In 1989, he rushed for 1,137 yards and 15 more touchdowns. First-round pick Cleveland Gary held out 56 days into training camp and never did put it together. Robert Delpino and Buford McGee both helped out, especially through the air, with 34 and 37 receptions, respectively. It'll be interesting to see if Cleveland Gary can make more of an impact as a second-year player and what kind of impact newly acquired Curt Warner may make for the Rams. There's also promise in third-round selection Latin Berry our of Oregon.

WR: You wouldn't know it by looking at his stats—70 receptions for 1,382 yards and eight touchdowns—but Henry Ellard missed time in 1989 because of a calf injury. Second-year players Willie "Flipper" Anderson and Aaron Cox began to make their marks in 1989, especially Anderson, who latched onto 44 receptions (25 during the last five games) for an unbelievable 1,146 yards and a 26.1-yard average. He is definitely a player to note as you prepare for your 1990 draft.

TE: Pete Holohan continues to produce receptions, with 51 in 1989. Damone Johnson saw his reception total drop to 25, but 5 were for scores. Both should be a big part of the Rams' offensive scheme again in 1990.

QB: Jim Everett, throwing in 1989 for 4,310 yards and 29 touchdowns, has not stopped putting together the big numbers. He's quickly developing into one of the league's premier signal callers.

K: Considering that four of Mike Lansford's seven missed field-goal attempts in 1989 were from beyond 50 yards (he was 23 for 30 [.706]), you have to admit that he had a good season. However, it was a bit of a surprise to see the Rams not protect him under Plan B free agency.

MIAMI DOLPHINS
Home Stadium: Joe Robbie Stadium
Playing Surface: Grass

RB: Injuries had a big impact on the Dolphins' running attack in 1989; Troy Stradford (knee), Lorenzo Hampton (knee), and Ron Davenport (groin) all missed time because of injury. A 57-day contract holdout got rookie first-round pick Sammie Smith off to a slow start, but by season's end he and Marc Logan had become the Dolphins' primary ground threats. I expect a lot from Sammie Smith in 1990. Lorenzo Hampton was lost to the Denver Broncos through Plan B free agency.

WR: Despite a 47-day contract holdout, Mark Clayton still produced some big year-end numbers—64 receptions for 1,011 yards and nine touchdowns. Mark Duper, however, was less than super. Bothered by a knee injury, Duper produced only 49 receptions and one touchdown. Utility man Jim Jensen put together an impressive '89 campaign with 61 receptions, 5 of which went for touchdowns. Look for this trio of reception machines, stoked by Dan Marino, to rack up the numbers again in 1990.

TE: Second-year man Ferrell Edmunds became the Dolphins' main tight end in 1989 and produced 32 receptions. Meanwhile, veteran Bruce Hardy was released.

QB: Dan Marino threw for just under 4,000 yards in 1989 and recorded 25 touchdown passes. Though these numbers are substantially lower than those he produced in the mid-1980s, he remains a top fantasy quarterback.

K: A groin injury knocked Fuad Reveiz out of the Dolphins' kicking job, so rookie Pete Stoyanovich got a shot. Stoyanovich's 19 of 26 on field-goal attempts (.731) may be good enough to lock him into the job for 1990. Reveiz, who missed the entire 1989 season, signed with the San Diego Chargers.

MINNESOTA VIKINGS
Home Stadium: Hubert H. Humphrey Metrodome
Playing Surface: AstroTurf

RB: The blockbuster trade that brought Herschel Walker to Minnesota was not the boost the Vikings had hoped it would be. Herschel didn't seem to fit into the offense. Or maybe the Vikings couldn't modify it to accomodate Herschel's strengths. If Walker remains a Viking, something has to be done to properly utilize this standout running back. In the Walker trade, the Vikings parted with Darrin Nelson, which left Rick Fenney, Alfred Anderson, D. J. Dozier, and Allen Rice to complement Walker. Fenney, a determined runner, produced well, rushing for 588 hard-earned yards and contributing 30 receptions.

WR: A very disgruntled Anthony Carter showed up late to training camp in 1989 and, though bothered by nagging injuries, still produced a 65-reception, 1,066-yard, four-touchdown season. Opposite Carter was Hassan Jones, who continued to mature and produced a decent 42-reception season for himself in 1989.

TE: Perennial all-pro tight end Steve Jordan was another Viking displeased with his contract and who showed up late to training camp. His year-end total of only 35 receptions may reflect both his contract displeasure and his tardiness in getting to camp. He may be pushed in 1990 by rookie third-round selection Mike Jones out of Texas A. & M. Jones comes to the Vikings with high expectations.

QB: The Vikings had settled on Wade Wilson over Tommy Kramer, but Wilson had a terrible year, which has the Vikings scratching their heads about what to do now. They released Kramer, making Rich Gannon their number-two man; Wilson will be given the initial call, although the Vikings have confidence in Gannon's ability.

K: Teddy Garcia started the '89 season as the Vikings' kicker, but after a horrendous 1-of-5 start (.200) through three games, he was released. The Vikes then brought in veteran Rich Karlis, who had been released by the Broncos. Karlis hit a spendid 31 of 39 field-goal attempts (.795) during the season's last 13 games and may have earned himself a job for 1990 as well.

NEW ENGLAND PATRIOTS
Home Stadium: Sullivan Stadium
Playing Surface: Super Turf

RB: The Pats have a good running back in John Stephens. Though an ankle injury sidelined Stephens for a couple of games in 1989, he still rushed for 833 yards and seven touchdowns. If he can stay healthy in 1990, he should be able to recapture his rookie-year magic and again top the 1,000-yard mark. Bob Perryman also continues to contribute rushing yardage—562 yards in 1989. The Pats let another significant contributor, Reggie Dupard, go during the 1989 season (he was picked up by Washington), so the bulk of the rushing load should continue to fall to Stephens and Perryman. They did, however, pick up former Redskin Jamie Morris as a Plan B free agent.

WR: Both primary wideouts, Irving Fryar (sprained knee) and Stanley Morgan (fractured fibula), missed plenty of action because of injuries in 1989. Their year-end stats reflect that, with Fryar grabbing only 29 receptions and Morgan only 28. Their absence presented opportunities for both Cedric Jones and rookie Hart Lee Dykes, and both responded well. Dykes, after a slow start, finished the season with 49 receptions and five touchdowns, while Jones grabbed 48 receptions, six for touchdowns. This could be the year the aging Morgan steps aside and yields to youth, as both Dykes and Jones seem ready and hungry to produce. That could spell trouble for Fryar. The Patriots also went out and chose Greg McMurtry out of Michigan as their third-round selection in this year's draft to further their youth movement.

TE: The Patriots used Plan B free agency effectively in acquiring Eric Sievers last season. The sure-handed Sievers became the primary tight end (ahead of Lin Dawson and rookie Marv Cook) and latched onto 54 aerials in 1989. The Pats have added another Plan B tight end this year—Zeke Mowatt of the Giants.

QB: Here's a real mess! The Patriots released Tony Eason during the '89 season, and he later signed with the New York Jets. From that point on, the Pats juggled veteran Steve Grogan and Doug Flutie and finished the year with Marc Wilson. This leaves the job wide open for 1990. And don't forget to throw in rookie third-round pick Tommy Hodson out of Louisiana State to jumble things up further.

K: Greg Davis was another Plan B player signed in 1989. Davis started the year as the Pats' kicker but was released after a 16-of-23 (.696) field-goal performance. The Pats then signed Jason Staurovsky, who hit 14 of his 17 attempts (.823), probably good enough to secure his job for the 1990 season.

NEW ORLEANS SAINTS
Home Stadium: Louisiana Superdome
Playing Surface: AstroTurf

RB: For Dalton Hilliard, 1989 was a banner year. With Rueben Mayes out for the season with a knee injury, Hilliard played spectacularly—1,262 yards rushing, 514 more on 52 receptions, and 18 touchdowns—and became the 1989 Fantasy Player of the Year. He got some support from Craig Heyward, Buford Jordan, and Paul Frazier, but Hilliard was the main man. Will the return of a healthy Rueben Mayes cut drastically into Hilliard's 1990 stats? Perhaps, but Hilliard really proved what he could do when given ample opportunity.

WR: The numbers for both Eric Martin (68 receptions, 1,079 yards, 8 touchdowns) and Lonzell Hill (48 receptions, 636 yards, 4 touchdowns) slipped somewhat in 1989. Both Brett Perriman (20 receptions) and rookie Floyd Turner (22 receptions) helped out, but each had an injury (Perriman, knee; Turner, broken arm) that hindered his production. In 1990, I'll keep a close watch on the effectiveness or ineffectiveness of the Saints' running game, led by Dalton Hilliard, which will dictate the production level of the Saints' receivers. With Hilliard very effective in 1989, the receivers' levels were down. Will that happen again in 1990?

TE: Hoby Brenner stayed healthy for most of the '89 season, and his stats reflect that in a 34-reception, four-touchdown year. Meanwhile, John Tice had a dismal nine receptions on the season. This was a flip-flop from 1988, when Brenner accounted for only 5 receptions and Tice had 26. Either or both should again provide offensive help for the Saints in 1990.

QB: Bobby Hebert started the first 13 games of 1989, but near season's end head coach Jim Mora thought the offense needed a boost and he turned the reins over to John Fourcade. Fourcade's impressive showing—829 passing yards, seven touchdown passes, and three wins—makes him the frontrunner for the 1990 season.

K: Another truly subpar season in 1989 for the usually consistent Morten Andersen, who connected on only 20 of 29 (.690) field-goal attempts. Still, it's hard to believe his job would be in jeopardy.

NEW YORK GIANTS
Home Stadium: Giants Stadium
Playing Surface: AstroTurf

RB: A season-ending knee injury to Joe Morris surely shook things up for the Giants at the outset of 1989. With Morris gone for the season, the aging O. J. Anderson was called on to be the Giants' primary ground gainer. Anderson responded in fine fashion, rushing for 1,023 yards and 14 touchdowns. A repeat of this performance shouldn't be expected in 1990; Anderson is just too old and Morris hopes to be back healthy. 1990 should also bring the continued development of two 1989 rookies. Fifth-round selection Dave Meggett really made his presence felt by grabbing 34 receptions, 4 of which were for touchdowns. Fourth-round selection Lewis Tillman was more of a disappointment, rushing for only 290 yards. The Giants in this year's draft secured Rodney Hampton out of Georgia as their first-round pick. If the veterans can't get it done, they'll look to Hampton.

WR: The Giants' offense stayed on the ground, utilizing running back O. J. Anderson in 1989, so none of the team's wide receivers had a big season. After a 65-reception, 1,029-yard season in 1988, the Giants' most prominent wide receiver, Lionel Manuel, had only 33 receptions in 1989. Odessa Turner got off to a strong start and finished the season as the Giants' leading receiver, but even he had only 38 receptions and four touchdowns. The Giants also got production from Mark Ingram (17 receptions), Stephen Baker (13 receptions), and Stacey Robinson (4 receptions). I think we'll see an upward swing in the reception level for the Giants' receivers in 1990, especially from Lionel Manuel and Odessa Turner, because the strength of the Giants' running attack is in question.

TE: Perennial all-pro Mark Bavaro was off to a good start with 22 receptions over the season's first seven games when a knee injury sidelined him for the season. Zeke Mowatt filled in, accounting for 27 receptions, but the Giants obviously hope to have Bavaro back and healthy in 1990. Meanwhile, the Giants have lost Mowatt via Plan B free agency to New England and have picked up veterans Thornton Chandler (Cowboys) and Bob Mrosko (Oilers) by the same means.

QB: Phil Simms threw for just over 3,000 yards and only 14 touchdowns in 1989, partly because an ankle injury kept him out of two games. This tough signal caller should rebound statistically if he can avoid the hard licks in 1990.

K: A leg injury sidelined Raul Allegre in the sixth game of 1989. His replacement was Bjorn Nittmo, who, despite hitting 9 of 12 (.750) field-goal attempts, did give way to a healthy Allegre in the playoffs. Nittmo signed with the Kansas City Chiefs, after being left unprotected through Plan B free agency. The Giants did, however, draft the only placekicker in this draft—Matt Stover of Louisiana Tech—in the twelfth round.

NEW YORK JETS
Home Stadium: Giants Stadium
Playing Surface: AstroTurf

RB: Freeman McNeil had a very poor season, rushing for only 342 yards through 10 games, and seemed to run himself out of a job. Roger Vick saw more playing time late in the year, after McNeil's benching, and finished the season with 434 yards and seven touchdowns. Although Johnny Hector got off to a very slow start, due to his 56-day contract holdout, he did finish the year as the Jets' leading rusher, with 702 yards. Nevertheless, he scored only five touchdowns. The Jets, under new leadership in 1990, will have to reexamine many things; one will definitely be their running game. As a first step toward that end, they chose Blair Thomas out of Penn State as the number-two overall pick. Thomas will be asked to revitalize a struggling ground attack.

WR: Al Toon had an unbelievable year. He came late into camp and missed much of the year with ankle and shoulder injuries. Catching passes in only 11 games, Toon still accounted for 63 receptions, proving that when he's healthy he's one of the game's best. Veteran Wesley Walker has seen his better days come and go, as he managed only eight receptions in a year when neck and ankle injuries took their toll; he has since been given his release. So where do the Jets turn for help? Jo Jo Townsell put together a decent 45-reception season in 1989. The Jets also picked up veterans Chris Burkett and Phillip Epps, with Burkett (18 receptions for the Jets) being more productive than Epps (only 9). Epps, too, was released. The Jets made a big move in this year's draft by selecting West Virginia's Reggie Rembert in the second round. Rembert could become an excellent complement to Al Toon as part of the Jets' receiving crew.

TE: Another great season was apparently in store for Mickey Shuler, as he accounted for 29 receptions through the first eight games of 1989. But a knee injury from which he hopes to bounce back in 1990 knocked him out of the second half of the season. In his absence, the Jets tried the likes of Billy Griggs (9 receptions), Chris Dressel (an acquisition from Kansas City who made 2 receptions as a Jet), and Keith Neubert, who played very well, accounting for 28 receptions over the season's last nine games. The Jets also added Plan B free agent Mark Boyer, who was the starting tight end for the Indianapolis Colts at the close of the '89 season.

QB: A new year, a new coaching staff, and a new-look offense. What's going to happen at quarterback? The Jets have Ken O'Brien, their perennial starter, but now they also have Tony Eason, whom they acquired during the 1989 season. They have released both other back-ups—Pat Ryan and Kyle Mackey. The O'Brien-Eason situation better sort itself out as the season opener draws near.

K: Pat Leahy has been with the Jets for a long time. His 1989 field-goal performance of 14 of 21 (.667) was quite a drop from his 23 of 28 (.821) in 1988. His 1990 job security is a question mark.

PHILADELPHIA EAGLES
Home Stadium: Veterans Stadium
Playing Surface: AstroTurf

RB: The Eagles' two primary backs produced mediocre rushing totals in 1988. Anthony Toney rushed for 582 yards, while Keith Byars rushed for 452. Byars did put in an outstanding year catching the football in 1989, however—721 yards on 68 receptions, an impressive followup to his 1988 tally of 705 yards on 72 receptions. The Eagles also got some support from Mark Higgs (184 yards), and rookies Heath Sherman (177 yards) and Robert Drummond (132 yards). But in 1990 it should again be Keith Byars and Anthony Toney leading the ground attack, with Byars again making his presence felt more through the air than on the ground.

WR: This marked the second straight season former Pro Bowl receiver Mike Quick missed most of the regular season. This time around, a knee injury forced him to miss the season's last 10 games. Can he return 100% healthy? That's a big question for 1990. Meanwhile, in Quick's absence Cris Carter continues to be the Eagles' big-play receiver, accounting for 11 touchdowns in 1990. The Eagles also have Ron Johnson and Greg Garrity and they acquired Carlos Carson during the '89 season; none of these, however, comes close to what Mike Quick does or what he means to this club. That may be why they took a shot at two wide receivers in the early rounds of this year's draft, latching onto Illinois's Mike Bellamy in the second round and Arkansas State's Fred Barnett in the third round.

TE: Even though he missed a few games because of knee and back injuries, Keith Jackson managed 63 receptions, evidence that he's still a player to be heard from in a big way.

QB: Randall Cunningham's 631 rushing yards led the team and may prove that the team asks just a little too much from him. Cunningham threw for 3,400 yards and 21 touchdowns, showing he can get it done in many ways.

K: The Eagles went through three kickers in 1989. Luis Zendejas started the year but his 9-of-15 (.600) field-goal performance lost him the job. Then Steve DeLine came in for three games, hitting only 3 of 7 (.429) attempts. Finally Roger Ruzek, who had been released by Dallas earlier in the year, managed to hit 8 of 11 (.727) field-goal attempts for the Eagles, but I wonder if it's enough to secure him the job for 1990.

PHOENIX CARDINALS
Home Stadium: Sun Devil Stadium
Playing Surface: Grass

RB: Stump Mitchell, the Cardinals' main ground weapon, suffered a knee injury in game #3 of the 1989 season and missed the last 13 games. His recovery may be a key to the Cardinals' 1990 running game. Unfortunately for the Cardinals, Earl Ferrell was unable to pick up the slack last year. His rushing-yards dropped from 924 in 1988 to only 502 in 1989. And during the offseason, Ferrell announced a surprise retirement after being tested positive for drugs and facing the prospect of having to miss the 1990 season. He can petition to return to the league if he remains clean for a year. If Mitchell doesn't return 100% healthy in 1990, where will the Cardinals turn? Certainly the likes of Tony Jordan, Vai Sikahema, or Tony Baker could fill his shoes in 1989. That may be why the Cardinals selected Indiana's Anthony Thompson in the first round of this year's draft. Thompson may get the opportunity to produce early on for the banged-up Cardinals.

WR: Wide receivers were another sore spot for the Cardinals in 1989, literally. Both standout receivers, J. T. Smith and Roy Green, suffered significant injuries. Smith was off to an unbelievable start with 62 receptions, for 778 yards and five touchdowns, in the season's first nine games, before suffering a season-ending fractured fibula. Green was sidelined for four weeks with a fractured collarbone. This left plenty of opportunity for the other receivers to shine. Ernie Jones did just that, grabbing 44 receptions for 823 yards and three touchdowns. His performance should get him more playing opportunity in 1990, regardless of the health of J. T. Smith and Roy Green. The Cardinals also got youth in Richard Proehl from Wake Forest in the third round of this year's draft.

TE: The Cardinals' two steady performers at tight end, Robert Awalt (33 receptions) and Jay Novacek (23 receptions), saw their production fall off somewhat in 1989. This could have been due to the loss of Neil Lomax as their signal caller. In 1990, only Awalt will be concerned, because Novacek is now a member of the Dallas Cowboys, courtesy of Plan B free agency. This could also open the door for last year's second-round pick, Walter Reeves.

QB: This could be a real question mark for the Cardinals in 1990. Neil Lomax has retired. Gary Hogeboom was the primary signal caller for the Cardinals in 1989, but will they look to youth in 1990? Tom Tupa and Timm Rosenbach may be given more of a shot by the Cardinals. This situation is well worth watching into the preseason.

K: It was no surprise when Al Del Greco was left unprotected under Plan B free agency. Del Greco followed his miserable 12-of-21 (.571) showing of 1988 with a dismal 18-of-26 (.692) performance in 1989. This should make the job wide open for 1990.

PITTSBURGH STEELERS
Home Stadium: Three Rivers Stadium
Playing Surface: AstroTurf

RB: Rookie Tim Worley got off to a slow start in 1989 but came on to rush for 491 yards over the season's last seven games. It's that kind of production the Steelers hope to see more of in 1990. Merril Hoge put in a second consecutive solid season, rushing for 621 yards and eight touchdowns and adding 271 more yards on 34 receptions. Both these players should be big weapons for the Steelers in 1990.

WR: Though a 36-day holdout in preseason, Louis Lipps put up some decent numbers, with a 50-reception, 944-yard, six-touchdown season. Lipps is a key to the Steeler passing game, and he seems to be regaining the productive ways of his early years in the league. The Steelers are still looking for a receiver to complement Lipps, a vacancy they've had since the retirement of John Stallworth. Derek Hill seems to be the leading candidate, although he produced only 28 receptions in 1989. You can also count rookie fourth-round selection Chris Calloway from Michigan as another candidate for the job.

TE: Tight end has been a spot the Steeler offense has seemed to ignore for years. However, Plan B free agent Mike Mularkey got into the offensive scheme and tallied 22 receptions for 326 yards; he may become more prominent in Pittsburgh's plans for 1990. Or the Steelers may turn immediately to their first-round selection, Eric Green out of Liberty, who could make an immediate impact.

QB: Bubby Brister has taken his knocks, but he may have helped this team start its turnaround. In 1989 the two games he missed with a knee injury were part of the reason his passing totals were low—2,365 yards and only nine touchdowns. With more experience and better health, he should be able to improve on those stats in 1990.

K: For one of the league's finest and most accurate kickers, Gary Anderson's 21 of 30 (.700) field-goal attempts in 1989 might seem a bit low, but I assume he'll be back.

SAN DIEGO CHARGERS
Home Stadium: Jack Murphy Stadium
Playing Surface: Grass

RB: The biggest story for the Chargers' running game in 1989 was the season-long holdout of Gary Anderson, an ingredient the Chargers sorely missed in their offense. In his absence, seventh-round draft choice Marion Butts got his shot and made the most of it. Butts rushed for 683 yards and more importantly, nine touchdowns. Tim Spencer also chipped in 521 rushing yards, while Darrin Nelson, an acquisition from Minnesota via Dallas, became a useful receiver out of the backfield. With Anderson now being dealt to Tampa Bay, I expect Butts will continue to see much of the rushing load. The Chargers have also added former Buffalo Bill Ronnie Harmon and former Chicago Bear Thomas Sanders through Plan B free agency.

WR: Anthony Miller in short order has placed himself among the league's best. In 1989 he amassed 1,242 yards on 75 receptions, 10 of which went for touchdowns. He's certain to be the Chargers' main receiving target again in 1990. But who do the Chargers have to go along with him? Jamie Holland saw plenty of action, producing 25 receptions through mid-year in 1989, but towards season's end, Wayne Walker took over to make 15 receptions during one four-game stretch. And the Chargers selected Walter Wilson of East Carolina as their third-round pick in this year's draft to battle for the job.

TE: Rod Bernstine was working out just the way the Chargers had hoped in 1989, latching onto 21 receptions through the first five games. A knee injury then eliminated him for the season. In Bernstine's absence, Arthur Cox (22 receptions), Joe Caravello (10 receptions), Craig McEwen (7 receptions), and Andy Parker (2 receptions) all filled in. Obviously, their play was not near Bernstine's standard, which is why the Chargers have their fingers crossed for his healthy return in 1990.

QB: The Chargers went out and got themselves a solid veteran quarterback in Jim McMahon prior to the 1989 season. McMahon, however, was not an immediate savior, and eventually his ineffectiveness lost him the starting job to Billy Joe Tolliver. Tolliver's strong late-season performance should give him the edge for retaining the job at the outset of the '90 season, especially now that the Chargers have released McMahon.

K: Chris Bahr became a Charger via Plan B free agency. His sporadic 17 of 25 (.680) field-goal attempts—he missed at least one field goal in eight different games—made the Chargers shop again. They signed former Miami Dolphin Fuad Reveiz and former Tampa Bay Buccaneer John Carney.

SAN FRANCISCO 49ers
Home Stadium: Candlestick Park
Playing Surface: Grass

RB: The 49ers' one-two punch—Roger Craig and Tom Rathman—was successful again in 1989. Craig rushed for 1,054 yards, added 473 more on 49 receptions, and scored seven touchdowns. Rathman was much more productive through the air. He latched onto 73 receptions for 616 yards and added 306 more rushing yards, but he scored only two touchdowns. Backup Terrence Flagler finally got dealt to the Dallas Cowboys. The 49ers went right out and drafted Dexter Carter out of Florida State in the first round as an investment for their future.

WR: Just incredible! That's what I think of Jerry Rice. Fortunately, I had him as a member of my fantasy team in 1989—another stellar season, with 82 receptions for 1,483 receiving yards and 17 touchdowns. The 49ers have found themselves another outstanding weapon to complement Rice. John Taylor is coming into his own, 60 receptions for 1,077 yards and 10 touchdowns in 1989 prove that. Besides Rice and Taylor in 1990, we may be seeing a bit more of Mike Sherrard, who was activated late in the year after a two-year layoff due to a leg injury.

TE: With the retirement of John Frank, the tight end position for the 49ers was in question. Brent Jones stepped in and became the answer. His total of 40 receptions for 500 yards and four touchdowns proved he was a worthy choice.

QB: Is there any better? Has there ever been? I don't think so. Joe Montana is a magician. I don't care what home team you cheer for, Montana is fun to watch. And at 33, when most quarterbacks are on the downside of their careers, Montana seems like he hasn't yet peaked. How many more years does he have? Two? Three? Four? That's a question his backup, Steve Young, must also be asking. Young, a very good quarterback in his own right, has to be frustrated. Though at one time his lack of playing time made him want to be traded, he now seems to have accepted his backup role and will stay on with the 49ers.

K: Mike Cofer had a strong 1989 regular season, hitting 29 of 36 (.855) of his field-goal attempts and 49 of 50 extra points for 136 total points and Fantasy Kicker of the Year honors.

SEATTLE SEAHAWKS
Home Stadium: Kingdome
Playing Surface: AstroTurf

RB: It seems like just a short time ago that Curt Warner made a big splash coming into the league, demonstrating his elusive cut-back moves. After his knee surgery, those moves aren't as crisp and Warner's play has taken a slide. In 1989, he rushed for only 631 yards and was left unprotected by the Seahawks under Plan B free agency. It's sad to see such diminished play from such a talented runner. Warner has since signed with the Los Angeles Rams, but the Seahawks still have J. L. Williams. Williams was slowed somewhat by an ankle injury in 1989, but he still managed 499 rushing yards and another 657 yards on 76 receptions. He should again be the Seahawks' primary weapon in 1990. Also given a shot to produce in 1990 should be Derrick Fenner, who looked impressive in minimal exposure in 1989. The Seahawks should also give rookie fourth-round selection Chris Warren out of Ferrum a good look.

WR: The Seahawks will be losing perennial standout receiver Steve Largent. He'll be sorely missed. However, they have to be ecstatic over the play of second-year receiver Brian Blades. Blades went from a 40-reception, 682-yard, eight-touchdown season as a rookie in 1988 to a fantastic 77-reception, 1,063-yard, five-touchdown season in 1989. 1990 should spell more of the same for this talented wideout. Who do the Seahawks have to team with him? There's Paul Skansi, who's built like Steve Largent and could be a great possession receiver. There's also Louis Clark, who contributed 25 receptions in 1989, and perhaps Tommy Kane, who doesn't, however, seem to be able to shrug off injuries.

TE: At tight end, the Seahawks started 1989 with Robert Tyler, but an ankle injury placed him on the sidelines for the last eight games. The Seahawks also have last year's rookie fourth-round selection, Travis McNeal, who stepped in late in the 1989 season, and they have added Ron Heller from Atlanta through Plan B free agency.

QB: When he's hot, he's hot; when he's not.... So goes the play of quarterback Dave Krieg. Can Krieg's inconsistent performance hold off the challenge of Kelly Stouffer? That's something to be given a closer look as the regular season draws near.

K: Neither the Seahawks nor Norm Johnson can be pleased with his poor showing in 1989, a miserable 15 of 25 (.600) field-goal attempts. Four of those misses were from beyond 50 yards, but you wonder if the Seahawks won't open their eyes to other kickers for the 1990 season.

TAMPA BAY BUCCANEERS
Home Stadium: Tampa Stadium
Playing Surface: Grass

RB: Since the virtual demise at running back of James Wilder, the Buccaneers haven't had a strong ground attack. Lars Tate again led the Bucs in rushing in 1989, but his 589-yard performance was small comfort. He did, however, contribute eight touchdowns. The Bucs also got contributions from William Howard (357 yards), James Wilder (244 yards), and Sylvester Stamps (141 yards). Both Wilder (36 receptions for 335 yards) and William Howard (30 receptions for 188 yards) helped out through the air. Wilder, however, was lost to the Washington Redskins via Plan B free agency, so he won't be around in 1990. The biggest story for the Bucs may be the acquisition of Gary Anderson from the San Diego Chargers. Anderson, who sat out the Chargers' entire 1989 season over a contract dispute, should give them plenty of firepower. Look for Anderson, Lars Tate, and possibly rookie second-round selection Reggie Cobb out of Tennessee to bear most of the rushing load.

WR: Mark Carrier took his statistics to a new level in 1989—86 receptions for 1,412 yards and nine touchdowns—establishing himself as one of the league's better wideouts. His receiving partner, Bruce Hill, also fared well with 50 receptions for 673 yards and five touchdowns. Those two should be back in 1990 to grab Vinny Testaverde's aerials. They should get some help from Willie Drewrey, Danny Peebles, and Frank Pillow, who missed the entire 1989 season with a broken foot.

TE: Ron Hall continues to be productive at tight end for the Bucs. His 1989 numbers dropped off somewhat from his previous year's results, but he could rebound in 1990. Or the Bucs may turn to rookie fourth-round selection Jesse Anderson out of Mississippi.

QB: It's time for Vinny Testaverde to shine, and last year he did. Testaverde threw for more than 3,100 yards and 20 touchdowns in 1989 and really limited the number of interceptions he threw. Look for continued maturity and progress in 1990.

K: Donald Igwebuike hit on 22 of 28 (.785) field-goal attempts in 1989; of his 6 misses, all were from beyond 40 yards and 5 were from beyond 46 yards. This short-range accuracy and consistency should keep him a Buccaneer.

WASHINGTON REDSKINS
Home Stadium: Robert F. Kennedy Stadium
Playing Surface: Grass

RB: The Redskins cannot be pleased with the outcome of their 1989 acquisition of Gerald Riggs. Riggs got off to a solid start, with 658 rushing yards through the season's first seven games, but chest, knee, ankle, and arch injuries cut into his play so much that he finished the year with only 834 rushing yards total. Is this the dominant back that the Redskins want? Does he lack durability? The Redskins in 1989 were also without Kelvin Bryant, who was hurt in an offseason auto accident and missed the entire season with a herniated disk. His healthy return remains questionable. So, without Riggs for part of the season and without Bryant the entire season, the Redskins turned to Earnest Byner. Byner, acquired in an offseason trade with Cleveland, was Washington's number-two rusher (580 yards) and added another 458 yards on 54 receptions. His nine touchdowns also tied him for the team lead. He may get a similar opportunity in 1990, especially with the uncertainty about Riggs's durability and about Bryant's healthy return. The Redskins lost Jamie Morris to the New England Patriots but picked up former Tampa Bay Buccaneer James Wilder, both via Plan B free agency.

WR: Here is one of the best three-receiver squads ever put together: Art Monk (86 receptions, 1,186 yards, eight touchdowns), Ricky Sanders (80 receptions, 1,138 yards, four touchdowns), and Gary Clark (79 receptions, 1,229 yards, seven touchdowns). All had incredible seasons in 1989, and the same would seem to be in store for 1990.

TE: Tight end was once an important position in the offensive scheme for the Redskins. In 1989 it sure wasn't. Don Warren led the Washington tight ends with a measly 15 receptions, while Terry Orr (3 receptions) and Mike Tice (1 reception) were even less productive.

QB: Doug Williams sat out the first half of the '89 season with back trouble. On his return, he was given a shot at regaining the starting role, but his ineffectiveness eventually led to his release by the Redskins. Meanwhile, Mark Rypien's numbers (3,768 passing yards and 22 touchdown passes) were especially impressive when we consider that he didn't play in two games. His problem, however, was fumbling. If he can overcome that tendency, he could become an excellent signal caller.

K: Chip Lohmiller had plenty of opportunity for a big year in 1989 with 40 field-goal attempts, but he was successful on only 29. This gave him a kicking percentage of 72.5, a figure the Skins would surely like him to improve on in 1990.

VIII
RATING THE PLAYERS:
BASIC SCORING METHOD

With the Basic Scoring Method, points are awarded to the players who actually score or throw touchdowns, with no consideration for the yardage a player may accumulate or the distance covered by a touchdown play.

The Basic Scoring Method is the simplest scoring method, but it may be the hardest to draft for. This method probably involves more luck than skill in predicting who will score touchdowns. When most sports enthusiasts sit down at their first Fantasy Football draft, they feel they are pretty much up on the game. Their tendency is to draft well-known, established names; they usually get a rude awakening. Their highly paid scatback rushes up and down the field week after week, but when it comes to the two-yard touchdown plunge, the ball is given to the big fullback. For years Freeman McNeil was the Jets' yardage man. When it came to the short touchdowns, however, Johnny Hector usually was called on. In recent years, however, more teams have left their quick-moving scatback players in near the goal line to reap some of the scoring rewards after laboring to pick up that yardage all the way down the field. Nevertheless, don't think the million-dollar players guarantee a successful Fantasy Football team.

In the following pages, I'm going to help you plan your basic drafting strategy. Then I'll follow with some things to keep in mind when choosing players. Next, I'll offer a statistical look at the players' 1989 results. Finally, I'll rate the players for the 1990 season. No rookies are included in my player ratings. It's too early to size up how they'll fit into each team's scheme. I rate the rookies separately, in Section V of this chapter.

Basic Scoring Method

DRAFTING STRATEGY BY ROUNDS

(A Guide for the Beginner)

1. The draft consists of 12 rounds.
2. Of the 12 players, 7 are starters and 5 are reserves.
3. The starting 7 comprise:

1 Quarterback		1 Quarterback
2 Running Backs	OR	2 Running Backs
2 Wide Receivers	FLEX OPTION	3 Receivers
1 Tight End		1 Kicker
1 Kicker		

4. The 5 reserves can be from any position.

5. Any player from any starting position can be drafted in any round.

What are the keys to drafting a successful Fantasy Football team? If luck plays such a big role in the Basic Scoring Method, why are some franchises consistent winners, year after year?

In studying the successful franchises of the league I participate in, I have found a number of success factors. One of these is preparation: Successful franchise owners are always ready for the unexpected. If a player they were hoping to get is grabbed just before their turn, they have an alternate choice. Following is a system that will give you the best chance of having a successful Fantasy Football draft.

ROUND 1: No matter whether you pick 1st or 16th in this round, grab the best six-point player available. This is often a running back because they are the most consistent at scoring touchdowns, though some wide receivers like Jerry Rice have also become consistent scorers and are also good picks. Quarterbacks may throw a lot of touchdown passes, but they are awarded only three points for each, as opposed to the six awarded to the player who actually has possession of the ball in the end zone. In studying successful fantasy teams, I've found the one constant factor was having at least one consistently scoring running back. Look under "Rating the Players for 1990" later in this running-backs section for help in determining whom to draft.

ROUND 2: This is the round in which to choose the best player available, staying with the players awarded six points for scoring—running backs, wide receivers, and tight ends. A second running back is in many instances your best choice, because they are the steadiest players. Wide receivers like Sterling Sharpe, Mark Clayton, and Anthony Miller, however, may also be available and are also good choices here. All are potential 10-plus touchdown scorers.

ROUND 3: Now it's time to consider a three-point player, either a quarterback or a kicker. I find that a trend usually develops in the third round. If the first two or three choices are quarterbacks, the rest of the franchises will panic and choose a quarterback. If the first few picks are kickers, the rest will follow that lead. Kickers and quarterbacks play important roles on your Fantasy Football team. I've seen kickers carry a fantasy team by averaging 15 points a week for two or three weeks. A quarterback who throws 30 touchdowns in a year averages two touchdown passes per week, giving you (on the average) six points weekly from that position.

ROUNDS 4 and 5: It's time to pick up at least one of your wide receivers. Although many are inconsistent, you must acquire at least one productive wide receiver. If you already have a wide receiver, you may want to take a shot at a tight end. Lately, tight ends have been getting more attention from quarterbacks, as well as from fans.

ROUNDS 6, 7, and 8: By the end of the eighth round, you should have your seven starting positions filled. Setting the eighth round instead of the seventh as a deadline, gives you one round to play with.

ROUNDS 9 through 12: This is the time to pick your reserves and take some long shots on rookies. Make sure that you have at least one backup quarterback, one backup running back, and one backup wide receiver, since these seem to be the most injury-prone positions. Don't let yourself believe these are unimportant picks. Many unexpected points come from players drafted in the late rounds.

NOTE: Another strategy to consider is drafting a receiver who is a favorite target of your quarterback. This provides for a nine-point play every time there is a touchdown completion between the two (three points for the pass and six points for the touchdown). This can make the difference in your season, especially if you have people like Marino and Clayton, who combined for touchdowns 18 times in 1984 and 14 times in 1988. You could also testify to the value of this nine-point combination if you had drafted Joe Montana and Jerry Rice in 1987, when Rice caught 22 touchdown passes and Montana threw 26, or if you had chosen both Don Majkowski and Sterling Sharpe in 1989, when Majkowski threw 27 touchdowns, 12 of which went to Sharpe.

Now let's take a look at what to consider in choosing players at the various positions.

Basic Scoring Method

A LOOK AT THE RUNNING BACKS

(A Guide for the Beginner)

Considerations in Choosing a Running Back

You should start your draft with running backs. Here, listed in order of usefulness, are some considerations for choosing the players. After this review are the 1989 statistics, followed by my 1990 player ratings.

1. First, look at players' previous performances.

2. The fast, solidly built runner is your best bet in selecting a running back. The big backs like Eric Dickerson and Greg Bell are usually left in the game in short-yardage touchdown situations; however, the fast scatback players like Dalton Hilliard and Barry Sanders are also starting to see plenty of scoring opportunities.

3. Your next choice should be a back used as a designated scorer, as Larry Kinnebrew was for years by the Cincinnati Bengals and as O. J. Anderson was in 1988 by the Giants. Another prime example is Robb Riddick of Buffalo, who produced 8 and 14 touchdowns in 1987 and 1988, respectively, while rushing for only 630 yards combined during those two seasons.

In looking at the 1989 statistics, you'll find the players ranked by their fantasy-point totals. Remember: In the Basic Scoring Method, fantasy points are calculated by scoring six points for every touchdown rushed or caught and three points for every touchdown pass thrown.

1989 STATISTICAL RESULTS
(Running Backs — Basic Scoring Method)

NAME	TEAM	GP	RSH	YARDS	REC	YARDS	TOTAL YARDS	TD PS THR	RSH TDs	PS REC TDs	TOTAL TDs	1989 FAN-TASY PTS
1. Hilliard	NO	16	344	1,262	52	514	1,776	0	13	5	18	108
2. N. Anderson	CHI	16	274	1,275	50	434	1,709	0	11	4	15	90
3. Bell	LARm	16	272	1,137	19	85	1,222	0	15	0	15	90
4. B. Sanders+	DET	15	280	1470	24	282	1,752	0	14	0	14	84
5. O.J. Anderson	NYG	16	325	1,023	28	268	1,291	0	14	0	14	84
6. Thomas	BUF	16	298	1,244	60	669	1,913	0	6	6	12	72
7. Okoye	KC	15	370	1,480	2	12	1,492	0	12	0	12	72
8. Metcalf+	CLE	16	187	633	54	397	1,030	0	6	4	10	60
9. Walker* **	MINN	16	250	915	40	423	1,338	0	7	2	10	60
10. Brooks	CIN	16	221	1,239	37	306	1,545	0	7	2	9	54
11. Butts+	SD	15	170	683	7	21	704	0	9	0	9	54
12. Tate	TB	15	167	589	11	75	664	0	8	1	9	54
13. Byner	WASH	16	134	580	54	458	1,038	0	7	2	9	54
14. Humphrey*+	DEN	16	294	1,151	22	156	1,307	1	7	1	8	51
15. Muster	CHI	16	82	327	32	259	586	0	5	3	8	48
16. Dickerson	IND	15	314	1,311	30	211	1,522	0	7	1	8	48
17. Hoge	PITT	16	186	621	34	271	892	0	8	0	8	48
18. Stephens	NE	14	244	833	21	207	1,040	0	7	0	7	42
19. Vick	NYJ	16	112	434	34	241	675	0	5	2	7	42
20. Craig	SF	16	271	1,054	49	473	1,527	0	6	1	7	42
21. J.L. Williams	SEAT	15	146	499	76	657	1,156	0	1	6	7	42
22. K. Jones+	ATL	12	52	202	41	396	598	0	6	0	6	36
23. Kinnebrew	BUF	13	132	534	5	60	594	0	6	0	6	36
24. Highsmith	HOUS	16	128	531	18	201	732	0	4	2	6	36
25. Sm. Smith+	MIA	13	200	659	7	81	740	0	6	0	6	36
26. Fenney	MINN	16	151	588	30	254	842	0	4	2	6	36
27. Ferrell	PHOE	15	149	502	18	122	624	0	6	0	6	36
28. Settle	ATL	15	179	690	39	316	1,006	0	3	2	5	30
29. C. Taylor+	CIN	8	30	111	4	44	155	0	3	2	5	30
30. Manoa	CLE	16	87	289	27	241	530	0	3	2	5	30
31. Fullwood	GB	15	204	821	19	214	1,035	0	5	0	5	30
32. White	HOUS	14	104	349	6	37	386	0	5	0	5	30
33. Bentley*	IND	16	75	299	52	525	824	0	1	3	5	30
34. McGee	LARm	15	21	99	37	363	462	0	1	4	5	30
35. Byars	PHIL	16	133	452	68	721	1,173	0	5	0	5	30
36. Meggett*+	NYG	16	28	117	34	531	648	0	0	4	5	30
37. Hector	NYJ	15	177	702	38	330	1,032	0	3	2	5	30
38. Worley+	PITT	15	195	770	15	115	885	0	5	0	5	30
39. R. Harmon	BUF	13	17	99	29	363	462	0	0	4	4	24
40. Bratton+	DEN	11	30	108	10	59	167	0	1	3	4	24
41. Fontenot	GB	16	17	69	40	362	431	0	1	3	4	24
42. Jackson	LARd	11	173	950	9	69	1,019	0	4	0	4	24
43. V. Mueller	LARd	12	46	153	18	240	393	0	2	2	4	24
44. Carter	PITT	14	12	10	38	267	277	0	1	3	4	24
45. Warner	SEAT	16	194	631	23	153	784	0	3	1	4	24
46. Riggs	WASH	12	201	834	7	67	901	0	4	0	4	24
47. Davis	BUF	9	29	149	6	92	241	0	1	2	3	18
48. Ball+	CIN	14	98	391	6	44	435	0	3	0	3	18
49. Jennings	CIN	14	83	293	10	119	412	0	2	1	3	18
50. Johnston+	DALL	12	67	212	16	133	345	0	0	3	3	18
51. Sewell	DEN	13	7	44	25	416	460	0	0	3	3	18
52. Saxon	KC	15	58	233	11	86	319	0	3	0	3	18
53. B. Jordan	NO	11	38	179	4	53	232	0	3	0	3	18
54. Toney	PHIL	14	172	582	19	124	706	0	3	0	3	18

1989 STATISTICAL RESULTS
(Running Backs — Basic Scoring Method)

NAME	TEAM	GP	RSH	YARDS	REC	YARDS	TOTAL YARDS	TD PS THR	RSH TDs	PS REC TDs	TOTAL TDs	1989 FAN-TASY PTS
55. McNeil	NYJ	10	79	342	32	320	662	0	2	1	3	18
56. Spencer	SD	14	134	521	18	112	633	0	3	0	3	18
57. Wilder	TB	13	70	244	36	335	579	0	0	3	3	18
58. Lang	ATL	15	47	176	39	436	612	0	1	1	2	12
59. Woods	CIN	2	29	94	0	0	94	0	2	0	2	12
60. T. Sanders*+	CHI	13	41	127	3	28	155	0	0	1	1	12
61. Suhey	CHI	10	20	51	9	73	124	0	1	1	2	12
62. Palmer	DALL	9	111	434	17	93	527	0	2	0	2	12
63. Winder	DEN	15	110	351	14	89	440	0	2	0	2	12
64. Alexander	DEN	13	45	146	8	84	230	0	2	0	2	12
65. Pinkett	HOUS	15	94	449	31	239	688	0	1	1	2	12
66. Rozier	HOUS	12	88	301	3	22	323	0	2	0	2	12
67. Mc. Allen	LARd	8	69	293	20	191	484	0	2	0	2	12
68. Delpino	LARm	16	78	368	34	344	712	0	1	1	2	12
69. Logan*	MIA	9	57	201	5	34	235	0	0	0	2	12
70. Perryman	NE	16	150	562	29	195	757	0	2	0	2	12
71. A. Anderson	MINN	11	52	189	20	193	382	0	2	0	2	12
72. Clack	DALL	2	14	40	3	60	100	0	2	0	2	12
73. Sherman+	PHIL	7	40	177	8	85	262	0	2	0	2	12
74. T. Jordan	PHOE	12	83	211	6	20	231	0	2	0	2	12
75. Rathman	SF	16	79	306	73	616	922	0	1	1	2	12
76. Howard	TB	13	110	357	30	188	545	0	1	1	2	12
77. Jm. Morris	WASH	10	124	336	8	85	421	0	2	0	2	12
78. Flowers	ATL	5	13	26	0	0	26	0	1	0	1	6
79. Gentry	CHI	15	17	106	39	463	569	0	0	1	1	6
80. M. Green+	CHI	6	5	46	5	48	94	0	1	0	1	6
81. K. Jones	CLE	10	43	160	15	126	286	0	1	0	1	6
82. Oliphant	CLE	5	15	97	3	22	119	0	1	0	1	6
83. Redden	CLE	12	40	180	6	34	214	0	1	0	1	6
84. Mack	CLE	4	37	130	2	7	137	0	1	0	1	6
85. Sargent	DALL	12	20	87	7	50	137	0	1	0	1	6
86. Haddix	GB	12	44	135	15	111	246	0	0	1	1	6
87. Woodside	GB	15	46	273	59	527	800	0	1	0	1	6
88. Heard	KC	15	63	216	25	246	462	0	0	1	1	6
89. McNair+	KC	13	23	121	34	372	493	0	0	1	1	6
90. St. Smith	LARd	16	117	471	19	140	611	0	1	0	1	6
91. Gary+	LARm	8	37	163	2	13	176	0	1	0	1	6
92. Stradford	MIA	7	66	240	25	233	473	0	1	0	1	6
93. Davenport	MIA	6	14	56	3	19	75	0	1	0	1	6
94. Mv. Allen	NE	3	11	51	0	0	51	0	1	0	1	6
95. Egu+	NE	2	3	20	0	0	20	0	1	0	1	6
96. Heyward	NO	12	49	183	13	69	252	0	1	0	1	6
97. Frazier	NO	8	25	103	3	25	128	0	1	0	1	6
98. Drummond+	PHIL	9	32	127	17	180	307	0	0	1	1	6
99. Wolfley	PHOE	8	13	36	5	38	74	0	1	0	1	6
100. W. Williams	PITT	5	37	131	6	48	179	0	1	0	1	6
101. Wallace	PITT	4	5	10	0	0	10	0	1	0	1	6
102. Flagler	SF	8	33	129	6	51	180	0	1	0	1	6
103. Henderson+	SF	3	5	21	3	130	151	0	1	0	1	6
104. Fenner	SEAT	2	11	41	3	23	64	0	1	0	1	6
105. Stamps	TB	10	29	141	15	82	223	0	1	0	1	6
106. Dupard**	WASH	8	37	111	6	70	181	0	1	0	1	6
107. Paterra+	ATL	4	9	32	5	42	74	0	0	0	0	0
108. J. Mueller	BUF	6	15	43	1	8	51	0	0	0	0	0

NAME	TEAM	GP	RSH	YARDS	REC	YARDS	TOTAL YARDS	TD PS THR	RSH TDs	PS REC TDs	TOTAL TDs	1989 FAN-TASY PTS
109. Holifield	CIN	1	11	20	2	8	28	0	0	0	0	0
110. B. Taylor	CHI	1	0	0	2	7	7	0	0	0	0	0
111. Scott	DALL	3	2	-4	9	63	59	0	0	0	0	0
112. Tautalatasi	DALL	8	6	15	17	157	172	0	0	0	0	0
113. Paige	DET	7	30	105	2	27	132	0	0	0	0	0
114. Painter	DET	5	15	64	3	41	105	0	0	0	0	0
115. Workman+	GB	2	3	5	1	3	8	0	0	0	0	0
116. Tc. Johnson+	HOUS	3	1	-1	4	25	24	0	0	0	0	0
117. Hunter+	IND	2	6	22	0	0	22	0	0	0	0	0
118. Carruth	KC	1	0	0	1	3	3	0	0	0	0	0
119. Agee	KC	1	0	0	1	3	3	0	0	0	0	0
120. Gamble	KC	2	6	24	2	2	26	0	0	0	0	0
121. G. Green	LARm	6	26	74	0	0	74	0	0	0	0	0
122. Porter	LARd	5	13	54	0	0	54	0	0	0	0	0
123. Hampton	MIA	6	17	48	7	28	76	0	0	0	0	0
124. T. Brown	MIA	7	13	29	12	100	129	0	0	0	0	0
125. Faaola	MIA	2	2	10	1	8	18	0	0	0	0	0
126. Tatupu	NE	6	11	49	9	43	92	0	0	0	0	0
127. Wonsley	NE	2	2	-2	0	0	-2	0	0	0	0	0
128. Dozier	MINN	11	46	207	14	148	355	0	0	0	0	0
129. Clark	MINN	3	20	99	2	14	113	0	0	0	0	0
130. Rice	MINN	3	7	15	4	29	44	0	0	0	0	0
131. Higgs	PHIL	10	49	184	3	9	193	0	0	0	0	0
132. Carthon	NYG	14	57	153	15	132	285	0	0	0	0	0
133. Rouson	NYG	11	11	51	7	121	172	0	0	0	0	0
134. Tillman+	NYG	12	79	290	1	9	299	0	0	0	0	0
135. Adams	NYG	5	9	29	2	7	36	0	0	0	0	0
136. A. Brown+	NYJ	4	9	48	4	10	58	0	0	0	0	0
137. S. Mitchell	PHOE	3	43	165	1	10	175	0	0	0	0	0
138. Sikahema	PHOE	12	38	145	23	245	390	0	0	0	0	0
139. Baker	PHOE	5	17	26	2	18	44	0	0	0	0	0
140. Stone	PITT	7	10	53	7	82	135	0	0	0	0	0
141. Tyrrell	PITT	1	1	3	0	0	3	0	0	0	0	0
142. Floyd+	SD	3	8	15	1	6	21	0	0	0	0	0
143. Nelson**	SD	14	67	321	38	380	701	0	0	0	0	0
144. Brinson	SD	7	17	64	12	71	135	0	0	0	0	0
145. Sydney	SF	5	7	32	9	71	103	0	0	0	0	0
146. Harris+	SEAT	4	8	23	3	26	49	0	0	0	0	0
147. J. Jones	SEAT	1	0	0	1	8	8	0	0	0	0	0
148. K. Harmon	SEAT	1	1	24	0	0	24	0	0	0	0	0
149. D. Smith	TB	7	6	31	7	110	141	0	0	0	0	0
150. A. Mitchell	TB	1	0	0	1	11	11	0	0	0	0	0
151. Reaves	WASH	1	1	-1	0	0	-1	0	0	0	0	0

+   DENOTES ROOKIES

*	Walker	(MINN)	—Scored TD on kickoff return of 93 yards.
*	Humphrey	(DEN)	—Threw TD pass of 17 yards.
*	Bentley	(IND)	—Scored TD on return of blocked punt.
*	Meggett	(NYG)	—Scored TD on punt return of 76 yards.
*	T. Sanders	(CHI)	—Scored TD on kickoff return of 96 yards.
*	Logan	(MIA)	—Scored TD on kickoff return of 97 yards.
			Scored TD on blocked-punt return of 2 yards.
**	Walker	(MINN)	—Played in 5 games with DALL.
**	Nelson	(SD)	—Played in 5 games with MINN.
**	Dupard	(WASH)	—Played in 6 games with NE.

RATING THE PLAYERS FOR 1990
(Running Backs—Basic Scoring Method)

GRAB ONE IF YOU CAN

1. Neal Anderson (Chicago Bears)
Over the past three seasons, Neal Anderson has seen his touchdown production grow from 6 in 1987, to 12 in 1988, and then to 15 last year. In 1990 he'll again be the Bears' main offensive weapon and should produce big touchdown numbers.

2. Greg Bell (Los Angeles Rams)
Since becoming a Ram, Bell has produced two consecutive big touchdown years, with 18 in '88 and 15 in '89, a range he should near or surpass in 1990.

3. Barry Sanders (Detroit Lions)
As a rookie in 1989, Sanders produced 14 touchdowns, despite being banged up at times. There's no lid on his 1990 potential.

4. Dalton Hilliard (New Orleans Saints)
With running mate Rueben Mayes out for the 1989 season due to injury, Hilliard went wild, scoring 18 times. He should again produce plenty of scores in 1990, but Mayes's healthy return could cut into his totals.

5. Christian Okoye (Kansas City Chiefs)
Okoye became a real scoring horse for the Chiefs in 1989, scoring 12 times. His big, punishing running style should again help him account for solid touchdown production in 1990.

6. Eric Dickerson (Indianapolis Colts)
Has Eric Dickerson slipped a notch? Well, his touchdown production did in 1989, dropping to 8 scores from the 15 he tallied in 1988. He was hampered by a hamstring injury in 1989, but perhaps he'll rebound to the numbers we're used to seeing from this perennial scorer.

7. Eric Metcalf (Cleveland Browns)
Although one season doesn't make a career, Metcalf's rookie season opened some eyes. As a rookie in '89, Metcalf produced 10 touchdowns, 6 on the ground and 4 through the air. This is just the beginning of even better things to come.

8. Roger Craig (San Francisco 49ers)
Craig, perhaps because he plays on such a diversely talented team, has seen his touchdown levels rollercoaster throughout his career. Craig has scored 12, 10, 15, 7, 1, 10, and 7 touchdowns over the past seven seasons, which has to keep him in the high-potential group.

9. Herschel Walker (Minnesota Vikings)
Regardless of where Walker plays, he finds a way to get into the end zone. In 1989, playing for both Dallas and Minnesota, Walker produced 10 touchdowns, a mark he could easily exceed in 1990, if the Vikings find a way to use him properly.

10. Ickey Woods (Cincinnati Bengals)
After scoring 15 touchdowns as a rookie in 1988, Woods missed most of the '89 campaign with a knee injury. If he can return from his injury in good shape, he should again be in double digits.

BEST OF THE REST

11. Bobby Humphrey (Denver Broncos)
As a rookie in 1989, Humphrey produced eight touchdowns, despite being taken out in many goal-line situations. Near the season's end he was being left in more often on those goal-line occasions, which should spell even more scores for Humphrey in 1990.

12. James Brooks (Cincinnati Bengals)
Despite not having Ickey Woods to compete with for scoring glory in 1989, Brooks produced only nine touchdowns. Just a year earlier, though, with Woods as a running mate, Brooks produced 14 TDs, demonstrating his scoring potential.

13. Thurman Thomas (Buffalo Bills)
After scoring only two touchdowns as a rookie in 1988, Thomas jumped up to 12 in 1989. This may be partly due to the absence of the Bills' designated scorer Robb Riddick, who missed the '89 season with a knee injury. Thomas is sure to score often in 1990, but if Riddick returns healthy, will he cut into Thomas's touchdown production?

14. Keith Byars (Philadelphia Eagles)
Byars saw his touchdown level drop from 10 in 1988 to 5 in 1989. I expect Byars again to near the double-digit touchdown range in 1990.

15. J. L. Williams (Seattle Seahawks)
Although he scored only seven touchdowns in each of the last two seasons, with running mate Curt Warner now in an LA Rams uniform Williams is really ripe to produce. The 10-touchdown range should be easily reachable.

16. John Stephens (New England Patriots)
As a rookie in 1988, Stephens scored four times. Last year he crossed the goal line seven times. As the Patriots' most consistent offensive force, Stephens may near or surpass the 10-touchdown range in 1990.

17. Lars Tate (Tampa Bay Buccaneers)
Tate scored eight times as a rookie in 1988 and then upped that one notch in 1989 by scoring nine times. I feel he'll continue his rise in touchdown production in 1990.

18. Sammie Smith (Miami Dolphins)
Smith got off to a slow start in 1989 but finished the year with six touchdowns in the season's last six games, a finish that may carry over into a big 1990 season.

19. Tim Worley (Pittsburgh Steelers)

Although Worley scored only five times as a rookie in 1989, four of those came in the last three games. This has me believing he could score in a big way in 1990, becoming a bigger part of the Steelers' offense.

20. Joe Morris (New York Giants)

Morris missed the entire '89 season with a knee injury. If he returns healthy in 1990, he could produce plenty of scores. O. J. Anderson, who has been the Giants' designated scorer the past two seasons, is perhaps beyond his prime. So look for a healthy Morris to fall short of the 21- and 15-touchdown plateaus he reached in '85 and '86 but to reach the double-digit range.

STRONG LONG SHOTS

21. Johnny Hector (New York Jets)

Hector's touchdown production dropped off to five in 1989. The previous three years he tallied 10, 11, and 8 touchdowns, respectively, levels I believe he'll near again in 1990.

22. Marcus Allen (Los Angeles Raiders)

Injuries have taken their toll on Allen lately, like the knee injury suffered last year. We have to look back to '83, '84, and '85, when Allen scored 12, 18, and 14 touchdowns, respectively, to recall his potential. Perhaps he won't reach 18, but if he can stay healthy, double digits are obtainable.

23. Marion Butts (San Diego Chargers)

With Gary Anderson out for the year as a contract holdout, Marion Butts scored nine times. Now, with Anderson traded to Tampa Bay, Butts should be assured of continued scoring opportunities in 1990.

24. John Settle (Atlanta Falcons)

After scoring eight times in 1988, Settle's touchdown production fell to only five in 1989. I look for Settle's scoring output to rebound in 1990, with him as the Falcons' primary ground weapon.

25. Stump Mitchell (Phoenix Cardinals)

If Mitchell can return 100% healthy from his season-ending knee injury of 1989, he should fare well—especially now that running mate Earl Ferrell has announced his surprise retirement after testing positive for drugs.

HAVE THE POTENTIAL

26. O. J. Anderson (New York Giants)

Although Anderson produced 14 touchdowns in 1989, I don't think this aging star will be able to continue to play with that kind of consistency and intensity in 1990. He may, however, produce near the eight-touchdown mark he tallied in 1988.

27. Earnest Byner (Washington Redskins)

With injuries to both Gerald Riggs and Kelvin Bryant in 1989, Earnest Byner was called on often. He produced nine touchdowns, which may be a good or poor indicator for 1990, depending on the health of Riggs and Bryant.

28. Gerald Riggs (Washington Redskins)

The Redskins had hoped Riggs would become a big part of their offense. Injuries limited him to only four touchdowns in 1989, however, and I wonder if injuries won't again hold down his scoring production in 1990.

29. Robb Riddick (Buffalo Bills)

His producing 8 touchdowns in 1987 and 14 in 1988 makes Riddick a fantasy player to bear in mind. He is recovering from a knee injury suffered in 1989, though, which also makes him a big question mark.

30. Curt Warner (Los Angeles Rams)

We all remember Warner's great moves and great years. But his play has slipped and his scoring only four touchdowns in 1989 makes him a questionable pick for 1990, especially since becoming a member of the Los Angeles Rams in the offseason.

KEEP AN EYE ON

31. Kevin Mack(Cleveland Browns)

If Mack can put his 1989 drug involvement behind him, he should return to success in 1990.

32. Gary Anderson (Tampa Bay Buccaneers)

Anderson took the '89 season off due to a contract dispute. If we look back to his 1986 production when he scored nine times, however, we remember his potential. Going to the Buccaneers should assure Anderson of seeing the ball often, and that should mean plenty of scoring opportunity.

33. Brent Fullwood (Green Bay Packers)

Fullwood needs season-long scoring consistency. In 1989 he scored all five of his touchdowns in the season's first three games and none thereafter.

34. Bo Jackson (Los Angeles Raiders)

Though only a half-season player, he's still more than worth having for those eight or nine games.

35. Brad Muster (Chicago Bears)

Muster's eight touchdowns in 1989 should have opened some eyes.

36. Merril Hoge (Pittsburgh Steelers)

His scoring six and eight touchdowns the last two years makes Hoge worth a look.

37. Roger Vick (New York Jets)

Vick's playing time and touchdowns (seven in 1989) should continue to increase, unless rookie Blair Thomas becomes the standout that many expect.

38. Dave Meggett (New York Giants)
He displayed plenty of potential as a rookie in 1989, scoring five times.

39. Rueben Mayes (New Orleans Saints)
Coming back from a knee injury is hard to do. Keep in mind, however, that as a rookie in 1986 Mayes tallied eight touchdowns.

40. Kelvin Bryant (Washington Redskins)
Bryant scored seven, six, and six touchdowns, respectively, from 1986 through 1988 before a neck injury sidelined him in 1989. The prospects for his 1990 return look dismal.

PRIME PROSPECTS

41.	Manoa (CLE)	46.	Johnston (DALL)
42.	Fenney (MINN)	47.	Bentley (IND)
43.	Rozier (HOUS)	48.	Bratton (DEN)
44.	Highsmith (HOUS)	49.	Perryman (NE)
45.	Toney (PHIL)	50.	White (HOUS)

DON'T BE SURPRISED   YOU NEVER KNOW

51.	Winder (DEN)	61.	Stradford (MIA)
52.	Flagler (DALL)	62.	Heyward (NO)
53.	Pinkett (HOUS)	63.	Hampton (DEN)
54.	C. Taylor (CIN)	64.	Kinnebrew (BUF)
55.	Delpino (LARm)	65.	Ball (CIN)
56.	T. Jordan (PHOE)	66.	Wilder (WASH)
57.	Rathman (SF)	67.	Fontenot (GB)
58.	Jm. Morris (NE)	68.	Carter (PITT)
59.	B. Jordan (NO)	69.	V. Mueller (LARd)
60.	St. Smith (LARd)	70.	K. Jones (ATL)

WORTH MENTIONING

71.	Jennings (CIN)	76.	Logan (MIA)
72.	Sewell (DEN)	77.	A. Anderson (MINN)
73.	Nelson (SD)	78.	Howard (TB)
74.	Palmer (CIN)	79.	Woodside (GB)
75.	Alexander (DEN)	80.	McNeil (NYJ)

A LOOK AT THE WIDE RECEIVERS
(A Guide for the Beginner)

Considerations in Choosing a Wide Receiver

If you have played Fantasy Football and used the Basic Scoring Method, you know that wide receivers were unpredictable scorers until Jerry Rice came along. It is a challenge to guess how they will perform from year to year. After a great year they tend to fall back to a mediocre or dismal season.

1. First, look at players' previous performances.

2. Look for receivers from pass-oriented teams like the 49ers or the Dolphins. Obviously, these players are more likely to have productive years.

3. Look for receivers who are favorites of a particular quarterback. Many quarterbacks single out a receiver whom they go to in clutch touchdown situations, such as Jerry Rice of the 49ers, who is a favorite target of Joe Montana. Sterling Sharpe of the Packers gets a lot of attention from Don Majkowski, and Mark Clayton is a favorite of Dan Marino.

4. If a wide receiver has a couple of good years or one great year, look for opposing teams to double- or triple-team him, perhaps drastically reducing his touchdown productivity. This could happen to Sterling Sharpe or Anthony Miller in 1990, but I think they're too good to get shut down.

5. Look for quarterback changes to have an adverse effect on wide receivers. When a quarterback and wide receiver have played together for years, the performance of the receiver may drop off if his regular quarterback leaves.

6. Keep an eye on rookie wide receivers, especially from teams looking for a starter at that position. Rookies don't usually draw much coverage, because they are unproven receivers. Such was the case with Seattle's Brian Blades in 1988, and he turned in a very productive eight-touchdown season.

In the 1989 statistics, players are ranked by their fantasy-point totals. Remember that Basic Scoring Method fantasy points are calculated by scoring six points for every touchdown rushed or caught and three points for every touchdown pass thrown.

1989 STATISTICAL RESULTS
(Wide Receivers — Basic Scoring Method)

NAME	TEAM	GP	RSH	YARDS	REC	YARDS	TOTAL YARDS	TD PS THR	RSH TDs	PS REC TDs	TOTAL TDs	1989 FAN-TASY PTS
1. Rice	SF	16	4	16	82	1,483	1,499	0	0	17	17	102
2. Sharpe*	GB	16	1	26	90	1,423	1,449	0	0	12	13	78
3. C. Carter	PHIL	14	1	11	45	605	616	0	0	11	11	66
4. Miller*	SD	16	4	21	75	1,242	1,263	0	0	10	11	66
5. Taylor	SF	15	1	6	60	1,077	1,083	0	0	10	10	60
6. Reed	BUF	15	2	31	88	1,312	1,343	0	0	9	9	54
7. Fernandez	LARd	16	2	16	57	1,069	1,085	0	0	9	9	54
8. Clayton	MIA	15	2	-2	64	1,011	1,009	0	0	9	9	54
9. Carrier	TB	16	0	0	86	1,412	1,412	0	0	9	9	54
10. G. Clark	WASH	15	2	19	79	1,229	1,248	0	0	9	9	54
11. Jensen*	MIA	14	4	32	61	557	589	1	0	6	6	51
12. McGee	CIN	16	2	36	65	1,211	1,247	0	0	8	8	48
13. R. Johnson	DET	16	12	38	70	1,091	1,129	0	0	8	8	48
14. Dr. Hill	HOUS	14	0	0	66	936	936	0	0	8	8	48
15. Ellard	LARm	14	6	23	70	1,382	1,405	0	0	8	8	48
16. E. Martin	NO	16	1	11	68	1,079	1,090	0	0	8	8	48
17. Monk	WASH	16	3	8	86	1,186	1,194	0	0	8	8	48
18. V. Johnson	DEN	15	0	0	76	1,095	1,095	0	0	7	7	42
19. Green	PHOE	11	0	0	44	703	703	0	0	7	7	42
20. E. Brown	CIN	15	0	0	52	814	814	0	0	6	6	36
21. Slaughter	CLE	16	0	0	65	1,236	1,236	0	0	6	6	36
22. C. Jones	NE	14	1	3	48	670	673	0	0	6	6	36
23. Lipps	PITT	15	13	180	50	944	1,124	0	1	5	6	36
24. Duncan	HOUS	15	1	0	43	613	613	0	0	5	5	30
25. Anderson	LARm	14	1	-1	44	1,146	1,145	0	0	5	5	30
26. A.B. Brown	MIA	11	0	0	24	410	410	0	0	5	5	30
27. Dykes+	NE	14	0	0	49	795	795	0	0	5	5	30
28. Townsell	NYJ	15	0	0	45	787	787	0	0	5	5	30
29. J.T. Smith	PHOE	9	1	10	62	778	788	0	0	5	5	30
30. Blades	SEAT	16	1	3	77	1,063	1,066	0	0	5	5	30
31. Skansi	SEAT	15	0	0	39	488	488	0	0	5	5	30
32. B. Hill	TB	14	0	0	50	673	673	0	0	5	5	30
33. Haynes	ATL	11	4	35	40	681	716	0	0	4	4	24
34. Brooks	IND	15	1	0	63	919	919	0	0	4	4	24
35. Rison+	IND	16	1	18	52	820	838	0	0	4	4	24
36. Gault	LARd	12	0	0	28	690	690	0	0	4	4	24
37. A. Carter	MINN	16	2	30	65	1,066	1,096	0	0	4	4	24
38. O. Turner	NYG	11	2	11	38	467	478	0	0	4	4	24
39. L. Hill	NO	15	1	-7	48	636	629	0	0	4	4	24
40. Sanders	WASH	16	4	19	80	1,138	1,157	0	0	4	4	24
41. Collins+	ATL	16	0	0	58	862	862	0	0	3	3	18
42. Lofton	BUF	6	0	0	8	166	166	0	0	3	3	18
43. McKinnon	CHI	14	1	3	28	433	436	0	0	3	3	18
44. Davis	CHI	12	0	0	27	405	405	0	0	3	3	18
45. Tillman*+	CLE	6	0	0	6	70	70	0	0	2	3	18
46. J. Dixon*	DALL	11	3	30	24	477	507	0	0	2	3	18
47. Givins	HOUS	15	0	0	55	794	794	0	0	3	3	18
48. Cox	LARm	7	0	0	20	340	340	0	0	3	3	18
49. Fryar	NE	10	2	15	29	537	552	0	0	3	3	18
50. Morgan	NE	9	1	7	28	486	493	0	0	3	3	18
51. E. Jones	PHOE	14	1	18	44	823	841	0	0	3	3	18
52. Largent	SEAT	10	0	0	28	403	403	0	0	3	3	18
53. F. Dixon	ATL	10	1	0	25	357	357	0	0	2	2	12
54. Beebe+	BUF	9	0	0	17	317	317	0	0	2	2	12

1989 STATISTICAL RESULTS
(Wide Receivers — Basic Scoring Method)

NAME	TEAM	GP	RSH	YARDS	REC	YARDS	TOTAL YARDS	TD PS THR	RSH TDs	PS REC TDs	TOTAL TDs	1989 FAN- TASY PTS
55. M. Martin	CIN	7	0	0	15	160	160	0	0	2	2	12
56. Langhorne	CLE	15	4	29	60	749	778	0	0	2	2	12
57. Irvin	DALL	5	1	6	26	378	384	0	0	2	2	12
58. K. Martin	DALL	11	0	0	46	644	644	0	0	2	2	12
59. M. Jackson	DEN	14	5	13	28	446	459	0	0	2	2	12
60. Young	DEN	11	0	0	22	402	402	0	0	2	2	12
61. R. Clark	DET	12	0	0	40	741	741	0	0	2	2	12
62. Bland*	GB	7	0	0	11	164	164	0	0	1	2	12
63. Query+	GB	11	0	0	23	350	350	0	0	2	2	12
64. Kemp	GB	14	4	29	48	611	640	0	0	2	2	12
65. Harris+	HOUS	5	0	0	13	194	194	0	0	2	2	12
66. Jeffires	HOUS	15	0	0	47	619	619	0	0	2	2	12
67. Verdin*	IND	12	3	34	20	381	415	0	0	1	2	12
68. Harry	KC	12	1	9	33	430	439	0	0	2	2	12
69. R. Thomas+	KC	5	0	0	8	58	58	0	0	2	2	12
70. Paige	KC	14	0	0	44	759	759	0	0	2	2	12
71. Schwedes*	MIA	3	0	0	7	174	174	0	0	1	2	12
72. Gustafson	MINN	9	0	0	14	144	144	0	0	2	2	12
73. Baker	NYG	10	0	0	13	255	255	0	0	2	2	12
74. Toon	NYJ	11	0	0	63	673	673	0	0	2	2	12
75. Quick	PHIL	6	0	0	13	228	228	0	0	0	0	10
76. Garrity	PHIL	13	0	0	13	209	209	0	0	2	2	12
77. F. Johnson	BUF	10	0	0	25	303	303	0	0	1	1	6
78. K. Smith+	CIN	7	0	0	10	140	140	0	0	1	1	6
79. Hillary	CIN	10	1	-2	17	162	160	0	0	1	1	6
80. Morris	CHI	14	1	-14	29	468	454	0	0	1	1	6
81. Gentry	CHI	15	17	106	39	463	569	0	0	1	1	6
82. Shepard**	DALL	10	2	19	20	304	323	0	0	1	1	6
83. B. Ford	DALL	4	0	0	7	78	78	0	0	1	1	6
84. Nattiel	DEN	6	0	0	10	183	183	0	0	1	1	6
85. Phillips+	DET	11	0	0	31	359	359	0	0	1	1	6
86. Pruitt	IND	3	0	0	5	71	71	0	0	1	1	6
87. Mandley	KC	12	1	-7	35	476	469	0	0	1	1	6
88. R. Brown	LARm	8	6	27	5	113	140	0	0	1	1	6
89. M. Alexander	LARd	9	0	0	15	295	295	0	0	1	1	6
90. Banks	MIA	12	0	0	30	520	520	0	0	1	1	6
91. Duper	MIA	13	0	0	49	717	717	0	0	1	1	6
92. H. Jones	MINN	16	1	37	42	694	731	0	0	1	1	6
93. Lewis	MINN	7	0	0	12	148	148	0	0	1	1	6
94. Manuel	NYG	14	0	0	33	539	539	0	0	1	1	6
95. Ingram	NYG	10	1	1	17	290	291	0	0	1	1	6
96. Burkett**	NYJ	11	1	-4	21	278	274	0	0	1	1	6
97. F. Turner+	NO	11	2	8	22	279	287	0	0	1	1	6
98. R. Johnson	PHIL	9	0	0	20	295	295	0	0	1	1	6
99. Holmes	PHOE	9	0	0	14	286	286	0	0	1	1	6
100. Dk. Hill+	PITT	15	0	0	28	455	455	0	0	1	1	6
101. Wn. Walker	SD	9	1	9	24	395	404	0	0	1	1	6
102. Wilson	SF	8	0	0	9	103	103	0	0	1	1	6
103. L. Clark	SEAT	11	0	0	25	260	260	0	0	1	1	6
104. Drewery	TB	9	0	0	14	157	157	0	0	1	1	6
105. Bailey	ATL	6	0	0	8	170	170	0	0	0	0	0
106. G. Thomas	ATL	3	0	0	4	46	46	0	0	0	0	0
107. Parker	CIN	1	0	0	1	45	45	0	0	0	0	0
108. Garrett	CIN	1	0	0	2	29	29	0	0	0	0	0

1989 STATISTICAL RESULTS
(Wide Receivers — Basic Scoring Method)

NAME	TEAM	GP	RSH	YARDS	REC	YARDS	TOTAL YARDS	TD PS THR	RSH TDs	PS REC TDs	TOTAL TDs	1989 FAN-TASY PTS
109. Kozlowski	CHI	3	0	0	3	74	74	0	0	0	0	0
110. Waddle	CHI	1	0	0	1	8	8	0	0	0	0	0
111. McNeil	CLE	7	0	0	10	114	114	0	0	0	0	0
112. Brennan	CLE	11	0	0	28	289	289	0	0	0	0	0
113. R. Alexander	DALL	1	0	0	1	16	16	0	0	0	0	0
114. Burbage	DALL	5	0	0	17	134	134	0	0	0	0	0
115. Gray	DET	3	3	22	2	47	69	0	0	0	0	0
116. Mobley	DET	5	0	0	13	158	158	0	0	0	0	0
117. T. Johnson	DET	2	0	0	2	29	29	0	0	0	0	0
118. Stanley	DET	11	0	0	24	304	304	0	0	0	0	0
119. McDonald	DET	4	1	-2	12	138	136	0	0	0	0	0
120. J. Ford+	DET	3	0	0	5	46	46	0	0	0	0	0
121. Matthews	GB	10	0	0	18	200	200	0	0	0	0	0
122. K. Jackson	HOUS	3	0	0	4	31	31	0	0	0	0	0
123. Worthen+	KC	2	0	0	5	69	69	0	0	0	0	0
124. Weathers**	KC	8	0	0	23	254	254	0	0	0	0	0
125. T. Brown	LARd	1	0	0	1	8	8	0	0	0	0	0
126. S. Martin	NE	7	0	0	13	229	229	0	0	0	0	0
127. Robinson	NYG	2	0	0	4	41	41	0	0	0	0	0
128. Ws. Walker	NYJ	4	0	0	8	89	89	0	0	0	0	0
129. Harper	NYJ	3	0	0	7	127	127	0	0	0	0	0
130. Epps	NYJ	4	1	14	9	116	130	0	0	0	0	0
131. Perriman	NO	9	1	-10	20	356	346	0	0	0	0	0
132. Williams	PHIL	3	0	0	4	32	32	0	0	0	0	0
133. Edwards	PHIL	1	0	0	2	74	74	0	0	0	0	0
134. Carson**	PHIL	6	0	0	9	98	98	0	0	0	0	0
135. McConkey	PHOE	2	0	0	2	18	18	0	0	0	0	0
136. Usher	PHOE	1	0	0	1	8	8	0	0	0	0	0
137. Thompson	PITT	3	0	0	4	74	74	0	0	0	0	0
138. Early	SD	4	1	19	11	126	145	0	0	0	0	0
139. Holland	SD	11	5	48	26	336	384	0	0	0	0	0
140. Allen	SD	2	0	0	2	19	19	0	0	0	0	0
141. Greer	SF	1	0	0	1	26	26	0	0	0	0	0
142. Kane	SEAT	4	0	0	7	94	94	0	0	0	0	0
143. Chadwick**	SEAT	7	0	0	8	95	95	0	0	0	0	0
144. Bouyer	SEAT	1	0	0	1	9	9	0	0	0	0	0
145. Peebles+	TB	7	2	6	10	176	182	0	0	0	0	0

+ DENOTES ROOKIES

*	Sharpe	(GB)	—Scored TD on fumble recovery of 5 yards.
*	Miller	(SD)	—Scored TD on kickoff return of 91 yards.
*	Jensen	(MIA)	—Threw TD pass of 19 yards.
*	Tillman	(CLE)	—Scored TD on recovery of blocked punt.
*	J. Dixon	(DALL)	—Scored TD on kickoff return of 97 yards.
*	Bland	(GB)	—Scored TD on fumble recovery.
*	Verdin	(IND)	—Scored TD on punt return of 49 yards.
*	Schwedes	(MIA)	—Scored TD on punt return of 70 yards.
**	Shepard	(DALL)	—Played in 2 games with NO.
**	Weathers	(KC)	—Played in 2 games with IND.
**	Burkett	(NYJ)	—Played in 2 games with BUF.
**	Carson	(PHIL)	—Played in 4 games with KC.
**	Chadwick	(SEAT)	—Played in 1 game with DET

RATING THE PLAYERS FOR 1990
(Wide Receivers—Basic Scoring Method)

GRAB ONE IF YOU CAN

1. Jerry Rice (San Francisco 49ers)
Who else would be number one? Rice has led all NFL wide receivers in touchdowns three out of the last four seasons. I look for him to near or top 15 touchdowns again in 1990.

2. Mark Clayton (Miami Dolphins)
Clayton has twice led the league's wide receivers in touchdowns. In 1984 he led the league with 18 touchdowns and in 1988 he led with 14. As a prime target of Dan Marino, he continues to be a potent threat.

3. Sterling Sharpe (Green Bay Packers)
Although he scored only one touchdown as a rookie in 1988, his 55 receptions were an inkling of his ability. In 1989 he upped his reception level to 90 and this time tallied 13 touchdowns, a hefty production I think he'll continue in 1990.

4. Henry Ellard (Los Angeles Rams)
Ellard grabbed 156 receptions for 18 touchdowns over the past two seasons as a favorite wideout of Jim Everett. This makes Ellard a prime fantasy pick again in 1990.

5. Anthony Miller (San Diego Chargers)
As a rookie in 1988, Miller scored only three times, but in 1989 he accounted for 75 receptions and 11 scores. I believe he'll be a double-digit scoring threat again in 1990.

6. Drew Hill (Houston Oilers)
Hill has scored 9, 5, 6, 10, and 8 touchdowns over the past six seasons, respectively. I feel he'll near 10 touchdowns again in '90.

7. Ricky Sanders (Washington Redskins)
His playing with two other great receivers—Art Monk and Gary Clark—makes predicting Sanders's touchdown production tough. Sanders's touchdown level dropped from 14 in 1988 to 4 in 1989, while his receptions actually went up, from 73 to 80. I think he's a potential double-digit scorer in 1990.

8. John Taylor (San Francisco 49ers)
John Taylor will not be overlooked anymore, even though he plays alongside Jerry Rice. His 60 receptions and 10 touchdowns of 1989 sure won't be ignored.

9. Andre Reed (Buffalo Bills)
Reed has fast become the favorite target of quarterback Jim Kelly. His touchdown production confirms that, as he continues to near that 10-touchdown plateau, scoring 7, 5, 6, and 9 times over the last four years, respectively.

10. Mark Duper (Miami Dolphins)
Duper has struggled the last two years, but remembering the healthy times—10 TDs in 1983, 8 TDs in 1984, 11 TDs in 1986, and 8 TDs in 1987—we better recognize his 1990 potential.

BEST OF THE REST

11. Mike Quick (Philadelphia Eagles)
If he can return healthy from his knee problems, Quick could return to the double-digit scoring he produced in the mid-1980s.

12. Mark Carrier (Tampa Bay Buccaneers)
Carrier improved his touchdown production from five in 1988 to nine in 1989, a level I believe he'll near or better in 1990 as Vinny Testaverde's favorite target.

13. Eddie Brown (Cincinnati Bengals)
A slow start, partly due to a 48-day contract holdout, may be why Brown's touchdown production dropped from nine in 1988 to six in 1989. I see him back on the upswing in 1990.

14. Cris Carter (Philadelphia Eagles)
Carter continues to reap the statistical benefits of Mike Quick's injuries, scoring 6 and 10 touchdowns over the last two seasons. His 1990 production could hinge on Quick's healthy return.

15. Willie Anderson (Los Angeles Rams)
Anderson is fast becoming a big scoring threat. Although he produced only five touchdowns in 1989, I believe the best is yet to come.

16. Brian Blades (Seattle Seahawks)
As a rookie in 1988, Blades scored eight touchdowns on only 40 receptions. In 1989, Blades saw his receptions jump to 77 and his touchdowns drop to five. He can easily get back on the upswing in 1990 as the Seahawks' primary wideout.

17. Al Toon (New York Jets)
Although he produced seasons of 46, 85, 68, 93, and 63 receptions since coming into the league in 1985, Toon has produced only three, eight, five, five, and two touchdowns over that same period. But anybody grabbing that many receptions has big touchdown potential.

18. Tim McGee (Cincinnati Bengals)
After playing second fiddle to Eddie Brown the last couple of years, Tim McGee came into his own with a 65-reception, eight-touchdown season in 1989. He could easily do as well in 1990.

19. Gary Clark (Washington Redskins)
Following three consecutive seasons of seven touchdowns, Clark jumped to nine scores in 1989. Playing alongside two other great wideouts—Art Monk and Ricky Sanders—he'll be hard pressed to reach that kind of touchdown production in 1990.

20. Roy Green (Phoenix Cardinals)
Surely the years like 1983 (14 TDs) and 1984 (12 TDs) are over for Roy Green. His 1989 season was slowed by a collarbone injury, but I still don't believe he'll reach double digits again.

STRONG LONG SHOTS

21. Mervyn Fernandez (Los Angeles Raiders)
In 1989, with nine touchdowns, Fernandez had his best year since coming over from the Canadian Football League. But if Tim Brown returns healthy from his knee injury in 1990, it should cut into Fernandez's year-end production.

22. Eric Martin (New Orleans Saints)
Martin has proven himself a very consistent receiver over the past two seasons. In 1988 he grabbed 85 receptions and seven touchdowns, while in 1989 he latched onto 68 receptions and eight scores, a consistency I see continuing in 1990.

23. Richard Johnson (Detroit Lions)
If anybody benefited from the Lions' run-and-shoot offense in 1989, it was Richard Johnson. Johnson latched onto 70 receptions and eight touchdowns and should continue to flourish in 1990.

24. Stephone Paige (Kansas City Chiefs)
Paige has a history of producing some big touchdown years, scoring 10, 11, 4, 8, and 2 over the past five seasons. Last year's drop to only two touchdowns was partly because of a late arrival in training camp, something he should hope to avoid in 1990.

25. Louis Lipps (Pittsburgh Steelers)
After a couple of injury-filled years, Lipps seems to be back on track, scoring seven and six touchdowns the last two seasons, respectively. Remembering his first two years in the league—1984 and 1985—when he scored 10 and 15 touchdowns, we have a feel for his potential.

26. J. T. Smith (Phoenix Cardinals)
Smith recorded seasons of 80, 76, and 83 receptions, along with six, eight, and five touchdowns from 1986 through 1988. A fractured fibula halted Smith's 1989 season after nine games. He still put together an unbelievable 62 receptions and five touchdowns in that short time. His healthy return should provide healthy numbers again in 1990.

27. Anthony Carter (Minnesota Vikings)
Carter has seen his touchdown production slowly decline over the past five seasons, scoring eight, seven, seven, six, and four touchdowns over that period. His reception level remains good—65 in 1989—so his scoring potential remains interesting.

28. Ernest Givins (Houston Oilers)
Since coming into the league in 1986, Givins has had consistent receptions, recording 61, 53, 60, and 66 catches over that period. He has trouble beating the six-touchdown mark, though, recording four, six, five and three scores in that same span.

29. Art Monk (Washington Redskins)
Although he's one of the league's most consistent receivers, with 106, 91, 73, 38, 72, and 86 receptions over the past six seasons, Monk's touchdown level just doesn't match. During that same stretch he has scored seven, two, four, six, five, and eight touchdowns, perhaps because there are only so many touchdowns to be spread among so much talent.

30. Tim Brown (Los Angeles Raiders)
As a rookie in 1988, Brown grabbed 46 receptions and six touchdowns. In 1989 a knee injury ended his season early. If he's healthy in 1990, there seems to be plenty of scoring potential for Brown.

KEEP AN EYE ON

31. Webster Slaughter (Cleveland Browns)
Slaughter has seen his touchdown production fluctuate right around the half-dozen mark since coming into the league in 1986, scoring five, seven, three, and six touchdowns through 1989. But anybody pushing the 65-reception mark, which is what he did in 1989, could exceed those touchdown levels.

32. Vance Johnson (Denver Broncos)
This "amigo" has produced seven, five, and seven touchdowns the last three seasons.

33. Lonzell Hill (New Orleans Saints)
As the receiving mate for Eric Martin, Hill saw his touchdown production drop from seven in 1988 to four in 1989.

34. Lionel Manuel (New York Giants)
Manuel, the Giants' most consistent wideout, needs to get his touchdown production on the upswing. He has scored six, four, and one touchdown, respectively, over the past three seasons.

35. Irving Fryar (New England Patriots)
Injuries and other distractions continue to prevent any possible consistency.

36. Billy Brooks (Indianapolis Colts)
Brooks peaked with eight touchdowns as a rookie in 1986, but he continues to be a consistent receiver.

37. Reggie Langhorne (Cleveland Browns)
Although he scored only twice on 60 receptions in 1989, just a year earlier he scored eight times on 56 catches.

38. Michael Irvin (Dallas Cowboys)
Five touchdowns as a rookie in 1988 gave us a glimpse of his potential. Will he return healthy from his knee injury?

39. Cedric Jones (New England Patriots)
With injuries to Stanley Morgan and Irving Fryar, Jones scored six times on 48 receptions, giving us a taste of his potential.

40. Andre Rison (Atlanta Falcons)
Four scores as a rookie in 1989 give us a clue of what possibly lies ahead, though he'll be running his routes for the Atlanta Falcons in 1990.

PRIME PROSPECTS

41. B. Hill (TB)
42. Morgan (NE)
43. McKinnon (DALL)
44. Dykes (NE)
45. H. Jones (MINN)

46. Haynes (ATL)
47. Jensen (MIA)
48. K. Martin (DALL)
49. Collins (ATL)
50. E. Jones (PHOE)

DON'T BE SURPRISED

51. Duncan (HOUS)
52. F. Dixon (ATL)
53. Townsell (NYJ)
54. Skansi (SEAT)
55. Gault (LARd)
56. Tillman (CLE)
57. Davis (CHI)
58. O. Turner (NYG)
59. Kemp (GB)
60. Morris (CHI)

YOU NEVER KNOW

61. Brennan (CLE)
62. Wn. Walker (SD)
63. Baker (NYG)
64. Nattiel (DEN)
65. R. Clark (DET)
66. M. Jackson (DEN)
67. Perriman (NO)
68. Phillips (DET)
69. A. B. Brown (MIA)
70. J. Dixon (DALL)

WORTH MENTIONING

71. Cox (LARm)
72. Lofton (BUF)
73. Jeffires (HOUS)
74. Young (DEN)
75. Query (GB)

76. Beebe (BUF)
77. Verdin (IND)
78. Harry (KC)
79. Mandley (KC)
80. Lewis (MINN)

A LOOK AT THE TIGHT ENDS

(A Guide for the Beginner)

Considerations in Choosing a Tight End

1. First, look at players' previous performances.

2. If a team has one or two good wide receivers, opponents are forced to double-cover them, leaving the tight end open more often, especially in close situations. Keith Jackson of the Philadelphia Eagles certainly benefits from the play of Mike Quick and Cris Carter, while Ferrell Edmunds benefits from the play of Mark Clayton and Mark Duper.

3. Tight ends from pass-oriented offenses have a better chance for a productive year than those from running teams.

4. Look for tight ends who seem to be favorite targets of a particular quarterback. Although tight ends are less likely to be receivers than some other players, scoring receptions by tight ends are more common than before, as tight ends have grown more important in many teams' offensive schemes. Rodney Holman, Mark Bavaro, and now Keith Jackson have brought tight ends more attention.

5. If a tight end had a great season last year, look for teams to start jamming him. Although good tight ends seem to be consistent during their careers, a great year may affect the following year's productivity a bit.

6. Quarterback changes have adverse effects on a tight end's productivity. If a tight end has been productive with a quarterback and that quarterback is traded, look for this to lower the tight end's effectiveness.

In the 1989 statistics, the players have been ranked by their fantasy-point totals. Remember that in the Basic Scoring Method fantasy points are calculated by scoring six points for every touchdown rushed or caught and three points for every touchdown pass thrown.

1989 STATISTICAL RESULTS
(Tight Ends — Basic Scoring Method)

NAME	TEAM	GP	REC	YARDS	RSH TDs	PS REC TDs	TOTAL TDs	1989 FANTASY POINTS
1. Holman	CIN	16	50	736	0	9	9	54
2. West	GB	7	22	269	0	5	5	30
3. D. Johnson	LARm	14	25	148	0	5	5	30
4. Brenner	NO	14	34	398	0	4	4	24
5. Jones	SF	14	40	500	0	4	4	24
6. Wilkins	ATL	6	6	145	0	3	3	18
7. Thornton	CHI	13	24	392	0	3	3	18
8. Edmunds	MIA	15	32	382	0	3	3	18
9. Jordan	MINN	12	35	506	0	3	3	18
10. Bavaro	NYG	6	22	278	0	3	3	18
11. Jackson	PHIL	13	63	648	0	3	3	18
12. McKeller	BUF	12	20	341	0	2	2	12
13. Metzelaars	BUF	10	18	179	0	2	2	12
14. Folsom	DALL	13	28	255	0	2	2	12
15. Kay	DEN	10	21	197	0	2	2	12
16. Beach	IND	10	14	77	0	2	2	12
17. Boyer	IND	8	11	58	0	2	2	12
18. Hayes	KC	9	18	229	0	2	2	12
19. Holohan	LARm	16	51	510	0	2	2	12
20. Dyal	LARd	14	27	499	0	2	2	12
21. Junkin	LARd	2	3	32	0	2	2	12
22. Novoselsky	MINN	4	4	11	0	2	2	12
23. Giles	PHIL	8	16	225	0	2	2	12
24. Bernstine	SD	5	21	222	1	1	2	12
25. Cox	SD	13	22	200	0	2	2	12
26. Hall	TB	11	30	331	0	2	2	12
27. Heller	ATL	11	33	324	0	1	1	6
28. Beckman	ATL	5	11	102	0	1	1	6
29. Rolle	BUF	1	1	1	0	1	1	6
30. Boso	CHI	11	17	182	0	1	1	6
31. Newsome	CLE	13	29	324	0	1	1	6
32. Tennell	CLE	1	1	4	0	1	1	6
33. Middleton	CLE	1	1	5	0	1	1	6
34. Didier	GB	6	6	81	0	1	1	6
35. Roberts	KC	7	8	55	0	1	1	6
36. Horton	LARd	4	4	44	0	1	1	6
37. Ingram+	MINN	2	5	47	0	1	1	6
38. Cross+	NYG	3	6	107	0	1	1	6
39. Neubert	NYJ	8	28	302	0	1	1	6
40. Dressel**	NYJ	6	12	191	0	1	1	6
41. J. Tice	NO	8	9	98	0	1	1	6
42. Little	PHIL	2	2	8	0	1	1	6
43. Novacek	PHOE	12	23	225	0	1	1	6
44. Mularkey	PITT	13	22	326	0	1	1	6
45. Walls+	SF	4	4	16	0	1	1	6
46. Harris	TB	6	11	85	0	1	1	6
47. Warren	WASH	9	15	167	0	1	1	6
48. Kattus	CIN	7	12	93	0	0	0	0
49. Riggs	CIN	4	5	29	0	0	0	0
50. Jennings+	DALL	2	6	47	0	0	0	0

1989 STATISTICAL RESULTS
(Tight Ends — Basic Scoring Method)

NAME	TEAM	GP	REC	YARDS	RSH TDs	PS REC TDs	TOTAL TDs	1989 FANTASY POINTS
51. Kelly	DEN	2	3	13	0	0	0	0
52. Mobley	DEN	8	17	200	0	0	0	0
53. Spagnola	GB	2	2	13	0	0	0	0
54. Mrosko+	HOUS	3	3	28	0	0	0	0
55. Verhulst	HOUS	3	4	48	0	0	0	0
56. Hardy	MIA	1	1	2	0	0	0	0
57. Kinchen	MIA	1	1	12	0	0	0	0
58. Sievers	NE	13	54	615	0	0	0	0
59. Cook+	NE	2	3	13	0	0	0	0
60. Dawson	NE	4	10	90	0	0	0	0
61. Mowatt	NYG	13	27	288	0	0	0	0
62. Shuler	NYJ	7	29	322	0	0	0	0
63. Griggs	NYJ	5	9	112	0	0	0	0
64. Dunn	NYJ	1	2	13	0	0	0	0
65. Werner	NYJ	3	8	115	0	0	0	0
66. Scales	NO	6	8	89	0	0	0	0
67. Awalt	PHOE	12	33	360	0	0	0	0
68. Reeves+	PHOE	1	1	5	0	0	0	0
69. O'Shea	PITT	1	1	8	0	0	0	0
70. Caravello	SD	5	10	95	0	0	0	0
71. McEwen	SD	3	7	99	0	0	0	0
72. Parker	SD	2	2	5	0	0	0	0
73. Williams	SF	1	3	38	0	0	0	0
74. Tyler	SEAT	8	14	148	0	0	0	0
75. McNeal+	SEAT	5	9	148	0	0	0	0
76. J. Johnson+	WASH	4	4	84	0	0	0	0
77. Orr	WASH	3	3	80	0	0	0	0
78. M. Tice	WASH	1	1	2	0	0	0	0

+ DENOTES ROOKIES

** Dressel (NYJ) —Played in 5 games with KC.

RATING THE PLAYERS FOR 1990
(Tight Ends—Basic Scoring Method)

GRAB ONE IF YOU CAN

1. Keith Jackson (Philadelphia Eagles)
As a rookie in 1988, Jackson caught 81 passes and scored six times. In 1989 his touchdown production fell to three and his reception level to 63, because he missed some action with knee and back injuries. I believe he'll see plenty of aerials in 1990, and good touchdown production should follow.

2. Rodney Holman (Cincinnati Bengals)
Holman produced a career-high nine touchdowns in 1989. Although I don't think he'll reach that level in 1990, he should be near six or seven.

3. Damone Johnson (Los Angeles Rams)
Johnson has produced two consecutive years of good touchdown totals. In 1988 he scored six times and last year, five. I believe he'll score similarly in 1990.

4. Mark Bavaro (New York Giants)
Bavaro has scored four, four, eight, four, and three touchdowns the last five seasons, respectively. He would have done far better than his three touchdowns in 1989 had he not missed the last nine games with a knee injury. His healthy return should push him near the six-touchdown range in 1990.

5. Mickey Shuler (New York Jets)
We'll overlook his performance in 1989, when a knee injury knocked him out for half the season. From 1984 through 1988, Shuler produced six, seven, four, three, and five touchdowns, respectively, and was among the league's top tight ends.

BEST OF THE REST

6. Steve Jordan (Minnesota Vikings)
A productive reception man tallying 38, 58, 35, 57, and 35 catches the last five years, respectively, Jordan has put together touchdown totals of only three, six, two, five, and three over that same period. Still, playing on the pass-oriented Vikings, for whom he's a prime target, Jordan gets lots of fantasy attention.

7. Ed West (Green Bay Packers)
West upped his touchdown production from three in 1988 to five in 1989. He is fast becoming a favorite among tight end fantasy prospects.

8. Ferrell Edmunds (Miami Dolphins)
Edmunds has scored three touchdowns in each of his two seasons in the NFL, a level I believe he could easily surpass playing on the very pass-oriented Dolphins.

9. Brent Jones (San Francisco 49ers)

After taking over the 49ers' tight-end duties in 1989, Jones scored four times. He can easily match or surpass that mark in 1990 for the offensively diverse 49ers.

10. Hoby Brenner (New Orleans Saints)

Brenner peaked with six touchdowns way back in 1984. In 1989, however, Brenner produced 34 receptions, four for touchdowns, proving that the scoring potential is still there.

STRONG LONG SHOTS

11. Eric Sievers (New England Patriots)

Although Sievers failed to score a touchdown for the Pats in 1989, he did produce 54 receptions. Back in 1985 with the Chargers, Sievers scored six times, showing the possibilities presented by an end who catches the ball as often as Sievers does.

12. Robert Awalt (Phoenix Cardinals)

Awalt scored six times as a rookie in 1987 but has seen his touchdowns drop to four in 1988 and zero in 1989. Perhaps another year's work with the new Cardinal quarterbacks will boost his numbers. Also, he will no longer have to share tight-end duties with Jay Novacek, who is off to Dallas.

13. Ron Hall (Tampa Bay Buccaneers)

Although Hall didn't score at all in 1988 and had only two touchdowns in 1989, his reception levels of 39 in 1988 and 30 in 1989 make him worthy of fantasy consideration.

14. Pete Holohan (Los Angeles Rams)

Holohan has produced 59 and 51 receptions the past two seasons, respectively. During those same two years he scored only three and two touchdowns. Still, anybody grabbing that many receptions has big scoring potential.

15. Rod Bernstine (San Diego Chargers)

Bernstine was on his way to his best season, scoring two times and racking up 21 receptions in the first five games of 1989, when a knee injury ended his season. The Chargers hope for his healthy return in 1990.

HAVE THE POTENTIAL

16. Jay Novacek (Dallas Cowboys)

Novacek's touchdown production fell to one in 1989, after three and four touchdowns, respectively, the previous years. His 23 receptions in '89 show he's still getting the football, and that may increase in 1990 as he plays for the Cowboys.

17. Jim Thornton (Chicago Bears)

Thornton stepped in to grab 24 receptions and score three touchdowns for the Bears in 1989, totals he should be able to match or surpass in 1990 as he is used more in the offense.

18. Clarence Kay (Denver Broncos)
Kay has tallied three, three, one, zero, four, and two touchdowns, respectively, in the last six years, showing his very promising scoring potential.

19. Mike Dyal (Los Angeles Raiders)
It's tough to replace a Todd Christensen. Mike Dyal hasn't quite done that yet, but his 27 receptions and two touchdowns in 1989 are a good start.

20. Ozzie Newsome (Cleveland Browns)
This aging standout has decided to hang around another year, so don't count him out.

KEEP AN EYE ON

21.	Beach (IND)	26.	J. Tice (NO)
22.	Wilkins (ATL)	27.	Heller (SEAT)
23.	Folsom (DALL)	28.	Mularkey (PITT)
24.	Hayes (KC)	29.	Mowatt (NE)
25.	Boyer (NYJ)	30.	Metzelaars (BUF)

YOU NEVER KNOW

31.	Tyler (SEAT)	39.	Jennings (DALL)
32.	Tennell (CLE)	40.	McKeller (BUF)
33.	Mobley (DEN)	41.	Higdon (ATL)
34.	Boso (CHI)	42.	Dawson (NE)
35.	Junkin (LARd)	43.	Giles (PHIL)
36.	Neubert (NYJ)	44.	Walls (SF)
37.	Warren (WASH)	45.	Dressel (NYJ)
38.	Kattus (CIN)		

A LOOK AT THE QUARTERBACKS

(A Guide for the Beginner)

Considerations in Choosing a Quarterback

1. First, look at players' previous performances.

2. Quarterbacks who play for passing teams have the edge. Look for a quarterback with a high number of pass attempts, one who will assure you of at least 25 to 30 touchdown passes for the year. Dan Marino, Joe Montana, and Jim Everett are all good examples.

3. Look for a quarterback who doesn't mind running the ball, especially near the goal line. Because six points are awarded for a touchdown run and only three points for throwing a touchdown, quarterbacks who like to rush for touchdowns are another plus. Young Randall Cunningham of Philadelphia and John Elway of the Broncos are prime examples.

4. Avoid situations in which the starting quarterback may change from week to week. Some teams use one quarterback one week and then switch, either during the game or the following week, depending on the player's performance. It would obviously hurt you if you didn't know whether your quarterback was going to play. For example, who'll start in 1990 among Grogan, Wilson, and Flutie for New England? Between Hebert and Fourcade in New Orleans? Among Hogeboom, Tupa, and Rosenbach in Phoenix?

In the 1989 statistics, players have been ranked by their fantasy-point totals. Remember that in the Basic Scoring Method fantasy points are calculated by scoring six points for every rushing touchdown and three points for every touchdown pass thrown. No yardage statistics are included because there are no points awarded in the Basic Scoring Method for yardage gained. It is not important how a player's team did or how he ranks in any category except fantasy points. A player may have a poor passing percentage and may not throw for many yards, but if he ranks high in throwing and rushing touchdowns, he will help you win.

1989 STATISTICAL RESULTS
(Quarterbacks — Basic Scoring Method)

NAME	TEAM	GP	RSH	COMP	ATT	PCT	RUSH TDs	TD PS	1989 FANTASY POINTS
1. Majkowski	GB	16	75	353	599	58.9	5	27	111
2. Montana	SF	13	50	271	386	70.2	3	26	96
3. Moon	HOUS	16	69	280	464	60.3	4	23	93
4. Everett	LARm	16	25	304	518	50.7	1	29	93
5. Kelly	BUF	13	29	228	391	58.3	2	25	87
6. Marino	MIA	16	14	308	550	56.0	2	25	87
7. Cunningham	PHIL	16	104	290	534	54.3	4	21	87
8. Esiason	CIN	16	47	258	455	56.7	0	28	84
9. Elway	DEN	15	48	223	416	53.6	3	18	72
10. Rypien	WASH	14	26	280	476	58.8	1	22	72
11. Krieg	SEAT	15	39	286	499	57.3	0	21	63
12. Kosar	CLE	16	30	303	513	59.1	1	18	60
13. Testaverde	TB	14	26	258	481	53.6	0	20	60
14. Trudeau	IND	13	35	190	362	52.5	2	15	57
15. Tomczak	CHI	14	25	156	306	51.0	1	16	54
16. Miller*	ATL	15	10	280	526	53.2	0	16	51
17. Simms	NYG	15	33	228	405	56.3	1	14	48
18. Hogeboom	PHOE	14	27	204	364	56.0	1	14	48
19. Hebert	NO	13	25	222	354	62.7	0	15	45
20. Gagliano	DET	11	41	117	232	50.4	4	6	42
21. Peete+	DET	8	33	103	195	52.8	4	5	39
22. Beuerlein	LARd	10	15	108	217	49.8	0	13	39
23. O'Brien	NYJ	15	9	289	478	60.4	0	12	36
24. Young	SF	9	39	64	92	69.6	2	8	36
25. Harbaugh	CHI	11	45	111	178	62.4	3	5	33
26. De Berg	KC	12	12	196	324	60.5	0	11	33
27. W. Wilson	MINN	14	32	194	362	53.6	1	9	33
28. McMahon	SD	12	29	176	318	55.3	0	10	30
29. Tolliver+	SD	5	4	89	185	48.1	0	5	30
30. Aikman+	DALL	11	38	155	292	53.1	0	9	27
31. Grogan	NE	7	9	133	261	51.0	0	9	27
32. Fourcade	NO	7	15	60	106	56.6	1	7	27
33. Brister	PITT	14	27	187	343	54.5	0	9	27
34. Schroeder	LARd	10	20	91	194	46.9	0	8	24
35. Reich	BUF	5	9	53	87	60.9	0	7	21
36. Kramer	MINN	7	12	77	136	56.6	0	7	21
37. Hostetler	NYG	5	11	20	39	51.3	2	3	21
38. Walsh+	DALL	8	5	109	219	49.8	0	5	15
39. Pelluer	KC	4	17	26	47	55.3	2	1	15
40. Wilhelm	CIN	5	6	30	56	53.6	0	4	12
41. Chandler	IND	3	7	39	80	48.8	1	2	12
42. Eason**	NYJ	5	3	79	141	56.0	0	4	12
43. M. Wilson	NE	5	7	75	150	50.0	0	3	9
44. Tupa	PHOE	6	15	65	134	48.5	0	3	9
45. Ferguson	TB	5	5	44	90	48.9	0	3	9
46. Kubiak	DEN	5	14	32	55	58.2	0	2	6
47. Hipple	DET	1	2	7	18	38.9	1	0	6
48. Ramsey	IND	6	4	24	50	48.0	0	1	6
49. Jaworski	KC	3	3	36	61	59.0	0	2	6
50. Flutie	NE	5	16	36	81	44.4	0	2	6

1989 STATISTICAL RESULTS
(Quarterbacks — Basic Scoring Method)

NAME	TEAM	GP	RSH	COMP	ATT	PCT	RUSH TDs	TD PS	1989 FANTASY POINTS
51. Millen	ATL	4	1	31	49	63.3	0	1	3
52. Pagel	CLE	4	2	5	14	35.7	0	1	3
53. Secules	MIA	4	4	22	50	44.0	0	1	3
54. Ryan	NYJ	4	1	15	30	50.0	0	1	3
55. Cavanaugh	PHIL	4	0	3	5	60.0	0	1	3
56. Blackledge	PITT	3	9	22	60	36.7	0	1	3
57. Bono	SF	1	0	4	5	80.0	0	1	3
58. Humphries	WASH	1	5	5	10	50.0	0	1	3
59. Williams	WASH	4	0	51	93	54.8	0	1	3
60. Schonert	CIN	1	0	0	2	0.0	0	0	0
61. Long	DET	1	3	2	5	40.0	0	0	0
62. Carlson	HOUS	6	3	15	31	48.4	0	0	0
63. Herrmann	LARm	3	2	2	5	40.0	0	0	0
64. Evans	LARd	1	1	2	2	100.0	0	0	0
65. Mackey	NYJ	3	2	11	25	44.0	0	0	0
66. Malone	NYJ	1	1	2	2	100.0	0	0	0
67. Rosenbach+	PHOE	2	6	9	22	40.9	0	0	0
68. Strom	PITT	2	3	0	0	0.0	0	0	0
69. Archer	SD	3	2	5	12	41.7	0	0	0
70. Stouffer	SEAT	3	2	29	59	49.2	0	0	0

+ DENOTES ROOKIES

* Miller (ATL) —Kicked a 25-yard field goal.
** Eason (NYJ) —Played in 3 games with NE.

RATING THE PLAYERS FOR 1990
(Quarterbacks—Basic Scoring Method)

GRAB ONE IF YOU CAN

1. Jim Everett (Los Angeles Rams)
Two years in a row Everett has led the league in touchdown passes, throwing 31 in 1988 and 29 in 1989. That consistency should keep him near the top of the heap again in 1990.

2. Randall Cunningham (Philadelphia Eagles)
Producing 45 touchdown passes and 10 rushing touchdowns over the past two seasons demonstrates an ability to score through the air and on the ground. That kind of consistent versatility is rare for a quarterback and is the edge Cunningham holds over many.

3. Joe Montana (San Francisco 49ers)
When he's healthy, Montana is the best in the game. His touchdown pass levels should always be near the 30 mark. In 1989, although he missed three games, he threw 26 touchdown passes and ran for 3 more. He hasn't lost a thing.

4. Dan Marino (Miami Dolphins)
We all fondly remember when Marino produced 48 touchdown passes in 1984 and 44 in 1986. Though those numbers may no longer be attainable, he's still one of the league's quickest arms, backed by plenty of receiving talent.

5. Don Majkowski (Green Bay Packers)
You've got to love the way Majkowski stepped in and took over the quarterback job for the Packers. Twenty-seven passing touchdowns and five rushing touchdowns later, he had his Packers on the brink of a playoff berth. What's in store for 1990?

BEST OF THE REST

6. Warren Moon (Houston Oilers)
During the last two seasons, Moon has placed fifth and third by this scoring method. He has done it not only on the strength of his arm (40 touchdown passes during the past two years), but also because of his ability to score on the ground (9 rushing touchdowns). I see his success continuing in the 1990 season.

7. Boomer Esiason (Cincinnati Bengals)
Here is another of the league's more consistent offensive performers over the last few years. Over the past four years, Esiason has thrown 27, 24, 28, and 28 touchdown passes, ranking him third, second, third, and eighth, respectively, during that period. There's nothing to keep him from repeating that kind of performance in 1990.

8. Jim Kelly (Buffalo Bills)
As the Bills opened up their offense a bit, Kelly expanded his numbers. Kelly progressed from throwing only 15 touchdowns in 1988 to throwing 25 in 1989, while adding two rushing scores. This is a level I believe this talented signal caller will near or maintain.

9. Dave Krieg (Seattle Seahawks)
When he's on, he's on! When he's off, he's awful! Krieg has produced as many as 32 touchdown passes (in 1984). If he can maintain some consistency and hold off the challenge of Kelly Stouffer, he could have a big season.

10. Mark Rypien (Washington Redskins)
Playing in only nine games in 1988, Rypien threw for 18 touchdowns. In 1989, plagued by fumbles, Rypien was benched for a couple of games but still managed 22 touchdown passes in 14 games. If he can avoid fumbles and retain his starting role, his numbers could pick up.

STRONG LONG SHOTS

11. Phil Simms (New York Giants)
Simms is usually a consistent low-20s producer in touchdown passes. Prior to 1989, Simms had thrown 22, 22, 21, 17, and 21 touchdowns, respectively. In 1989 he dropped off to only 14 scoring passes, a level I think he'll rebound from in 1990.

12. John Elway (Denver Broncos)
Elway has built his reputation on his strong arm, and doesn't rate among the league's top fantasy quarterbacks. Over the past seven seasons he has thrown for 18, 22, 19, 19, 19, 17, and 18 touchdowns, respectively. Only in 1987 and 1989, when he rushed for four and three touchdowns, respectively, has he cracked the league's top 10 by this scoring method.

13. Bernie Kosar (Cleveland Browns)
Surprisingly, only once in his career has Kosar thrown more than 20 touchdown passes—in 1987, when he launched 22. With targets like Webster Slaughter, Reggie Langhorne, and now Eric Metcalf, that has to be a very attainable number.

14. Vinny Testaverde (Tampa Bay Buccaneers)
Testaverde lowered his number of interceptions in 1989, and in turn his touchdown passes went up—from 13 in 1988 to 20 in 1989. He should reach or exceed that number in 1990, as he continues to mature.

15. John Fourcade/Bobby Hebert (New Orleans Saints)
Can either now hold the job all season? Hebert sometimes struggled in 1989 and eventually gave way to Fourcade. Fourcade took full advantage, throwing for seven touchdowns and leading the Saints to three straight wins to end the season. Either will realize some success in 1990 but a close eye should be kept on the situation as the season nears.

HAVE THE POTENTIAL

16. Ken O'Brien/Tony Eason (New York Jets)
When healthy, O'Brien has produced seasons like 1985 and 1986, when he threw for 25 touchdowns each year. But that was then, and this is now. He now has to contend with poor pass protection and the challenge of Tony Eason. Eason has also experienced reasonable success in the NFL with the New England Patriots. His presence on the Jets clouds the quarterback situation for 1990.

17. Chris Miller (Atlanta Falcons)
This young signal caller upped his touchdown production from 11 in 1988 to 16 last year. I believe he'll continue to improve in 1990, but he'll also have to contend with the league's toughest schedule.

18. Andre Ware/Rodney Peete/Bob Gagliano (Detroit Lions)
Playing in just eight games because of injuries in 1989, Peete threw for only five touchdowns and ran for four more. In Peete's absence, Bob Gagliano filled in admirably, also running for four touchdowns and adding six through the air. The Lions hope to keep Peete healthy in 1990, but I believe it's only a matter of time anyway before Andre Ware runs the show.

19. Gary Hogeboom/Timm Rosenbach/Tom Tupa (Phoenix Cardinals)
The Cardinals still face replacing the retired Neil Lomax. Last year veteran Gary Hogeboom came in and was the starter most of the season. Will the Cardinals stay with Hogeboom or turn to youth in Timm Rosenbach or Tom Tupa? Whoever gets the call, targets like Roy Green, J. T. Smith, and Robert Awalt should help his productivity.

20. Jeff George/Chris Chandler/Jack Trudeau (Indianapolis Colts)
Chris Chandler started out the '89 season as the team's starter, but a knee injury ended his season. Jack Trudeau took over and fared well, throwing for 15 touchdowns and running for 2 more. Will a healthy Chris Chandler return to his starting role in 1990? Or will 15-million-dollar rookie Jeff George work his way into the starting role?

KEEP AN EYE ON

21. Steve Beuerlein/Jay Schroeder (Los Angeles Raiders)
Will Steve Beuerlein retain his starting role in 1990? Jay Schroeder started the '89 season as the team's starter but lost the job due to ineffectiveness. Beuerlein then started the last six games, leading the Raiders to a 3-3 record, while throwing for eight touchdowns.

22. Wade Wilson (Minnesota Vikings)
Wilson has been an unimpressive fantasy player the last two seasons. He has thrown only 14 and 9 touchdowns, respectively. He did run for five scores in 1988, however.

23. Steve De Berg/Steve Pelluer (Kansas City Chiefs)

Steve De Berg was an on-and-off starter for the Chiefs in 1989. Starting the season's last six games, he led the Chiefs to four wins and a tie, however, which should give him the inside track for the starting role in 1990.

24. Bubby Brister (Pittsburgh Steelers)

Following 1988, when he ran for 6 touchdowns and threw for 11 more, Brister's touchdowns fell off in 1989. He failed to run for a score and threw only nine. He should rebound as he continues to mature in 1990.

25. Troy Aikman (Dallas Cowboys)

Aikman should be able to improve on the nine touchdown passes he produced as a rookie in 1989, if he and his receivers can stay healthy.

26. Mike Tomczak/Jim Harbaugh (Chicago Bears)

Playing on a team that would rather run Neal Anderson than pass makes either quarterback a questionable fantasy choice. Neither seems consistent enough to hold the starting job.

27. Billy Joe Tolliver (San Diego Chargers)

McMahon's inconsistency lost him the job in 1989. Then he was released. Will Tolliver play well enough to hold the position?

28. Steve Grogan/Marc Wilson/Doug Flutie (New England Patriots)

This situation just doesn't interest me!

A LOOK AT THE KICKERS

(A Guide for the Beginner)

Considerations in Choosing a Kicker

1. First, look at players' previous productivity.

2. A kicker can't score points without opportunities to score, so one of our main concerns is the team he's playing for. You're well off with a kicker from a good offensive team that will get close enough for a field-goal attempt. Even a good defensive team will provide its kicker with plenty of scoring opportunities.

3. A kicker who has played for the same team for a few years is a good bet. Kickers are treated as if they were a dime a dozen, so if one has been with a team a few years, there must be some confidence that he will be consistent year after year.

4. Consider the opposition a kicker will face in 1990. Favor the kickers who will face an easy schedule. (See Section VI, "Rating the 1990 NFL Team Schedules.")

In the 1989 statistics, the players have been ranked by the number of fantasy points accumulated. Remember that in both the Basic Scoring Method and the Performance Point Method fantasy points are calculated by scoring three points for each field goal and one point for each extra point.

1989 STATISTICAL RESULTS
(Kickers — Basic Scoring Method and
Performance Point Method)

NAME	TEAM	GP	EXTRA PTS	EXTRA PT ATT	PCT	FIELD GOALS	FIELD GOAL ATT	ACC RATE	1989 FANTASY POINTS
1. Cofer	SF	16	49	50	.980	29	36	.806	136
2. Lohmiller	WASH	16	41	42	.976	29	40	.725	128
3. Treadwell	DEN	16	39	40	.975	27	33	.818	120
4. Lansford	LARm	16	51	51	1.000	23	30	.767	120
5. Karlis	MINN	13	27	28	.964	31	39	.795	120
6. Norwood	BUF	16	46	48	.958	23	30	.767	115
7. T. Zendejas	HOUS	16	40	40	1.000	25	37	.676	115
8. Jacke+	GB	16	42	42	1.000	22	28	.786	108
9. Lowery	KC	16	34	35	.971	24	33	.727	106
10. Andersen	NO	16	44	46	.956	20	29	.690	104
11. Jaeger	LARd	16	34	34	1.000	23	24	.958	103
12. Igwebuike	TB	16	33	35	.943	22	28	.786	99
13. Murray	DET	16	36	36	1.000	20	21	.952	96
14. Davis**	ATL	15	26	28	.928	23	34	.677	95
15. Stoyanovich+	MIA	16	38	39	.974	19	26	.731	95
16. Biasucci	IND	16	31	33	.939	21	27	.778	94
17. Anderson	PITT	16	28	28	1.000	21	30	.700	91
18. M. Bahr	CLE	16	40	40	1.000	16	24	.667	88
19. Butler	CHI	16	43	45	.956	15	19	.789	86
20. Allegre	NYG	10	23	24	.958	20	26	.769	83
21. Del Greco	PHOE	16	28	29	.966	18	26	.692	82
22. C. Bahr	SD	16	29	31	.935	17	25	.680	80
23. L. Zendejas**	DALL	15	33	33	1.000	14	24	.583	75
24. Breech	CIN	12	37	39	.949	12	14	.857	73
25. Johnson	SEAT	16	27	27	1.000	15	25	.600	72
26. Leahy	NYJ	16	29	30	.967	14	21	.667	71
27. Ruzek**	PHIL	14	28	29	.966	13	22	.591	67
28. McFadden	ATL	9	18	18	1.000	15	20	.750	63
29. Staurovsky	NE	7	14	14	1.000	14	17	.823	56
30. Nittmo	NYG	6	12	13	.923	9	12	.750	39
31. Gallery	CIN	4	13	13	1.000	2	6	.333	19
32. Deline	PHIL	3	3	3	1.000	3	7	.429	12
33. Garcia	MINN	3	8	8	1.000	1	5	.200	11
34. Miller	ATL	1	0	0	.000	1	1	1.000	3

+ DENOTES ROOKIES

** Davis   (ATL)   —Played in 9 games with NE.
** L. Zendejas (DALL)   —Played in 8 games with PHIL.
** Ruzek   (PHIL)   —Played in 9 games with DALL.

RATING THE PLAYERS FOR 1990
(Kickers—Basic Scoring and Performance Point Methods)

GRAB ONE IF YOU CAN

1. Mike Cofer (San Francisco 49ers)
Cofer upped his field-goal percentage from .711 in 1988 to .806 in 1989. With that improvement, Cofer moved from number two in the league to number one, a standing that he could retain in 1990, kicking for this potent offensive machine.

2. Scott Norwood (Buffalo Bills)
After hitting a very solid 32 of 37 (.865) field-goal attempts in 1988, leading all kickers in scoring, Norwood's 1989 performance dropped a bit. He still hit on 23 of 30 (.767) attempts. He can certainly improve in 1990, as the Bills continue to give him plenty of scoring opportunity.

3. Chip Lohmiller (Washington Redskins)
Although Lohmiller's field-goal percentage did not actually increase (.731 in 1988, .725 in 1989) his field-goal attempts did. The Redskins provided him with 40 chances in 1989, as compared to 26 in 1988. Although there's no assurance of that happening again, I believe the Redskins will continue to provide Lohmiller with plenty of scoring opportunity in 1990.

4. David Treadwell (Denver Broncos)
You have to be impressed with this rookie's 1989 performance. Treadwell hit 27 of 33 field-goal attempts for a very promising .818 kicking percentage, accuracy that could keep him around for a long time.

5. Dean Biasucci (Indianapolis Colts)
Until 1989's dropoff, when his Colts faced the league's toughest schedule, Biasucci had placed third and fifth by this scoring method the two previous years, respectively. I believe he'll rebound in 1990, since the Colts won't face such tough opponents.

BEST OF THE REST

6. Mike Lansford (Los Angeles Rams)
Lansford's 24 of 32 (.750) field-goal attempts in 1988 and 23 of 30 (.767) in 1989 have helped him to fourth place by this scoring method the last two seasons. Although I see another steady performance from Lansford in 1990, the Rams' facing the league's fifth toughest schedule may drop him a few notches.

7. Rich Karlis (Minnesota Vikings)

Before being released by the Broncos prior to the '89 season, Karlis had kicked well enough to be a top-10 finisher by this scoring method for three consecutive years. Karlis, picked up by the Vikings to kick in the season's last 13 games, had plenty of scoring opportunity. In 39 field-goal attempts he hit 31, for a .795 kicking percentage. He added 27 extra points for a total of 120 points, tying him for fourth in the league. Although I don't believe he'll see that many scoring opportunities in 1990, if he remains the kicker for Minnesota, he'll again have plenty of scoring success.

8. Raul Allegre (New York Giants)

Before a groin injury sidelined him for the last six games of 1989, Allegre hit on 20 of 26 (.769) field-goal attempts. He totaled 83 points in his 10 games and probably would have wound up in the 120-point range had he remained healthy. I believe he'll near 120 points in 1990.

9. Tony Zendejas (Houston Oilers)

Over the past three seasons, Zendejas has placed fifth (91 points in a 12-game season), fifth (114 points), and sixth (115 points), respectively. That success level may drop a bit in 1990, with Houston facing the league's fifth toughest schedule.

10. Chris Jacke (Green Bay Packers)

As a rookie in 1989, Jacke hit a solid 22 of 28 (.786) field-goal attempts and all 42 extra-point attempts, to score 108 total points. The improving Packers should continue to give him scoring opportunity in 1990, which ought to result in another top-10 finish.

STRONG LONG SHOTS

11. Morten Andersen (New Orleans Saints)

Andersen has placed 5th, 5th, 1st, 8th, and 10th by this scoring method over the past five years, respectively. In 1989, this usually accurate kicker hit only 20 of 29 field-goal attempts for a woeful .690 percentage. I expect him to improve in 1990, which should again put him in or near the top 10.

12. Gary Anderson (Pittsburgh Steelers)

Anderson had been a pretty consistent top-10 performer by this scoring method prior to 1989. He had placed 5th, 3rd, 2nd, 12th, 7th, and 3rd, respectively, the previous six years. Then in 1989 he dropped to 17th, hitting only 21 of 30 (.700) field-goal attempts. I'm looking for a rebound to a near top-10 finish in 1990.

13. Nick Lowery (Kansas City Chiefs)

Lowery's ranking by this scoring method has hovered right around the bottom of the top 10 for the past six years. He placed 9th, 10th, 10th, 11th, 13th, and 9th, respectively, during that period. Then this normally very accurate kicker's field-goal percentage dropped to .727 in 1989, from .826 and .828, respectively, the previous two years. Although his aging leg may lack some of its previous accuracy, I still believe he'll be battling to reach or near the top 10 again in 1990.

14. Donald Igwebuike (Tampa Bay Buccaneers)
As the Bucs slowly improve, so does Donald Igwebuike. Igwebuike has progressively placed 24th, 22nd, and 12th, respectively, over the past three seasons. I believe he'll continue to score well in 1990, as the Bucs face the league's second easiest schedule.

15. Pete Stoyanovich (Miami Dolphins)
As a rookie in 1989, Stoyanovich took over for the injured Fuad Reveiz and produced some fair numbers. He hit on 19 of 26 (.731) field-goal attempts and added 38 of 39 (.974) extra-point attempts. Kicking for the offensively very potent Dolphins, who face the league's fifth easiest schedule in 1990, should provide plenty more scoring opportunities.

HAVE THE POTENTIAL

16. Eddie Murray (Detroit Lions)
Murray's hitting 20 of 21 (.952) field-goal attempts in 1989 certainly reconfirmed his accuracy. Murray's only drawback was that he kicked for the offensively weak Lions. The Lions may not be so weak anymore, though, which may give Murray a scoring boost.

17. Kevin Butler (Chicago Bears)
Butler has seen his standing by this scoring method take a dive. Over the past five seasons Butler has placed 1st, 2nd, 8th, 19th, and 19th, respectively. The once-proud Bears are in a state of semi-rebuilding, and I don't see a drastic improvement.

18. Matt Bahr (Cleveland Browns)
Bahr was given only 24 field-goal opportunities in 1989, of which he hit 16. Scoring opportunity plays a big role for kickers, and in 1990 Bahr and the Browns face the league's third toughest schedule, which will continue to spell problems for Bahr's scoring chances.

19. Jeff Jaeger (Los Angeles Raiders)
Jaeger's field-goal percentage hasn't been the best. For Cleveland in 1987 he hit 12 of 20 (.600) attempts. For the Raiders in 1989 he hit 23 of 34 (.677) attempts. Scoring opportunities in 1990 may be infrequent, because the Raiders face the league's seventh toughest schedule.

20. Jim Breech (Cincinnati Bengals)
After being released by the Bengals in 1989 at the season's outset, Breech returned to kick in the last 12 games. His kicking percentage was an impressive .857—12 of 14 attempts. A drawback kicking for the Bengals is that they find a way to get into the end zone, rather than settle for field goals. Compare Breech's 39 extra-point attempts to his 14 field-goal attempts. Regardless, kicking for the Bengals should provide scoring opportunity one way or another.

KEEP AN EYE ON

21. Pat Leahy (New York Jets)
Although the Jets face the league's easiest schedule, their erratic 1989 play makes me leery.

22. Paul McFadden/Greg Davis (Atlanta Falcons)
McFadden's thigh injury led to the acquisition of Greg Davis in 1989. The uncertainty of whose job this may be and the Falcons' facing the league's toughest schedule have me shying away.

23. Norm Johnson (Seattle Seahawks)
Johnson's 15 of 25 (.600) on field-goal attempts in 1989 has me worried that his job is in jeopardy.

24. Al Del Greco (Phoenix Cardinals)
Del Greco's field-goal percentage has been less than impressive the last two seasons. In 1988 he hit 12 of 21 attempts (.571) and in 1989 he hit 18 of 26 (.692) attempts. He'll have to improve his accuracy to improve his standing.

25. Jason Staurovsky (New England Patriots)
This team is trying to find a permanent quarterback, a new head coach, and itself, which makes me hesitant. Staurovsky himself was impressive, hitting 14 of 17 (.823) field-goal attempts for the Pats.

26. Roger Ruzek (Philadelphia Eagles)
After being released by the Cowboys, Ruzek finished out the year with Philadelphia. His 13 of 22 (.591) on field-goal tries has me wondering if he'll finish the 1990 season at Philadelphia.

27. Luis Zendejas (Dallas Cowboys)
His kicking for a young team facing the league's fourth toughest schedule will keep me away.

28. Chris Bahr/Fuad Reveiz (San Diego Chargers)
Bahr's 17-of-25 (.680) field-goal kicking in 1989 has lost him a job. The Chargers say they won't re-sign Bahr and will be looking for a new placekicker. Fuad Reveiz is one who'll be brought into camp.

A 1990 MOCK DRAFT
(My Top-16 Overall Picks for the Basic Scoring Method)

NAME	TEAM	POSITION
1. Jerry Rice	San Francisco 49ers	Wide Receiver
2. Neal Anderson	Chicago Bears	Running Back
3. Greg Bell	Los Angeles Rams	Running Back
4. Barry Sanders	Detroit Lions	Running Back
5. Dalton Hilliard	New Orleans Saints	Running Back
6. Christian Okoye	Kansas City Chiefs	Running Back
7. Eric Dickerson	Indianapolis Colts	Running Back
8. Mark Clayton	Miami Dolphins	Wide Receiver
9. Sterling Sharpe	Green Bay Packers	Wide Receiver
10. Jim Everett	Los Angeles Rams	Quarterback
11. Randall Cunningham	Philadelphia Eagles	Quarterback
12. Eric Metcalf	Cleveland Browns	Running Back
13. Roger Craig	San Francisco 49ers	Running Back
14. Herschel Walker	Minnesota Vikings	Running Back
15. Ickey Woods	Cincinnati Bengals	Running Back
16. Joe Montana	San Francisco 49ers	Quarterback

I don't normally put wide receivers at the top of my list, but Jerry Rice is just too consistent and too good not to be there.

Neal Anderson, Greg Bell, Barry Sanders, and Dalton Hilliard are potential 15-touchdown scorers.

Then Christian Okoye, Eric Dickerson, Mark Clayton, and Sterling Sharpe are very likely 12-plus touchdown scorers.

Now two quarterbacks: Jim Everett may be picked now because he has led the league in touchdown passes two consecutive years. Randall Cunningham combines running ability with his gifted arm to be a very prominent fantasy pick.

The next group, who are all running backs, includes Eric Metcalf, Roger Craig, Herschel Walker, and Ickey Woods, all double-digit probables.

Joe Montana rounds out my top picks. If he's healthy, he's the best, and 30 touchdown passes are probable.

IX
RATING THE PLAYERS:
PERFORMANCE POINT METHOD

To begin forming a drafting strategy for the Performance Point Method of scoring, let's recall how points are awarded in this system. In this method, unlike the Basic Scoring Method, actual touchdowns scored are meaningless. Points are awarded on the basis of a player's yardage performance.

This method of scoring may be the least frustrating to use because it relies least on chance. Pro football teams go into games with a plan for how they are going to use their skilled players to move the ball up and down the field. They often have specialists, however, to score the one-yard touchdowns. The skilled players who worked hard to get the yardage between the 20-yard lines may not get the satisfaction of crossing the goal line. The Performance Point Method rewards the skilled players for what they accomplished.

In drafting for this method you are going after the yardage players. You know their names: Dickerson, Rice, Marino, and so on. As you can see, the well-known, highly paid players are the first to consider.

As with the Basic Scoring Method, we will take a look at some basic drafting strategy, followed by a list of positive and negative qualities to consider in choosing your players. Then we will take a look at the players' 1989 statistics, and finally I will rate the players for the 1990 season.

No rookies are included in my player ratings. It's too early to judge how they'll fit into each team's scheme. I rate the rookies separately, in Section V of this chapter.

Performance Point Method

DRAFTING STRATEGY BY ROUNDS

(A Guide for the Beginner)

1. The draft consists of 12 rounds.
2. Of the 12 players, 7 are starters and 5 are reserves.
3. The starting 7 comprise:

1 Quarterback		1 Quarterback
2 Running Backs	OR	2 Running Backs
2 Wide Receivers	FLEX OPTION	3 Receivers
1 Tight End		1 Kicker
1 Kicker		

4. The 5 reserves can be from any position.

5. Any player from any starting position can be drafted in any round.

ROUND 1: Remember that running backs, wide receivers, and tight ends are awarded one point for every 10 yards rushing or pass-receiving, while quarterbacks receive one point for every 20 yards passed. A good first-round pick would be a 15-point-per-game player. That means a running back, wide receiver, or tight end who averages 150 yards rushing or pass-receiving per game, or a quarterback who has many 300-yard games. Overall, a running back has a better chance to perform consistently at that level than a player at any other position. Therefore, a top-notch running back—someone with a combined rushing and receiving total between 1,500 and 2,000 yards for a season—should be your first pick. Eric Dickerson of the Indianapolis Colts and Roger Craig of the 49ers come to mind, and both of them surpassed the 2,000-yard mark in 1988. In 1989, only Thurman Thomas neared that 2,000-yard plateau, with 1,913 total yards. You might also go with a wide receiver who could attain that 1,500–2,000-yard level, although there aren't many in that category.

ROUND 2: This round should just be a repetition of round one. Again, running backs are the most consistent scorers, so take the best one available.

ROUND 3: By this time, most of the better running backs will be gone. As I mentioned in my remarks about the Basic Scoring Method, I have found that, although a few receivers are consistently above the rest, most tend to be unpredictable from year to year. Tight ends are not as likely to accumulate 1,000-yard seasons as running backs are, so try to select a top-yardage quarterback, one who plays for a pass-oriented offense. Dan Marino comes to mind first, but he probably won't be around this late in the draft; look for a quarterback who could surpass the 4,000-yard mark. Randall Cunningham, Joe Montana, and Jim Everett are possibilities.

ROUND 4: It's time to pick a good wide receiver. A consistent one like Jerry Rice, Mark Clayton, or Mike Quick comes to mind, but they may have disappeared from the draft list by this round.

ROUND 5: Let's make this the free round. Grab the best player available, no matter what position, or take a shot at a rookie.

ROUNDS 6, 7, and 8: Use these middle rounds to fill in your seven-man lineup. If you're missing a tight end, a kicker, or a player for some other position, use these rounds to pick one up.

ROUNDS 9 through 12: These last four rounds are used to pick up reserves and maybe to take a chance on some rookie prospects. Be sure to have at least one backup at quarterback, running back, and wide receiver, because players at these positions are prone to injury. Now let's take a look at how to fill the various positions on your team.

A LOOK AT THE RUNNING BACKS

(A Guide for the Beginner)

Considerations in Choosing a Running Back

As I did with the Basic Scoring Method, I will first list some positive and negative qualities to check in choosing draft picks. Then I'll show the players' 1989 statistics, followed by the player ratings for 1990.

1. First, look at players' previous performances.

2. In the Performance Point Method, where yardage is your only concern, seek an all-purpose running back who can rush for 1,000 yards in a season and catch the ball to pick up additional yardage. He should get you many games in which his combined rushing-receiving yardage comes to at least 150. Eric Dickerson, Roger Craig, and now Thurman Thomas top this list.

3. If you don't have a shot at a good all-purpose back, your next choice should be a 1,000-yard running back. He will get you 100-plus yards in several games. John Stephens, Barry Sanders, and Bobby Humphrey are all prime examples.

4. Try for rookies on teams that will use them as regulars. Rookies play hard in order to prove themselves. Look at how Barry Sanders, Bobby Humphrey, and Eric Metcalf fared in 1989.

5. Yardage is the key with this method, so the big backs who specialize in short-yardage touchdowns and do not have many 100-yard games will not be good picks.

6. As was mentioned in the Basic Scoring Method, older backs tend to be less productive. Their battered bodies can no longer take the punishment, and their desire to excel may have fallen off.

7. Injury-prone players should always be viewed suspiciously. Although they may have good games, you can't depend on them for a full season.

In the 1989 statistics, the players have been ranked by their fantasy-point totals. Remember that in the Performance Point Method, fantasy points are calculated by scoring one point for every 10 yards rushing, one point for every 10 yards pass-receiving, and one point for every 20 yards passing.

1989 STATISTICAL RESULTS
(Running Backs — Performance Point Method)

NAME	TEAM	GP	RSH	YARDS	AVG PER GM	PS REC	YARDS	AVG PER GM	TOTAL YARDS	AVG PER GM	1989 FAN-TASY PTS
1. Thomas	BUF	16	298	1,244	77.8	60	669	41.8	1,913	119.6	178
2. Hilliard	NO	16	344	1,262	78.9	52	514	32.1	1,776	111.0	165
3. B. Sanders+	DET	15	280	1,470	98.0	24	282	18.8	1,752	116.8	163
4. N. Anderson	CHI	16	274	1,275	79.7	50	434	27.1	1,709	106.8	157
5. Dickerson	IND	16	314	1,311	87.4	30	211	14.1	1,522	101.5	143
6. Okoye	KC	15	370	1,480	98.7	2	12	0.8	1,492	99.5	143
7. Brooks	CIN	16	221	1,239	77.4	37	306	19.1	1,545	96.6	141
8. Craig	SF	16	271	1,054	65.9	49	473	29.6	1,527	95.4	141
9. Humphrey+	DEN	16	294	1,151	71.9	22	156	9.8	1,307	81.7	121
10. Walker**	MINN	16	250	915	57.2	40	423	26.4	1,338	83.6	119
11. Bell	LARm	16	272	1,137	71.1	19	85	5.3	1,222	76.4	115
12. O.J. Anderson	NYG	16	325	1,023	63.9	28	268	16.8	1,291	80.7	115
13. J.L. Williams	SEAT	15	146	499	33.3	76	657	43.8	1,156	77.1	104
14. Byars	PHIL	16	133	452	28.3	68	721	45.1	1,173	73.3	102
15. Jackson	LARd	11	173	950	86.4	9	69	6.3	1,019	92.6	94
16. Stephens	NE	14	244	833	59.5	21	207	14.8	1,040	74.3	93
17. Byner	WASH	16	134	580	36.3	54	458	28.6	1,038	64.9	93
18. Hector	NYJ	15	177	702	46.8	38	330	22.0	1,032	68.8	91
19. Fullwood	GB	15	204	821	54.7	19	214	14.3	1,035	69.0	90
20. Settle	ATL	15	179	690	46.0	39	316	21.1	1,006	67.1	87
21. Riggs	WASH	12	201	834	69.5	7	67	5.6	901	75.1	85
22. Metcalf+	CLE	16	187	633	39.6	54	397	24.8	1,030	64.4	83
23. Worley+	PITT	15	195	770	51.3	15	115	7.7	885	59.0	80
24. Rathman	SF	16	79	306	19.1	73	616	38.5	922	57.6	79
25. Hoge	PITT	16	186	621	38.8	34	271	16.9	892	55.8	74
26. Warner	SEAT	16	194	631	39.4	23	153	9.6	784	49.0	69
27. Bentley	IND	16	75	299	18.7	52	525	32.8	824	51.5	68
28. Woodside	GB	15	46	273	18.2	59	527	35.1	800	53.3	67
29. Sm. Smith+	MIA	13	200	659	50.6	7	81	6.2	740	56.9	67
30. Fenney	MINN	16	151	588	36.8	30	254	15.9	842	52.6	66
31. Perryman	NE	16	150	562	35.1	29	195	12.2	757	47.3	64
32. Butts+	SD	15	170	683	45.5	7	21	1.4	704	46.9	63
33. Highsmith	HOUS	16	128	531	33.2	18	201	12.6	732	45.8	61
34. Nelson**	SD	14	67	321	22.9	38	380	27.1	701	50.1	61
35. Toney	PHIL	14	172	582	12.3	19	124	8.9	706	50.4	60
36. Pinkett	HOUS	15	94	449	29.9	31	239	15.9	688	45.9	59
37. Delpino	LARm	16	78	368	23.0	34	344	21.5	712	44.5	59
38. McNeil	NYJ	10	79	342	34.2	32	320	32.0	662	66.2	56
39. Tate	TB	15	167	589	39.3	11	75	5.0	664	44.3	56
40. Meggett+	NYG	16	28	117	7.3	34	531	33.2	648	40.5	53
41. Vick	NYJ	16	112	434	27.1	34	241	15.1	675	42.2	53
42. Kinnebrew	BUF	13	132	534	41.1	5	60	4.6	594	45.7	52
43. Ferrell	PHOE	15	149	502	33.5	18	122	8.1	624	41.6	51
44. St. Smith	LARd	16	117	471	29.4	19	140	8.8	611	38.2	50
45. Wilder	TB	13	70	244	18.8	36	335	25.8	579	44.5	50
46. K. Jones+	ATL	12	52	202	16.8	41	396	33.0	598	49.8	49
47. Spencer	SD	14	134	521	37.2	18	112	8.0	633	45.2	48
48. Muster	CHI	16	82	327	20.4	32	259	16.2	586	36.6	47
49. Palmer	DALL	9	111	434	48.2	17	93	10.3	527	58.6	46
50. Lang	ATL	15	47	176	11.7	39	436	29.1	612	40.8	45

1989 STATISTICAL RESULTS
(Running Backs — Performance Point Method)

NAME	TEAM	GP	RSH	YARDS	AVG PER GM	PS REC	YARDS	AVG PER GM	TOTAL YARDS	AVG PER GM	1989 FAN-TASY PTS
51. Gentry	CHI	15	17	106	7.1	39	463	30.9	569	37.9	44
52. Howard	TB	13	110	357	27.5	30	188	14.5	545	41.9	44
53. Mc. Allen	LARd	8	69	293	36.6	20	191	23.9	484	60.5	43
54. Manoa	CLE	16	87	289	18.1	27	241	15.1	530	33.1	42
55. McNair+	KC	13	23	121	9.3	34	372	28.6	493	37.9	41
56. Stradford	MIA	7	66	240	34.3	25	233	33.3	473	67.6	41
57. R. Harmon	BUF	13	17	99	7.6	29	363	27.9	462	35.5	39
58. Sewell	DEN	13	7	44	4.8	25	416	32.0	460	35.4	37
59. Heard	KC	15	63	216	14.4	25	246	16.4	462	30.8	37
60. Jm. Morris	WASH	10	124	336	33.6	8	85	8.5	421	42.1	36
61. Ball+	CIN	14	98	391	27.9	6	44	3.1	435	31.1	34
62. Winder	DEN	15	110	351	23.4	14	89	5.9	440	29.3	33
63. Fontenot	GB	16	17	69	4.3	40	362	22.6	431	26.9	33
64. Jennings	CIN	14	83	293	20.9	10	119	8.5	412	29.4	32
65. White	HOUS	14	104	349	24.9	6	37	2.6	386	37.6	31
66. V. Mueller	LARd	12	46	153	12.8	18	240	20.0	393	32.8	31
67. McGee	LARm	15	21	99	6.6	37	363	24.2	462	30.8	30
68. Dozier	MINN	11	46	207	18.8	14	148	13.5	355	32.3	29
69. Sikahema	PHOE	12	38	145	12.1	23	245	20.4	390	32.5	29
70. A. Anderson	MINN	11	52	189	17.2	20	193	17.5	382	34.7	28
71. Johnston+	DALL	12	67	212	17.7	16	133	11.1	345	28.8	26
72. Rozier	HOUS	12	88	301	25.1	3	22	1.8	323	26.9	26
73. Tillman+	NYG	12	79	290	24.2	1	9	0.8	299	24.9	26
74. Drummond+	PHIL	9	32	127	14.1	17	180	20.0	307	34.1	25
75. K. Jones	CLE	10	43	160	16.0	15	126	12.6	286	28.6	22
76. Saxon	KC	15	58	233	15.5	11	86	5.7	319	21.3	22
77. Carter	PITT	14	12	10	0.7	38	267	19.1	277	19.8	22
78. Sherman+	PHIL	7	40	177	25.3	8	85	12.1	262	37.4	21
79. Logan	MIA	9	57	201	22.3	5	34	3.8	235	26.1	19
80. B. Jordan	NO	11	38	179	16.3	4	53	4.8	232	21.1	19
81. Davis	BUF	9	29	149	16.6	6	92	10.2	241	26.8	19
82. Haddix	GB	12	44	135	11.3	15	111	9.3	246	20.5	18
83. Heyward	NO	12	49	183	15.3	13	69	5.8	252	21.0	18
84. Alexander	DEN	13	45	146	11.2	8	84	6.5	230	17.7	17
85. Carthon	NYG	14	57	153	10.9	15	132	9.4	285	20.4	17
86. Redden	CLE	12	40	180	15.0	6	34	2.8	214	17.8	16
87. T. Jordan	PHOE	12	83	211	17.6	6	20	1.7	231	19.3	16
88. S. Mitchell	PHOE	3	43	165	55.0	1	10	3.3	175	58.3	16
89. Flagler	SF	8	33	129	16.1	6	51	6.4	180	22.5	16
90. Stamps	TB	10	29	141	14.1	15	82	8.2	223	22.3	16
91. Dupard**	WASH	8	37	111	13.9	6	70	8.8	181	22.6	15
92. W. Williams	PITT	5	37	131	26.2	6	48	9.6	179	35.8	14
93. Henderson+	SF	3	5	21	7.0	3	130	43.3	151	50.3	14
94. Gary+	LARm	8	37	163	20.4	2	13	1.6	176	22.0	13
95. Higgs	PHIL	10	49	184	18.4	3	9	0.9	193	19.3	13
96. C. Taylor+	CIN	8	30	111	13.9	4	44	5.5	155	19.4	12
97. Mack	CLE	4	37	130	32.5	2	7	1.8	137	34.3	12
98. Tautalatasi	DALL	8	6	15	1.9	17	157	19.6	172	21.5	12
99. Paige	DET	7	30	105	15.0	2	27	3.9	132	18.9	11
100. T. Brown	MIA	7	13	29	4.1	12	100	14.3	129	18.4	11

1989 STATISTICAL RESULTS
(Running Backs — Performance Point Method)

	NAME	TEAM	GP	RSH	YARDS	AVG PER GM	PS REC	YARDS	AVG PER GM	TOTAL YARDS	AVG PER GM	1989 FAN-TASY PTS
101.	Oliphant	CLE	5	15	97	19.4	3	22	4.4	119	23.8	10
102.	Clark	MINN	3	20	99	33.0	2	14	4.7	113	37.7	10
103.	Frazier	NO	8	25	103	12.9	3	25	3.1	128	16.0	10
104.	Stone	PITT	7	10	53	7.6	7	82	11.7	135	19.3	10
105.	D. Smith	TB	7	6	31	4.4	7	110	15.7	141	20.1	10
106.	Woods	CIN	2	29	94	47.0	0	0	0.0	94	47.0	9
107.	T. Sanders+	CHI	13	41	127	9.8	3	28	2.2	155	11.9	9
108.	Clack	DALL	2	14	40	20.0	3	60	30.0	100	50.0	9
109.	Rouson	NYG	11	11	51	4.6	7	121	11.0	172	15.6	9
110.	Sydney	SF	5	7	32	6.4	9	71	14.2	103	20.6	9
111.	Sargent	DALL	12	20	87	7.3	7	50	4.2	137	11.4	8
112.	Bratton+	DEN	11	30	108	9.8	10	59	5.4	167	15.2	8
113.	M. Green+	CHI	6	5	46	7.7	5	48	8.0	94	15.7	7
114.	Suhey	CHI	10	20	51	5.5	9	73	7.3	124	12.4	7
115.	Tatupu	NE	6	11	49	8.2	9	43	7.2	92	15.3	7
116.	Brinson	SD	7	17	64	9.1	12	71	10.1	135	19.3	7
117.	Paterra+	ATL	4	9	32	8.0	5	42	10.5	74	18.5	6
118.	Scott	DALL	3	2	-4	-0.8	9	63	21.0	59	19.7	5
119.	Painter	DET	5	15	64	12.8	3	41	8.2	105	21.0	5
120.	G. Green	LARm	6	26	74	12.3	0	0	0.0	74	12.3	4
121.	Mv. Allen	NE	3	11	51	17.0	0	0	0.0	51	17.0	4
122.	A. Brown+	NYJ	4	9	48	12.0	4	10	2.5	58	14.5	4
123.	Wolfley	PHOE	8	13	36	4.5	5	38	4.8	74	9.3	4
124.	Fenner+	SEAT	2	11	41	20.5	3	23	11.5	64	32.0	4
125.	Porter	LARd	5	13	54	10.8	0	0	0.0	54	10.8	3
126.	Hampton	MIA	6	17	48	8.0	7	28	4.7	76	12.7	3
127.	Davenport	MIA	6	14	56	9.3	3	19	3.2	75	12.5	3
128.	Rice	MINN	3	7	15	5.0	4	29	9.7	44	14.7	3
129.	Adams	NYG	5	9	29	5.8	2	7	1.8	36	7.2	3
130.	Holifield	CIN	1	11	20	20.0	2	8	8.0	28	28.0	2
131.	Gamble	KC	2	6	24	12.0	2	2	1.0	26	13.0	2
132.	Harris+	SEAT	4	8	23	5.8	3	26	6.5	49	12.3	2
133.	K. Harmon	SEAT	1	1	24	24.0	0	0	0.0	24	24.0	2
134.	Flowers	ATL	5	13	26	5.2	0	0	0.0	26	5.2	1
135.	J. Mueller	BUF	6	15	43	7.2	1	8	1.3	51	8.5	1
136.	Tc. Johnson+	HOUS	3	1	-1	-0.3	4	25	8.3	24	8.3	1
137.	Hunter+	IND	2	6	22	11.0	0	0	0.0	22	11.0	1
138.	Egu+	NE	2	3	20	10.0	0	0	0.0	20	10.0	1
139.	Baker	PHOE	5	17	26	5.2	2	18	3.6	44	8.8	1
140.	Floyd+	SD	3	8	15	5.0	1	6	6.0	21	7.0	1
141.	A. Mitchell	TB	1	0	0	0.0	1	11	11.0	11	11.0	1
142.	B. Taylor	CHI	1	0	0	0.0	2	7	7.0	7	7.0	0
143.	Workman+	GB	2	3	5	2.5	1	3	3.0	8	4.0	0
144.	Carruth	KC	1	0	0	0.0	1	3	3.0	3	3.0	0
145.	Agee	KC	1	0	0	0.0	1	3	3.0	3	3.0	0
146.	Faaola	MIA	2	2	10	5.0	1	8	8.0	18	9.0	0
147.	Wonsley	NE	2	2	-2	-1.0	0	0	0.0	-2	-1.0	0
148.	Wallace	PITT	4	5	10	2.5	0	0	0.0	10	2.5	0
149.	Tyrrell	PITT	1	1	3	3.0	0	0	0.0	3	3.0	0
150.	J. Jones	SEAT	1	0	0	0.0	1	8	8.0	8	8.0	0
151.	Reaves	WASH	1	1	-1	-1.0	0	0	0.0	-1	-1.0	0

+ DENOTES ROOKIES

** Walker   (MINN) —Played in 5 games with DALL.
** Nelson   (SD) —Played in 5 games with MINN.
** Dupard   (WASH) —Played in 6 games with NE.

RATING THE PLAYERS FOR 1990
(Running Backs—Performance Point Method)

GRAB ONE IF YOU CAN

1. Neal Anderson (Chicago Bears)
Anderson's rushing-receiving production continues to climb. He produced 1,051, 1,477, and 1,709 yards, respectively, over the past three seasons, a climb I see continuing as he remains the Bears' primary offensive weapon.

2. Thurman Thomas (Buffalo Bills)
After producing 1,089 rushing-receiving yards as a rookie in 1988, Thomas totaled 1,913 yards in 1989. Watch out in 1990, because he continued to play well in the '89 playoffs.

3. Eric Dickerson (Indianapolis Colts)
Even though hampered by a hamstring injury, Dickerson still rushed for 1,311 yards and tallied over 1,500 rushing-receiving yards. He has been a 2,000-combined-yardage man four times, making him a prime fantasy candidate again in 1990.

4. Barry Sanders (Detroit Lions)
1,470 rushing yards and another 282 receiving yards as a rookie in 1989 show unlimited potential for this prime fantasy pick.

5. Roger Craig (San Francisco 49ers)
Craig can help you both on the ground (1,054 rushing yards in 1989) and through the air (49 receptions, for another 473 yards). As a two-time 2,000-combined-yardage back, he has obvious possibilities.

6. Bobby Humphrey (Denver Broncos)
After taking over the starting role from Sammy Winder in 1989, Humphrey went on to accumulate 1,307 rushing-receiving yards. This is just a glimpse of what 1990 may have in store for this elusive back.

7. Dalton Hilliard (New Orleans Saints)
With Rueben Mayes out for the year with a knee injury, Hilliard exploded for 1,776 rushing-receiving yards in 1989. He could fare well again in 1990, but the healthy return of Mayes may bite into his production.

8. Christian Okoye (Kansas City Chiefs)
Okoye, despite missing one game with a thigh injury, led the league in rushing in 1989 with 1,480 yards. You can count on him being a major force for the Chiefs again in 1990.

9. Herschel Walker (Minnesota Vikings)
As a Dallas Cowboy, Walker produced seasons of 1,574, 1,606, and 2,019 rushing-receiving yards from 1986 through 1988. Then in 1989 when he joined the Vikings five games into the season, he managed only 1,338 combined yards. You'd think the Vikes would devise a way to revitalize Walker's stats in 1990.

10. James Brooks (Cincinnati Bengals)
Brooks has produced 1,505, 1,773, 562, 1,218, and 1,545 rushing-receiving yards over the past five seasons, respectively. His 1990 total may depend on Ickey Woods. If Woods returns healthy from his knee injury, he could cut into Brooks's yardage.

BEST OF THE REST

11. J. L. Williams (Seattle Seahawks)
In 1988 Williams rushed for 877 yards and added 651 more on 58 receptions, for a standout 1,528-yard season. In 1988 he saw his rushing production drop off to 499 yards, but he remained a standout receiver, with 657 yards on 76 receptions. I feel that, with Curt Warner now a Los Angeles Ram, Williams will have a very productive year in 1990.

12. Greg Bell (Los Angeles Rams)
Bell has rushed for 1,212 and 1,137 yards over the past two seasons, respectively. Although he doesn't help himself very much with receiving production, he should again near the 1,200-yard mark in 1990.

13. John Settle (Atlanta Falcons)
Settle's rushing-receiving numbers dropped from a big 1,594-yard season in 1988 to 1,006 yards in 1989. I believe he'll rebound some in 1990, even though he and the Falcons face the league's toughest schedule.

14. Ickey Woods (Cincinnati Bengals)
Woods rushed for over 1,000 yards as a rookie in 1988, but in 1989 a knee injury sidelined him for most of the season. A healthy return could spell another big year in 1990, but he'll have to compete in the backfield with James Brooks.

15. John Stephens (New England Patriots)
As a rookie in 1988, Stephens rushed for over 1,100 yards. In 1989, Stephens's rushing mark dropped to 833 yards, as he missed two games with an ankle injury. Look for a healthy Stephens to produce a healthy set of rushing stats in 1990.

16. Keith Byars (Philadelphia Eagles)
Byars produced 1,222 and 1,173 combined yardage in 1988 and 1989, respectively. Over 700 receiving yards, which have really become his forte, were produced in each season. Look for similar contributions from Byars in 1990.

17. Joe Morris (New York Giants)
Until a knee injury ended his season in 1989, Morris was a top producer by this scoring method three out of four years. His healthy return should also spell a healthy return statistically in 1990.

18. Gerald Riggs (Washington Redskins)
Through seven games of 1989, Riggs rushed for 658 yards. But numerous injuries took their bite, and he finished the year with only 834 yards. If he can avoid injuries, 1990 could be a much better year.

19. Eric Metcalf (Cleveland Browns)
His rookie numbers—633 rushing yards and 397 receiving yards—should be just stepping stones for this talented back.

20. Stump Mitchell (Phoenix Cardinals)
Just two short years ago, Mitchell produced 1,178 rushing-receiving yards in 1987's 12-game season. This shows his potential, but the question is, How strong can he come back from the knee injury that knocked him out of the '89 season?

STRONG LONG SHOTS

21. Gary Anderson (Tampa Bay Buccaneers)
As the Chargers' big-yardage man in 1986, Anderson ran and received for 1,313 yards. In 1988 he combined for 1,301 yards, giving us an idea of his 1990 potential. However, now he has become a Tampa Bay Buccaneer, so much uncertainty remains.

22. Sammie Smith (Miami Dolphins)
Although Smith's year-end total of 659 rushing yards isn't very impressive, 492 of those came in the season's last eight games, perhaps an inkling of what Smith could do over a full season.

23. Marcus Allen (Los Angeles Raiders)
Prior to 1989, when Allen totaled only 484 rushing-receiving yards, he had been one of the league's most consistent backs. From 1983 through 1988 he produced seasons of 1,594, 1,928, 2,314, 1,212, 1,164 and 1,134 yards. If he can avoid injuries, we should see a return to much better productivity in 1990.

24. Earnest Byner (Washington Redskins)
Byner produced over 1,000 rushing-receiving yards in 1989. His 1990 potential, however, rests heavily on the health of both Gerald Riggs and Kelvin Bryant, who were injury-riddled in 1989.

25. Johnny Hector (New York Jets)
Hector in recent years has been more of a scorer than a big-yardage man for the Jets. Then in 1989 he surpassed the 1,000-yard mark in rushing-receiving yards and now he seems to have ousted Freeman McNeil as the Jets' primary ground gainer. However, the Jets have strengthened their ground game even more with the acquisition of Blair Thomas in this year's draft. If Thomas fares as expected, both Hector and McNeil may have to take a backseat.

HAVE THE POTENTIAL

26. Bo Jackson (Los Angeles Raiders)
Even though he only hung around for nine games in 1989, Jackson rushed for over 950 yards. Okay, you don't get to use him for an entire season, but look what he can produce for you when he plays.

27. Mike Rozier (Houston Oilers)

As a latecomer to training camp in 1989, Rozier got off to a slow start and finished the year with a dismal 301 rushing yards. In the two years prior to '89, Rozier produced over 1,100 rushing-receiving yards in each season, which is much more indicative of his play.

28. Brent Fullwood (Green Bay Packers)

Fullwood just seems to lack consistency. In 1989 he again got off to a strong start, rushing for 528 yards over the season's first eight games, but he finished with only 821 yards total. As the improving Packers' primary runner, Fullwood's potential is big, but his inconsistency remains his downfall. The Packers' having drafted rookie Darrell Thompson out of Minnesota should either force Fullwood to play harder or force him out of a job.

29. Tim Worley (Pittsburgh Steelers)

Worley got off to a slow start as a rookie in 1989, but came on to rush for 491 yards over the season's last seven games, perhaps a sign of big things to come in 1990.

30. Curt Warner (Los Angeles Rams)

Once one of the league's slickest rushers, Warner's play has been on the wane. Warner has twice surpassed the 1,800 combined-yardage mark, but in 1988 and 1989 we saw those numbers drop to 1,179 and 784 yards, respectively. 1990 sure seems to be a big question mark, especially since Warner became a Los Angeles Ram in the offseason, via Plan B free agency.

KEEP AN EYE ON

31. Tom Rathman (San Francisco 49ers)

You have to be really impressed with his 616 yards on 73 receptions in 1989. If his rushing yards pick up, he could have a big year in 1990.

32. Kevin Mack (Cleveland Browns)

Mack should put his 1989 season behind him and regain his old form.

33. Brad Muster (Chicago Bears)

Muster continues to become more a part of the Bear offense, which should continue to build his stats.

34. Lars Tate (Tampa Bay Buccaneers)

Tate got 589 rushing yards in 1989 as the Buccaneers' leading rusher. Are bigger numbers just around the corner?

35. Marion Butts (San Diego Chargers)

Butts rushed for 683 yards as a rookie in 1989. That may increase in 1990, as Gary Anderson has been traded off to Tampa Bay. Butts should continue to see the ball often.

36. Rueben Mayes (New Orleans Saints)

He has to come back from a knee injury and compete with Dalton Hilliard for playing time.

37. O. J. Anderson (New York Giants)
I don't believe Anderson will be the main focus of the Giants' rushing attack in 1990.

38. Merril Hoge (Pittsburgh Steelers)
Hoge has become a steady performer for the Steelers.

39. Robert Perryman (New England Patriots)
Perryman continues to produce and complement running mate John Stephens well.

40. Alonzo Highsmith (Houston Oilers)
He could fare much better if he becomes a stronger focus of the Oiler offense.

PRIME PROSPECTS

41.	Bentley (IND)	46.	Delpino (LARm)
42.	Fenney (MINN)	47.	Woodside (GB)
43.	Toney (PHIL)	48.	Vick (NYJ)
44.	Meggett (NYG)	49.	Bryant (WASH)
45.	Johnston (DALL)	50.	Pinkett (HOUS)

DON'T BE SURPRISED   YOU NEVER KNOW

51.	B. Jordan (NO)	61.	Riddick (BUF)
52.	McNeil (NYJ)	62.	Lang (ATL)
53.	Manoa (CLE)	63.	St. Smith (LARd)
54.	Stradford (MIA)	64.	Spencer (SD)
55.	Winder (DEN)	65.	Wilder (WASH)
56.	Heyward (NO)	66.	K. Jones (ATL)
57.	Jm. Morris (NE)	67.	Ball (CIN)
58.	Flagler (DALL)	68.	Fontenot (GB)
59.	Howard (TB)	69.	White (HOUS)
60.	Nelson (SD)	70.	Hampton (DEN)

WORTH MENTIONING

71.	Kinnebrew (BUF)	76.	C. Taylor (CIN)
72.	Tillman (NYG)	77.	Bratton (DEN)
73.	Palmer (CIN)	78.	Dozier (MINN)
74.	Logan (MIA)	79.	Heard (KC)
75.	T. Jordan (PHOE)	80.	Carter (PITT)

A LOOK AT THE WIDE RECEIVERS
(A Guide for the Beginner)

Considerations in Choosing a Wide Receiver

You will find it easier to pick your wide receivers for the Performance Point Method than for the Basic Scoring Method. Wide receivers, though inconsistent scorers, show more consistency in yardage gained. Let's take a look at some positive and negative characteristics to look for in drafting wide receivers.

1. First, look at players' previous performances.

2. Look for the wide receivers who have consistently produced good yardage over the years. Jerry Rice and Henry Ellard are excellent examples.

3. Look for wide receivers who play on predominantly passing teams. It's obviously wise to stay away from receivers on teams like the Chicago Bears, who'd much rather run than pass.

4. Look for wide receivers with the speed to go downtown. It takes only one or two long receptions in a game for those yardage points to add up.

5. Keep an eye on rookie wide receivers, especially from teams that are looking for a starter in that position. Rookies Shawn Collins from Atlanta (862 yards), Andre Rison from Indianapolis (820 yards), and Hart Lee Dykes from New England (795 yards) all had productive years in 1989.

6. Expect quarterback changes to have an adverse effect on wide receivers. Quarterbacks develop great precision with certain receivers over the years. Any quarterback change is likely to disrupt the timing of a passing attack, and a receiver's performance may suffer.

In the 1989 statistics, you'll find the players ranked by their fantasy-point totals. Remember, in the Performance Point Method fantasy points are calculated by scoring one point for every 10 yards rushing, one point for every 10 yards pass-receiving, and one point for every 20 yards passing.

1989 STATISTICAL RESULTS
(Wide Receivers — Performance Point Method)

NAME	TEAM	GP	RSH	YARDS	AVG PER GM	PS REC	YARDS	AVG PER GM	TOTAL YARDS	AVG PER GM	1989 FAN- TASY PTS
1. Rice	SF	16	4	16	1.0	82	1,483	92.7	1,499	93.7	143
2. Carrier	TB	16	0	0	0.0	86	1,412	88.3	1,412	88.3	136
3. Sharpe	GB	16	1	26	1.6	90	1,423	88.9	1,449	90.6	135
4. Ellard	LARm	14	6	23	1.6	86	1,382	98.7	1,405	100.3	134
5. Reed	BUF	15	2	31	2.1	88	1,312	87.5	1,343	89.5	125
6. Miller	SD	16	4	21	1.3	75	1,242	77.6	1,263	78.9	120
7. G. Clark	WASH	15	2	19	1.3	79	1,229	81.9	1,248	83.2	118
8. McGee	CIN	16	2	36	2.3	65	1,211	75.7	1,247	77.9	115
9. Slaughter	CLE	16	0	0	0.0	65	1,236	77.3	1,236	77.3	115
10. Monk	WASH	16	3	8	0.5	86	1,186	74.1	1,194	74.6	111
11. Anderson	LARm	14	1	-1	-1.0	44	1,146	81.9	1,145	81.8	107
12. Sanders	WASH	16	4	19	1.2	80	1,138	71.1	1,157	72.3	107
13. R. Johnson	DET	16	12	38	2.4	70	1,091	68.2	1,129	70.6	105
14. Lipps	PITT	15	13	180	12.0	50	944	62.9	1,124	74.9	103
15. V. Johnson	DEN	15	0	0	0.0	76	1,095	73.0	1,095	73.0	102
16. E. Martin	NO	16	1	11	0.7	68	1,079	67.4	1,090	68.1	102
17. Taylor	SF	15	1	6	0.4	60	1,077	71.8	1,083	72.2	101
18. Fernandez	LARd	16	2	16	1.0	57	1,069	66.8	1,085	67.8	100
19. A. Carter	MINN	16	2	30	1.9	65	1,066	66.6	1,096	68.5	100
20. Blades	SEAT	16	1	3	0.2	77	1,063	66.4	1,066	66.4	99
21. Clayton	MIA	15	2	-2	-0.1	64	1,011	67.4	1,009	67.3	94
22. Brooks	IND	15	1	0	0.0	63	919	61.3	919	61.3	88
23. Dr. Hill	HOUS	14	0	0	0.0	66	936	66.9	936	66.9	85
24. Collins+	ATL	16	0	0	0.0	58	862	53.9	862	53.9	78
25. E. Jones	PHOE	14	1	18	1.3	44	823	58.8	841	60.1	78
26. E. Brown	CIN	15	0	0	0.0	52	814	54.3	814	54.3	75
27. Rison+	IND	16	1	18	1.1	52	820	51.3	838	52.4	75
28. J.T. Smith	PHOE	9	1	10	0.9	62	778	86.4	788	86.4	75
29. Givins	HOUS	15	0	0	0.0	55	794	52.9	794	52.9	73
30. Dykes+	NE	14	0	0	0.0	49	795	56.8	795	56.8	73
31. Townsell	NYJ	15	0	0	0.0	45	787	52.5	787	52.5	72
32. Paige	KC	14	0	0	0.0	44	759	54.2	759	54.2	70
33. Langhorne	CLE	15	4	29	1.9	60	749	49.9	778	51.9	69
34. R. Clark	DET	12	0	0	0.0	40	741	61.8	741	61.8	69
35. Haynes	ATL	11	4	35	3.2	40	681	61.9	716	65.1	67
36. Duper	MIA	13	0	0	0.0	49	717	55.2	717	55.2	66
37. H. Jones	MINN	16	1	37	2.3	42	694	43.4	731	45.7	65
38. Green	PHOE	11	0	0	0.0	44	703	63.9	703	63.9	65
39. Gault	LARd	12	0	0	0.0	28	690	57.5	690	57.5	63
40. Toon	NYJ	11	0	0	0.0	63	673	61.2	673	61.2	61
41. K. Martin	DALL	11	0	0	0.0	46	644	58.5	644	58.5	60
42. B. Hill	TB	14	0	0	0.0	50	673	48.1	673	48.1	60
43. C. Jones	NE	14	1	3	0.2	48	670	47.9	673	48.1	59
44. L. Hill	NO	15	1	-7	-0.5	48	636	42.4	629	41.9	56
45. Jeffires	HOUS	15	0	0	0.0	47	619	41.3	619	41.3	56
46. Kemp	GB	14	4	29	2.1	48	611	43.6	640	45.7	55
47. C. Carter	PHIL	14	1	11	0.8	45	605	43.2	616	44.0	54
48. Duncan	HOUS	15	1	0	0.0	43	613	40.9	613	40.9	54
49. Jensen	MIA	14	4	32	2.3	61	557	39.8	589	42.1	51
50. Fryar	NE	10	2	15	1.5	29	537	53.7	552	55.2	50

NAME	TEAM	GP	RSH	YARDS	AVG PER GM	PS REC	YARDS	AVG PER GM	TOTAL YARDS	AVG PER GM	1989 FAN-TASY PTS
51. J. Dixon	DALL	11	3	30	2.7	24	477	43.4	507	46.1	46
52. Manuel	NYG	14	0	0	0.0	33	539	38.5	539	38.5	46
53. Banks	MIA	12	0	0	0.0	30	520	43.3	520	43.3	45
54. Gentry	CHI	15	17	106	7.1	39	463	30.9	569	37.9	44
55. Mandley	KC	12	1	-7	-0.6	35	476	39.7	469	39.1	44
56. Morgan	NE	9	1	7	0.8	28	486	54.0	493	54.8	44
57. O. Turner	NYG	11	2	11	1.0	38	467	42.5	478	43.5	42
58. Skansi	SEAT	15	0	0	0.0	39	488	32.5	488	32.5	42
59. Morris	CHI	14	1	-14	-1.0	29	468	33.4	454	32.4	40
60. M. Jackson	DEN	14	5	13	0.9	28	446	31.8	459	32.8	40
61. Harry	KC	12	1	9	0.8	33	430	35.8	439	36.6	39
62. Dk. Hill+	PITT	15	0	0	0.0	28	455	30.3	455	30.3	39
63. A.B. Brown	MIA	11	0	0	0.0	24	410	37.3	410	37.3	37
64. McKinnon	CHI	14	1	3	0.2	28	433	30.9	436	30.9	36
65. Irvin	DALL	5	1	6	1.2	26	378	75.6	384	76.8	36
66. Verdin	IND	12	3	34	2.8	20	381	31.8	415	34.6	36
67. Wn. Walker	SD	9	1	9	1.0	24	395	43.9	404	44.9	36
68. Largent	SEAT	10	0	0	0.0	28	403	40.3	403	40.3	36
69. Young	DEN	11	0	0	0.0	22	402	36.5	402	36.5	34
70. Holland	SD	11	5	48	4.4	26	336	30.5	384	34.9	34
71. Davis	CHI	12	0	0	0.0	27	405	33.8	405	33.8	32
72. Cox	LARm	7	0	0	0.0	20	340	48.6	340	48.6	32
73. F. Dixon	ATL	10	1	0	0.0	25	357	35.7	357	35.7	31
74. Phillips+	DET	11	0	0	0.0	31	359	32.6	359	32.6	31
75. Perriman	NO	9	1	-10	-0.9	20	356	39.6	346	38.4	31
76. Query+	GB	11	0	0	0.0	23	350	31.8	350	31.8	30
77. Beebe+	BUF	9	0	0	0.0	17	317	35.2	317	35.2	28
78. M. Alexander	LARd	9	0	0	0.0	15	295	32.8	295	32.8	27
79. Stanley	DET	11	0	0	0.0	24	304	27.6	304	27.6	26
80. R. Johnson	PHIL	9	0	0	0.0	20	295	32.8	295	32.8	26
81. F. Johnson	BUF	10	0	0	0.0	25	303	30.3	303	30.3	25
82. Brennan	CLE	11	0	0	0.0	28	289	26.3	289	26.3	25
83. Ingram	NYG	10	1	1	0.1	17	290	29.0	291	29.1	25
84. Burkett**	NYJ	11	1	-4	-0.4	21	278	25.3	274	24.9	25
85. F. Turner+	NO	11	2	8	0.7	22	279	25.4	287	26.1	25
86. Shepard**	DALL	10	2	19	1.9	20	304	30.4	323	32.3	24
87. Holmes	PHOE	9	0	0	0.0	14	286	31.8	286	31.8	24
88. Weathers**	KC	8	0	0	0.0	23	254	31.8	254	31.8	22
89. L. Clark	SEAT	11	0	0	0.0	25	260	23.6	260	23.6	22
90. Quick	PHIL	6	0	0	0.0	13	228	38.0	228	38.0	21
91. Baker	NYG	10	0	0	0.0	13	255	25.5	255	25.5	20
92. S. Martin	NE	7	0	0	0.0	13	229	32.7	229	32.7	19
93. Garrity	PHIL	13	0	0	0.0	13	209	16.1	209	16.1	19
94. Harris+	HOUS	5	0	0	0.0	13	194	38.8	194	38.8	17
95. Schwedes	MIA	3	0	0	0.0	7	174	58.0	174	58.0	16
96. Lewis	MINN	7	0	0	0.0	12	148	21.1	148	21.1	16
97. Nattiel	DEN	6	0	0	0.0	10	183	30.5	183	30.5	15
98. Matthews	GB	10	0	0	0.0	18	200	20.0	200	20.0	15
99. Bailey	ATL	6	0	0	0.0	8	170	28.3	170	28.3	14
100. Lofton	BUF	6	0	0	0.0	8	166	27.7	166	27.7	14

1989 STATISTICAL RESULTS
(Wide Receivers — Performance Point Method)

NAME	TEAM	GP	RSH	YARDS	AVG PER GM	PS REC	YARDS	AVG PER GM	TOTAL YARDS	AVG PER GM	1989 FAN-TASY PTS
101. Mobley	DET	5	0	0	0.0	13	158	31.6	158	31.6	14
102. Bland	GB	7	0	0	0.0	11	164	23.4	164	23.4	14
103. Peebles+	TB	7	2	6	0.9	10	176	25.1	182	26.0	14
104. Drewrey	TB	9	0	0	0.0	14	157	17.4	157	17.4	13
105. K. Smith+	CIN	7	0	0	0.0	10	140	20.0	140	20.0	12
106. McDonald	DET	4	1	-2	-0.5	12	138	34.5	136	34.0	12
107. Gustafson	MINN	9	0	0	0.0	14	144	16.0	144	16.0	12
108. Harper	NYJ	3	0	0	0.0	7	127	42.3	127	42.3	12
109. M. Martin	CIN	7	0	0	0.0	15	160	22.9	160	22.9	11
110. Hillary	CIN	10	1	-2	-0.2	17	162	16.2	160	16.0	11
111. Burbage	DALL	5	0	0	0.0	17	134	26.8	134	26.8	11
112. Early	SD	4	1	19	4.8	11	126	31.5	145	36.3	11
113. R. Brown	LARm	8	6	27	3.4	5	113	14.1	140	17.5	10
114. Epps	NYJ	4	1	14	3.5	9	116	29.0	130	32.5	10
115. Carson**	PHIL	6	0	0	0.0	9	98	16.3	98	16.3	8
116. Kane	SEAT	4	0	0	0.0	7	94	23.5	94	23.5	8
117. McNeil	CLE	7	0	0	0.0	10	114	16.3	114	16.3	7
118. Ws. Walker	NYJ	4	0	0	0.0	8	89	22.3	89	22.3	7
119. Edwards	PHIL	1	0	0	0.0	2	74	74.0	74	74.0	7
120. Thompson	PITT	3	0	0	0.0	4	74	24.7	74	24.7	7
121. Wilson	SF	8	0	0	0.0	9	103	12.9	103	12.9	7
122. Chadwick**	SEAT	7	0	0	0.0	8	95	13.6	95	13.6	7
123. Kozlowski	CHI	3	0	0	0.0	3	74	24.7	74	24.7	6
124. Pruitt	IND	3	0	0	0.0	5	71	23.7	71	23.7	6
125. Worthen+	KC	2	0	0	0.0	5	69	34.5	69	34.5	6
126. B. Ford	DALL	4	0	0	0.0	7	78	19.5	78	19.5	5
127. Gray	DET	3	3	22	7.3	2	47	15.7	69	23.0	5
128. Parker	CIN	1	0	0	0.0	1	45	45.0	45	45.0	4
129. Tillman+	CLE	6	0	0	0.0	6	70	11.7	70	11.7	4
130. G. Thomas	ATL	3	0	0	0.0	4	46	15.3	46	15.3	3
131. J. Ford+	DET	3	0	0	0.0	5	46	15.3	46	15.3	3
132. R. Thomas+	KC	5	0	0	0.0	8	58	11.6	58	11.6	3
133. Robinson	NYG	2	0	0	0.0	4	41	20.5	41	20.5	3
134. Garrett	CIN	1	0	0	0.0	2	29	29.0	29	29.0	2
135. T. Johnson	DET	2	0	0	0.0	2	29	14.5	29	14.5	2
136. Greer	SF	1	0	0	0.0	1	26	26.0	26	26.0	2
137. R. Alexander	DALL	1	0	0	0.0	1	16	16.0	16	16.0	1
138. K. Jackson	HOUS	3	0	0	0.0	4	31	10.3	31	10.3	1
139. Williams	PHIL	3	0	0	0.0	4	32	10.7	32	10.7	1
140. McConkey	PHOE	2	0	0	0.0	2	18	9.0	18	9.0	1
141. Allen	SD	2	0	0	0.0	2	19	9.5	19	9.5	1
142. Waddle	CHI	1	0	0	0.0	1	8	8.0	8	8.0	0
143. T. Brown	LARd	1	0	0	0.0	1	8	8.0	8	8.0	0
144. Usher	PHOE	1	0	0	0.0	1	8	8.0	8	8.0	0
145. Bouyer	SEAT	1	0	0	0.0	1	9	9.0	9	9.0	0

+ DENOTES ROOKIES

** Burkett (NYJ) —Played in 2 games with BUF.
** Shepard (DALL) —Played in 2 games with NO.
** Weathers (KC) —Played in 2 games with IND.
** Carson (PHIL) —Played in 4 games with KC.
** Chadwick (SEAT) —Played in 1 game with DET.

RATING THE PLAYERS FOR 1990
(Wide Receivers—Performance Point Method)

GRAB ONE IF YOU CAN

1. Jerry Rice (San Francisco 49ers)
You can't argue with success, and that's exactly what Jerry Rice has produced, ranking first by this scoring method three of the last four years. The other year he ranked second. Last year's total of 1,483 yards is about his norm, which is why I expect him to near 1,500 yards again in 1990.

2. Sterling Sharpe (Green Bay Packers)
As a rookie in 1988, Sterling Sharpe tallied 791 receiving yards. In 1989 he nearly doubled that total with 1,423 yards, becoming a real receiving force. This was not fluke, and Sharpe should continue faring well in 1990.

3. Henry Ellard (Los Angeles Rams)
Ellard has produced two consecutive 1,400-yard seasons. His amassing 1,421 yards in 1988 and 1,405 in 1989 shows a consistency that needs little explanation.

4. Gary Clark (Washington Redskins)
After producing 1,313 and 1,066 receiving yards in 1986 and 1987, respectively, Clark's production fell off to 892 yards in 1988. In 1989 Clark came back strong with 1,229 yards. He's capable of producing the same in 1990, but playing alongside the likes of Art Monk and Ricky Sanders keeps his totals somewhat questionable.

5. Mark Clayton (Miami Dolphins)
Clayton seems to be a household name year after year. It's no wonder, since his receiving yardage for the past six seasons averages 1,075.5 yards per year. As a favorite target of Dan Marino, he should continue his success in 1990.

6. Anthony Miller (San Diego Chargers)
In just his second year in the NFL, Miller more then doubled his 526-yard total of 1988, accumulating 1,242 receiving yards in 1989. Fast becoming one of the league's more feared deep threats, Miller should continue to do well in 1990.

7. Andre Reed (Buffalo Bills)
Reed totaled 968 receiving yards in 1988. With a more open offense in 1989, Reed produced 1,312 yards and should become a prime fantasy consideration for 1990.

8. Anthony Carter (Minnesota Vikings)
Carter placed seventh and fourth by this scoring method in 1987 (922 receiving yards) and 1988 (1,255), respectively. But in 1989, when he came into training camp late, Carter wound up tied for 18th, with 1,066 receiving yards. He'll push to improve that ranking and production in 1990.

9. Mike Quick (Philadelphia Eagles)
Quick has been sidelined most of the last two seasons with leg and knee injuries. Remembering his big years from 1983 through 1985, when he produced seasons of 1,409, 1,052, and 1,247 receiving yards, respectively, we get a hint of his potential. There's still a big question as to whether he will return healthy after last year's knee injury.

10. Mark Carrier (Tampa Bay Buccaneers)
Carrier's 970 yards in 1988 left him just short of the 1,000-yard mark. In 1989 he pushed those numbers far higher to have a 1,412-yard season. Although he may not quite reach that level in 1990, he should again easily reach the 1,000–1,300-yard range.

BEST OF THE REST

11. Webster Slaughter (Cleveland Browns)
After recording 806 receiving yards in a 12-game season in 1987, Slaughter missed much of the 1988 season with a broken forearm. In 1989, however, Slaughter came back in grand fashion, producing 1,236 receiving yards, the kind of numbers he can produce when healthy.

12. John Taylor (San Francisco 49ers)
Are there enough yards to go around? Apparently, because in 1989, even though Jerry Rice led the league with 1,483 receiving yards, John Taylor accounted for 1,077 of his own. Taylor has certainly come into his own and should again get his share of receiving yards in 1990.

13. Drew Hill (Houston Oilers)
1989 marked the first year in five that Hill didn't place among the nine top wide receivers by this scoring method. This could be attributed to both a late arrival into training camp and a midseason back injury. Looking at his production the previous four years (1985: sixth, 1,169 yards; 1986: ninth, 1,112 yards; 1987: fourth, 989 yards; 1988: seventh, 1,141 yards), we better see his true potential.

14. Ricky Sanders (Washington Redskins)
Pretty consistent production characterized Sanders the last two seasons, with 1,148 receiving yards in 1988 and 1,138 in 1989, despite competition from two other standout receivers—Gary Clark and Art Monk. I see Sanders stretching his two-year streak to three in 1990.

15. Eric Martin (New Orleans Saints)
Martin has produced two consistent years in receiving yards. He has produced 1,079 and 1,083 yards the past two seasons, respectively, a standard he should meet or exceed in 1990.

16. Eddie Brown (Cincinnati Bengals)
After putting together a fantastic 1,273-yard season in 1988, Brown produced only 814 yards in 1989. This, I believe, was partly due to his late arrival in training camp because of contract problems and the emergence of Tim McGee. I look for the very talented Brown to rebound statistically in 1990.

17. Al Toon (New York Jets)
Toon placed 7th, 5th, and 11th by this scoring method in 1986, 1987, and 1988, respectively. During that stretch he produced 85, 68, and 93 receptions and 1,176, 976, and 1,083 yards. In 1989 shoulder and ankle injuries limited him to 673 yards, even though he had 63 receptions in only 11 games. Healthy again in 1990, Toon should recapture his healthy set of stats.

18. Art Monk (Washington Redskins)
In 1989 Monk gained 1,186 yards, his fourth 1,000-yard season in the last six. Totals like that are no small feat if you play alongside Gary Clark and Ricky Sanders.

19. Tim McGee (Cincinnati Bengals)
McGee stepped out from the shadow of Eddie Brown in 1989 to produce 65 receptions and 1,211 receiving yards. Although I don't feel he'll reach that yardage level in 1990, he will still experience success.

20. J. T. Smith (Phoenix Cardinals)
Until suffering a fractured fibula in 1989, Smith was probably on his way to his best season. Before the injury, he recorded 62 receptions for 778 yards over nine games. Combining that with his previous three years of 80, 76, and 83 receptions, for 1,014, 900, and 986 yards, respectively, we have quite a consistent receiver, if he returns healthy in 1990.

STRONG LONG SHOTS

21. Mark Duper (Miami Dolphins)
Three times in his career Duper has produced 1,000-yard seasons. In 1983, he had 1,003 yards, in 1984, 1,306 yards, and in 1986, 1,313 yards. Injuries and drug involvement have hampered his production for the past two years, though, and they make him questionable still for 1990.

22. Willie Anderson (Los Angeles Rams)
After producing just 319 receiving yards as a rookie in 1988, Anderson exploded for 1,146 yards on only 44 receptions in 1989. He seems to have truly arrived as an NFL receiver and will be highly sought after by fantasy owners in 1990.

23. Louis Lipps (Pittsburgh Steelers)
After two injury-plagued years in 1986 and 1987, Lipps has produced well again the last two years. In 1988, Lipps had 973 receiving yards and added 129 rushing yards for 1,102 total. In 1989, Lipps again led wide receivers in the league in rushing yards with 180 and added 944 receiving yards for 1,124 total. We get an idea of the numbers he's capable of, if he stays healthy.

24. Brian Blades (Seattle Seahawks)
As a rookie in 1988, Blades produced 682 receiving yards on 40 receptions. In 1989, he boosted those totals to 77 receptions and 1,066 yards, levels I believe he'll again near in 1990.

25. Vance Johnson (Denver Broncos)
Johnson produced 896 yards on 68 receptions in 1988 and then pushed those totals over the 1,000-yard mark with 1,095 yards on 76 receptions in 1989. As the most consistent of the "three amigos," Johnson should again log more than 1,000 yards in 1990.

26. Ernest Givins (Houston Oilers)
Until last year's dropoff to 794 receiving yards, Givins seemed to be always pushing 1,000 yards. From 1986 through 1988 Givins produced 1,062, 933, and 976 yards, respectively, yardage I believe he'll rebound to in 1990.

27. Roy Green (Phoenix Cardinals)
This aging star has produced seasons like 1983 when he had 1,221 receiving yards, 1984 (1,555 yards), and 1988 (1,097). He may again have been headed for the 1,000-plus level in 1989, but he suffered a broken collarbone, missed four games, and wound up with 703 yards. Can he rebound in 1990?

28. Richard Johnson (Detroit Lions)
As the main target of the Lions' run-and-shoot offense, Johnson produced 1,091 receiving yards on 70 receptions in 1989, a level he should near again in 1990 as the Lions continue to fine-tune their offense.

29. Billy Brooks (Indianapolis Colts)
Brooks has seen his reception yardage go steadily up over the last three seasons, from 722 in 1987 to 869 in 1988 to 919 in 1989. Will he top that 1,000-yard mark in 1990? Perhaps he will, now that Andre Rison has been dealt to Atlanta.

30. Cris Carter (Philadelphia Eagles)
Although he produced only 761 and 605 receiving yards the last two seasons, respectively, Carter may see the ball much more often in 1990, if receiving mate Mike Quick can't come back 100% from his knee injury.

KEEP AN EYE ON

31. Bruce Hill (Tampa Bay Buccaneers)
Although Hill produced only 673 receiving yards in 1988, just one year earlier he had 1,040 yards.

32. Lionel Manuel (New York Giants)
Manuel had an off season in 1989, with only 539 yards. The previous year, however, he racked up 1,029 yards.

33. Mervyn Fernandez (Los Angeles Raiders)
I wonder if the injury to Tim Brown didn't help boost Fernandez over the 1,000-yard mark in 1989. Brown's healthy return in 1990 may cut into those numbers.

34. Stephone Paige (Kansas City Chiefs)
Paige has flirted with 1,000-yard seasons a couple of times, producing 943, 829, 697, 905, and 759 yards, respectively, the last five seasons.

35. Shawn Collins (Atlanta Falcons)
Collins's 58 receptions and 862 yards as a rookie in 1989 may be just a taste of what's to come.

36. Andre Rison (Atlanta Falcons)
Want an idea of Rison's potential? Consider his 820 yards on 52 receptions as a rookie in 1989 with the Colts. In 1990, however, he'll be wearing an Atlanta uniform.

37. Reggie Langhorne (Cleveland Browns)
Langhorne has produced 772 and 749 yards the last two seasons. Perhaps it's time to exceed those numbers.

38. Michael Irvin (Dallas Cowboys)
Irvin had 378 yards after only six games in 1989 when a knee injury ended his season. His healthy return remains the big question.

39. Lonzell Hill (New Orleans Saints)
Hill has produced seasons of 703 and 636 receiving yards the past two seasons, numbers he'd like to improve on in 1990.

40. Tim Brown (Los Angeles Raiders)
As a rookie in 1988, Brown produced 725 receiving yards on 43 receptions, but in 1989 a knee injury in the season opener ended his play for the year. His recovery from that injury is the key to his 1990 season.

PRIME PROSPECTS

41. Fryar (NE)	46. Morgan (NE)
42. Haynes (ATL)	47. R. Clark (DET)
43. H. Jones (MINN)	48. Gault (LARd)
44. Dykes (NE)	49. McKinnon (CHI)
45. K. Martin (DALL)	50. C. Jones (NE)

DON'T BE SURPRISED   YOU NEVER KNOW

51. Kemp (GB)	61. Jeffires (HOUS)
52. Jensen (MIA)	62. Skansi (SEAT)
53. O. Turner (NYG)	63. Wn. Walker (SD)
54. E. Jones (PHOE)	64. Dk. Hill (PITT)
55. Nattiel (DEN)	65. Verdin (IND)
56. Brennan (CLE)	66. Davis (CHI)
57. Morris (CHI)	67. Bailey (ATL)
58. M. Jackson (DEN)	68. Phillips (DET)
59. Townsell (NYJ)	69. Tillman (CLE)
60. Sherrard (SF)	70. Perriman (NO)

WORTH MENTIONING

71. F. Dixon (ATL)	76. Ingram (NYG)
72. Mandley (KC)	77. L. Clark (SEAT)
73. Young (DEN)	78. Baker (NYG)
74. Cox (LARm)	79. Lewis (MINN)
75. Duncan (HOUS)	80. J. Dixon (DALL)

A LOOK AT THE TIGHT ENDS

(A Guide for the Beginner)

Considerations in Choosing a Tight End

In evaluating tight ends, you will find that they are often among the league leaders in receptions, but not in yardage. Let's take a look at some qualities to consider when drafting a tight end.

1. First, look at players' previous performances.

2. Look for a tight end from a predominantly passing team. Examples would be Rodney Holman of Cincinnati and Brent Jones of San Francisco, both of whom fared well in 1989 while playing on pass-oriented teams.

3. Look for a tight end who is used frequently in the passing attack. Two good examples are Keith Jackson of the Eagles and Mark Bavaro of the Giants. Some teams use their tight ends as they use their other receivers; other teams expect their tight ends to do more blocking than receiving.

4. Look for a tight end from a team that has two good wide receivers. Opponents are often forced to double-cover the wide receivers, thus leaving the tight end open. Young Ferrell Edmunds of the Miami Dolphins should benefit from playing between Mark Clayton and Mark Duper.

5. Expect opposing teams to keep a close eye on a tight end who is coming off a great year. The chance of increased double coverage may hurt his yardage

6. Quarterback changes can have an adverse effect on a tight end's productivity.

In the 1989 statistics, players have been ranked by their fantasy-point totals. Remember that in the Performance Point Method, fantasy points are calculated by scoring one point for every 10 yards rushing, one point for every 10 yards pass-receiving, and one point for every 20 yards passing.

1989 STATISTICAL RESULTS
(Tight Ends — Performance Point Method)

NAME	TEAM	GP	RSH	YARDS	REC	YARDS	TOTAL YARDS	AVG PER GM	1989 FANTASY POINTS
1. Holman	CIN	16	0	0	50	736	736	46.0	67
2. Sievers	NE	13	0	0	54	615	615	47.3	57
3. Jackson	PHIL	13	0	0	63	648	648	49.8	57
4. Holohan	LARm	16	1	3	51	510	513	32.1	44
5. Dyal	LARd	14	0	0	27	499	499	35.6	44
6. Jordan	MINN	12	0	0	35	506	506	42.2	43
7. Jones	SF	14	0	0	40	500	500	35.7	42
8. Thornton	CHI	13	1	4	24	392	396	30.5	34
9. Brenner	NO	14	0	0	34	398	398	28.4	34
10. Edmunds	MIA	15	0	0	32	382	382	25.5	33
11. Bernstine	SD	5	15	137	21	222	359	71.8	32
12. Awalt	PHOE	12	0	0	33	360	360	30.0	31
13. McKeller	BUF	12	0	0	20	341	341	28.4	30
14. Shuler	NYJ	7	0	0	29	322	322	46.0	29
15. Neubert	NYJ	8	0	0	28	302	302	37.8	28
16. Mularkey	PITT	13	0	0	22	326	326	25.1	28
17. Hall	TB	11	0	0	30	331	331	30.1	28
18. Heller	ATL	11	0	0	33	324	324	29.5	27
19. Newsome	CLE	13	0	0	29	324	324	24.9	27
20. Bavaro	NYG	6	0	0	22	278	278	46.3	26
21. West	GB	7	0	0	22	269	269	38.4	24
22. Mowatt	NYG	13	0	0	27	288	288	22.2	24
23. Hayes	KC	9	0	0	18	229	229	25.4	20
24. Folsom	DALL	13	0	0	28	255	255	19.6	19
25. Giles	PHIL	8	0	0	16	225	225	28.1	17
26. Novacek	PHOE	12	0	0	23	225	225	18.8	17
27. Mobley	DEN	8	0	0	17	200	200	25.0	16
28. Dressel**	NYJ	6	0	0	12	191	191	31.8	16
29. Cox	SD	13	0	0	22	200	200	15.4	16
30. Kay	DEN	10	0	0	21	197	197	19.7	15
31. Wilkins	ATL	6	0	0	6	145	145	24.2	14
32. Warren	WASH	9	0	0	15	167	167	18.6	14
33. Metzelaars	BUF	10	0	0	18	179	179	17.9	13
34. Boso	CHI	11	0	0	17	182	182	16.5	13
35. McNeal+	SEAT	5	0	0	9	148	148	29.6	12
36. Werner	NYJ	3	0	0	8	115	115	38.3	11
37. Tyler	SEAT	8	0	0	14	148	148	18.5	11
38. Cross+	NYG	3	0	0	6	107	107	35.7	9
39. Beckman	ATL	5	0	0	11	102	102	20.4	8
40. D. Johnson	LARm	14	0	0	25	148	148	10.6	8
41. Griggs	NYJ	5	0	0	9	112	112	22.4	8
42. Caravello	SD	5	1	0	10	95	95	19.0	8
43. McEwen	SD	3	0	0	7	99	99	33.0	8
44. Dawson	NE	4	0	0	10	90	90	22.5	7
45. Harris	TB	6	0	0	11	85	85	14.2	7
46. Orr	WASH	3	0	0	3	80	80	26.7	7
47. Kattus	CIN	7	0	0	12	93	93	13.3	6
48. Scales	NO	6	0	0	8	89	89	14.8	6
49. J. Tice	NO	8	0	0	9	98	98	12.3	6
50. J. Johnson+	WASH	4	0	0	4	84	84	21.0	6

1989 STATISTICAL RESULTS
(Tight Ends — Performance Point Method)

NAME	TEAM	GP	RSH	YARDS	REC	YARDS	TOTAL YARDS	AVG PER GM	1989 FANTASY POINTS
51. Didier	GB	6	0	0	6	81	81	13.5	5
52. Jennings+	DALL	2	0	0	6	47	47	23.5	4
53. Horton	LARd	4	0	0	4	44	44	11.0	4
54. Ingram+	MINN	2	0	0	5	47	47	23.5	4
55. Verhulst	HOUS	3	0	0	4	48	48	16.0	3
56. Roberts	KC	7	0	0	8	55	55	7.9	3
57. Junkin	LARd	2	0	0	3	32	32	16.0	3
58. Williams	SF	1	0	0	3	38	38	38.0	3
59. Beach	IND	10	0	0	14	77	77	7.7	2
60. Boyer	IND	8	0	0	11	58	58	7.3	2
61. Riggs	CIN	4	0	0	5	29	29	7.3	1
62. Kelly	DEN	2	0	0	3	13	13	6.5	1
63. Spagnola	GB	2	0	0	2	13	13	6.5	1
64. Mrosko	HOUS	3	0	0	3	28	28	9.3	1
65. Kinchen	MIA	1	0	0	1	12	12	12.0	1
66. Dunn	NYJ	1	0	0	2	13	13	13.0	1
67. Rolle	BUF	1	0	1	1	1	1	1.0	0
68. Tennell	CLE	1	0	0	1	4	4	4.0	0
69. Middleton	CLE	1	0	0	1	5	5	5.0	0
70. Hardy	MIA	1	0	0	1	2	2	2.0	0
71. Novoselsky	MINN	4	0	0	4	11	11	2.8	0
72. Cook+	NE	2	0	0	3	13	13	6.5	0
73. Little	PHIL	2	0	0	2	8	8	4.0	0
74. Reeves+	PHOE	1	0	0	1	5	5	5.0	0
75. O'Shea	PITT	1	0	0	1	8	8	8.0	0
76. Parker	SD	2	0	0	2	5	5	2.5	0
77. Walls+	SF	4	0	0	4	16	16	4.0	0
78. M. Tice	WASH	1	0	0	1	2	2	2.0	0

+ DENOTES ROOKIES

** Dressel (NYJ) —Played in 5 games with KC.

RATING THE PLAYERS FOR 1990
(Tight Ends—Performance Point Method)

GRAB ONE IF YOU CAN

1. Keith Jackson (Philadelphia Eagles)
As a rookie in 1988, Jackson led all tight ends with 869 receiving yards. Last year his yardage dipped to 648, partly because he missed time with knee and back injuries. A healthy Jackson is sure to produce exceptionally well in 1990.

2. Steve Jordan (Minnesota Vikings)
Before dropping off to sixth by this scoring method in 1989, Jordan had placed third, third, fifth, and third the previous four years. From 1985 through 1989, he recorded seasons of 818, 859, 490, 756, and 506 yards, respectively. I believe he'll rebound statistically in 1990 from his '89 performance, because this time around with any luck he'll have his contract problems worked out before the season.

3. Rodney Holman (Cincinnati Bengals)
Holman ranked first by this scoring method in 1989 with 736 receiving yards. Success comes as no surprise for Holman. In the three years prior to 1989, he finished seventh, seventh, and ninth respectively, while amassing 570, 438, and 527 yards during that period.

4. Mark Bavaro (New York Giants)
Bavaro, sidelined by a knee injury for a good part of the 1989 season, had placed second, first, and fourth the previous four years, with yardages of 1,001, 867, and 672 during that stretch. If healthy he'll be a prime fantasy prospect for 1990.

5. Eric Sievers (New England Patriots)
Although Sievers had tasted some success when playing for both the Los Angeles Rams and San Diego Chargers, none of it could compare to the great season that gave him second place by this scoring method in 1989. His 54 receptions for 615 yards will surely draw him fantasy attention for 1990.

BEST OF THE REST

6. Pete Holohan (Los Angeles Rams)
Holohan has really made the last two years productive since coming over to the Rams from San Diego. He grabbed 59 receptions for 640 yards in 1988 and 51 receptions for 510 yards last year, consistency that should continue in 1990.

7. Mickey Shuler (New York Jets)
Before 1989, Shuler had been a consistent top-10 tight end by this scoring method. He finished fifth, second, sixth, seventh, and second from 1984 through 1988. During that stretch he produced seasons of 782, 879, 675, 434, and 805 receiving yards, respectively, and he could again near those numbers in 1990 if he can return healthy from his 1989 knee injury.

8. Ferrell Edmunds (Miami Dolphins)
As a rookie in 1988, Edmunds produced 575 yards on 33 receptions. In 1989 his yardage fell to 382 while his reception level dropped by just 1, to 32. I believe he'll continue to see plenty of aerials in 1990, and with them will come the yards.

9. Rod Bernstine (San Diego Chargers)
Bernstine was off to a great start, with 222 yards on 21 receptions in 1989 through just five games, when a knee injury ended his season. If he can return healthy, his receiving yardage could be high.

10. Robert Awalt (Phoenix Cardinals)
Awalt has seen his pass-reception yardage slowly decline over the last three years. From his rookie season in 1987, when he produced 526 yards, he has slipped to 444 and 360 yards the last two seasons. I believe he can rebound to over 500 yards in 1990, as the new Phoenix quarterbacks become better adjusted to the offense and with Jay Novacek now off to Dallas.

STRONG LONG SHOTS

11. Brent Jones (San Francisco 49ers)
In taking over the regular tight-end duties in 1989, Jones produced 500 receiving yards on 40 receptions, levels he should near again in 1990.

12. Ron Hall (Tampa Bay Buccaneers)
Hall's production fell from 555 yards on 39 receptions in 1988 to 331 yards on 30 receptions in 1989. Look for Hall to be in the 30-plus reception range again in 1990, and for his yardage statistics to be rewarding.

13. Mike Dyal (Los Angeles Raiders)
In becoming the replacement tight end for Todd Christensen, Dyal began to make a name for himself. His finishing the year with 499 receiving yards has captured fantasy owners' attention.

14. Mike Mularkey (Pittsburgh Steelers)
The Steelers finally added the tight end position to their offensive scheme in 1989, when Mularkey came over as a Plan B free agent. Mularkey's solid play, which produced 326 receiving yards, makes him a player to keep in mind for 1990.

15. Hoby Brenner (New Orleans Saints)
Brenner placed ninth by this method back in 1985 with 652 yards. The next few seasons he did not fare well until he rebounded to another ninth-place finish in 1989 with 398 yards. That productive season gives him plenty of fantasy promise for 1990.

HAVE THE POTENTIAL

16. Jim Thornton (Chicago Bears)
Thornton came on for the Bears in 1989, producing 392 yards on 24 receptions. His playing on the run-oriented Bears makes me a bit skeptical of his potential for 1990.

17. Jay Novacek (Dallas Cowboys)
Seventh place by this scoring method came with Novacek's 560 yards on
38 receptions in 1988, totals that hinted at some interesting potential. In
1989 Novacek's production fell to 225 yards on 23 catches. However, in
1990 Novacek may see more playing opportunity with the Dallas
Cowboys.

18. Ed West (Green Bay Packers)
Missing a portion of the 1989 season limited West to 269 receiving yards
on 22 receptions, levels he could easily exceed in 1990 if he stays healthy.

19. Clarence Kay (Denver Broncos)
Although Kay's production has been on the decline (440, 352, and 191
yards the last three seasons, respectively), I believe he's capable of turning
it around in 1990.

20. Pete Metzelaars (Buffalo Bills)
Metzelaars placed 10th, 14th, and 10th by this scoring method from 1986
through 1988 before falling way off in 1989. His dropoff was partially due
to splitting production with Keith McKeller, which could also affect
Metzelaars's 1990 statistics.

KEEP AN EYE ON

21. Newsome (CLE)
22. McKeller (BUF)
23. Hayes (KC)
24. Folsom (DALL)
25. Heller (SEAT)

26. Mowatt (NE)
27. Mobley (DEN)
28. D. Johnson (LARm)
29. Dawson (NE)
30. J. Tice (NO)

YOU NEVER KNOW

31. Wilkins (ATL)
32. Warren (WASH)
33. Tyler (SEAT)
34. Beach (IND)
35. Neubert (NYJ)
36. Cox (SD)
37. Boyer (NYJ)
38. Tennell (CLE)

39. Higdon (ATL)
40. Cook (NE)
41. Giles (PHIL)
42. Dressel (NYJ)
43. Kattus (CIN)
44. Beckman (ATL)
45. Jennings (DALL)

A LOOK AT THE QUARTERBACKS

(A Guide for the Beginner)

Considerations in Choosing a Quarterback

1. First, look at players' previous performances.

2. Our first criterion for selecting a quarterback is whether he plays for a predominantly passing team. Remember: We don't care if the quarterback plays for a winning team, has a good passing percentage, or anything else, as long as he throws for a lot of yards. Dan Marino and the pass-happy Dolphins come to mind first. However, that list may also include Joe Montana and now Jim Everett of the Rams and Don Majkowski of the Packers.

3. Look for a quarterback who has a deep-threat receiver on his team. A couple of long completions rack up a lot of points in this scoring system. Certainly Joe Montana benefits from having Jerry Rice and John Taylor, both of whom often burn defenses deep.

4. The next step is to look at quarterbacks who run fairly often. In our Performance Point Method, quarterbacks can earn points with their rushing yardage as well as their passing yardage. Here Randall Cunningham of the Philadelphia Eagles comes to mind, along with Boomer Esiason of Cincinnati and John Elway of Denver, who aren't afraid to tuck the ball away and run with it.

5. Stay away from quarterbacks who are not guaranteed a starting assignment week after week. Some teams use one quarterback one week and then switch to another the following week, depending on the players' performances. Quarterbacks in that situation are risky draft choices in Fantasy Football. Such is the case with the New England Patriots, who may field Marc Wilson, Steve Grogan, or Doug Flutie on any given week.

6. Stay away from a quarterback on a team that prefers the run to the pass. Even though this quarterback may win a lot of games, he won't give you the passing statistics that you need to be successful with the Performance Point Method. A run-oriented approach that comes to mind is that of the Chicago Bears; Neal Anderson is the featured back and the Bears choose to pass only when necessary.

In the 1989 statistics, the players have been ranked by the number of fantasy points they accumulated. Remember that in the Performance Point Method, fantasy points are calculated by scoring one point for every 20 yards passed and one point for every 10 yards rushed. Touchdowns are of no concern; this method deals strictly with yardage.

1989 STATISTICAL RESULTS
(Quarterbacks — Performance Point Method)

	NAME	TEAM	GP	RSH	RSH YDS	AVG PER GM	COMP	ATT	PCT	PS YDS	AVG PER GM	1989 FAN- TASY PTS
1.	Majkowski	GB	16	75	358	22.4	353	599	58.9	4,318	269.9	234
2.	Cunningham	PHIL	16	104	631	39.4	290	534	54.3	3,400	212.5	221
3.	Everett	LARm	16	25	31	1.9	304	518	58.7	4,310	269.4	210
4.	Moon	HOUS	16	60	268	16.8	280	464	60.3	3,631	226.9	193
5.	Marino	MIA	16	14	-5	-0.3	308	550	56.0	3,997	249.8	191
6.	Esiason	CIN	16	47	278	17.4	258	455	56.7	3,525	220.3	189
7.	Montana	SF	13	50	226	17.4	271	386	70.2	3,521	270.8	188
8.	Rypien	WASH	14	26	56	4.0	280	476	58.8	3,868	269.1	184
9.	Kosar	CLE	16	30	70	4.4	303	513	59.1	3,533	220.8	173
10.	Krieg	SEAT	15	39	161	10.7	286	499	57.3	3,309	220.6	167
11.	Elway	DEN	15	48	244	16.3	223	416	53.6	3,051	203.4	164
12.	O'Brien	NYJ	15	9	18	1.2	289	478	60.4	3,356	223.7	162
13.	Kelly	BUF	13	29	137	10.5	228	391	58.3	3,130	240.8	161
14.	Testaverde	TB	14	26	139	9.9	258	481	53.6	3,133	223.8	161
15.	Miller	ATL	15	10	20	1.3	280	526	53.2	3,459	230.6	156
16.	Simms	NYG	15	33	141	9.4	228	405	56.3	3,061	204.1	156
17.	Hebert	NO	13	25	87	6.7	222	354	62.7	2,686	206.6	132
18.	W. Wilson	MINN	14	32	132	9.4	194	362	53.6	2,541	181.5	131
19.	Hogeboom	PHOE	14	27	89	6.4	204	364	56.0	2,591	185.1	129
20.	De Berg	KC	12	12	6	0.5	196	324	60.5	2,529	210.8	121
21.	Brister	PITT	14	27	43	3.1	187	343	54.5	2,365	168.9	118
22.	Trudeau	IND	13	35	91	7.0	190	362	52.5	2,317	178.2	115
23.	McMahon	SD	12	29	136	11.3	176	318	55.3	2,132	177.7	111
24.	Aikman+	DALL	11	38	302	27.5	155	292	53.1	1,749	159.0	109
25.	Tomczak	CHI	14	25	66	4.7	156	306	51.0	2,058	147.0	102
26.	Gagliano	DET	11	41	192	17.5	117	232	50.4	1,671	151.9	95
27.	Grogan	NE	7	9	19	2.7	133	261	51.0	1,697	242.4	82
28.	Harbaugh	CHI	11	45	276	25.1	111	178	62.4	1,219	110.8	80
29.	Beuerlein	LARd	10	15	41	4.1	108	217	49.8	1,677	167.7	80
30.	Schroeder	LARd	10	20	79	7.9	91	194	46.9	1,550	155.0	77
31.	Peete+	DET	8	33	148	18.5	103	195	52.8	1,479	184.9	76
32.	Walsh+	DALL	8	5	2	0.3	109	219	49.8	1,362	170.3	66
33.	Young	SF	9	39	124	13.8	64	92	69.6	1,001	111.2	57
34.	Tupa	PHOE	6	15	75	12.5	65	134	48.5	973	162.2	53
35.	Tolliver+	SD	5	4	-5	-1.0	89	185	48.1	1,097	219.4	53
36.	Fourcade	NO	7	15	90	12.9	60	106	56.6	919	131.3	51
37.	M. Wilson	NE	5	7	42	8.4	75	150	50.0	1,006	201.2	49
38.	Eason**	NYJ	5	3	-2	-0.4	79	141	56.0	1,016	203.2	49
39.	Kramer	MINN	7	12	9	1.3	77	136	56.6	906	129.4	43
40.	Millen	ATL	4	1	0	0.0	31	49	63.3	432	108.0	42
41.	Reich	BUF	5	9	30	6.0	53	87	60.9	701	140.2	36
42.	Chandler	IND	3	7	57	19.0	39	80	48.8	537	179.0	31
43.	Flutie	NE	5	16	87	17.4	36	81	44.4	490	98.0	30
44.	Williams	WASH	4	0	0	0.0	51	93	54.8	585	146.3	28
45.	Pelluer	KC	4	17	143	35.8	26	47	55.3	301	75.3	26
46.	Ferguson	TB	5	5	6	1.2	44	90	48.9	533	106.6	26
47.	Wilhelm	CIN	5	6	21	4.2	30	56	53.6	425	85.0	20
48.	Hostetler	NYG	5	11	71	14.2	20	39	51.3	294	58.8	19
49.	Jaworski	KC	3	3	1	0.3	36	61	59.0	385	128.3	18
50.	Kubiak	DEN	5	14	40	8.0	32	55	58.2	284	56.8	14

1989 STATISTICAL RESULTS
(Quarterbacks — Performance Point Method)

NAME	TEAM	GP	RSH	RSH YDS	AVG PER GM	COMP	ATT	PCT	PS YDS	AVG PER GM	1989 FAN-TASY PTS
51. Secules	MIA	4	4	39	9.8	22	50	44.0	286	71.5	14
52. Blackledge	PITT	3	9	20	6.7	22	60	36.7	282	94.0	14
53. Ramsey	IND	6	4	5	0.8	24	50	48.0	280	46.7	12
54. Stouffer	SEAT	3	2	11	3.7	29	59	49.2	270	90.0	12
55. Carlson	HOUS	6	3	-5	-0.5	15	31	48.4	155	25.8	6
56. Ryan	NYJ	4	1	-1	-0.3	15	30	50.0	153	38.3	6
57. Mackey	NYJ	3	2	3	1.0	11	25	44.0	125	41.7	5
58. Rosenbach+	PHOE	2	6	26	13.0	9	22	40.9	95	47.5	5
59. Archer	SD	3	2	14	4.7	5	12	41.7	62	20.7	4
60. Humphries	WASH	1	5	10	10.0	5	10	50.0	91	91.0	4
61. Bono	SF	1	0	0	0.0	4	5	80.0	62	62.0	3
62. Pagel	CLE	4	2	-1	-0.3	5	14	35.7	60	15.0	2
63. Long	DET	1	3	2	2.0	2	5	40.0	42	42.0	2
64. Herrmann	LARm	3	2	-1	-0.3	2	5	40.0	59	19.7	2
65. Evans	LARd	1	1	16	16.0	2	2	100.0	50	50.0	2
66. Hipple	DET	1	2	11	11.0	7	18	38.9	90	90.0	1
67. Schonert	CIN	1	0	0	0.0	0	2	0.0	0	0.0	0
68. Malone	NYJ	1	1	0	0.0	2	2	100.0	13	13.0	0
69. Cavanaugh	PHIL	4	0	0	0.0	3	5	60.0	33	8.3	0
70. Strom	PITT	2	3	-2	-1.0	0	0	0.0	0	0.0	0

+ DENOTES ROOKIES

** Eason   (NYJ)   —Played in 3 games with NE.

RATING THE PLAYERS FOR 1990
(Quarterbacks—Performance Point Method)

GRAB ONE IF YOU CAN

1. Randall Cunningham (Philadelphia Eagles)

Cunningham has placed second, first, and second by this scoring method over the last three seasons, respectively. He has combined good passing seasons of 2,786, 3,808, and 3,400 yards with an ability to run (505, 628, and 631 rushing yards) unmatched by any other quarterback. His versatility should keep him at the top again in 1990.

2. Dan Marino (Miami Dolphins)

In 1989, Marino tallied 3,997 passing yards. But looking back to 1984, when he threw for an incredible 5,084 yards, 1985 (4,134 yards), 1986 (4,746 yards), and 1988 (4,434 yards) we recall his potential.

3. Jim Everett (Los Angeles Rams)

Jim Everett has converted a team that was very run-oriented to a very diverse run-pass team. Over the past two seasons he has produced 3,964 and 4,310 yards, respectively, while placing third by this scoring method both seasons. I believe he will continue to succeed in 1990.

4. Boomer Esiason (Cincinnati Bengals)

Hobbled somewhat by ankle trouble, Esiason took sixth place with a 3,525-yard performance in 1989—his worst in four years. In the three years prior to 1989, he placed second, first, and fourth, respectively, with 3,966, 3,321 (12-game season), and 3,572 yards. Producing 146, 241, 238, and 278 rushing yards during that same stretch has also helped. If he stays healthy in 1990, he'll again place among the league's best.

5. Don Majkowski (Green Bay Packers)

Not only did Majkowski capture the Green Bay starting-quarterback job in 1989 but he also led the league in passing yards with 4,318. He may not do as well in 1990, but he could get close, as he and the Packers continue to improve.

BEST OF THE REST

6. Joe Montana (San Francisco 49ers)

Injuries have certainly played a big part in Montana's fallen production the last few years. From 1983 through 1985, Montana placed third, sixth, and fifth, respectively, by this scoring method, throwing for 3,910, 3,630, and 3,653 yards. But in 1986, due to a serious back injury, his production fell way off. He returned in 1987 to place ninth with 2,657 yards. In 1988 he produced 2,846 yards, placing 12th, and in 1989 he threw for 2,521 yards, placing 7th. If he is to remain among the league leaders, he'll have to avoid the nagging injuries that have plagued him the last few years.

7. John Elway (Denver Broncos)

Over the past five seasons, Elway has ranked 1st, 4th, 2nd, 5th, and 11th, respectively, by this scoring method. He rushed for 258, 257, 304, 234, and 244 yards during that period. His passing stats have been much more erratic—3,891, 3,482, 1,728, 3,309, and 3,051 yards over the same stretch. 1990 should be more of the same, with a solid rushing performance guiding the way.

8. Warren Moon (Houston Oilers)

Four times in the last six years, Moon has been a top-10 finisher by this scoring method. He placed eighth (1984), eighth (1986), eighth (1987), and fourth (1989) during that stretch. He should fare as well in 1990.

9. Bernie Kosar (Cleveland Browns)

Only in 1988, when an elbow injury forced him to miss much of the season, has Kosar not placed in the top 10 by this scoring method over the past four seasons. In 1986 he placed fifth with 3,854 passing yards; in 1987, seventh with 3,033 yards; and in 1989, ninth with 3,533 yards. He should reach that success range again in 1990, if he avoids injury.

10. Mark Rypien (Washington Redskins)

With the likes of Gary Clark, Art Monk, and Ricky Sanders to throw to, success should be easy. Rypien proved that by throwing for 3,868 yards in 1989, despite being benched for two games. His benching resulted from his habit of fumbling when sacked, and if he can avoid that in 1990, he can have a big year.

STRONG LONG SHOTS

11. Jim Kelly (Buffalo Bills)

After finishing sixth by this scoring method for three consecutive years, Kelly fell off to 13th in 1989. This was due to two reasons—missing three games with a shoulder injury and the emergence of Thurman Thomas as a big running threat. I look for a healthy Kelly to rebound to the top 10 in 1990.

12. Dave Krieg (Seattle Seahawks)

Krieg rebounded to his first top-10 finish by this scoring method since 1984, placing 10th with a 3,309-yard season in 1989. He remains an inconsistent performer, but when he's on, he's very good. If he can hold off the challenge of Kelly Stouffer in 1990, he could have another solid year.

13. Ken O'Brien/Tony Eason (New York Jets)

Perhaps under new coaching direction the Jets' offense can get back on track. O'Brien has seen his passing yardage fall off the last couple of seasons, something he hopes to improve on in 1990 under new leadership. He'll also have to contend with the challenge of Tony Eason, whom the Jets signed in midseason in 1989.

14. Vinny Testaverde (Tampa Bay Buccaneers)

Throwing for 3,240 and 3,133 yards, respectively, Testaverde has placed 10th and 14th the past two seasons, a success level I see continuing in 1990.

15. Phil Simms (New York Giants)

With the Giants relying more on defense and the run in recent years, Simms has seen his passing yardage slowly slide. He has thrown for 4,044, 3,829, 3,487, 3,359, and 3,061 yards over the past six seasons, respectively, skipping 1987 when he was injured. I believe the decline is over, but he'll again place near where he finished in 1989, 16th by this scoring method.

HAVE THE POTENTIAL

16. Gary Hogeboom/Timm Rosenbach/Tom Tupa (Phoenix Cardinals)

The Cardinals, with Roy Green, J. T. Smith, Robert Awalt, Ernie Jones, and company sure have the receiving talent to make any of these quarterbacks statistically healthy. Veteran Gary Hogeboom ran the offense most of the '89 season, but the Cardinals may want to turn it over to a younger arm.

17. Chris Miller (Atlanta Falcons)

Staying free from injury seems to be Miller's toughest task. In missing only one game in 1989, Miller produced 3,459 passing yards, thus giving us an idea of what a healthy season can be like.

18. Wade Wilson (Minnesota Vikings)

Wilson has produced 2,111, 2,746, and 2,541 passing yards over the last three seasons. These levels are less than impressive from a quarterback throwing for a team that's known for its pass offense.

19. Andre Ware/Rodney Peete/Bob Gagliano (Detroit Lions)

Though both Rodney Peete and Bob Gagliano proved they could run-and-shoot well in 1989, I believe it will be only a short time until Andre Ware is at the helm showcasing his talent.

20. Bubby Brister (Pittsburgh Steelers)

Brister's passing totals dipped a bit in 1989 to 2,365 yards from his 2,634-yard total of 1988. He's a young quarterback on an improving team, though, and he should see his production rebound in 1990.

BEST OF THE REST

21. Bobby Hebert/John Fourcade (New Orleans Saints)

Hebert threw for 3,156 yards in 1988 as the Saints' season-long starter. In 1989, Hebert's ineffectiveness resulted in the appearance of John Fourcade, who started and won the last three games, throwing for 829 yards, and giving us an idea of what he can produce if he becomes the Saints' starter in 1990.

22. Troy Aikman (Dallas Cowboys)
Aikman threw for only 1,749 yards as a rookie in 1989, missing five games with a throwing-hand injury. If he can remain healthy in 1990, perhaps the Cowboys will get more of what they had hoped for from Aikman.

23. Steve Beuerlein/Jay Schroeder (Los Angeles Raiders)
Though the potential for either of these quarterbacks is much higher than this ranking suggests, the uncertainty of either holding the job for the entire season drops their fantasy value.

24. Steve De Berg/Steve Pelluer (Kansas City Chiefs)
De Berg was the starter for most of the '89 season. Will he continue to hold that position? The Chiefs also plan to rely on their running game, led by Christian Okoye.

25. Billy Joe Tolliver (San Diego Chargers)
McMahon's ineffectiveness led to Tolliver's late-season appearance as the Chargers' starter. Is Tolliver ready to take over this young team on a permanent basis? McMahon, now released, won't be around to challenge him for the job.

26. Jeff George/Jack Trudeau/Chris Chandler (Indianapolis Colts)
Throwing on a team that features Eric Dickerson is not usually statistically very rewarding for a quarterback. That's one obstacle that one of these three will face in 1990. With the Colts dishing out $15 million to rookie Jeff George, I wouldn't think it will be too long until he's given a shot at earning his keep.

27. Mike Tomczak/Jim Harbaugh (Chicago Bears)
The Bears are usually content to feature the running attacks of Neal Anderson and Brad Muster. Neither Tomczak nor Harbaugh has consistently impressed me.

28. Steve Grogan/Marc Wilson/Doug Flutie (New England Patriots)
Too many questions here!

A LOOK AT THE KICKERS

(A Guide for the Beginner)

Considerations in Choosing a Kicker

The scoring for kickers is identical for both the Basic Scoring Method and the Performance Point Method. (See the section on the Basic Scoring Method).

A 1990 MOCK DRAFT
(My Top-16 Overall Picks for the Performance Point Method)

NAME	TEAM	POSITION
1. Neal Anderson	Chicago Bears	Running Back
2. Thurman Thomas	Buffalo Bills	Running Back
3. Eric Dickerson	Indianapolis Colts	Running Back
4. Barry Sanders	Detroit Lions	Running Back
5. Roger Craig	San Francisco 49ers	Running Back
6. Bobby Humphrey	Denver Broncos	Running Back
7. Dalton Hilliard	New Orleans Saints	Running Back
8. Christian Okoye	Kansas City Chiefs	Running Back
9. Herschel Walker	Minnesota Vikings	Running Back
10. James Brooks	Cincinnati Bengals	Running Back
11. J. L. Williams	Seattle Seahawks	Running Back
12. Jerry Rice	San Francisco 49ers	Wide Receiver
13. Sterling Sharpe	Green Bay Packers	Wide Receiver
14. Henry Ellard	Los Angeles Rams	Wide Receiver
15. Randall Cunningham	Philadelphia Eagles	Quarterback
16. Jim Everett	Los Angeles Rams	Quarterback

Neal Anderson, Thurman Thomas, Eric Dickerson, Barry Sanders, and Roger Craig, all running backs, have the potential to top the 2,000-yard combined rushing-receiving level.

Then the next group, Bobby Humphrey, Dalton Hilliard, Christian Okoye, Herschel Walker, James Brooks, and J. L. Williams, again all running backs, I believe will fall in the 1,400–1,700-yard range.

Then come three wide receivers—Jerry Rice, Sterling Sharpe, and Henry Ellard—all possessing the potential to near the 1,500-yard mark.

I round off my top picks with two quarterbacks, Randall Cunningham and Jim Everett. Cunningham rates well because of his ability to pick up yards on the ground as well as through the air, while Everett is becoming a consistent 4,000–4,500-yard passing man.

X
RATING THE PLAYERS:
DISTANCE SCORING METHOD

Let's review how scoring is done using the Distance Scoring Method. As in the Basic Scoring Method, points are awarded for touchdowns scored by players on offense. The difference between this method and the Basic Scoring Method is that in the Distance Scoring Method the yardage covered on the touchdown play is used to calculate the points to be awarded; the longer the touchdown, the more points awarded. This scoring method favors exciting touchdowns and rewards players for the yardage they covered in making the play.

The Distance Scoring Method presents unique challenges for your draft selection. It's difficult to determine who is going to score the actual touchdowns. In addition, you must predict who is going to score from enough distance to give you the winning edge.

As we did in the preceding methods, we will now look at basic drafting strategies and review the players' 1989 statistics; finally I will rate the players for 1990.

No rookies are included in my player ratings. It's too early to size up how they'll fit into each team's scheme. I rate the rookies separately, in Section V of this chapter.

Distance Scoring Method

DRAFTING STRATEGY BY ROUNDS
(A Guide for the Beginner)

1. The draft consists of 12 rounds.
2. Of the 12 players chosen, 7 are starters and 5 are reserves.
3. The starting 7 comprise:

1 Quarterback		1 Quarterback
2 Running Backs	OR	2 Running Backs
2 Wide Receivers	FLEX OPTION	3 Receivers
1 Tight End		1 Kicker
1 Kicker		

4. The 5 reserves can be from any position.

5. Any player from any starting position may be drafted in any round.

Preparation for your draft will play a big part in making you a successful Fantasy Football coach. Let's look at the basic strategy used in drafting players for the Distance Scoring Method.

ROUND 1: Remember that points are awarded for actual touchdowns scored. Players are awarded two points for every 10 yards on touchdown plays. Our first concern, therefore, is to get a consistent two-point player.

As in the Basic Scoring Method, running backs are usually the highest-scoring players. Although many touchdowns scored by running backs may be in short-yardage situations, you still need a player who scores consistently. Favor quick backs who can break into long scoring runs, rather than big running backs who plow over from inside the five-yard line. Prime first-round picks are Eric Dickerson, Herschel Walker, and Neal Anderson. Grabbing a James Brooks can give you that occasional long touchdown, along with consistent scoring, so he may also be a good choice.

ROUND 2: Because more points are awarded for long touchdown plays, this round should be where you take a shot at a wide receiver. Most passing touchdowns are from distances that can run up a good score quickly using this scoring method. Choose a receiver who consistently scores 10 touchdowns per year, like Jerry Rice, Mark Clayton, or Mike Quick.

ROUND 3: In this round let's try to grab a good quarterback, one who will throw 25 or more touchdown passes during the year. A consistent quarterback will put points on the scoreboard week after week. Dan Marino and Joe Montana fall into this category. By the end of the third round, you should have a consistently scoring running back and quarterback, along with a deep-threat wide receiver—a good start at a balanced offense.

ROUND 4: In this round, pick up a scatback who will give you that long touchdown run.

ROUND 5: Now it's important to pick up a kicker. Look for a consistent scorer who plays on a team good enough to give him plenty of scoring chances.

ROUNDS 6, 7, and 8: Fill in the starting positions you have left open. If you have followed my suggestions, you lack a tight end and a wide receiver. But if you notice that a player you really like is available at a position you have already partially filled, pick him up, even if you haven't filled all your starting positions. You'll feel better about your lineup, and at the very worst you'll have either a high-powered reserve or some attractive trade bait.

ROUNDS 9 through 12: These rounds are used to fill in your reserves. It's a good time to take a shot at a rookie. In choosing your reserves, be sure to draft backups for the more injury-prone positions—quarterback, running back, and wide receiver. Even though you're into the less important players by this time, keep alert. Many good picks happen in these late rounds.

Let's now take a look at what to consider when choosing players for each position.

A LOOK AT THE RUNNING BACKS

(A Guide for the Beginner)

Considerations in Choosing a Running Back

Here are some considerations to bear in mind when selecting a running back. Following this will be the 1989 statistics, and then I rate the players for 1990.

1. First, consider players' performance records.

2. Our first priority in selecting a running back is choosing one who not only will score consistently but also is capable of long touchdown runs. Our first choice is a big, fast back. Eric Dickerson and Neal Anderson can score from anywhere, and both fit the mold perfectly.

3. If a big, quick back is not available on your turn, you should forget about speed and take a consistent, high-scoring big back. Although his touchdown runs may be shorter, he provides you with consistent scoring. Ickey Woods of Cincinnati is built like a fullback and has good speed; he is a solid choice here, if he returns healthy from his 1989 knee injury.

4. Our next preference is the back who will probably not score many touchdowns but is likely to get some big yardage when he does score. These are the scatback runners who excel in the open but give way to the bigger backs in bruising goal-line situations. This type of player may work out as a good second back in your offense. Here James Brooks would be a great pick. Brooks gives you breakaway speed, and if you had him in 1988 when he scored 14 times, you did well.

5. Next is a top rookie. There seems always to be at least one first-year running back who makes it big. Look at Barry Sanders, Eric Metcalf, Bobby Humphrey, or Marion Butts in 1989.

6. In most cases, shy away from old running backs. If they have been in the league for many years, they probably won't last a full season without injury. In addition, their desire to excel may be dwindling this late in their careers.

7. Keep an eye out for running backs who like to throw the option pass. Because this pass catches the defense off guard, it can produce a long-yardage touchdown, thus rewarding you with some additional passing points.

8. Finally, beware of players who have injury after nagging injury. They may be good backs, but they can't help you if they are out of the lineup more often than in it.

In looking at the 1989 statistics, you'll find the players ranked by their fantasy-point totals. Remember that in the Distance Scoring Method, fantasy points are calculated by the length of the touchdown scored; the longer the touchdown play, the more points earned.

1989 STATISTICAL RESULTS
(Running Backs — Distance Scoring Method)

NAME	TEAM	GP	TD PS	RSH	RSH TDs	AVG LGTH	PS REC	PS REC TDs	AVG LGTH	TOTAL TDs	AVG LGTH	1989 FAN-TASY PTS
1. N. Anderson	CHI	16	0	274	11	12.7	50	4	25.0	15	16.0	68
2. Hilliard	NO	16	0	344	13	5.0	52	5	29.8	18	11.9	68
3. Meggett*+	NYG	16	0	28	0	0.0	34	4	51.3	5	56.2	62
4. Thomas	BUF	16	0	298	6	7.5	60	6	23.3	12	15.4	52
5. Walker* **	MINN	16	0	250	7	8.4	40	2	17.5	10	18.7	50
6. Brooks	CIN	16	0	221	7	22.4	37	2	11.5	9	20.0	46
7. Metcalf+	CLE	16	0	187	6	12.2	54	4	25.0	10	17.3	46
8. B. Sanders+	DET	15	0	280	14	8.3	24	0	0.0	14	8.3	40
9. Jackson	LARd	11	0	173	4	43.5	9	0	0.0	4	43.5	40
10. Bell	LARm	16	0	272	15	5.1	19	0	0.0	15	5.1	38
11. O.J. Anderson	NYG	16	0	325	14	5.9	28	0	0.0	14	5.9	38
12. Butts+	SD	15	0	170	9	12.1	7	0	0.0	9	12.1	38
13. Okoye	KC	15	0	370	12	6.8	2	0	0.0	12	6.8	30
14. Humphrey*+	DEN	16	1	294	7	9.0	22	1	12.0	8	9.4	28
15. J.L. Williams	SEAT	15	0	146	1	4.0	76	6	15.0	7	13.4	28
16. Vick	NYJ	16	0	112	5	16.2	34	2	11.0	7	14.7	28
17. R. Harmon	BUF	13	0	17	0	0.0	29	4	23.0	4	23.0	24
18. T. Sanders*+	CHI	13	0	41	0	0.0	3	1	16.0	2	56.0	24
19. Stephens	NE	14	0	244	7	9.0	21	0	0.0	7	9.0	24
20. Tate	TB	15	0	167	8	5.6	11	1	10.0	9	6.1	24
21. Muster	CHI	16	0	82	5	4.8	32	3	8.7	8	6.3	22
22. Logan*	MIA	9	0	57	0	0.0	5	2	0.0	2	50.5	22
23. Byner	WASH	16	0	134	7	4.1	54	2	6.5	9	4.7	22
24. Fontenot	GB	16	0	17	1	1.0	40	3	27.3	4	20.8	20
25. Dickerson	IND	15	0	314	7	4.6	30	1	8.0	8	5.0	20
26. Ferrell	PHOE	15	0	149	6	9.3	18	0	0.0	6	9.3	20
27. Settle	ATL	16	0	179	3	2.7	39	2	21.5	5	10.2	16
28. Gentry	CHI	15	0	17	0	0.0	39	1	79.0	1	79.0	16
29. Palmer	DALL	9	0	111	2	32.5	17	0	0.0	2	32.5	16
30. V. Mueller	LARd	12	0	46	2	3.5	18	2	25.2	4	14.5	16
31. Worley+	PITT	15	0	195	5	10.6	15	0	0.0	5	10.6	16
32. Hoge	PITT	16	0	186	8	2.1	34	0	0.0	8	2.1	16
33. Carter	PITT	14	0	12	1	1.0	38	3	17.0	4	13.0	16
34. Riggs	WASH	12	0	201	4	14.3	7	0	0.0	4	14.3	16
35. K. Jones+	ATL	12	0	52	6	3.8	41	0	0.0	6	3.8	14
36. Jennings	CIN	14	0	83	2	3.0	10	1	43.3	3	16.3	14
37. Sewell	DEN	13	0	7	0	0.0	25	3	18.3	3	18.3	14
38. Highsmith	HOUS	16	0	128	4	6.0	18	2	4.0	6	5.3	14
39. Fenney	MINN	16	0	151	4	3.3	30	2	9.5	6	5.3	14
40. Hector	NYJ	15	0	177	3	1.0	38	2	16.0	5	7.0	14
41. Craig	SF	16	0	271	6	1.8	49	1	4.0	7	2.1	14
42. Woodside	GB	15	0	46	1	68.0	59	0	0.0	1	68.0	14
43. Kinnebrew	BUF	13	0	132	6	1.2	5	0	0.0	6	1.2	12
44. Fullwood	GB	15	0	204	5	4.0	19	0	0.0	5	4.0	12
45. White	HOUS	14	0	104	5	3.2	6	0	0.0	5	3.2	12
46. McGee	LARm	15	0	21	1	5.0	37	4	6.8	5	6.4	12
47. Sm. Smith+	MIA	13	0	200	6	2.3	7	0	0.0	6	2.3	12
48. Byars	PHIL	16	0	133	5	4.6	68	0	0.0	5	4.6	12
49. McNeil	NYJ	10	0	79	2	10.0	32	1	25.0	3	15.0	12
50. Davis	BUF	9	0	29	1	17.0	6	2	12.0	3	13.7	10
51. C. Taylor+	CIN	8	0	30	3	3.0	4	2	9.5	5	5.6	10
52. Manoa	CLE	16	0	87	3	2.3	27	2	6.0	5	3.4	10
53. Bratton+	DEN	11	0	30	1	5.0	10	3	7.3	4	6.8	10
54. Bentley*	IND	16	0	75	1	1.0	52	3	6.0	5	3.8	10

1989 STATISTICAL RESULTS
(Running Backs — Distance Scoring Method)

NAME	TEAM	GP	TD PS	RSH	RSH TDs	AVG LGTH	PS REC	PS REC TDs	AVG LGTH	TOTAL TDs	AVG LGTH	1989 FAN-TASY PTS
55. Delpino	LARm	16	0	78	1	32.0	34	1	9.0	2	20.5	10
56. M. Green+	CHI	6	0	5	1	37.0	5	0	0.0	1	37.0	8
57. Redden	CLE	12	0	40	1	38.0	6	0	0.0	1	38.0	8
58. Johnston+	DALL	12	0	67	0	0.0	16	3	11.0	3	11.0	8
59. Warner	SEAT	16	0	194	3	2.7	23	1	1.0	4	2.3	8
60. Lang	ATL	15	0	47	1	10.0	39	1	9.0	2	9.5	6
61. Ball+	CIN	14	0	98	3	2.7	6	0	0.0	3	2.7	6
62. Oliphant	CLE	5	0	15	1	21.0	3	0	0.0	1	21.0	6
63. Pinkett	HOUS	15	0	94	1	2.0	31	1	10.0	2	6.0	6
64. Saxon	KC	15	0	58	3	4.7	11	0	0.0	3	4.7	6
65. B. Jordan	NO	11	0	38	3	1.3	4	0	0.0	3	1.3	6
66. Toney	PHIL	14	0	172	3	2.0	19	0	0.0	3	2.0	6
67. Spencer	SD	14	0	134	3	5.0	18	0	0.0	3	5.0	6
68. Flagler	SF	8	0	33	1	29.0	6	0	0.0	1	29.0	6
69. Stamps	TB	10	0	29	1	21.0	15	0	0.0	1	21.0	6
70. Wilder	TB	13	0	70	0	0.0	36	3	7.7	3	7.7	6
71. Woods	CIN	2	0	29	2	3.0	0	0	0.0	2	3.0	4
72. Suhey	CHI	10	0	20	1	1.0	9	1	1.0	2	1.0	4
73. Winder	DEN	15	0	110	2	1.5	14	0	0.0	2	1.5	4
74. Alexander	DEN	13	0	45	2	1.0	8	0	0.0	2	1.0	4
75. Rozier	HOUS	12	0	88	2	1.0	3	0	0.0	2	1.0	4
76. McNair+	KC	13	0	23	0	0.0	34	1	11.0	1	11.0	4
77. Mc. Allen	LARd	8	0	69	2	1.0	20	0	0.0	2	1.0	4
78. St. Smith	LARd	16	0	117	1	11.0	19	0	0.0	1	11.0	4
79. Perryman	NE	16	0	150	2	2.0	29	0	0.0	2	2.0	4
80. Egu+	NE	2	0	3	1	15.0	0	0	0.0	1	15.0	4
81. A. Anderson	MINN	11	0	52	2	3.0	20	0	0.0	2	3.0	4
82. Sherman+	PHIL	7	0	40	2	4.5	8	0	0.0	2	4.5	4
83. T. Jordan	PHOE	12	0	83	2	1.0	6	0	0.0	2	1.0	4
84. Rathman	SF	16	0	79	1	1.0	73	1	8.0	2	4.5	4
85. Jm. Morris	WASH	10	0	124	2	4.5	8	0	0.0	2	4.5	4
86. Howard	TB	13	0	110	1	1.0	30	1	9.0	2	5.0	4
87. Henderson+	SF	3	0	5	1	11.0	3	0	0.0	1	11.0	4
88. Flowers	ATL	5	0	13	1	1.0	0	0	0.0	1	1.0	2
89. K. Jones	CLE	10	0	43	1	9.0	15	0	0.0	1	9.0	2
90. Mack	CLE	4	0	37	1	4.0	2	0	0.0	1	4.0	2
91. Sargent	DALL	12	0	20	1	1.0	7	0	0.0	1	1.0	2
92. Clack	DALL	2	0	14	2	1.0	3	0	0.0	2	2.0	2
93. Haddix	GB	12	0	44	0	0.0	15	1	6.0	1	6.0	2
94. Heard	KC	15	0	63	0	0.0	25	1	8.0	1	8.0	2
95. Gary+	LARm	8	0	37	1	5.0	2	0	0.0	1	5.0	2
96. Stradford	MIA	7	0	66	1	1.0	25	0	0.0	1	1.0	2
97. Davenport	MIA	6	0	14	1	5.0	3	0	0.0	1	5.0	2
98. Mv. Allen	NE	3	0	11	1	1.0	0	0	0.0	1	1.0	2
99. Heyward	NO	12	0	49	1	1.0	13	0	0.0	1	1.0	2
100. Frazier	NO	8	0	25	1	1.0	3	0	0.00	1	1.0	2
101. Drummond+	PHIL	9	0	32	0	0.0	17	1	4.0	1	4.0	2
102. Wolfley	PHOE	8	0	13	1	5.0	5	0	0.0	1	5.0	2
103. W. Williams	PITT	5	0	37	1	1.0	6	0	0.0	1	1.0	2
104. Wallace	PITT	4	0	5	1	2.0	0	0	0.0	1	2.0	2
105. Fenner+	SEAT	2	0	11	1	5.0	3	0	0.0	1	5.0	2
106. Dupard**	WASH	8	0	37	1	4.0	6	0	0.0	1	4.0	2
107. Paterra+	ATL	4	0	9	0	0.0	5	0	0.0	0	0.0	0
108. J. Mueller	BUF	6	0	15	0	0.0	1	0	0.0	0	0.0	0

1989 STATISTICAL RESULTS
(Running Backs — Distance Scoring Method)

NAME	TEAM	GP	TD PS	RSH	RSH TDs	AVG LGTH	PS REC	PS REC TDs	AVG LGTH	TOTAL TDs	AVG LGTH	1989 FAN-TASY PTS
109. Holifield	CIN	1	0	11	0	0.0	2	0	0.0	0	0.0	0
110. B. Taylor	CHI	1	0	0	0	0.0	2	0	0.0	0	0.0	0
111. Scott	DALL	3	0	2	0	0.0	9	0	0.0	0	0.0	0
112. Tautalatasi	DALL	8	0	6	0	0.0	17	0	0.0	0	0.0	0
113. Paige	DET	7	0	30	0	0.0	2	0	0.0	0	0.0	0
114. Painter	DET	5	0	15	0	0.0	3	0	0.0	0	0.0	0
115. Workman+	GB	2	0	3	0	0.0	1	0	0.0	0	0.0	0
116. Tc. Johnson+	HOUS	3	0	1	0	0.0	4	0	0.0	0	0.0	0
117. Porter	LARd	5	0	13	0	0.0	0	0	0.0	0	0.0	0
118. Hunter+	IND	2	0	6	0	0.0	0	0	0.0	0	0.0	0
119. Carruth	KC	1	0	0	0	0.0	1	0	0.0	0	0.0	0
120. Agee	KC	1	0	0	0	0.0	1	0	0.0	0	0.0	0
121. G. Green	LARm	6	0	26	0	0.0	0	0	0.0	0	0.0	0
122. Hampton	MIA	6	0	17	0	0.0	7	0	0.0	0	0.0	0
123. T. Brown	MIA	7	0	13	0	0.0	12	0	0.0	0	0.0	0
124. Tatupu	NE	6	0	11	0	0.0	9	0	0.0	0	0.0	0
125. Wonsley	NE	2	0	2	0	0.0	0	0	0.0	0	0.0	0
126. Dozier	MINN	11	0	46	0	0.0	14	0	0.0	0	0.0	0
127. Faaola	MIA	2	0	2	0	0.0	1	0	0.0	0	0.0	0
128. Gamble	KC	2	0	6	0	0.0	2	0	0.0	0	0.0	0
129. Rice	MINN	3	0	7	0	0.0	4	0	0.0	0	0.0	0
130. Clark	MINN	3	0	20	0	0.0	2	0	0.0	0	0.0	0
131. Higgs	PHIL	10	0	49	0	0.0	3	0	0.0	0	0.0	0
132. Carthon	NYG	14	0	57	0	0.0	15	0	0.0	0	0.0	0
133. Rouson	NYG	11	0	11	0	0.0	7	0	0.0	0	0.0	0
134. Tillman+	NYG	12	0	79	0	0.0	1	0	0.0	0	0.0	0
135. Adams	NYG	5	0	9	0	0.0	2	0	0.0	0	0.0	0
136. A. Brown+	NYJ	4	0	9	0	0.0	4	0	0.0	0	0.0	0
137. S. Mitchell	PHOE	3	0	43	0	0.0	1	0	0.0	0	0.0	0
138. Sikahema	PHOE	12	0	38	0	0.0	23	0	0.0	0	0.0	0
139. Stone	PITT	7	0	10	0	0.0	7	0	0.0	0	0.0	0
140. Tyrrell	PITT	1	0	1	0	0.0	0	0	0.0	0	0.0	0
141. Floyd+	SD	3	0	8	0	0.0	1	0	0.0	0	0.0	0
142. Nelson**	SD	14	0	67	0	0.0	38	0	0.0	0	0.0	0
143. Brinson	SD	7	0	17	0	0.0	12	0	0.0	0	0.0	0
144. Sydney	SF	5	0	7	0	0.0	9	0	0.0	0	0.0	0
145. Harris+	SEAT	4	0	8	0	0.0	3	0	0.0	0	0.0	0
146. J. Jones	SEAT	1	0	0	0	0.0	1	0	0.0	0	0.0	0
147. K. Harmon	SEAT	1	0	1	0	0.0	0	0	0.0	0	0.0	0
148. D. Smith	TB	7	0	6	0	0.0	7	0	0.0	0	0.0	0
149. A. Mitchell	TB	1	0	0	0	0.0	1	0	0.0	0	0.0	0
150. Reaves	WASH	1	0	1	0	0.0	0	0	0.0	0	0.0	0
151. Baker	PHOE	5	0	17	0	0.0	2	0	0.0	0	0.0	0

+ DENOTES ROOKIES

*	Meggett	(NYG)	—Scored TD on punt return of 76 yards.
*	Walker	(MINN)	—Scored TD on kickoff return of 93 yards.
*	Humphrey	(DEN)	—Threw TD pass of 17 yards.
*	T. Sanders	(CHI)	—Scored TD on kickoff return of 96 yards.
*	Logan	(MIA)	—Scored TD on blocked-punt return of 2 yards.
			Scored TD on kickoff return of 97 yards.
*	Bentley	(IND)	—Scored TD on return of blocked punt.
**	Walker	(MINN)	—Played in 5 games with DALL.
**	Nelson	(SD)	—Played in 5 games with MINN.
**	Dupard	(WASH)	—Played in 6 games with NE.

RATING THE PLAYERS FOR 1990
(Running Backs—Distance Scoring Method)

GRAB ONE IF YOU CAN

1. Neal Anderson (Chicago Bears)
With the ability to score both running and receiving, Anderson can score at any time. He has placed first by this method both of the last two seasons. Being the Bears' main offensive weapon in 1990 should allow him another big year.

2. Barry Sanders (Detroit Lions)
As a rookie in 1989, Sanders scored 14 times and demonstrated some very elusive moves. I believe he'll be even more involved in the Lions' offense in 1990 and will be a threat to break one often.

3. Eric Dickerson (Indianapolis Colts)
Normally a strong finisher by this scoring method, Dickerson had placed 1st, 3rd, 19th, 4th, 11th, and 2nd, respectively, in recent years, before winding up 24th in 1989. If he can avoid the nagging injuries that have taken a toll the last couple of years, he should rebound to his productive ways in 1990.

4. James Brooks (Cincinnati Bengals)
As one of the league's more feared breakaway runners, Brooks has placed in the top-six running backs four out of the last five seasons. That's a consistency to buy into when selecting Brooks for your fantasy team.

5. Dalton Hilliard (New Orleans Saints)
Of Hilliard's 18 touchdowns in 1989, five came through the air. He averaged just under 30 yards on each of those five scores, which should make him a prime candidate for this scoring method.

6. Greg Bell (Los Angeles Rams)
With Bell's punishing running style, he's less likely to break a big one. But his consistent scoring (18 and 15 touchdowns over the last two years, respectively) still makes him a good choice for this scoring method.

7. Thurman Thomas (Buffalo Bills)
With Robb Riddick out for the year with a knee injury, Thomas really became a scoring force for the Bills in 1989. His six touchdowns rushing and six touchdowns receiving prove he can get it done both ways.

8. Eric Metcalf (Cleveland Browns)
As a rookie in 1989, Metcalf proved he's a back who can score both on the ground (six TDs) and through the air (four TDs). With his exceptional quickness, he's always a threat to go the distance.

9. Herschel Walker (Minnesota Vikings)
Even though the Vikings struggled to find a way to utilize him, Walker still fared well by this scoring method. He can also get it done through the air, as well as on the ground. And remember, he can occasionally be used for kickoff returns, which could really rack up the fantasy points.

10. Ickey Woods (Cincinnati Bengals)

Woods was a real scoring force as a rookie in 1988, scoring 15 times. But in 1989 a knee injury forced him to miss much of the season. Be sure not to overlook this big scoring threat as a potential standout for your 1990 fantasy team.

BEST OF THE REST

11. Bobby Humphrey (Denver Broncos)

As a rookie in 1989, Humphrey seemed to be just a step away from breaking a long one many times. He scored eight times and in 1990 may expand on that, with some touchdowns from good distances.

12. J. L. Williams (Seattle Seahawks)

Of Williams's 14 touchdowns over the past two seasons, nine have come via the air. This proves his versatility, and with him taking more of the backfield load now that Curt Warner is gone, his scoring production should rise.

13. Christian Okoye (Kansas City Chiefs)

Although Okoye is not likely to break many long touchdown runs, his 12 touchdowns in 1989 prove he's a back whom the Chiefs will use often in scoring situations.

14. Gary Anderson (Tampa Bay Buccaneers)

Anderson took a year off in 1989, due to a contract dispute with the Chargers. If we look back to 1986, when he placed third by this scoring method, averaging over 20 yards on nine touchdowns, we get a feel for what he's capable of. However, in 1990 he'll be producing for a new team, the Bucs.

15. Roger Craig (San Francisco 49ers)

Though his scoring has lagged in recent years, we can look back to 1984 and 1985, when he placed fourth and second by this scoring method, to know he's capable of a big season. I wouldn't let him get out of my hands at this point.

16. Keith Byars (Philadelphia Eagles)

In 1989 Byars scored only four short touchdowns, which limited his totals by this scoring method. But in 1988, 4 of his 10 touchdowns came through the air. So don't get locked into his 1989 performance. He has much potential.

17. Joe Morris (New York Giants)

Morris placed number one by this scoring method in 1985, when he scored 21 touchdowns. His primary concern for 1990 will be returning from the knee injury suffered in last year's preseason.

18. John Stephens (New England Patriots)

Stephens upped his total from four touchdowns in 1988 to seven in 1989. I believe that, as a main ingredient of the Patriots' offense again in 1990, his total will continue to rise.

19. Bo Jackson (Los Angeles Raiders)
Although he may show up for only eight or nine games again in 1990, his 43.5-yard average on four touchdowns in 1989 proves he's a back to give plenty of consideration.

20. Gerald Riggs (Washington Redskins)
The Redskins hope to have Riggs stay free from injury in 1990, so he can become more of a contributor and scorer, which will help him expand on his four touchdowns of 1989.

STRONG LONG SHOTS

21. Lars Tate (Tampa Bay Buccaneers)
Eight touchdowns as a rookie in 1988 and nine last year prove his scoring capability. As a continued main ingredient of the Bucs' offense in 1990, Tate should continue to score.

22. Marcus Allen (Los Angeles Raiders)
Twice Allen has been a top-10 finisher by this scoring method. That was back in 1984 and 1985, however. If he is to recapture some of that scoring glory, he must somehow stay clear of the injuries that have plagued him in recent years.

23. Kevin Mack (Cleveland Browns)
The Browns would like to have Mack around for the entire 1990 season, after having him miss 12 games of the '89 season due to drug involvement. He could again become a big scoring force.

24. John Settle (Atlanta Falcons)
Settle saw his touchdown production drop from eight in 1988 to only five scores in 1989. The Falcons hope to get Settle into the end zone more often in 1990, which may be a struggle because they face the league's toughest schedule.

25. Stump Mitchell (Phoenix Cardinals)
With the surprise retirement announcement by Earl Ferrell, the Cardinals are hoping for a healthy return by Mitchell. If Mitchell is healthy, he should certainly show his talent for scoring well in this method.

HAVE THE POTENTIAL

26. Johnny Hector (New York Jets)
Always a prime scoring threat for the Jets, Hector may also steal more of the rushing load from Freeman McNeil in 1990, which could spell even more scoring. Rookie Blair Thomas, however, may stand in his way.

27. Tim Worley (Pittsburgh Steelers)
As a rookie in 1989, Worley crossed the goal line only five times, but four of those came in the season's last three games, as he became a very big contributor to the Steeler offense.

28. Marion Butts (San Diego Chargers)
Butts scored nine times in 1989, as he became the Chargers' main ground force in the absence of Gary Anderson, who sat out the season over a contract dispute. And now that Anderson is with Tampa Bay, Butts should have continued success in 1990.

29. Curt Warner (Los Angeles Rams)
The years have taken their toll on Curt Warner, once a very good breakaway runner, and his knees. Warner saw his touchdown production drop from 12 scores in 1988 to only 4 in 1989. And now as a member of the Los Angeles Rams, his playing time is a big question.

30. O. J. Anderson (New York Giants)
Although he scored 14 times in 1989, I don't believe Anderson will again be the Giants' main back in 1990, which should really limit his touchdown potential.

KEEP AN EYE ON

31. Earnest Byner (Washington Redskins)
Byner scored nine touchdowns in 1989. His 1990 scoring potential rests a great deal on the health of Gerald Riggs and Kelvin Bryant, both of whom were injury-ridden in 1989.

32. Sammie Smith (Miami Dolphins)
Smith came on late in 1989, scoring all six of his touchdowns in the last six games.

33. Brent Fullwood (Green Bay Packers)
Fullwood is always a potential big scorer but continues to lack season-long consistency.

34. Roger Vick (New York Jets)
Vick's seven scores in 1989 demonstrate that the Jets are beginning to give him more scoring opportunities.

35. Dave Meggett (New York Giants)
His fantastic 56.2-yard average on five touchdowns in 1989 really opened some eyes.

36. Brad Muster (Chicago Bears)
In taking over the bulk of the fullback chores for the Bears in 1989, Muster scored eight times, a sign of things to come.

37. Alonzo Highsmith (Houston Oilers)
Highsmith carries plenty of scoring potential as the Oilers' "Big Back."

38. Albert Bentley (Indianapolis Colts)
Although he plays behind Eric Dickerson, Bentley should get some scoring chances. Remember, in 1987 he placed first by this scoring method.

39. Rueben Mayes (New Orleans Saints)
Are his knees healthy?

40. Anthony Toney (Philadelphia Eagles)
Has the potential to score often and do well in this scoring method.

PRIME PROSPECTS

41. Rozier (HOUS)
42. Winder (DEN)
43. Manoa (CLE)
44. Johnston (DALL)
45. Hoge (PITT)

46. Bryant (WASH)
47. Rathman (SF)
48. Perryman (NE)
49. Fenney (MINN)
50. White (HOUS)

DON'T BE SURPRISED

51. Logan (MIA)
52. Pinkett (HOUS)
53. Stradford (MIA)
54. Delpino (LARm)
55. Flagler (DALL)
56. B. Jordan (NO)
57. Carter (PITT)
58. Riddick (BUF)
59. Woodside (GB)
60. K. Jones (ATL)

YOU NEVER KNOW

61. Sewell (DEN)
62. Kinnebrew (BUF)
63. McGee (LARm)
64. McNeil (NYJ)
65. Bratton (DEN)
66. Wilder (WASH)
67. Hampton (DEN)
68. Ball (CIN)
69. St. Smith (LARd)
70. Anderson (MINN)

WORTH MENTIONING

71. T. Jordan (PHOE)
72. Jm. Morris (NE)
73. Howard (TB)
74. Heard (KC)
75. Heyward (NO)

76. Palmer (CIN)
77. Dozier (MINN)
78. Tillman (NYG)
79. Fontenot (GB)
80. Williams (PITT)

A LOOK AT THE WIDE RECEIVERS
(A Guide for the Beginner)

Considerations in Choosing a Wide Receiver

This method is like the Basic Scoring Method in that the player must score a touchdown to be awarded points. The difference is that a deep-threat receiver will be more valuable, since more points are awarded for the long touchdown play.

1. First, look at players' performance histories.

2. First priority is a receiver, preferably a speedy, deep-threat receiver from a predominantly passing team. Jerry Rice of San Francisco and Mark Clayton of Miami come to mind.

3. Look for rookie wide receivers who have a chance to start, especially if they're fast. Defenses pay little attention to rookies until they become established receivers. This certainly was the case for Brian Blades of Seattle in 1988, when he managed eight scores.

4. Opposing defenses try to clamp down on wide receivers who have just had a great year or consecutive good years.

5. Be leery of receivers on a team going through a quarterback change. If a wide receiver has had a few good years, much of the credit belongs to his timing with his quarterback. A new quarterback will require a period of adjustment, and during that time the wide receiver's productivity may fall off.

In the 1989 statistics, remember that the players are ranked by their fantasy-point totals. In the Distance Scoring Method fantasy points are calculated by the length of the touchdown play, with more points going for long touchdown plays.

NAME	TEAM	GP	TD PS	RSH	RSH TDs	AVG LGTH	PS REC	PS REC TDs	AVG LGTH	TOTAL TDs	AVG LGTH	1989 FAN-TASY PTS
1. Rice	SF	16	0	4	0	0.0	82	17	27.1	17	27.1	104
2. Taylor	SF	15	0	1	0	0.0	60	10	44.3	10	44.3	82
3. Miller*	SD	16	0	4	0	0.0	75	10	24.1	11	30.2	78
4. Slaughter	CLE	16	0	0	0	0.0	65	6	56.3	6	56.3	74
5. Sharpe*	GB	16	0	1	0	0.0	90	12	22.6	13	20.8	70
6. McGee	CIN	16	0	2	0	0.0	65	8	35.5	8	35.5	66
7. Fernandez	LARd	16	0	2	0	0.0	57	9	31.3	9	31.3	66
8. Clayton	MIA	15	0	2	0	0.0	64	9	30.7	9	30.7	64
9. Reed	BUF	15	0	2	0	0.0	88	9	29.4	9	29.4	62
10. Lipps	PITT	15	0	13	1	5.8	50	5	43.8	6	46.2	60
11. G. Clark	WASH	15	0	2	0	0.0	79	9	26.0	9	26.0	58
12. R. Johnson	DET	16	0	12	0	0.0	70	8	30.0	8	30.0	56
13. Carrier	TB	16	0	0	0	0.0	86	9	27.6	9	27.6	56
14. Anderson	LARm	14	0	1	0	0.0	44	5	44.4	5	44.4	50
15. Townsell	NYJ	15	0	0	0	0.0	45	5	43.6	5	43.6	48
16. Ellard	LARm	14	0	6	0	0.0	70	8	24.8	8	24.8	46
17. E. Martin	NO	16	0	1	0	0.0	68	8	23.5	8	23.5	46
18. Monk	WASH	16	0	3	0	0.0	86	8	23.4	8	23.4	46
19. J. Dixon*	DALL	11	0	3	0	0.0	24	2	55.0	3	69.0	44
20. Gault	LARd	12	0	0	0	0.0	28	4	45.8	4	45.8	40
21. Green	PHOE	11	0	0	0	0.0	44	7	33.1	7	33.1	40
22. Dr. Hill	HOUS	14	0	0	0	0.0	66	8	18.6	8	18.6	38
23. C. Carter	PHIL	14	0	1	0	0.0	45	11	11.5	11	11.5	38
24. V. Johnson	DEN	15	0	0	0	0.0	76	7	20.1	7	20.1	36
25. E. Brown	CIN	15	0	0	0	0.0	52	6	24.0	6	24.0	34
26. Duncan	HOUS	15	0	1	0	0.0	43	5	27.0	5	27.0	32
27. C. Jones	NE	14	0	1	0	0.0	48	6	20.2	6	20.2	32
28. E. Jones	PHOE	14	0	1	0	0.0	44	3	48.3	3	48.3	32
29. Haynes	ATL	11	0	4	0	0.0	40	4	32.0	4	32.0	30
30. Schwedes*	MIA	3	0	0	0	0.0	7	1	65.0	1	65.0	30
31. Sanders	WASH	16	0	4	0	0.0	80	4	34.0	4	34.0	30
32. Beebe+	BUF	9	0	0	0	0.0	17	2	63.0	2	63.0	28
33. A.B. Brown	MIA	11	0	0	0	0.0	24	5	23.4	5	23.4	28
34. Blades	SEAT	16	0	1	0	0.0	77	5	22.6	5	22.6	28
35. Verdin*	IND	12	0	3	0	0.0	20	1	82.0	2	65.5	28
36. Brooks	IND	15	0	1	0	0.0	63	4	26.0	4	26.0	26
37. Fryar	NE	10	0	2	0	0.0	29	3	38.7	3	38.7	26
38. Morgan	NE	9	0	1	0	0.0	28	3	34.7	3	34.7	24
39. Dykes+	NE	14	0	0	0	0.0	49	5	16.4	5	16.4	24
40. J.T. Smith	PHOE	9	0	1	0	0.0	62	5	17.2	5	17.2	24
41. Langhorne	CLE	15	0	4	0	0.0	60	2	47.0	2	47.0	22
42. Rison+	IND	16	0	1	0	0.0	52	4	21.5	4	21.5	22
43. Cox	LARm	7	0	0	0	0.0	20	3	30.7	3	30.7	22
44. A. Carter	MINN	16	0	2	0	0.0	65	4	21.8	4	21.8	22
45. Davis	CHI	12	0	0	0	0.0	27	3	27.7	3	27.7	20
46. L. Hill	NO	15	0	1	0	0.0	48	4	17.5	4	17.5	20
47. F. Dixon	ATL	10	0	1	0	0.0	25	2	39.5	2	39.5	18
48. Lofton	BUF	6	0	0	0	0.0	8	3	24.3	3	24.3	18
49. McKinnon	CHI	14	0	1	0	0.0	28	3	22.0	3	22.0	18
50. Jensen*	MIA	14	1	4	0	0.0	61	6	9.0	6	9.0	18
51. O. Turner	NYG	11	0	2	0	0.0	38	4	17.8	4	17.8	18
52. Skansi	SEAT	15	0	0	0	0.0	39	5	13.6	5	13.6	18
53. B. Hill	TB	14	0	0	0	0.0	50	5	10.4	5	10.4	18
54. Gentry	CHI	15	0	17	0	0.0	39	1	79.0	1	79.0	16

1989 STATISTICAL RESULTS
(Wide Receivers — Distance Scoring Method)

NAME	TEAM	GP	TD PS	RSH	RSH TDs	AVG LGTH	PS REC	PS REC TDs	AVG LGTH	TOTAL TDs	AVG LGTH	1989 FAN-TASY PTS
55. Irvin	DALL	5	0	1	0	0.0	26	2	35.0	2	35.0	16
56. Baker	NYG	10	0	0	0	0.0	13	2	37.0	2	37.0	16
57. Holmes	PHOE	9	0	0	0	0.0	14	1	77.0	1	77.0	16
58. Largent	SEAT	10	0	0	0	0.0	28	3	21.3	3	21.3	16
59. M. Jackson	DEN	14	0	5	0	0.0	28	2	28.5	2	28.5	14
60. Jeffires	HOUS	15	0	0	0	0.0	47	2	29.0	2	29.0	14
61. Paige	KC	14	0	0	0	0.0	44	2	29.0	2	29.0	14
62. Morris	CHI	14	0	1	0	0.0	29	1	58.0	1	58.0	12
63. R. Clark	DET	12	0	0	0	0.0	40	2	24.0	2	24.0	12
64. Phillips+	DET	11	0	0	0	0.0	31	1	55.0	1	55.0	12
65. Bland*	GB	7	0	0	0	0.0	11	1	46.0	2	46.0	12
66. Givins	HOUS	15	0	0	0	0.0	55	3	15.3	3	15.3	12
67. Toon	NYJ	11	0	0	0	0.0	63	2	24.5	2	24.5	12
68. F. Turner+	NO	11	0	2	0	0.0	22	1	54.0	1	54.0	12
69. Collins+	ATL	16	0	0	0	0.0	58	3	14.7	3	14.7	10
70. K. Smith+	CIN	7	0	0	0	0.0	10	1	41.0	1	41.0	10
71. K. Martin	DALL	11	0	0	0	0.0	46	2	18.5	2	18.5	10
72. Young	DEN	11	0	0	0	0.0	22	2	20.5	2	20.5	10
73. Harris+	HOUS	5	0	0	0	0.0	13	2	17.0	2	17.0	10
74. Banks	MIA	12	0	0	0	0.0	30	1	43.0	1	43.0	10
75. H. Jones	MINN	16	0	1	0	0.0	42	1	46.0	1	46.0	10
76. Ingram	NYG	10	0	1	0	0.0	17	1	41.0	1	41.0	10
77. Shepard**	DALL	10	0	2	0	0.0	20	1	37.0	1	37.0	8
78. Kemp	GB	14	0	4	0	0.0	48	2	15.5	2	15.5	8
79. R. Brown	LARm	8	0	6	0	0.0	5	1	39.0	1	39.0	8
80. Duper	MIA	13	0	0	0	0.0	49	1	35.0	1	35.0	8
81. Garrity	PHIL	13	0	0	0	0.0	13	2	14.0	2	14.0	8
82. F. Johnson	BUF	10	0	0	0	0.0	25	1	26.0	1	26.0	6
83. M. Martin	CIN	7	0	0	0	0.0	15	2	11.0	2	11.0	6
84. Tillman*+	CLE	6	0	0	0	0.0	6	2	12.0	3	8.0	6
85. Query+	GB	11	0	0	0	0.0	23	2	9.0	2	9.0	6
86. Harry	KC	12	0	1	0	0.0	33	2	8.5	2	8.5	6
87. R. Thomas+	KC	5	0	0	0	0.0	8	2	8.0	2	8.0	6
88. Lewis	MINN	7	0	0	0	0.0	12	1	28.0	1	28.0	6
89. Burkett**	NYJ	11	0	1	0	0.0	21	1	29.0	1	29.0	6
90. L. Clark	SEAT	11	0	0	0	0.0	25	1	27.0	1	27.0	6
91. Hillary	CIN	10	0	1	0	0.0	17	1	10.0	1	10.0	4
92. B. Ford	DALL	4	0	0	0	0.0	7	1	10.0	1	10.0	4
93. M. Alexander	LARd	9	0	0	0	0.0	15	1	12.0	1	12.0	4
94. Gustafson	MINN	9	0	0	0	0.0	14	2	5.0	2	5.0	4
95. Manuel	NYG	14	0	0	0	0.0	33	1	11.0	1	11.0	4
96. Quick	PHIL	6	0	0	0	0.0	13	2	5.0	2	5.0	4
97. R. Johnson	PHIL	9	0	0	0	0.0	20	1	13.0	1	13.0	4
98. Nattiel	DEN	6	0	0	0	0.0	10	1	5.5	1	5.5	2
99. Pruitt	IND	3	0	0	0	0.0	5	1	5.0	1	5.0	2
100. Mandley	KC	12	0	1	0	0.0	35	1	8.0	1	8.0	2
101. Dk. Hill+	PITT	15	0	0	0	0.0	28	1	7.0	1	7.0	2
102. Wn. Walker	SD	9	0	1	0	0.0	24	1	5.0	1	5.0	2
103. Wilson	SF	8	0	0	0	0.0	9	1	7.0	1	7.0	2
104. Drewrey	TB	9	0	0	0	0.0	14	1	6.0	1	6.0	2
105. Bailey	ATL	6	0	0	0	0.0	8	0	0.0	0	0.0	0
106. G. Thomas	ATL	3	0	0	0	0.0	4	0	0.0	0	0.0	0
107. Parker	CIN	1	0	0	0	0.0	1	0	0.0	0	0.0	0
108. Garrett	CIN	1	0	0	0	0.0	2	0	0.0	0	0.0	0

1989 STATISTICAL RESULTS
(Wide Receivers — Distance Scoring Method)

NAME	TEAM	GP	TD PS	RSH	RSH TDs	AVG LGTH	PS REC	PS REC TDs	AVG LGTH	TOTAL TDs	AVG LGTH	1989 FAN-TASY PTS
109. Kozlowski	CHI	3	0	0	0	0.0	3	0	0.0	0	0.0	0
110. Waddle	CHI	1	0	0	0	0.0	1	0	0.0	0	0.0	0
111. McNeil	CLE	7	0	0	0	0.0	10	0	0.0	0	0.0	0
112. Brennan	CLE	11	0	0	0	0.0	28	0	0.0	0	0.0	0
113. R. Alexander	DALL	1	0	0	0	0.0	1	0	0.0	0	0.0	0
114. Burbage	DALL	5	0	0	0	0.0	17	0	0.0	0	0.0	0
115. Gray	DET	3	0	0	0	0.0	2	0	0.0	0	0.0	0
116. Mobley	DET	5	0	0	0	0.0	13	0	0.0	0	0.0	0
117. T. Johnson	DET	2	0	0	0	0.0	2	0	0.0	0	0.0	0
118. Stanley	DET	11	0	0	0	0.0	24	0	0.0	0	0.0	0
119. McDonald	DET	4	0	1	0	0.0	12	0	0.0	0	0.0	0
120. J. Ford+	DET	3	0	0	0	0.0	5	0	0.0	0	0.0	0
121. Matthews	GB	10	0	0	0	0.0	18	0	0.0	0	0.0	0
122. K. Jackson	HOUS	3	0	0	0	0.0	4	0	0.0	0	0.0	0
123. Worthen+	KC	2	0	0	0	0.0	5	0	0.0	0	0.0	0
124. Weathers**	KC	8	0	0	0	0.0	23	0	0.0	0	0.0	0
125. T. Brown	LARd	1	0	0	0	0.0	1	0	0.0	0	0.0	0
126. S. Martin	NE	7	0	0	0	0.0	13	0	0.0	0	0.0	0
127. Robinson	NYG	2	0	0	0	0.0	4	0	0.0	0	0.0	0
128. Ws. Walker	NYJ	4	0	0	0	0.0	8	0	0.0	0	0.0	0
129. Harper	NYJ	3	0	0	0	0.0	7	0	0.0	0	0.0	0
130. Epps	NYJ	4	0	0	0	0.0	9	0	0.0	0	0.0	0
131. Perriman	NO	9	0	0	0	0.0	20	0	0.0	0	0.0	0
132. Williams	PHIL	3	0	0	0	0.0	4	0	0.0	0	0.0	0
133. Edwards	PHIL	1	0	0	0	0.0	2	0	0.0	0	0.0	0
134. Carson**	PHIL	6	0	0	0	0.0	9	0	0.0	0	0.0	0
135. McConkey	PHOE	2	0	0	0	0.0	2	0	0.0	0	0.0	0
136. Usher	PHOE	1	0	0	0	0.0	1	0	0.0	0	0.0	0
137. Thompson	PITT	3	0	0	0	0.0	4	0	0.0	0	0.0	0
138. Early	SD	4	0	0	0	0.0	11	0	0.0	0	0.0	0
139. Holland	SD	11	0	0	0	0.0	26	0	0.0	0	0.0	0
140. Allen	SD	2	0	0	0	0.0	2	0	0.0	0	0.0	0
141. Greer	SF	1	0	0	0	0.0	1	0	0.0	0	0.0	0
142. Kane	SEAT	4	0	0	0	0.0	7	0	0.0	0	0.0	0
143. Chadwick**	SEAT	7	0	0	0	0.0	8	0	0.0	0	0.0	0
144. Bouyer	SEAT	1	0	0	0	0.0	1	0	0.0	0	0.0	0
145. Peebles+	TB	7	0	0	0	0.0	10	0	0.0	0	0.0	0

+ DENOTES ROOKIES

* Miller	(SD)	—Scored TD on kickoff return of 91 yards.
* Sharpe	(GB)	—Scored TD on fumble recovery of 5 yards.
* J. Dixon	(DALL)	—Scored TD on kickoff return of 97 yards.
* Schwedes	(MIA)	—Scored TD on punt return of 70 yards.
* Verdin	(IND)	—Scored TD on punt return of 49 yards.
* Bland	(GB)	—Scored TD on fumble recovery.
* Tillman	(CLE)	—Scored TD on recovery of blocked punt.
** Shepard	(DALL)	—Played in 2 games with NO.
** Weathers	(KC)	—Played in 2 games with IND.
** Burkett	(NYJ)	—Played in 2 games with BUF.
** Carson	(PHIL)	—Played in 4 games with KC.
** Chadwick	(SEAT)	—Played in 1 game with DET.

RATING THE PLAYERS FOR 1990
(Wide Receivers—Distance Scoring Method)

GRAB ONE IF YOU CAN

1. Jerry Rice (San Francisco 49ers)
Four years running, Rice has been number one by this scoring method. Last year he averaged 27.1 yards on 17 scores. The year before, he averaged an unbelievable 47.9 yards on 10 touchdowns. He's just incredible.

2. Sterling Sharpe (Green Bay Packers)
One year doesn't usually make a player, but what a year it was. Sharpe recorded 90 receptions and averaged just over 20 yards on 13 touchdowns, establishing himself as a gifted receiver.

3. Mark Clayton (Miami Dolphins)
Clayton has been a top-10 finisher by this scoring method four out of the last five seasons, placing 2nd, 40th, 5th, 10th, and 8th, respectively. His 30.7-yard average on nine scores in 1989 proves he's still a real game breaker.

4. John Taylor (San Francisco 49ers)
As a rookie in 1988, Taylor placed sixth by this scoring method, averaging an unbelievable 78.3 yards on four touchdowns. In 1989 he upped his touchdown production to 10, averaging 44.3 yards on each, reason enough to give him prime fantasy consideration in 1990.

5. Anthony Miller (San Diego Chargers)
In only his second NFL season, Miller averaged 30.2 yards on 11 touchdowns. He has fast become one of league's more feared deep threats.

6. Eddie Brown (Cincinnati Bengals)
After averaging 44.0 yards on nine scores in 1988, while placing second by this scoring method, Brown saw his production drop off in 1989. He scored only six times, with a 24.0-yard average. I'm sure he'll rebound as one of Boomer Esiason's prime targets in 1990.

7. Henry Ellard (Los Angeles Rams)
In 1987 Ellard proved his big-play ability when scoring only three times but averaging 50.0 yards on each. Ellard then placed fifth by this scoring method, scoring 10 touchdowns in 1988, averaging 29.4 yards on each. In 1989 his touchdown production dropped to eight, but I think he can easily get back to healthier numbers in 1990.

8. Webster Slaughter (Cleveland Browns)
Slaughter has had two top-10 finishes by this scoring method in the last three seasons. In 1987 Slaughter finished eighth by this method, averaging 30.1 yards on seven touchdowns. Then his 56.3-yard average on six touchdowns in 1989 placed him fourth and reconfirmed his long-ball ability.

9. Andre Reed (Buffalo Bills)
Reed just seems to get better and better. His 88 receptions and nine touchdowns, with a lengthy 29.4 average, proved he has big deep-threat potential.

10. Louis Lipps (Pittsburgh Steelers)
Back in 1984 and 1985, when Lipps first came into the league, he placed third and first by this scoring method. Then came a two-year struggle with injuries. Lipps has returned to top-10 form the last two seasons, placing 3rd and 10th, respectively, a level of play he should maintain in 1990, if he stays free of injury.

BEST OF THE REST

11. Willie "Flipper" Anderson (Los Angeles Rams)
Anderson seems to be really coming into his own. Averaging 44.4 yards on five touchdowns in 1989, he gave us a glimpse of what he can do.

12. Ricky Sanders (Washington Redskins)
Sanders seems to be the best deep threat of the Redskins receivers, including Gary Clark and Art Monk. In 1988 he placed fourth by this scoring method, averaging 25.3 yards on 12 scores. In 1989 he dropped way off, scoring only four times. His touchdown members could easily rebound in 1990.

13. Mark Carrier (Tampa Bay Buccaneers)
In 1988 Carrier averaged 29.2 yards on five touchdowns. In 1989 he neared the top 10 by this scoring method (13th), averaging 27.6 yards on nine touchdowns, and his 86 receptions demonstrate that he's seeing the ball often enough to produce plenty of scores.

14. Drew Hill (Houston Oilers)
Although averaging only 18.6 yards on eight touchdowns in 1989, Hill is a proven big-play receiver. He has placed 10th, 24th, 10th, 6th, and 22nd by this scoring method over the past five years, respectively. As a prime target of Warren Moon in 1990, he should continue his success.

15. Tim McGee (Cincinnati Bengals)
Prior to 1989, Eddie Brown was the featured big-play receiver for the Bengals. But in '89, McGee went big-time, averaging over 35 yards on eight touchdowns, thus earning himself big consideration for your 1990 fantasy team.

16. Mark Duper (Miami Dolphins)
Top-10 showings by this scoring method in 1983 (fourth), 1984 (ninth), 1986 (third), and 1987 (seventh) prove his potential. However, if he is to rebound to prominence, he'll have to stay free of drugs and the injuries that have plagued him the last two years.

17. Al Toon (New York Jets)

Toon's best season by this scoring method came in 1986, when he averaged 34.9 yards on eight touchdowns, finishing sixth by this scoring method. He hasn't reached the top 10 since. In 1990 he hopes to rebound from the injuries that plagued him in 1989.

18. Mike Quick (Philadelphia Eagles)

Prior to two consecutive years of injuries, Quick was a top-11 finisher five consecutive years. He placed 1st, 11th, 2nd, 6th, and 3rd, respectively, by this scoring method from 1983 through 1987. His 1990 performance will depend heavily on his healthy return from the knee injury he suffered in 1989.

19. Gary Clark (Washington Redskins)

Clark has become a very consistent receiver, despite playing alongside the likes of Ricky Sanders and Art Monk. He has finished 4th, 24th, and 11th by this scoring method the last three seasons. Clark should fare well again in 1990.

20. Roy Green (Phoenix Cardinals)

Despite missing five games in 1989 with a fractured collarbone, Green managed seven touchdowns, averaging 33.1 yards on each. This shows he can still score on the long one. His potential remains if he can stay healthy.

STRONG LONG SHOTS

21. Eric Martin (New Orleans Saints)

Martin went from averaging only 13.3 yards on seven scores in 1988 to averaging 23.5 yards on eight touchdowns in 1989. As the Saints' leading receiver three consecutive years, he should continue to succeed.

22. Anthony Carter (Minnesota Vikings)

Carter is truly one of the league's foremost game breakers. In 1985 he placed seventh by this scoring method, averaging 36.1 yards on eight touchdowns. In 1987 he placed third by this method, with an astounding 43.1-yard average on seven scores, giving us an idea of his potential.

23. Mervyn Fernandez (Los Angeles Raiders)

In his best year since coming into the NFL, Fernandez scored nine times in 1989, averaging 31.3 yards. His success was partly due to Tim Brown's season-ending knee injury suffered in last year's season opener. Brown's healthy return could cut into Fernandez's 1990 success.

24. Richard Johnson (Detroit Lions)

We can expect more of the same from the Lion's run-and-shoot offense and Richard Johnson in 1990. In 1989 Johnson averaged 30.0 yards on eight touchdowns.

25. Brian Blades (Seattle Seahawks)

Blades saw his touchdown production drop in 1989 to only five scores, despite latching onto 77 receptions. As a rookie in 1988, Blades crossed the goal line eight times on only 40 receptions. With his reception level expected to stay up in 1990, his touchdown production should rebound.

26. Art Monk (Washington Redskins)

Monk is the least likely of Washington's trio of top receivers to break the long one. He has never been a top-10 finisher by this scoring method. His consistent ability to rack up receptions makes him a continued big-potential fantasy pick just the same.

27. Michael Irvin (Dallas Cowboys)

Irvin averaged 28.2 yards on five touchdowns as a rookie in 1988. Then in 1989 he was off to a good start, scoring twice in the early season and averaging a hefty 35.0 yards on each, until a knee injury knocked him out for the year. If he recovers, he could have a big 1990 season.

28. Tim Brown (Los Angeles Raiders)

Brown placed ninth by this scoring method as a rookie in 1988, averaging 40.3 yards on six touchdowns. A knee injury sidelined him early in 1989, but his healthy return should spell some healthy numbers in 1990.

29. Cris Carter (Philadelphia Eagles)

As a rookie in 1988, Carter averaged 36.2 yards on six scores, demonstrating his big-play ability. In 1989 he upped his touchdown level to 11, but the average on each was only 11.5 yards. I believe this happened because he became the Eagles' prime wideout when Mike Quick got hurt, and Quick's healthy return will dictate much of Carter's 1990 fate.

30. Vance Johnson (Denver Broncos)

Johnson finished in the top 10 by this scoring method once, in 1987 when he placed ninth and averaged 270 yards on seven scores in a shortened 12-game season. As the best and most consistent of the "amigos," Johnson should continue to score well.

KEEP AN EYE ON

31. Stephone Paige (Kansas City Chiefs)

In 1985 Paige placed 5th by this scoring method, averaging 31.2 yards on 10 scores. In the last couple of years his performances have slid, as in 1989, when he scored only two touchdowns. He'll have to recapture some of his scoring ways to rebound statistically in 1990.

32. Ernest Givins (Houston Oilers)

A one-time top-10 finisher by this method, Givins placed ninth in 1987. He needs more touchdowns.

33. J. T. Smith (Kansas City Chiefs)

Smith's not much of a big-play receiver, but his consistent receptions should make him a consideration for your fantasy team.

34. Reggie Langhorne (Cleveland Browns)

Langhorne placed ninth by this method in 1988 but fell way off in '89, scoring only twice, though averaging 47.0 yards on each.

35. Bruce Hill (Tampa Bay Buccaneers)

Hill placed 11th by this scoring method in 1988 before dropping way off in 1989.

36. Billy Brooks (Indianapolis Colts)
Brooks has fantasy promise as the Colts' most consistent receiver. And with Andre Rison off to Atlanta, Brooks should have increased opportunity.

37. Lionel Manuel (New York Giants)
His best finish came in 1987, when he placed 10th by this scoring method, averaging 31.2 yards on six scores. He lacks the consistency to make me believe that he can reach that level in 1990.

38. Andre Rison (Atlanta Falcons)
As a rookie in 1989, he gave us plenty of reason for giving him fantasy consideration in 1990, even though he'll be playing for the Atlanta Falcons this time around.

39. Irving Fryar (New England Patriots)
He averaged 38.7 yards on three touchdowns in 1989, but Fryar lacks scoring consistency.

40. Lonzell Hill (New Orleans Saints)
Hill's certainly a receiver with plenty of fantasy potential.

PRIME PROSPECTS

41.	C. Jones (NE)	46.	H. Jones (MINN)
42.	Morgan (NE)	47.	O. Turner (NYG)
43.	M. Jackson (DEN)	48.	Nattiel (DEN)
44.	Collins (ATL)	49.	Haynes (ATL)
45.	K. Martin (DALL)	50.	Gault (LARd)

DON'T BE SURPRISED   YOU NEVER KNOW

51.	Dykes (NE)	61.	F. Dixon (ATL)
52.	McKinnon (DALL)	62.	Jensen (MIA)
53.	E. Jones (PHOE)	63.	Skansi (SEAT)
54.	Townsell (NYJ)	64.	Baker (NYG)
55.	Verdin (IND)	65.	Jeffires (HOUS)
56.	Bailey (ATL)	66.	Morris (CHI)
57.	J. Dixon (DALL)	67.	Phillips (DET)
58.	Schwedes (MIA)	68.	Kemp (GB)
59.	R. Clark (DET)	69.	Tillman (CLE)
60.	Cox (LARm)	70.	Dk. Hill (PITT)

WORTH MENTIONING

71.	Wn. Walker (SD)	76.	Beebe (BUF)
72.	Duncan (HOUS)	77.	F. Turner (NO)
73.	A. B. Brown (MIA)	78.	Ingram (NYG)
74.	Lofton (BUF)	79.	Lewis (MINN)
75.	Gentry (CHI)	80.	Davis (CHI)

A LOOK AT THE TIGHT ENDS

(A Guide for the Beginner)

Considerations in Choosing a Tight End

The following list of recommendations resembles that for the Basic Scoring Method, except that here we must recognize the importance of the deep threat.

1. First, consider players' previous performances.

2. When choosing a tight end, first check on who his fellow receivers are. A tight end between two good wide receivers will often be left open while opponents double-cover the wide receivers. Such is the case in San Francisco, where Brent Jones is sandwiched between Jerry Rice and John Taylor.

3. Your second priority should be to pick up a good tight end from a predominantly passing team.

4. Any tight end who has the speed to sneak behind the defense for a long touchdown play will reward you with a lot of points. Kenny Jackson of Philadelphia and Ferrell Edmunds of Miami come to mind.

5. Consistency is common among tight ends. The ranks of the top tight ends seem to change little, with an occasional new name creeping onto the list. The Mark Bavaros, Steve Jordans, Mickey Shulers, and now Keith Jacksons always seem to top the list.

6. If a tight end is coming off an outstanding year, look for teams to double-cover him. This may choke off some of his productivity.

7. As with wide receivers, look for quarterback changes to have an adverse effect on a tight end. In a quarterback–tight end combination that has clicked well for many years, the departure of the quarterback is likely to reduce the tight end's productivity. This may explain why Phoenix tight ends Robert Awalt and Jay Novacek had such a dropoff in 1989, when Neil Lomax was unable to play.

In the 1989 statistics, the players have been ranked by their fantasy-point totals. Remember that in the Distance Scoring Method, fantasy points are calculated by touchdowns scored or thrown, with more points going for long scoring plays.

1989 STATISTICAL RESULTS
(Tight Ends — Distance Scoring Method)

NAME	TEAM	GP	TD PS	RSH	RSH TDs	AVG LGTH	PS REC	PS REC TDs	AVG LGTH	TOTAL TDs	AVG LGTH	1989 FAN-TASY PTS
1. Holman	CIN	16	0	0	0	0.0	50	9	24.9	9	24.9	52
2. Jones	SF	14	0	0	0	0.0	40	4	22.0	4	22.0	22
3. Dyal	LARd	14	0	0	0	0.0	27	2	44.5	2	44.5	20
4. Thornton	CHI	13	0	1	0	0.0	24	3	21.0	3	21.0	16
5. Giles	PHIL	8	0	0	0	0.0	16	2	34.5	2	34.5	16
6. Wilkins	ATL	6	0	0	0	0.0	6	3	20.3	3	20.3	14
7. West	GB	7	0	0	0	0.0	22	5	7.4	5	7.4	14
8. Brenner	NO	14	0	0	0	0.0	34	4	8.5	4	8.5	14
9. McKeller	BUF	12	0	0	0	0.0	20	2	25.0	2	25.0	12
10. D. Johnson	LARm	14	0	0	0	0.0	25	5	2.6	5	2.6	10
11. Holohan	LARm	16	0	1	0	0.0	51	2	19.0	2	19.0	10
12. Bavaro	NYG	6	0	0	0	0.0	22	3	16.3	3	16.3	10
13. Dressel**	NYJ	6	0	0	0	0.0	12	1	49.0	1	49.0	10
14. Bernstine	SD	5	0	15	1	32.0	21	1	1.0	2	16.5	10
15. Hall	TB	11	0	0	0	0.0	30	2	17.5	2	17.5	10
16. Kay	DEN	10	0	0	0	0.0	21	2	11.0	2	11.0	8
17. Edmunds	MIA	15	0	0	0	0.0	32	3	10.0	3	10.0	8
18. Neubert	NYJ	8	0	0	0	0.0	28	1	35.0	1	35.0	8
19. Jackson	PHIL	13	0	0	0	0.0	63	3	8.7	3	8.7	8
20. Heller	ATL	11	0	0	0	0.0	33	1	28.0	1	28.0	6
21. Didier	GB	6	0	0	0	0.0	6	1	24.0	1	24.0	6
22. Hayes	KC	9	0	0	0	0.0	18	2	9.0	2	9.0	6
23. Jordan	MINN	12	0	0	0	0.0	35	3	2.3	3	2.3	6
24. Cox	SD	13	0	0	0	0.0	22	2	8.5	2	8.5	6
25. Metzelaars	BUF	10	0	0	0	0.0	18	2	5.0	2	5.0	4
26. Folsom	DALL	13	0	0	0	0.0	28	2	4.5	2	4.5	4
27. Beach	IND	10	0	0	0	0.0	14	2	1.0	2	1.0	4
28. Boyer	IND	8	0	0	0	0.0	11	2	4.0	2	4.0	4
29. Junkin	LARd	2	0	0	0	0.0	3	2	2.0	2	2.0	4
30. Novoselsky	MINN	4	0	0	0	0.0	4	2	1.5	2	1.5	4
31. Cross+	NYG	3	0	0	0	0.0	6	1	16.0	1	16.0	4
32. J. Tice	NO	8	0	0	0	0.0	9	1	12.0	1	12.0	4
33. Mularkey	PITT	13	0	0	0	0.0	22	1	15.0	1	15.0	4
34. Beckman	ATL	5	0	0	0	0.0	11	1	3.0	1	3.0	2
35. Rolle	BUF	1	0	0	0	0.0	1	1	1.0	1	1.0	2
36. Boso	CHI	11	0	0	0	0.0	17	1	3.0	1	3.0	2
37. Newsome	CLE	13	0	0	0	0.0	29	1	4.0	1	4.0	2
38. Tennell	CLE	1	0	0	0	0.0	1	1	4.0	1	4.0	2
39. Middleton	CLE	1	0	0	0	0.0	1	1	5.0	1	5.0	2
40. Roberts	KC	7	0	0	0	0.0	8	1	2.0	1	2.0	2
41. Horton	LARd	4	0	0	0	0.0	4	1	1.0	1	1.0	2
42. Ingram+	MINN	2	0	0	0	0.0	5	1	2.0	1	2.0	2
43. Little	PHIL	2	0	0	0	0.0	2	1	1.0	1	1.0	2
44. Novacek	PHOE	12	0	0	0	0.0	23	1	2.0	1	2.0	2
45. Walls+	SF	4	0	0	0	0.0	4	1	1.0	1	1.0	2
46. Harris	TB	6	0	0	0	0.0	11	1	3.0	1	3.0	2
47. Warren	WASH	9	0	0	0	0.0	15	1	3.0	1	3.0	2
48. Kattus	CIN	7	0	0	0	0.0	12	0	0.0	0	0.0	0
49. Riggs	CIN	4	0	0	0	0.0	5	0	0.0	0	0.0	0
50. Jennings+	DALL	2	0	0	0	0.0	6	0	0.0	0	0.0	0

1989 STATISTICAL RESULTS
(Tight Ends — Distance Scoring Method)

NAME	TEAM	GP	TD PS	RSH	RSH TDs	AVG LGTH	PS REC	PS REC TDs	AVG LGTH	TOTAL TDs	AVG LGTH	1989 FAN-TASY PTS
51. Kelly	DEN	2	0	0	0	0.0	3	0	0.0	0	0.0	0
52. Mobley	DEN	8	0	0	0	0.0	17	0	0.0	0	0.0	0
53. Spagnola	GB	2	0	0	0	0.0	2	0	0.0	0	0.0	0
54. Mrosko+	HOUS	3	0	0	0	0.0	3	0	0.0	0	0.0	0
55. Verhulst	HOUS	3	0	0	0	0.0	4	0	0.0	0	0.0	0
56. Hardy	MIA	1	0	0	0	0.0	1	0	0.0	0	0.0	0
57. Kinchen	MIA	1	0	0	0	0.0	1	0	0.0	0	0.0	0
58. Sievers	NE	13	0	0	0	0.0	54	0	0.0	0	0.0	0
59. Cook+	NE	2	0	0	0	0.0	3	0	0.0	0	0.0	0
60. Dawson	NE	4	0	0	0	0.0	10	0	0.0	0	0.0	0
61. Mowatt	NYG	13	0	0	0	0.0	27	0	0.0	0	0.0	0
62. Shuler	NYJ	7	0	0	0	0.0	29	0	0.0	0	0.0	0
63. Griggs	NYJ	5	0	0	0	0.0	9	0	0.0	0	0.0	0
64. Dunn	NYJ	1	0	0	0	0.0	2	0	0.0	0	0.0	0
65. Werner	NYJ	3	0	0	0	0.0	8	0	0.0	0	0.0	0
66. Scales	NO	6	0	0	0	0.0	8	0	0.0	0	0.0	0
67. Awalt	PHOE	12	0	0	0	0.0	33	0	0.0	0	0.0	0
68. Reeves+	PHOE	1	0	0	0	0.0	1	0	0.0	0	0.0	0
69. O'Shea	PITT	1	0	0	0	0.0	1	0	0.0	0	0.0	0
70. Caravello	SD	5	0	0	0	0.0	10	0	0.0	0	0.0	0
71. McEwen	SD	3	0	0	0	0.0	7	0	0.0	0	0.0	0
72. Parker	SD	2	0	0	0	0.0	2	0	0.0	0	0.0	0
73. Williams	SF	1	0	0	0	0.0	3	0	0.0	0	0.0	0
74. Tyler	SEAT	8	0	0	0	0.0	14	0	0.0	0	0.0	0
75. McNeal+	SEAT	5	0	0	0	0.0	9	0	0.0	0	0.0	0
76. J. Johnson+	WASH	4	0	0	0	0.0	4	0	0.0	0	0.0	0
77. Orr	WASH	3	0	0	0	0.0	3	0	0.0	0	0.0	0
78. M. Tice	WASH	1	0	0	0	0.0	1	0	0.0	0	0.0	0

+ DENOTES ROOKIES

** Dressel   (NYJ)   —Played in 5 games with KC.

RATING THE PLAYERS FOR 1990
(Tight Ends—Distance Scoring Method)

GRAB ONE IF YOU CAN

1. Rodney Holman (Cincinnati Bengals)
The 1989 season marked the second time in five years that Holman ranked first by this scoring method. He has placed first, fifth, second, ninth, and first for those same five years, respectively. With the ability to get deep occasionally, Holman's consistent touchdown production makes him a prime fantasy prospect again in 1990.

2. Mark Bavaro (New York Giants)
Here is another consistent tight end by this scoring method. He placed seventh, eighth, first, and sixth from 1984 through 1988. Then because of a knee injury after just six games of 1989, he dropped to 10th. Imagine where he would have been had he not fallen victim to injury.

3. Keith Jackson (Philadelphia Eagles)
Jackson placed fourth by this scoring method as a rookie in 1988 on the strength of six touchdowns. But in 1989, slowed by back and knee injuries, Jackson's performance dropped well off. I believe he may currently be the league's best tight end, so I see his 1990 production rebounding in a big way.

4. Brent Jones (San Francisco 49ers)
Jones took over as the 49ers' starting tight end in 1989 and responded in good fashion. Grabbing 40 receptions—four for touchdowns—and averaging 22.0 yards, Jones has quickly established himself among Fantasy Football followers.

5. Ferrell Edmunds (Miami Dolphins)
As a rookie in 1988, Edmunds averaged an astounding 34.7 yards on three touchdowns. Although he again scored three times in 1989, Edmunds's average dropped to only 10.0 yards per score. I believe he may surpass the three-touchdown plateau in 1990, and he's certainly proved he can score a long one.

BEST OF THE REST

6. Ed West (Green Bay Packers)
West scored five touchdowns in 1989, despite missing much of the season with a knee injury. If he can remain healthy, his touchdown production could expand in 1990.

7. Mickey Shuler (New York Jets)
Until a knee injury sidelined him in 1989, Shuler had been one of the league's most consistent tight ends. In the five years prior to 1989 he finished eighth, second, eighth, fifth, and fifth by this scoring method, respectively, success I believe he'll return to if he's healthy in 1990.

8. Robert Awalt (Phoenix Cardinals)

Awalt placed third by this scoring method as a rookie in 1987 and first in 1988. Last year, possibly partly due to the loss of quarterback Neil Lomax, his performance dropped way off. I'm looking for a rebound in 1990, as the new Cardinal quarterbacks make their adjustments and with Jay Novacek now a member of the Dallas Cowboys.

9. Damone Johnson (Los Angeles Rams)

Though he may not score long touchdowns, Johnson's scoring consistency makes him a prime fantasy candidate. Johnson scored six and five touchdowns, respectively, in 1988 and 1989.

10. Steve Jordan (Minnesota Vikings)

Jordan has finished in the top 10 by this scoring method twice—first in 1986, averaging 24.0 yards on six touchdowns, and ninth in 1988, averaging only 6.0 yards on five scores. Playing on the very pass-oriented Vikings, he's sure to see plenty of aerials again in 1990, providing him many scoring opportunities.

STRONG LONG SHOTS

11. Rod Bernstine (San Diego Chargers)

Bernstine was well on his way to a big season in 1989 when a knee injury abruptly ended it after just five games. If he's healthy in 1990, perhaps we'll see where he was headed in 1989.

12. Hoby Brenner (New Orleans Saints)

Following a dismal 1988 season, when injuries played a role, Brenner rebounded to score four times on 34 receptions in 1989, characteristic of how he performs when healthy.

13. Jay Novacek (Dallas Cowboys)

After tying for first place by this scoring method with teammate Robert Awalt in 1988, Novacek's performance dropped way off in 1989. However, as a Dallas Cowboy in 1990, Novacek should see a rebound in his production.

14. Jim Thornton (Chicago Bears)

In 1989 Thornton's three touchdowns showed he can find his way into the end zone, and his 21.0-yard average shows he can also cover some ground.

15. Eric Sievers (New England Patriots)

Although he failed to score for New England in 1989, Sievers latched onto 54 receptions. A reception total like that proves his effectiveness and should create plenty of scoring opportunity.

HAVE THE POTENTIAL

16. Mike Dyal (Los Angeles Raiders)

Averaging 44.5 yards on two touchdowns in 1989 shows Dyal's downfield possibilities. And his 27 receptions show he's being looked at fairly often.

17. Clarence Kay (Denver Broncos)

Kay has placed 9th and 16th the last two years, scoring four and two touchdowns, respectively, in 1988 and 1989. Always a threat to score, Kay should do well again in 1990.

18. Pete Holohan (Los Angeles Rams)

Though he's caught only five touchdowns over the past two seasons, he has latched onto 110 receptions over that same period. Anybody catching the ball that often should get plenty of fantasy consideration.

19. Ron Hall (Tampa Bay Buccaneers)

In 1989, Hall averaged 17.5 yards on two touchdowns while grabbing 30 receptions—numbers he should be able to meet or beat in 1990.

20. Alex Higdon (Atlanta Falcons)

Don't forget about Higdon. Though he hasn't played since injuring his knee during the second game of the 1988 season, he has plenty of potential if he can return healthy.

KEEP AN EYE ON

21. Hayes (KC)
22. Beach (IND)
23. Mularkey (PITT)
24. Heller (SEAT)
25. Mobley (DEN)
26. Newsome (CLE)
27. Mowatt (NE)
28. Wilkins (ATL)
29. Giles (PHIL)
30. Boyer (NYJ)

YOU NEVER KNOW

31. J. Tice (NO)
32. Metzelaars (BUF)
33. Folsom (DALL)
34. Tennell (CLE)
35. McKeller (BUF)
36. Warren (WASH)
37. Dawson (NE)
38. Dressel (NYJ)
39. Cox (SD)
40. Boso (CHI)
41. Neubert (NYJ)
42. Junkin (LARd)
43. Walls (SF)
44. Jennings (DALL)
45. Ingram (MINN)

A LOOK AT THE QUARTERBACKS
(A Guide for the Beginner)

Considerations in Choosing a Quarterback

What factors should we bear in mind when selecting a quarterback?

1. First, consider a player's previous performances.

2. Next, does the quarterback's team like to put the ball in the air? The more a team throws the ball, the greater the chance that the quarterback will have a high-scoring year. The Dolphins' Dan Marino and San Francisco's Joe Montana are obvious early picks.

3. Look for a quarterback who likes to throw deep for those high-scoring, long-touchdown passes. Remember, the longer the touchdown, the more points awarded. A quarterback who has a proven deep-threat receiver among his targets is an asset to your team.

4. Next, we should consider quarterbacks who aren't afraid to run the ball in for a touchdown. This opens up an area of scoring possibilities not available to the gimpy-legged quarterback who stays in the pocket. Randall Cunningham of Philadelphia and John Elway of Denver come to mind.

5. If you start a quarterback who gets yanked after the first quarter or half of a game, your fantasy team will suffer. Stay away from teams that are struggling to find that weekly signal caller.

In the 1989 results, the players were ranked by the number of fantasy points they scored. Remember: In the Distance Scoring Method, fantasy points are calculated by touchdowns scored or thrown, with more points going for long scoring plays.

1989 STATISTICAL RESULTS
(Quarterbacks — Distance Scoring Method)

NAME	TEAM	GP	RSH TDs	TD PS	AVG LGTH	COMP	YARDS	AVG YARDS COMP	1989 FANTASY POINTS
1. Montana	SF	13	3	26	29.7	271	3,521	13.0	98
2. Kelly	BUF	13	2	25	27.2	228	3,130	13.7	84
3. Everett	LARm	16	1	29	22.0	304	4,310	14.2	83
4. Esiason	CIN	16	0	28	24.3	258	3,525	13.7	81
5. Majkowski	GB	16	5	27	19.1	353	4,318	12.2	78
6. Marino	MIA	16	2	25	23.1	308	3,997	13.0	72
7. Rypien	WASH	14	1	22	23.5	280	3,768	13.5	67
8. Kosar	CLE	16	1	18	30.5	303	3,533	11.7	66
9. Moon	HOUS	16	4	23	18.8	280	3,631	13.0	64
10. Elway	DEN	15	3	18	18.4	223	3,051	13.7	56
11. Tomczak	CHI	14	1	16	24.8	156	2,058	13.2	53
12. Miller*	ATL	15	0	16	24.7	280	3,459	12.4	52
13. Simms	NYG	15	1	14	30.1	228	3,061	13.4	52
14. Krieg	SEAT	15	0	21	16.8	286	3,309	11.6	49
15. Cunningham	PHIL	16	4	21	11.5	290	3,400	11.7	46
16. Hogeboom	PHOE	14	1	14	25.6	204	2,591	8.8	45
17. Gagliano	DET	11	4	6	44.0	117	1,671	14.3	40
18. Hebert	NO	13	0	15	20.1	222	2,686	12.1	40
19. Schroeder	LARd	10	0	8	43.4	91	1,550	17.0	39
20. Testaverde	TB	14	0	20	13.6	258	3,133	12.1	38
21. O'Brien	NYJ	15	0	12	26.2	289	3,356	11.6	37
22. Beuerlein	LARd	10	0	13	21.2	108	1,677	15.5	35
23. Trudeau	IND	13	2	15	13.9	190	2,317	12.2	33
24. Brister	PITT	14	0	9	30.9	187	2,365	12.6	32
25. Grogan	NE	7	0	9	26.7	133	1,697	12.8	28
26. McMahon	SD	12	0	10	22.1	176	2,132	12.1	28
27. Young	SF	9	2	8	24.3	64	1,001	15.6	28
28. Aikman+	DALL	11	0	9	25.3	155	1,749	11.3	27
29. De Berg	KC	12	0	11	16.4	196	2,529	12.9	24
30. Fourcade	NO	7	1	7	24.4	60	919	15.3	24
31. Harbaugh	CHI	11	3	5	19.4	111	1,219	10.9	23
32. W. Wilson	MINN	14	1	9	15.6	194	2,541	13.1	21
33. Peete+	DET	8	4	5	16.0	103	1,479	14.4	20
34. Tupa	PHOE	6	0	3	62.3	65	973	15.0	20
35. Reich	BUF	5	0	7	18.3	53	701	13.2	17
36. Wilhelm	CIN	5	0	4	32.8	30	425	14.1	16
37. Eason**	NYJ	5	0	4	30.8	79	1,016	12.9	16
38. Hostetler	NYG	5	2	3	22.7	20	294	14.7	15
39. Walsh+	DALL	8	0	5	21.0	109	1,362	12.5	13
40. Chandler	IND	3	1	2	52.0	39	537	13.8	13
41. Ferguson	TB	5	0	3	10.4	44	533	12.1	12
42. M. Wilson	NE	5	0	3	29.3	75	1,006	13.4	11
43. Kramer	MINN	7	0	7	9.4	77	906	11.8	10
44. Tolliver+	SD	5	0	5	8.8	89	1,097	12.3	8
45. Secules	MIA	4	0	1	44.0	22	286	13.0	5
46. Flutie	NE	5	0	2	17.5	36	490	13.6	5
47. Bono	SF	1	0	1	45.0	4	62	15.5	5
48. Pelluer	KC	4	2	1	5.0	26	301	11.6	4
49. Williams	WASH	4	0	1	34.0	51	585	11.5	4
50. Ryan	NYJ	4	0	1	23.0	15	153	10.2	3

1989 STATISTICAL RESULTS
(Quarterbacks — Distance Scoring Method)

NAME	TEAM	GP	RSH TDs	TD PS	AVG LGTH	COMP	YARDS	AVG YARDS COMP	1989 FANTASY POINTS
51. Pagel	CLE	4	0	1	14.0	5	60	12.0	2
52. Kubiak	DEN	5	0	2	3.0	32	284	8.9	2
53. Hipple	DET	1	1	0	0.0	7	90	12.9	2
54. Jaworski	KC	3	0	2	3.5	36	385	10.7	2
55. Cavanaugh	PHIL	4	0	1	13.0	3	33	11.0	2
56. Blackledge	PITT	3	0	1	14.0	22	282	12.8	2
57. Humphries	WASH	1	0	1	14.0	5	91	18.2	2
58. Millen	ATL	4	0	1	3.0	31	432	13.9	1
59. Ramsey	IND	6	0	1	1.0	24	280	11.7	1
60. Schonert	CIN	1	0	0	0.0	0	0	0.0	0
61. Long	DET	1	0	0	0.0	2	42	21.0	0
62. Carlson	HOUS	6	0	0	0.0	15	155	10.3	0
63. Herrmann	LARm	3	0	0	0.0	2	59	29.5	0
64. Evans	LARd	1	0	0	0.0	2	50	25.0	0
65. Mackey	NYJ	3	0	0	0.0	11	125	11.4	0
66. Malone	NYJ	1	0	0	0.0	2	13	6.5	0
67. Rosenbach+	PHOE	2	0	0	0.0	9	95	10.6	0
68. Strom	PITT	2	0	0	0.0	0	0	0.0	0
69. Archer	SD	3	0	0	0.0	5	62	12.4	0
70. Stouffer	SEAT	3	0	0	0.0	29	270	9.3	0

+ DENOTES ROOKIES

* Miller   (ATL) —Kicked a 25-yard field goal.
** Eason   (NYJ) —Played in 3 games with NE.

RATING THE PLAYERS FOR 1990
(Quarterbacks—Distance Scoring Method)

GRAB ONE IF YOU CAN

1. Joe Montana (San Francisco 49ers)
How consistent is Joe Montana by this scoring method? Skipping 1986, when he missed most of the season with a back injury, Montana has placed fourth, third, fourth, second, fourth, and first over the past seven years. Having receivers like Jerry Rice and John Taylor should help continue that success.

2. Jim Everett (Los Angeles Rams)
Everett has placed third by this scoring method two consecutive years. There are two reasons why he should continue that kind of success. First, he has led the league in touchdown passes two straight years with 31 and 29, respectively. The other reason: He has two speedy deep-threat wideouts in Henry Ellard and Willie "Flipper" Anderson.

3. Dan Marino (Miami Dolphins)
Marino is a very solid performer by this scoring method, placing first, third, fourth, sixth, and sixth, respectively, the last five seasons. If he can get Mark Duper back on track, to combine with Mark Clayton's efforts, he should easily continue his success.

4. Boomer Esiason (Cincinnati Bengals)
Esiason has twice been number one by this scoring method in the last five years, in 1985 and 1983. The other three seasons produced 7th-, 11th-, and 4th-place finishes. With targets like Eddie Brown, Tim McGee, Rodney Holman, and James Brooks in the backfield, 1990 should be another statistical success.

5. Randall Cunningham (Philadelphia Eagles)
Although he fell way off to 16th in 1990, Cunningham had placed 1st and 2nd, respectively, the previous two years. Part of his dropoff may have been due to the absence of Mike Quick, who missed most of the season with knee trouble. Quick's healthy return should help Cunningham's 1990 performance.

BEST OF THE REST

6. Warren Moon (Houston Oilers)
With targets like Drew Hill, Ernest Givins, Curtis Duncan, and Haywood Jeffires, it's no surprise that Moon has placed third, seventh, and ninth by this scoring method over the past three seasons, a success level I see continuing in 1990.

7. Jim Kelly (Buffalo Bills)

Prior to his 2nd-place finish by this scoring method in 1989, Kelly placed 19th and 20th the two previous years. His improvement was boosted by the deep-threat scoring of Andre Reed and the emergence of Thurman Thomas as a receiver (5 receiving touchdowns in 1989). These two receivers will help Kelly maintain his healthy standing in 1990.

8. Don Majkowski (Green Bay Packers)

Majkowski's 1989 performance was no less than fantastic. He threw for 27 touchdowns and ran for five more. Having Sterling Sharpe to throw to in 1990 should spell more success.

9. Mark Rypien (Washington Redskins)

Gary Clark, Ricky Sanders, and Art Monk are formidable deep threats. Throwing to these wideouts in 1989, Rypien tallied 22 touchdowns, which could have been more had he not been benched for two games. If he can retain the job all year in 1990, he should attain considerable success.

10. Bernie Kosar (Cleveland Browns)

Having wideouts like Webster Slaughter and Reggie Langhorne helped Kosar to a hefty 30.5-yard average on his 18 touchdown passes in 1989. Though that average may drop a bit in 1990, his touchdowns should climb over the 20 mark, which will help maintain his success.

STRONG LONG SHOTS

11. John Elway (Denver Broncos)

Although throwing to the likes of Vance Johnson, Ricky Nattiel, and Mark Jackson, Elway has been a top-10 finisher only twice in the last five years. Those performances came in 1987, when he placed 6th, and last year, when he finished 10th. With targets like the "three amigos," we must consider his top-10 potential.

12. Gary Hogeboom/Timm Rosenbach/Tom Tupa (Phoenix Cardinals)

Will Hogeboom, who started most of the Cardinals' games in 1989, continue to be their starter? Will the Cardinals turn to youth? Whoever gets the call will enjoy the talents of Roy Green, J. T. Smith, and Ernie Jones and company to throw to.

13. Dave Krieg/Kelly Stouffer (Seattle Seahawks)

After placing 2nd, 6th, 5th, and 7th, respectively, from 1984 through 1987, Krieg has dropped to 15th and 14th the last two years. Having a target like Brian Blades will help, but Krieg's biggest task will be fighting inconsistency and the challenge of Kelly Stouffer.

14. Phil Simms (New York Giants)

From 1984 through 1986, Simms ranked a consistent ninth, eighth, and eighth by this scoring method. Over the last three seasons his levels have again remained consistent, dropping to 15th, 14th, and 13th, respectively, a range I believe they'll be in in 1990.

15. Chris Miller (Atlanta Falcons)

Miller's touchdown production improved from 11 in 1988 to 16 in 1989. That improvement should continue as Miller and his young Falcons mature. They do face the league's toughest schedule in 1990, though.

HAVE THE POTENTIAL

16. Vinny Testaverde (Tampa Bay Buccaneers)

Though Testaverde improved, from 13 touchdown passes in 1988 to 20 in 1989, his 13.6-yard average proved that many of those scores didn't come on long plays. I expect him to continue his decent touchdown pace in 1990, which should place him somewhere in the same range.

17. Steve Beuerlein/Jay Schroeder (Los Angeles Raiders)

Targets like Mervyn Fernandez, Willie Gault, and Tim Brown provide long-ball potential. Either of these quarterbacks hanging onto the job for the whole season looms as a question mark in my mind.

18. Bubby Brister (Pittsburgh Steelers)

Although he threw for only nine touchdowns in 1990, Brister averaged 30.9 yards on each. A year earlier he averaged a very impressive 44.1 yards on 11 touchdown passes, while running for 6 more. With a target like Louis Lipps, Brister certainly has plenty of fantasy potential, but he has to stay free from injury and develop more consistency.

19. Ken O'Brien/Tony Eason (New York Jets)

Back in 1985 and 1986, Ken O'Brien ranked fifth and second by this scoring method, respectively. Over the past three seasons, due to a variety of reasons, he has seen his standing fall to 13th, 24th, and 21st. This makes me leery of O'Brien as a 1990 fantasy pick. And now he may have Tony Eason to compete with.

20. Andre Ware/Rodney Peete/Bob Gagliano (Detroit Lions)

The Lions feel they got the perfect man to run their run-and-shoot offense—Andre Ware. Though both Peete and Gagliano demonstrated reasonable success in 1989, Ware should become the Lions' number-one signal caller in short order.

KEEP AN EYE ON

21. John Fourcade/Bobby Hebert (New Orleans Saints)

Bobby Hebert relinquished his starting role to John Fourcade late in the 1989 season. Inconsistency and ineffectiveness led to Hebert's benching and Fourcade's appearance. Fourcade responded in strong fashion, leading the Saints to three wins in his three starts, while throwing for seven scores. Can Fourcade provide that kind of consistency in 1990 and hold onto the job?

22. Wade Wilson (Minnesota Vikings)
With targets like Anthony Carter and Hassan Jones, you would think that Wilson would fare much better, especially quarterbacking on a team that relies on the pass. But Wilson averaged only 15.6 yards, while throwing only nine touchdowns in 1989. Not very impressive.

23. Mike Tomczak/Jim Harbaugh (Chicago Bears)
Do you feel comfortable with either of these quarterbacks running your fantasy team? First of all, will either play consistently enough to hold onto the job all year? Second, because of their passing inconsistency, the Bears prefer to run the football.

24. Steve De Berg/Steve Pelluer (Kansas City Chiefs)
De Berg has to play well enough to hold the job, something he did only occasionally in 1989.

25. Billy Joe Tolliver (San Diego Chargers)
A target like Anthony Miller certainly helps in this scoring method. The question for me is, Can young Tolliver hold the job? He doesn't have to worry about a challenge from Jim McMahon anymore.

26. Jeff George/Chris Chandler/Jack Trudeau (Indianapolis Colts)
Chandler lost his job in 1989 when a knee injury abruptly ended his season. Another item that should again weigh heavily in the Colts' 1990 plans will be Eric Dickerson's running, which always limits a team's passing needs. However, the biggest question is about how long it will take the Colts' new 15-million-dollar man, Jeff George, to take over.

27. Troy Aikman (Dallas Cowboys)
Surely improvement is in store for both young Aikman and his Cowboys in 1990. Just how much raises a big question.

28. Steve Grogan/Marc Wilson/Doug Flutie (New England Patriots)
This situation won't unravel itself until much closer to the season's outset.

A LOOK AT THE KICKERS

(A Guide for the Beginner)

Considerations in Choosing a Kicker

1. First, look at players' histories.

2. A kicker needs scoring opportunities, and one of our main concerns is the team he's playing for. Get a kicker who plays for a team that consistently moves the ball deep into enemy territory.

3. Go for a kicker who has played for the same team for a few years. Kickers are treated as if they were a dime a dozen. If they have been with a team a few years, it's a sign of confidence in their consistency.

4. Look at the schedule to gauge the strength of the opposition a kicker will face in 1990. A soft schedule means a lot of points for a kicker. (See Section VI for 1990 schedules.)

5. A consideration that is unique to this method is the length of the field goal. If it comes to choosing between two kickers, go with the one who is more consistent from long distances.

In the 1989 statistics, the players have been ranked by their fantasy-point totals. Remember that in the Distance Scoring Method for kickers, fantasy points are calculated by the length of the field goal (see the following table), and one point is awarded for each successful extra point.

FIELD GOALS

0 – 9 yards... 1 point	40 – 49 yards... 5 points
10 – 19 yards... 2 points	50 – 59 yards... 6 points
20 – 29 yards... 3 points	60 – 69 yards... 7 points
30 – 39 yards... 4 points	70 & over......10 points

1989 STATISTICAL RESULTS
(Kickers — Distance Scoring Method)

NAME	TEAM	GP	EXTRA PTS	EXTRA PT ATT	ACC RATE	10-19	20-29	30-39	40-49	50-59	60 & OVER	FG	ATT	ACC RATE	1989 FANTASY POINTS
1. Coler	SF	16	49	50	.980	3/3	9/9	7/8	10/15	0/1	NA	29	36	.806	160
2. Lohmiller	WASH	16	41	42	.976	2/2	11/11	13/15	3/11	0/1	NA	29	40	.725	145
3. Norwood	BUF	16	46	48	.958	2/2	5/6	8/9	10/15	NA	NA	23	30	.767	143
4. Lansford	LARm	16	51	51	1.000	1/1	7/8	7/7	8/10	0/4	NA	23	30	.767	142
5. Karlis	MINN	13	27	28	.964	3/3	14/15	5/6	8/12	1/3	NA	31	39	.795	141
6. T. Zendejas	HOUS	16	40	40	1.000	1/1	8/9	9/14	5/11	2/2	NA	25	37	.676	139
7. Treadwell	DEN	16	39	40	.975	3/3	13/14	8/8	3/7	0/1	NA	27	33	.818	131
8. Lowery	KC	16	34	35	.971	1/1	6/6	10/15	6/8	1/3	NA	24	33	.727	130
9. Jacke+	GB	16	42	42	1.000	1/1	9/9	4/6	7/9	1/3	NA	22	28	.786	128
10. Davis**	ATL	15	26	28	.928	1/1	6/6	8/12	7/14	1/2	NA	23	34	.677	123
11. Murray	DET	16	36	36	1.000	NA	3/3	8/9	8/8	1/1	NA	20	21	.952	123
12. Jaeger	LARd	16	34	34	1.000	1/1	8/10	8/9	5/12	1/2	NA	23	24	.958	123
13. Igwebuike	TB	16	33	35	.943	NA	9/9	6/6	5/10	2/3	NA	22	28	.786	121
14. Andersen	NO	16	44	46	.956	NA	7/8	10/11	3/7	0/3	NA	20	29	.690	120
15. Anderson	PITT	16	28	28	1.000	2/2	5/5	5/8	9/15	NA	NA	21	30	.700	112
16. Biasucci	IND	16	31	33	.939	2/2	6/6	9/10	3/5	1/4	NA	21	27	.778	110
17. Stoyanovich+	MIA	16	38	39	.974	1/1	8/8	5/6	4/8	1/3	NA	19	26	.731	110
18. M. Bahr	CLE	16	40	40	1.000	NA	5/5	6/8	4/9	1/2	NA	16	24	.667	105
19. Allegre	NYG	10	23	24	.958	NA	6/6	8/9	5/9	1/2	NA	20	26	.769	104
20. Butler	CHI	16	43	45	.956	NA	6/6	6/7	3/5	0/1	NA	15	19	.789	100
21. Del Greco	PHOE	16	28	29	.966	NA	7/7	5/6	5/11	1/2	NA	18	26	.692	100
22. C. Bahr	SD	16	29	31	.935	NA	6/6	6/9	4/6	1/4	NA	17	25	.680	97
23. L. Zendejas**	DALL	15	33	33	1.000	1/1	3/3	4/6	6/12	0/2	NA	14	24	.583	88
24. Johnson	SEAT	16	27	27	1.000	1/1	6/7	3/4	4/8	1/5	NA	15	25	.600	85
25. Leahy	NYJ	16	29	30	.967	1/1	6/7	4/5	3/7	0/1	NA	14	21	.667	80
26. McFadden	ATL	9	18	18	1.000	1/1	4/4	6/7	2/6	2/2	NA	15	20	.750	78
27. Ruzek**	PHIL	14	28	29	.966	2/2	3/4	6/10	2/5	0/1	NA	13	22	.591	75
28. Staurovsky	NE	7	14	14	1.000	NA	4/4	5/7	4/5	1/1	NA	14	17	.823	72
29. Breech	CIN	12	37	39	.949	NA	9/9	3/4	0/1	1/1	NA	12	14	.857	46
30. Nittmo	NYG	6	12	13	.923	NA	4/5	5/5	0/2	1/2	NA	9	12	.750	44
31. Gallery	CIN	4	13	13	1.000	NA	1/1	0/1	1/4	0/1	NA	3	6	.333	21
32. Deline	PHIL	3	3	3	1.000	NA	1/1	1/2	2/5	NA	NA	3	7	.429	17
33. Garcia	MINN	3	8	8	1.000	NA	NA	1/4	2/5	0/1	NA	2	5	.200	12
34. Miller	ATL	1	0	0	.000	NA	1/1	NA	NA	NA	NA	1	1	1.000	3

+ DENOTES ROOKIES
** Davis (ATL) — Played in 9 games with NE.
** L. Zendejas (DALL) — Played in 8 games with PHIL
** Ruzek (PHIL) — Played in 9 games with DALL

RATING THE PLAYERS FOR 1990
(Kickers—Distance Scoring Method)

GRAB ONE IF YOU CAN

1. Mike Cofer (San Francisco 49ers)
Cofer has placed third and first by this scoring method the last two years, respectively. Although his kicking from beyond 40 yards has been less than impressive (18 of 31—.581—over the last two years), I believe the 49ers will continue to provide enough scoring opportunity to keep Cofer's stats healthy.

2. Scott Norwood (Buffalo Bills)
Norwood has been highly ranked by this scoring method, placing first and third for the past two years, respectively. His 16 of 25 (.640) on field-goal attempts from beyond 40 yards isn't exceptional, but has been sound enough to maintain his solid standing.

3. Tony Zendejas (Houston Oilers)
Zendejas has placed fifth, fourth, and sixth by this scoring method over the past three seasons. During that period the Oilers have shown they are not afraid to let Zendejas try the long one. He has hit 5 of 7 (.714) attempts from beyond 50 yards. Long-distance success like this should help him maintain his healthy production in 1990.

4. Mike Lansford (Los Angeles Rams)
Lansford continues to fare well by this scoring method. In 1988 he finished fourth and in 1989, seventh. Although he missed all 5 of his attempts from beyond 50 yards during that period, he hit 14 of 20 (.700) between 40 and 49 yards. That should help him continue his success in 1990.

5. Nick Lowery (Kansas City Chiefs)
You can't argue with consistent success. Over the past seven seasons, Lowery has placed fifth, sixth, sixth, ninth, eighth, sixth, and eighth, respectively, by this scoring method. Kicking for the improving Chiefs, he'll do well again in 1990.

BEST OF THE REST

6. Chip Lohmiller (Washington Redskins)
Although Lohmiller placed second by this scoring method in 1989, and the Redskins face the league's sixth easiest schedule, I'm somewhat leery of rating Lohmiller any higher for 1990. His 3-of-12 (.250) performance on field-goal attempts beyond 40 yards in 1989 is a big reason for my skepticism.

7. David Treadwell (Denver Broncos)
You have to be impressed with Treadwell's overall 1989 performance—27 of 33 field-goal attempts for a hefty .818 kicking percentage. Although he hit only 3 of 8 (.375) kicks from beyond 40 yards, his accuracy inside the 40 was an astounding 24 of 25 (.960). That should provide him continued success in 1990.

8. Eddie Murray (Detroit Lions)
In 1989, Murray couldn't miss from anywhere, almost! Murray hit all nine of his attempts from beyond 40 yards, including one from beyond 50 yards. For the season, he hit an incredible 20 of 21 (.952) field-goal attempts. The only thing he needs for 1990 is more scoring opportunities provided by the Lion offense.

9. Rich Karlis (Minnesota Vikings)
Karlis came on to kick for the Vikings in the last 13 games of 1989. He had an outstanding year, hitting 8 of 12 (.667) field-goal attempts from beyond 40 yards and 1 of 3 (.333) beyond 50. I expect him to realize success again in 1990, perhaps dropping a few notches because the Vikings and Atlanta face the league's toughest schedules.

10. Gary Anderson (Pittsburgh Steelers)
For Anderson, 1989 marked the first year in seven that he missed finishing in the top 10 by this scoring method. The previous six years he finished 4th, 5th, 1st, 10th, 6th, and 5th, respectively. That's consistency that shouldn't be ignored, and I see Anderson, kicking for an improving Pittsburgh team, climbing back in or near the top 10 in 1990.

STRONG LONG SHOTS

11. Morten Andersen (New Orleans Saints)
Andersen saw his accuracy and his standing fall in 1989. Prior to '89, Andersen had placed 2nd, 7th, 1st, and 10th, respectively, by this scoring method. During those four years Andersen was a very accurate long-distance kicker. He hit 30 of 38 (.789) attempts from 40 to 49 yards and 9 of 20 (.450) from beyond 50 yards. In 1989 he hit only 3 of 7 (.429) from 40 to 49 yards and 0 of 3 from beyond 50. He'll have to improve in 1990 to climb back in or near the top 10.

12. Chris Jacke (Green Bay Packers)
The Packers have to be very pleased with their rookie's 1989 kicking performance. After they struggled with four different kickers in 1988, Jacke's 22 of 28 (.786) field-goal attempts were welcome. His 7 of 9 (.778) from 40 to 49 yards and 1 of 3 (.333) from beyond 50 yards proved he's also got some distance in his leg. The Packers and I look for 1990 to put him in or near a top-10 standing.

13. Dean Biasucci (Indianapolis Colts)
Biasucci enjoyed two successful years in a row by this scoring method, placing second in 1987 and 1988. In 1989 that standing fell way off. His incredible long-range accuracy produced 13 of 16 (.813) field-goal attempts from 40 to 49 yards and 8 of 11 (.727) from beyond 50 yards in '87 and '88. A dropoff in that accuracy played a big part in Biasucci's 1989 demise. He hit on only 3 of 5 (.600) attempts from 40 to 49 yards and on 1 of 4 (.250) from beyond 50 yards.

14. Raul Allegre (New York Giants)
A leg injury forced Allegre to miss six games in 1989. I expect a healthy return to put Allegre in this range in 1990, since his long-distance accuracy—16 of 39 (.410) field-goal attempts beyond 40 yards over the past four seasons—is not impressive.

15. Donald Igwebuike (Tampa Bay Buccaneers)
Igwebuike has placed 15th, 22nd, 18th, 18th, and 13th, respectively, by this scoring method over the past five seasons. His hitting 2 of 3 attempts from beyond 50 yards in 1989 gives us an idea of his range. The Bucs face the league's second easiest schedule in 1990, and Igwebuike should continue to realize success.

HAVE THE POTENTIAL

16. Pete Stoyanovich (Miami Dolphins)
A groin injury to Fuad Reveiz was the stepping stone for Stoyanovich to become the Dolphin's kicker in 1989. Although his long-range accuracy is lacking—only 5 of 11 (.454) field-goal attempts from beyond 40 yards—he did hit an impressive 14 of 15 (.933) inside the 40. If he can improve a bit on his long-range kicking in 1990, working for the Dolphins should bring him continued success.

17. Kevin Butler (Chicago Bears)
There's a definite parallel between the rise and fall of the Bears and the productivity of Kevin Butler. Back in 1985 and 1986, Butler ranked third and second. Over the past three seasons Butler's standing has dropped to 11th, 21st, and 20th, respectively, as the Bears have dropped as a team. I don't see a drastic improvement in 1990.

18. Matt Bahr (Cleveland Browns)
Not including 1987, when he was out most of the year injured, Bahr has placed 14th, 20th, 24th, 20th, 12th, and 18th, respectively, over the past seven years. I see more of the same in 1990, as the Browns face the league's third toughest schedule.

19. Jim Breech (Cincinnati Bengals)
Will Breech be back in 1990? The Bengals released him in 1989 but brought him back five games into the season. He only attempted one kick from beyond 40 yards, which he missed, but his overall 12-of-14 (.857) kicking performance was a pleasant surprise for Cincinnati.

20. Jeff Jaeger (Los Angeles Raiders)
Although Jaeger improved to 12th place by this scoring method in 1989, from 22nd place as a rookie for the Browns in 1987, I don't believe he'll fare that well in 1990. Jaeger and the Raiders face the league's seventh toughest schedule in 1990.

KEEP AN EYE ON

21. Paul McFadden/Greg Davis (Atlanta Falcons)
McFadden missed seven games of the 1989 season due to a thigh injury, which led to the signing of Davis. Either will have trouble realizing any huge success because the Falcons face the league's toughest schedule in 1990.

22. Pat Leahy (New York Jets)
Leahy and the Jets face the league's easiest schedule, but I lost confidence in the Jet offense in 1989.

23. Norm Johnson (Seattle Seahawks)
Since hitting 5 of 7 (.714) field-goal attempts from beyond 50 yards in 1986, Johnson has hit only 1 of 6 (.167) since. He was also successful on only 4 of 8 (.500) attempts from 40 to 49 yards in 1989. It looks like he's losing his range.

24. Luis Zendejas (Dallas Cowboys)
Besides his kicking for the young Cowboys, Zendejas's long-range accuracy—he hit only 6 of 14 (.429) attempts from beyond 40 yards in 1989—makes me leery.

25. Jason Staurovsky (New England Patriots)
Staurovsky's 12 of 14 (.857) field-goal attempts in 1989 was quite impressive, but I'd like to see him do that over a longer stretch. The Pats' being in a big turnover mode doesn't excite me either.

26. Al Del Greco (Phoenix Cardinals)
Although Phoenix will face the league's eighth easiest schedule, Del Greco's field-goal percentages of .571 and .692 over the past two seasons may not suffice to maintain his job.

27. Roger Ruzek (Philadelphia Eagles)
The Eagles face the league's fourth easiest schedule, which is good. Ruzek's long-range field-goal kicking has me skeptical, though. In 1989 he hit only 6 of 10 (.600) from 30 to 39 yards and 2 of 5 (.400) from 40 to 49 yards, and he missed his only attempt from beyond 50 yards.

28. Chris Bahr/Fuad Reveiz (San Diego Chargers)
The Chargers face the league's third easiest schedule, but they've said Bahr will not be re-signed for 1990 kicking duties. If they go with a proven veteran you may want to move him up quite a few notches. Fuad Reveiz is one veteran who'll be in camp.

A 1990 MOCK DRAFT
(My Top-16 Overall Picks for the Distance Scoring Method)

NAME	TEAM	POSITION
1. Jerry Rice	San Francisco 49ers	Wide Receiver
2. Neal Anderson	Chicago Bears	Running Back
3. Barry Sanders	Detroit Lions	Running Back
4. Eric Dickerson	Indianapolis Colts	Running Back
5. James Brooks	Cincinnati Bengals	Running Back
6. Dalton Hilliard	New Orleans Saints	Running Back
7. Sterling Sharpe	Green Bay Packers	Wide Receiver
8. Mark Clatyon	Miami Dolphins	Wide Receiver
9. Greg Bell	Los Angeles Rams	Running Back
10. Thurman Thomas	Buffalo Bills	Running Back
11. Eric Metcalf	Cleveland Browns	Running Back
12. Herschel Walker	Minnesota Vikings	Running Back
13. John Taylor	San Francisco 49ers	Wide Receiver
14. Randall Cunningham	Philadelphia Eagles	Quarterback
15. Ickey Woods	Cincinnati Bengals	Running Back
16. Bobby Humphrey	Denver Broncos	Running Back

At the top, Jerry Rice gives you both long-distance capabilities and consistent scoring.

The next group of five running backs—Neal Anderson, Barry Sanders, Eric Dickerson, James Brooks, and Dalton Hilliard—should provide plenty of touchdowns and the potential to break the long one.

Sterling Sharpe and Mark Clayton also have the potential for big touchdown numbers, some of which should come on long passes.

Greg Bell provides consistent short-range scores.

The next four choices—Thurman Thomas, Eric Metcalf, Herschel Walker, and John Taylor—are all potential big-play touchdown scorers.

Quarterback Randall Cunningham can score on the ground as well as through the air.

Ickey Woods, trying to rebound from a 1989 knee injury, should be a big scoring threat again, if he's healthy.

Bobby Humphrey showed plenty of breakaway potential and should be a big scoring threat for the Broncos.

XI
RATING OPPOSING NFL DEFENSES:
WHO ARE YOUR PLAYERS UP AGAINST?

Once you've selected your fantasy team, the opposing defensive statistics will prove useful in determining which players to start in a given game.

If you have three good running backs and can only play two, decide which two to play based on the defenses they'll face. If one of the three will face a team very strong against the run, the choice is simple—bench him and play the other two. The same holds true for selecting a quarterback. Look for the defense that is weak against the pass or has allowed more passing touchdowns.

Defenses change. In recent years the Chicago Bears, New York Giants, and Minnesota Vikings have gotten plenty of attention. Going into the '90s, some other formidable defenses are starting to come together. The Kansas City Chiefs and the New Orleans Saints placed first in defense against the pass and the rush, respectively, in 1989. When these teams are playing well defensively, they are to be avoided. Since the stats I'm providing are based on last year's defenses, they'll be useful for only the first few games of 1990. To evaluate current NFL defenses, you must know how they're doing week to week. Read a publication that documents the current defensive standings. This will definitely help in selecting your fantasy lineup.

In the following charts I have listed the defensive rankings according to touchdowns allowed via the pass or rush and according to yardage allowed via the pass or rush. The defensive touchdown statistics will show fantasy owners who use the Basic or Distance Scoring Method which teams are toughest to score against via the pass or run. The defensive yardage stats will help fantasy teams playing the Performance Point Method to judge which teams are harder to move the ball against via passing and rushing.

The best defenses—the teams tough to score on or pick up yardage against—are on top and the easier defenses are toward the bottom. Obviously, the higher a defense rates, the less eager you will be to start a player against it.

These statistics show us which defenses were hardest to score on in 1989. Therefore, if your league uses the Basic or Distance Scoring Method and you have to choose between two quarterbacks, one playing against the New York Jets and the other facing the Buffalo Bills, choose the one facing the Jets; they allowed 31 passing touchdowns in 1989, compared to only 14 allowed by the Bills.

How about making a choice between two running backs, one playing the Cleveland Browns and the other facing the Atlanta Falcons? This should be an easy choice because the Browns allowed only 8 rushing touchdowns in 1989, compared to the 25 that the Falcons allowed. Choose the player facing the Falcons.

If your league uses the Performance Point Method or one similar, choosing between a quarterback facing the Los Angeles Rams, who allowed an average of 268.8 passing yards per game in 1989, and one facing the Kansas City Chiefs, who allowed an average of only 176.2 passing yards a game, the choice would be easy.

Deciding between two running backs, one facing the stingy New Orleans Saints defense (which allowed only 82.8 rushing yards per game in 1989) and one facing the Phoenix Cardinals (who allowed an average of 149.3 rushing yards) would also be simple. Use the back who'll be running against the more porous Phoenix defense.

1989 NFL DEFENSES
RUSHING TOUCHDOWNS ALLOWED

(For Leagues Using the Basic and Distance Scoring Methods)

TEAM	RUSHING TDs ALLOWED
1. Philadelphia	6
2. Cleveland	8
3. Washington	8
4. Cincinnati	9
5. Kansas City	9
6. San Francisco	9
7. Indianapolis	10
8. New Orleans	10
9. NY Giants	10
10. Denver	11
11. Seattle	11
12. LA Rams	12
13. Phoenix	12
14. San Diego	12
15. Minnesota	14
16. Buffalo	15
17. Green Bay	15
18. LA Raiders	15
19. NY Jets	16
20. Pittsburgh	16
21. Dallas	17
22. Detroit	18
23. Tampa Bay	18
24. Miami	18
25. Houston	19
26. New England	19
27. Chicago	21
28. Atlanta	25

1989 NFL DEFENSES
PASSING TOUCHDOWNS ALLOWED

(For Leagues Using the Basic and Distance Scoring Methods)

TEAM	PASSING TDs ALLOWED
1. Denver	12
2. Buffalo	14
3. Indianapolis	15
4. NY Giants	15
5. San Diego	15
6. San Francisco	15
7. Kansas City	16
8. Pittsburgh	17
9. LA Raiders	18
10. Minnesota	18
11. Atlanta	19
12. Detroit	19
13. Cleveland	20
14. Chicago	21
15. Dallas	21
16. Miami	21
17. Cincinnati	22
18. Green Bay	22
19. New Orleans	23
20. Seattle	23
21. LA Rams	24
22. Phoenix	24
23. Washington	25
24. Philadelphia	26
25. New England	27
26. Houston	28
27. Tampa Bay	29
28. NY Jets	31

1989 NFL DEFENSES
RUSHING YARDAGE ALLOWED

(For Leagues Using the Performance Point Method)

TEAM	RUSHING YARDS ALLOWED	AVG YARDS ALLOWED PER GAME
1. New Orleans	1,326	82.8
2. Washington	1,350	84.3
3. San Francisco	1,359	84.9
4. NY Giants	1,529	95.5
5. LA Rams	1,546	96.6
6. Philadelphia	1,593	99.5
7. Detroit	1,611	100.6
8. Houston	1,662	103.8
9. Cleveland	1,670	104.3
10. Minnesota	1,716	107.2
11. Buffalo	1,737	108.5
12. Kansas City	1,769	110.5
13. Denver	1,791	111.9
14. Chicago	1,897	118.5
15. San Diego	1,913	119.5
16. LA Raiders	1,921	120.0
17. New England	1,978	123.6
18. Green Bay	2,008	125.5
19. Pittsburgh	2,008	125.5
20. Tampa Bay	2,034	127.1
21. Miami	2,045	127.8
22. Indianapolis	2,067	129.1
23. Dallas	2,084	130.2
24. Seattle	2,113	132.0
25. NY Jets	2,135	133.4
26. Phoenix	2,390	149.3
27. Atlanta	2,471	154.4
28. Cincinnati	3,252	203.2

1989 NFL DEFENSES
PASSING YARDAGE ALLOWED

(For Leagues Using the Performance Point Method)

TEAM	PASSING YARDS ALLOWED	AVG YARDS ALLOWED PER GAME
1. Kansas City	2,820	176.2
2. Minnesota	3,003	187.6
3. Detroit	3,193	199.5
4. Denver	3,201	200.0
5. San Diego	3,311	206.9
6. LA Raiders	3,321	207.5
7. Seattle	3,332	208.2
8. Cincinnati	3,383	211.4
9. NY Giants	3,427	214.1
10. Buffalo	3,495	218.4
11. Cleveland	3,520	220.0
12. Green Bay	3,553	222.0
13. San Francisco	3,559	222.4
14. Tampa Bay	3,663	228.9
15. Philadelphia	3,721	232.0
16. Pittsburgh	3,721	232.5
17. Atlanta	3,737	233.5
18. Dallas	3,748	234.2
19. Phoenix	3,794	237.1
20. Miami	3,811	238.1
21. Houston	3,817	238.5
22. Washington	3,875	242.1
23. New England	3,905	244.0
24. Indianapolis	3,918	244.8
25. NY Jets	4,035	252.1
26. Chicago	4,079	254.9
27. New Orleans	4,222	263.8
28. LA Rams	4,302	268.8

Although these stats can be useful as guidelines, choosing your starting lineup is rarely a cut-and-dried situation. If you have a hot player, you may want to go with him no matter what. This requires a feel for the game. With time and experience you'll become good at it.

XII
HELPFUL HINTS FOR
VARIATIONS ON THE GAME

DRAFTING A COACH

Each team drafts a coach as an eighth player and is awarded three points when its coach's team wins. The strategy is simple: Choose the coach you feel will win the most games. For help in making your selection, take a look at Section VI in this chapter, which gives you last year's team standings.

DRAFTING A TEAM DEFENSE

Another variation uses a whole team's defense as an eighth scorer. Points are awarded for every touchdown scored by interception (6 points) or fumble recovery (6 points) and for every safety (2 points). When selecting a defense, look for opportunistic teams that score on their opponents' mistakes. To aid you in selecting a team defense, I'll do two things. First I'll list last year's defensive fantasy-point totals. Then I'll give you a listing of how the NFL's opportunistic defenses have done over the past three seasons. This cumulative look should give you a better feel for the consistent defensive performers.

TEAM DEFENSIVE RANKING FOR 1989

TEAM	INTER-CEPTIONS for TDs	FUMBLES RUN IN for TDs	SAFETIES	FANTASY POINTS
1. Minnesota	2	4	2	40
2. Cleveland	4	2	0	36
3. LA Raiders	3	2	1	32
4. Denver	2	2	1	26
5. NY Jets	2	2	1	26
6. Washington	3	0	3	24
7. Philadelphia	2	1	1	20
8. Dallas	0	3	0	18
9. Indianapolis	2	1	0	18
10. LA Rams	3	0	0	18
11. New Orleans	2	0	3	18
12. NY Giants	2	0	2	16
13. Tampa Bay	2	0	2	16
14. Kansas City	0	2	1	14
15. Phoenix	2	0	1	14
16. Cincinnati	1	1	0	12
17. Detroit	1	1	0	12
18. San Diego	0	2	0	12
19. Green Bay	0	1	1	8
20. Atlanta	0	1	0	6
21. Buffalo	1	0	0	6
22. Chicago	1	0	0	6
23. New England	1	0	0	6
24. Pittsburgh	0	1	0	6
25. San Francisco	0	1	0	6
26. Seattle	0	1	0	6
27. Houston	0	0	2	4
28. Miami	0	0	1	2

TEAM DEFENSIVE RANKING
3-YEAR CUMULATIVE
(1987, 1988, 1989)

TEAM	INTER-CEPTIONS for TDs	FUMBLES RUN IN for TDs	SAFETIES	FANTASY POINTS
1. LA Rams	8	4	2	76
2. Cleveland	6	5	0	66
3. Denver	6	4	3	66
4. Pittsburgh	6	3	2	58
5. Kansas City	4	5	1	56
6. LA Raiders	5	3	2	52
7. Minnesota	4	4	2	52
8. New England	4	3	1	56
9. San Francisco	5	2	0	42
10. Washington	4	2	3	42
11. Atlanta	2	4	1	38
12. Dallas	3	3	0	36
13. NY Jets	2	3	3	36
14. San Diego	2	3	3	36
15. Buffalo	1	4	2	34
16. Philadelphia	2	3	2	34
17. Tampa Bay	3	2	2	34
18. Chicago	3	1	2	28
19. NY Giants	4	0	2	28
20. New Orleans	3	0	5	28
21. Cincinnati	2	2	1	26
22. Indianapolis	2	2	1	26
23. Houston	0	3	2	22
24. Detroit	2	1	1	20
25. Phoenix	2	1	1	20
26. Seattle	2	1	0	18
27. Green Bay	1	1	1	14
28. Miami	0	0	1	2

SUDDEN-DEATH TIE BREAKER

If you use the sudden-death tie-breaker option, here's a little strategy:

OPTION #1: This option has changed this year. In previous years, any player scoring a single point in overtime would break the tie. This meant that if a kicker booted just one extra point, the tie would be broken. It made sense, then, to place your kicker at the top of your reserves. It was almost automatic that the kicker would break the tie.

But that rule has changed somewhat. The rule now states that when a kicker is used as a reserve, he can only break the tie if he kicks a field goal. This, as explained in the rule section (see Chapter 2), better reflects true NFL overtimes. With this change, the strategy for listing the order of reserves may also change. I see the kicker as still the best choice, but the quarterback has gained considerable importance as a reserve player. Is your kicker more likely to kick a field goal than your quarterback is to throw a touchdown pass? Slightly. A decent quarterback having an average season throws around 20 touchdown passes, and a respectable kicker having an average season will have a field-goal total somewhere in the mid-20s. So, I recommend choosing a kicker before a quarterback when choosing the order of reserves. A quarterback would be a good second choice, though, followed by your best six-point players.

OPTION #2: Another option is to break a tie by adding the scores of all the players on each team's reserve list. If, after you have tabulated each team's reserves, the score remains tied, the teams revert to the sudden-death tie breaker. In that case, the advice listed above under option #1 can be used here, too.

PLAYER AUCTIONING

This drafting method adds another dimension to the strategy of player selection. Here's what's important:

- You'll probably be able to afford only one high-priced player, so he should be someone who will assure you of a productive season. Only a few players in the league are worth big money. Make sure you know who they are! (See my picks for the top 10 in each scoring method.)

- Try to find unpublicized players with good potential, since they will cost you less. This will enable you to save money so that you can outbid others for more sought-after players.

PLAYOFF REDRAFTING

After watching NFL games for the 16-game regular season, you should have a good feel for which players are playing well. The trick is to select from teams you feel will go the furthest in the playoffs, since players can only produce points for as long as they play. Study the 12 teams in the playoffs to determine which have the best chance of making it to the Super Bowl, then select players according to your basic drafting strategy.

WEEKLY OFFICE POOLS

When you play Fantasy Football in a weekly office pool, here are a few things to keep in mind as you draft:

- Don't draft an injured player! Get a weekly football magazine, which will have the player injuries listed.

- Keep player statistics up to date, so you know who's playing well.

- Follow the drafting strategy for the scoring method your pool uses.

CHAPTER 2

FANTASY FOOTBALL BASICS

OPTIONS TO HELP TACKLE
THE NEW NFL SCHEDULE EXPANSION
FORMING A LEAGUE
PLAYING THE GAME
RULE CHANGES
OR ADDITIONS FOR 1990

Again last year I received many letters
and suggested rules from Fantasy Football participants. A number of them
were well thought out and may help
fantasy leagues, so I'm again going to
incorporate some of these changes into
this year's book. To identify them, look
for the text highlighted by stars (★★★)
in this chapter.

OPTIONS TO HELP TACKLE
THE NFL SCHEDULE EXPANSION

Based on all the phone calls and letters I received in the offseason, the foremost thing on most fantasy participants' minds is how to handle the new NFL schedule. The NFL proposes a 16-game schedule, to be played over 17 weeks in 1990 and 18 weeks thereafter, causing havoc in Fantasy Football leagues. No longer will all 28 teams play every weekend. After filtering the many suggestions sent my way, I'm sharing with you what I feel will best maintain the game's concept as we know it.

I have a few good starting points for you and I welcome ideas from you and your league. They will help me better address the problem in next year's book. Next year's changes will be even more involved because the 16-game schedule will be played over 18 weeks. I'll address that situation then. These suggestions deal with the immediate problems the schedule presents for 1990.

Tackling the New NFL Schedule

SCHEDULING OPTION #1 (for leagues of 10 or fewer teams)

With smaller leagues, you have more options because you have more players from whom to choose.

1. ROSTER
Expand your original roster from 15 to 20 players.

2. WEEKLY LINEUP SIZE
Maintain the seven-player starting lineup.

3. WEEKLY GAMES
Fantasy teams are allowed to field NFL players only from teams that are playing that week (which is why I don't like this method). For instance, in week #4 you would field from your 15-member fantasy roster a 7-member team of players who are playing that week. If you have Jerry Rice, and the San Francisco 49ers are not playing that week, Rice can't be used. You have to choose from your roster another wide receiver who does play that week.

Leagues using this method should be limited to 10 or fewer teams, because each team has to have at least two starting quarterbacks and two place kickers. Each franchise should be sure not to draft both of its quarterbacks or both of its kickers from the same division. Because the NFL has scheduled its byes divisionally, a fantasy team that concentrates its players in a single division might not be able to field a certain position if both of its players are off at the same time.

Option #1's Good Points:
This option maintains the immediacy that we fantasy participants have become accustomed to.

Option #1's Drawbacks:
The prime reason I don't care for this option is that there will be one or two weeks when you won't be able to field your top player(s). Worse yet, depending on the NFL schedule, you may be without a quarterback or other player because it just happens that none of your players from that position play that week.

SCHEDULING OPTION #2 (for leagues of any size)

This option provides both immediate results and much of the playing tradition that our fantasy leagues are used to. It is the option my league will use because it's the least confusing and easiest to use.

1. ROSTER
No changes are necessary.

2. WEEKLY LINEUP SIZE
Maintain the seven-player weekly lineup.

3. WEEKLY GAMES
In all the schedules in this book, the first 16 weeks of the 17-week NFL season are used. Weekly scores are tabulated as usual, but if a fantasy player doesn't play on a given week he can be put in the lineup before the previous week's game, with that week's performance counting for both weeks. For instance, after all 28 NFL teams have played three weeks into the 1990 season, teams begin to get byes. If one of your prime players is scheduled to bye on week #4 because his team is off that week, you can insert him for week #4 the previous week. His week-#3 performance is used for both week #3 and week #4. Commissioners should be prepared in week #3 to begin taking lineups for week #3 and week #4.

If a player who doesn't play on week #4 isn't listed for week #4 the previous week (week #3), his points cannot be used. Another player who **IS** playing must be used for week #4. The benefit for fantasy leagues is immediate weekly results. All fantasy games end on the same weekend.

4. SUDDEN-DEATH TIE BREAKERS
Commissioners, please note: For players not playing in a given week, the previous week's performances are used. This means that all players on NFL teams that bye on a given week **MUST** be inserted the previous week. This ensures that all players are given a spot on the following week's lineup card. Commissioners should insist on getting a positive comment from every Fantasy Franchise as to where in the following week's lineup it wants players that bye the following week. **Any team not heard from must omit from its lineup players who bye that week.**

5. LINEUP CHANGES

Lineup changes in this option are twofold. First, concerning the week at hand, only one lineup change is allowed after the weekly lineup is submitted. Second, regarding players who are submitted one week to account for a bye the next week, one lineup change is allowed. Remember, this change must be made before the player's previous week's game has started.

EXAMPLE: If a player is submitted to play on both week #4 and week #5, and his NFL team byes on week #5, he may be replaced for either week until game time of week #4. Remember, one lineup change is allowed for the current week and another for the next week's players. If a player is replaced in the next week's lineup because of a bye, this **DOES NOT** count as the following week's lineup change. So, two lineup changes are allowed per week—one change in the current lineup and one change among the players submitted the previous week.

6. TRADE NIGHT

A weekly trade night is allowed, and the standard guidelines apply. The trade deadline does not change.

7. SCHEDULING

See the appropriate scheduling formats in Section III of this chapter.

8. PLAYOFFS

See the appropriate playoff formats in Section III of this chapter.

Option #2's Good Points:
This procedure provides both immediate weekly results and much of the playing tradition that our fantasy leagues are used to.

Option #2's Drawbacks:
This option's only drawback is that a player's performance may count for two games, even if he plays poorly.

Tackling the New NFL Schedule

SCHEDULING OPTION #3 (for leagues of any size)

Although this option has its drawbacks, it continues my league's playing tradition. It's complicated, but the year's outcome is decided more or less as it was in years past.

1. ROSTER

Expand the roster from 12 players, or whatever your league currently uses, by two additional players.

2. WEEKLY LINEUP SIZE

Maintain the seven-player weekly lineup.

3. WEEKLY GAMES

A fantasy game begins when the first NFL teams begin their games for that week. The fantasy game ends when all 28 NFL teams finish play for that week.

EXAMPLE: If only 24 of the 28 NFL teams meet on week #4 of the NFL season, the fantasy teams with players from the four teams that don't play won't have their final scores until the following week. That makes for a long wait, but at least all fantasy teams will always be able to use all their players. On fantasy week #5 all fantasy teams from your league submit their lineups. The scores for the week-#5 fantasy games are tabulated using only the players on the teams that are playing their fifth NFL game. The rest of the points are tallied the following week, when the rest of the league finishes their fifth game. It's a little difficult for the commissioners, but they'll grow into it.

The season continues like this, with fantasy teams submitting their weekly lineups for whatever game will begin that week. When the first NFL team to play its seventh game begins to play, that is the kickoff for fantasy week #7. When the final NFL team plays its seventh game, fantasy week #7 ends. Included in the NFL schedule in the back of this book is a number in parentheses that indicates which game of the season it is for each NFL team. This should help commissioners in determining and updating game scores and in taking lineups. I recommend that commissioners show, in the league's weekly newsletter, the current standings, final scores of completed games, scores of games in progress, and how many players each team has left to play in those games that are still in progress.

Please note: Eventually you'll end up with 4 teams or so that haven't yet byed on a given week. The other 12 games with the other 24 teams won't be played until the following week, when you'll have your fantasy game results.

4. LINEUP CHANGES

Any fantasy team that has submitted its lineup may change any player from any position with another player, as long asneither player's NFL game has been played. If you submit your week-#10's starting lineup on week #10, and one of your running backs doesn't play until the following week, you can replace him up to game time, if you have a running back who also will play his week-#10 game on week #11. (This can be done in addition to the one lineup change allowed in section VIII of this chapter.) So, each fantasy team is allowed one lineup change in the first week of action and one additional change of a player who doesn't play in a given week's game until the following week.

5. TRADE NIGHT

A weekly trade is allowed. Once the season has started, trade nights must be numbered (trade #1, trade #2, and so on), and the following rule applies: A player picked up in a trade does not officially become a member of your fantasy team until his NFL team plays its game whose number equals the trade number plus one.

- Any player picked up on a trade night can be used for the following weekend's games if that player is playing in an NFL game that week.

- No player picked up by a fantasy team can be used on a given weekend if he is playing in the NFL game from the previous week.

EXAMPLE: Assume that James Brooks of Cincinnati is acquired on the trade night following week #5 (trade #5), and the Bengals drew a bye on week #5. Their NFL game #5 is therefore actually being played on week #6. A player acquired in trade #5 cannot join a new fantasy squad until his NFL team plays its sixth game (5 + 1 = 6), so Brooks cannot be used until week #7, when the Bengals play their sixth game. If Brooks is picked up in trade #5, and the Bengals did not bye that week, he officially joins his new fantasy squad without having to wait a week.

6. TRADE DEADLINE

I recommend keeping the trade deadline at midseason, after which you can use the Player-Addition Draft and Playoff-Expansion Draft. (See the appropriate sections for details.)

7. SCHEDULING

See the appropriate scheduling formats in Section III of this chapter.

8. PLAYOFFS

See the appropriate playoff formats in Section III of this chapter.

Option #3's Good Points:

Not many. It will probably get confusing; that's why I highly recommend Game Option #2. If, however, you have a strong distaste for carrying a player's stats over from one week to the next and making them count for two games, Game Option #3 might be worth trying.

Option #3's Drawbacks:

In many cases, you're forced to wait until the following week for game results. And sometimes playoff formats must be altered.

NOTE

I highly recommend that commissioners review the consequences of this new scheduling format. Address all of your rule issues, including lineups, lineup changes, weekly games, roster transactions, scheduling, and playoff format. Prepare carefully for this season because it presents new situations. And again, please feel free to send me your suggestions. I will certainly look them over for ideas to share with other Fantasy Football participants.

THE FUNDAMENTAL CONCEPT

- A group of 4 to 16 football fans get together to form a fantasy league. Each member of the group is awarded a franchise for the team he will put together.

- The newly founded league selects a commissioner and decides on an amount for a franchise entry fee.

- A predetermined schedule is set up or selected so the teams can meet in head-to-head competition.

- The commissioner organizes a fantasy draft where each franchise owner selects scoring players such as quarterbacks, running backs, receivers, and place kickers. These player selections are made from actual NFL player rosters.

- Trading and picking up players is allowed after the draft; all such transactions are subject to the trade guidelines and deadlines of the league.

- Each franchise submits its weekly starting lineup, before the franchises meet in head-to-head competition.

- Following the scoring method selected by the league, the weekly results of scores and standings are determined and posted or mailed out to each franchise by the commissioner.

- The season culminates with playoffs and a Fantasy Bowl, using a predetermined playoff structure as a guideline.

I
FORMING A FANTASY LEAGUE

1. NUMBER OF FRANCHISES:
   Any number of franchises from 4 to 16 can be used in forming a fantasy league. Staying with an even number of franchises, however, makes scheduling for your league easier.

2. ENTRY FEES:
   Another item to touch on when forming your league is whether to have an entry fee. It is totally up to the league franchises whether to set up some kind of wager system. There are many leagues that do have some sort of payoff system for the season's winners; there also are many leagues, especially those involving young members, that play the game just for fun.

II
THE LEAGUE COMMISSIONER

1. RESPONSIBILITIES:
   A. Coordinating draft day
   B. Keeping league standings and statistics
   C. Logging trade transactions
   D. Logging weekly team lineups
   E. Serving as league treasurer

2. TERM OF OFFICE:
   The length of time served by the commissioner should be determined by a vote of all the franchise owners, with the majority ruling. NOTE: In many leagues the commissioner serves until he no longer wants the job.

3. FEES:
   As an added incentive for taking and keeping the job, the commissioner is usually paid a fee by the league. NOTE: One good form of compensation for a commissioner's services is for him to be exempt from paying the initial franchise fees.

4. OPTIONS:
   If the opportunity presents itself, the ideal situation would be to have someone who is not a franchise owner serve as your commissioner. Finding someone to agree to this won't be easy but will prevent many hassles.

III
LEAGUE SCHEDULING

1. NUMBER OF TEAMS IN YOUR LEAGUE:

Obviously, your league scheduling will depend upon the number of franchises (teams) you wish to have in your league. There are a few things to consider in selecting the number of teams you will allow in your league. The first thing is how much time your commissioner wishes to spend with league involvement. Don't overload him to the point at which he personally won't enjoy the game. I have 16 teams in the league for which I serve as commissioner, and I often wish I could cut back to 12 or even 10. In the leagues I'm familiar with, the most common number of teams is either 8 or 10.

Another consideration is the availability of quarterbacks. Each team usually drafts two NFL starting quarterbacks, one as the starter and the other one as the reserve in case of injury. There are only 28 NFL teams, so if you have more than 14 Fantasy Football league franchises, some of your franchises will be without an NFL starting quarterback as a reserve.

Finally, I would like to emphasize that it would be much better to go with an even number of teams. This would provide far easier scheduling and no byes. Most Fantasy Football players are too addicted to the game to survive a bye.

2. SCHEDULING FOR LEAGUES OF VARIOUS SIZES:

The first consideration you should have in devising a schedule is that there are 16 games in the regular NFL season. If you decide to have playoffs in your league, you would have to shorten your regular season to, let's say, 12 or 14 games and then use the remaining weeks for your playoffs.

★★

Another major consideration is the now-expanded 16-game NFL schedule, to be played over 17 weeks in 1990 and 18 weeks thereafter. See the beginning of this chapter and the scheduling instructions below for suggestions on tackling this issue.

★★

You will be drafting players from all 28 NFL teams. Once the 16-game NFL regular season is complete, only the members from the NFL playoff teams will continue playing. This means that if you want all the players for your NFL teams to participate in your playoffs, these playoffs must take place before the end of the 16-game NFL regular season. Again, your playoffs would occur sometime during the last four weeks, depending upon how many of your teams will be involved in them.

In the event you decide not to have playoffs and a yearly Fantasy Bowl, you can just play the full 16-game schedule and declare that the winner is the fantasy franchise with the best record.

The following pages demonstrate various scheduling options for leagues with various numbers of teams:

FOUR-TEAM LEAGUE

REGULAR SEASON:
Play a 15-game regular season. Teams play each other five times. (Two teams have seven home games, and the other two have eight.)

PLAYOFFS:
The top two teams after 15 games advance to the Fantasy Bowl, which is played during week #17. A bye is observed in week #16 by leagues using Scheduling Option #1 or #2. Leagues using Scheduling Option #3 must use week #16 to wait for every NFL team to complete its 15th game of the season. (For determining who should advance based on record, see Section IV, Playoffs .)

Key: 1. Read down for week #.
2. Read across top for team # and then down for opponents.
3. The asterisk (*) indicates a home game for the team heading the column.

FOUR-TEAM LEAGUE

Team #	1	2	3	4
Week #				
1	2	1*	4*	3
2	3*	4*	1	2
3	4*	3	2*	1
4	2	1*	4	3*
5	3	4*	1*	2
6	4	3	2*	1*
7	2*	1	4	3*
8	3*	4*	1	2
9	4*	3	2*	1
10	2	1*	4	3*
11	3	4*	1*	2
12	4	3	2*	1*
13	2*	1	4	3*
14	3*	4*	1	2
15	4	3	2*	1*
	Scheduling Options #1 and #2		Scheduling Option #3	
16	Bye		Complete Game #15	
17	Fantasy Bowl		Fantasy Bowl	

SIX-TEAM LEAGUE

REGULAR SEASON:
Play a 15-game regular season. Teams play each other three times each. (Three teams have seven home games, and the other three have eight.)

PLAYOFFS:
The top two teams after 15 games advance to the Fantasy Bowl, which is played during week #17. A bye is observed in week #16 by leagues using Scheduling Option #1 or #2. Leagues using Scheduling Option #3 must use week #16 to wait for every NFL team to complete its 15th game of the season. (For determining who should advance based on record, see Section IV, Playoffs.)

Key: 1. Read down for week #.
     2. Read across top for team # and then down for opponents.
     3. The asterisk (*) indicates a home game for the team heading the column.

SIX-TEAM LEAGUE

Team #	1	2	3	4	5	6
Week #						
1	2*	1	4*	3	6*	5
2	3*	6*	1	5*	4	2
3	4	5	6	1*	2*	3*
4	5	3*	2	6	1*	4*
5	6*	4	5*	2*	3	1
6	2	1*	4	3*	6	5*
7	3	6	1*	5	4*	2*
8	4*	5*	6*	1	2	3
9	5*	3	2*	6*	1	4
10	6	4*	5	2	3*	1*
11	2*	1	4*	3	6*	5
12	3*	6*	1	5*	4	2
13	4	5	6	1*	2*	3*
14	5	3*	2	6	1*	4*
15	6*	4	5*	2*	3	1
	Scheduling Options #1 and #2			Scheduling Option #3		
16	Bye			Complete Game #15		
17	Fantasy Bowl			Fantasy Bowl		

EIGHT-TEAM LEAGUE

REGULAR SEASON:

Play a 14-game regular season. Teams play each other twice. (Each team has seven home games.)

For Scheduling Options #1 and #2, the regular fantasy season is over at the end of week #14. For Scheduling Option #3, the regular fantasy season of 14 games is not actually over until the end of week #15, by which time every NFL team will have played 14 games.

PLAYOFFS:

Following the 14-game regular season, the top four teams are seeded 1 through 4, as determined by their records. The #1 seed would be the team with the best record, and so on. Then during the first round of the playoffs (held during week #16), the schedule would have seed #1 vs. seed #4 and seed #2 vs. seed #3. The winners of round one would advance to the Fantasy Bowl during week #17. (For determining who should advance based on record, see Section IV, Playoffs.)

Leagues using Scheduling Options #1 or #2 should have a league-wide bye during week #15. Leagues using Scheduling Option #3 must use week #15 to wait for every NFL team to complete its 14th game of the season.

Key: 1. Read down for week #.
2. Read across top for team # and then down for opponents.
3. The asterisk (*) indicates a home game for the team heading the column.

EIGHT-TEAM LEAGUE

Team #	1	2	3	4	5	6	7	8
Week #								
1	2*	1	4*	3	6*	5	8*	7
2	3*	4*	1	2	8	7*	6	5*
3	4	8*	6*	1*	7	3	5*	2
4	5	6	8	7*	1*	2*	4	3*
5	6*	5*	7*	8	2	1	3	4*
6	7	3	2*	5	4*	8*	1*	6
7	8*	7	5	6*	3*	4	2*	1
8	2	1*	4	3*	6	5*	8	7*
9	3	4	1*	2*	8*	7	6*	5
10	4*	8	6	1	7*	3*	5	2*
11	5*	6*	8*	7	1	2	4*	3
12	6	5	7	8*	2*	1*	3*	4
13	7*	3*	2	5*	4	8	1	6*
14	8	7*	5*	6	3	4*	2	1*

	Scheduling Options #1 and #2	Scheduling Option #3
15	Bye	Complete Game #14
16	Playoffs	Playoffs
17	Fantasy Bowl	Fantasy Bowl

TEN-TEAM LEAGUE

DIVISIONS:
Split league into two divisions of five teams each.

REGULAR SEASON:
Play a 13-game regular season. Play each of the four other teams within the division twice, for eight games, each team being home once. Then play the teams in the other division once each for the other five games. (Five teams will have six home games, and the other five will have seven.)

With Scheduling Options #1 and #2, the regular fantasy season is over at the end of week #13. For leagues using Scheduling Option #3, the 13-game regular fantasy season does not actually end until week #14, by the end of which every NFL team will have played 13 games.

PLAYOFFS:
The top three of the five teams in each division advance to the playoffs. For week #15, the first-place teams in each division would be awarded byes. The second- and third-place teams would play, with the winner advancing to play the first-place team for the division title during week #16. The two winners advance to the Fantasy Bowl in week #17. To simplify the assignment of team numbers and divisions, we will designate the divisions by using the suits in a deck of cards. (For determining who should advance based on record, see Section IV, Playoffs.)

Note that leagues using Scheduling Option #1 or #2 should take a league-wide bye in week #14. Leagues using Scheduling Option #3 must use week #14 to wait for every NFL team to complete its 13th game of the season.

Key: 1. Read down for week #.
2. Read across top for team # and then down for opponents.
3. The asterisk (*) indicates a home game for the team heading the column.

TEN-TEAM LEAGUE

	SPADE DIVISION					CLUB DIVISION			
Team #	1	2	3	4	5	6	7	8	9	10
Week #										
1	2*	1	4*	3	6*	5	8*	7*	10	9
2	3*	5*	1	7*	2	10*	4	9*	8	6
3	4	8*	5*	1*	3	9	10	2	6*	7*
4	5	4	9	2*	1*	7	6*	10*	3*	8
5	10	3	2*	5	4*	8*	9*	6	7	1*
6	2	1*	5	6*	3*	4	10*	9	8*	7
7	3	5	1*	9	2*	7*	6	10	4*	9*
8	5*	7*	4	3*	1	8	2	6*	10	9*
9	4*	3*	2	1	10*	9*	8	7*	6	5
10	8	9	7	5*	4	10	3*	1*	2*	6*
11	6	4*	10*	2	8	1*	9	5*	7*	3
12	9*	10	6*	8*	7	3	5*	4	1	2*
13	7*	6	8	10	9*	2*	1	3*	5	4*

	Scheduling Options		Scheduling Option
	#1 and #2		#3
14	Bye		Complete Game #13
15	Playoffs		Playoffs
16	Playoffs		Playoffs
17	Fantasy Bowl		Fantasy Bowl

TWELVE-TEAM LEAGUE

DIVISIONS:
Split league into three divisions of four teams each.

REGULAR SEASON:
Play a 14-game regular season. Each of the four teams in a division plays the other three twice, for a total of six games. Each team also plays all the other eight teams once, for a total of eight games. This makes up the 14-game regular-season schedule.

With Scheduling Options #1 and #2, the regular fantasy season is over at the end of week #14. With Scheduling Option #3, the regular fantasy season is not over until the end of week #15, by which time every NFL team will have played its 14th game of the season.

PLAYOFFS:
The top team in each division advances to the playoffs, along with one wild-card team (whichever second-place team has the best record). The four teams are seeded 1 through 4. Again, #1 seed would be the team with the best record and so on. Seed #1 would play seed #4 and seed #2 would play seed #3 during week #16. The winners would advance to the Fantasy Bowl in week #17. To simplify the assignment of team numbers and divisions, we will designate the divisions by using suits in a deck of cards. (For determining who should advance based on record, see Section IV, Playoffs.)

Note that leagues using Scheduling Option #1 or #2 have a league-wide bye in week #15. Leagues using Scheduling Option #3 must use week #15 to wait for every NFL team to complete its 14th game of the season.

Key: 1. Read down for week #.
2. Read across top for team # and then down for opponents.
3. The asterisk (*) indicates a home game for the team heading the column.

TWELVE-TEAM LEAGUE

Team #	SPADE DIVISION				CLUB DIVISION				HEART DIVISION			
	1	2	3	4	5	6	7	8	9	10	11	12
Week #												
1	2*	1	4*	3	6	5*	8	7*	10	9*	12	11*
2	3*	4*	1	2	7*	8*	5	6	11*	12*	9	10
3	4	3	2*	1*	8	7	6*	5*	12	11	10*	9*
4	5	6*	11	12*	1*	2	9*	10	7	8*	3*	4
5	6	7*	9	10*	11*	1*	2	12*	3*	4	5	8
6	12*	11	8*	6	9	4*	10*	3	5*	7	2*	1
7	11*	10	6*	5	4*	3	12	9*	8	2*	1	7*
8	7	8*	12	9*	10	11	1*	2	4	5*	6*	3*
9	8*	9	7*	11*	12*	10*	3	1	2*	6	4	5
10	10*	12	5*	7	3	9*	4*	11*	6	1	8	2*
11	9	5*	10	8	2	12	11	4*	1*	3*	7*	6*
12	2	1*	4	3*	6*	5	8*	7	10*	8	12*	11
13	3	4	1*	2*	7	8	5*	6*	11	12	9*	10*
14	4*	3*	2	1	8*	7*	6	5	12*	11	10	9
	Scheduling Options #1 and #2								Scheduling Option #3			
15	Bye								Complete Game #14			
16	Playoffs								Playoffs			
17	Fantasy Bowl								Fantasy Bowl			

FOURTEEN-TEAM LEAGUE

DIVISIONS:
Split league into two divisions of seven teams each.

REGULAR SEASON:
Play a 14-game regular season. Each of the six teams within a division plays every other twice, for a total of 12 games. Each team also plays two teams at random from the other division, thus making up the 14-game schedule.

With Scheduling Options #1 and #2, the regular fantasy season is over at the end of week #14. With Scheduling Option #3, the regular season isn't over until the end of week #15, by which time every NFL team will have completed its 14th game of the season.

PLAYOFFS:
At the end of the 14-game regular season, the top two teams from each division are awarded playoff spots. The four playoff teams are then seeded 1 through 4, as determined by record. During week #16 the first round of playoffs would be seed #1 vs. seed #4 and seed #2 vs. seed #3. The winners would then advance to the Fantasy Bowl in week #17. (For determining who should advance based on record, see Section IV, Playoffs.)

Note that leagues using Scheduling Option #1 or #2 have a league-wide bye in week #15. Leagues using Scheduling Option #3 must use week #15 to wait for every NFL team to complete its 14th game of the season.

Key: 1. Read down for week #.
2. Read across top for team # and then down for opponents.
3. The asterisk (*) indicates a home game for the team heading the column.

FOURTEEN-TEAM LEAGUE

Team #	SPADE DIVISION							CLUB DIVISION						
	1	2	3	4	5	6	7	8	9	10	11	12	13	14
Week #														
1	2*	1	4*	3	6*	5	14	9	8*	11	10*	13	12*	7*
2	3	7*	1*	5*	4	13	2	10*	14	8	12	11*	6*	9*
3	4*	6	7	1	12	2*	3*	11	13*	14*	8*	5*	9	10
4	5	3*	2	11	1*	7*	6	12*	10	9*	4*	8	14	13*
5	6*	4	10	2*	7	1	5*	13	11*	3	9	14*	8*	12
6	7	9	5*	6*	3	4	1*	14*	2*	12	13*	10*	11	8
7	8	5*	6	7	2	3*	4*	1*	12	13*	14	9*	10	11*
8	5*	4*	11*	2	1	7	6*	14	13	12*	3	10	9*	8*
9	2	1*	7*	6	8*	4*	3	5	14*	13	12*	11	10*	9
10	3*	12*	1	7*	6	5*	3	9*	8	14	13	2	11*	10*
11	4	3	2*	1*	7*	9*	5	10	6	8*	14*	13*	12	11
12	13*	7	6*	5	4*	3	2*	11*	10*	9	8	14	1	12*
13	6	5	4	3*	2*	1*	10*	12	11	7	9*	8*	14*	13
14	7*	6*	5	14*	3*	2	1	13*	12*	11*	10	9	8	4
	Scheduling Options #1 and #2							Scheduling Option #3						
15	Bye							Complete Game #14						
16	Playoffs							Playoffs						
17	Fantasy Bowl							Fantasy Bowl						

SIXTEEN-TEAM LEAGUE

DIVISIONS:
   Split league into four divisions of four teams each.

REGULAR SEASON:
   Play a 12-game regular season. Each of the four teams within a division plays the other three twice, for a total of six games. Each team also plays two teams from each of the other three divisions once, for a total of six more games, which round out the 12-game schedule.

PLAYOFFS: OPTION #1
(12-Team Playoff, Usable Only With Scheduling Option #1 or #2
   The top team in each division automatically advances to the playoffs by winning its division. The second- and third-place teams in each division are also awarded playoff spots. This excludes only the last-place team in each division and keeps all of the teams in the race as long as possible, leaving 12 playoff teams.

   In the first week of the playoffs, the first-place teams are awarded byes. Then the teams that finished second and third in the division meet in the divisional wild-card games.

★★★

   Combined-Weeks Playoff Rule:

   Because a given NFL team might have a bye in either week #13 or #14, we will combine these two weeks into a single playoff week. For this combined-weeks playoff, lineups must be submitted before the lineup deadline for week #13. If a player in your lineup for the first week of playoffs is with an NFL team playing during both week #13 and week #14, only his week #13 performance can be used. **Here's the rule: Only a player's performance in his first game of this two-week period can count toward your fantasy playoff score.**

★★★

   The winners advance to meet the divisional champs in week #15. The divisional wild-card winners meet their respective divisional champions to determine who will represent the division in the semifinals.

   The winners advance to the semifinals in week #16. The teams representing the Spade and Club divisions meet, as do the teams representing the Diamond and Heart divisions.

The winners become the black and red conference champions, respectively, and meet in the Fantasy Bowl in week #17. To determine who should advance based on record, see Playoffs and Payoffs (Section IV).

PLAYOFFS: OPTION #2
(12-Team Playoff, Usable Only With Scheduling Option #1 or #2)

The top team from each division automatically advances to the playoffs for winning its division. The second- and third-place teams in each division are also awarded playoff spots. This excludes only the last-place team in each division and keeps every team in the race longer throughout the season.

In the first playoff week the first-place teams are awarded byes. Then the teams that finished in second or third place in their divisions are seeded 1 through 8 to play off for the four wild-card spots. Seeding is determined by record, the team with the best record being #1 and so on. Seed #1 plays seed #8, seed #2 plays seed #7, seed #3 plays seed #6, and seed #4 plays seed #5.

Because a given NFL team might have a bye in either week #13 or week #14, these two weeks are combined into a single playoff week. For details, see the Combined-Weeks Playoff Rule on the previous page.

The winners advance to meet division champs in week #15. In this round the division champs are seeded 1 through 4 and the wild-card winners are seeds 5 through 8. Again it will be seed #1 vs. seed #8, seed #2 vs. seed #7, seed #3 vs. seed #6, and seed #4 vs. seed #5. The winners advance to the semifinals, this time seeded 1 through 4, again based on record. Seed #1 meets seed #4, and seed #2 meets seed #3, with the winners advancing to the Fantasy Bowl in week #17. (For determining who should advance based on record, see Section IV, Playoffs.)

PLAYOFFS: OPTION #3
(8-Team Playoff, Usable With All Scheduling Options)

The top team in each division automatically advances to the playoffs. Of the teams that did not win their divisions, the four teams with the best records are also included in the playoff structure. These four teams can be one from each of the four divisions, or two or three can be from the same divisions, depending on how they finish. (Example: If the second- and third-place teams from the Spade Division have better records than the second-place team from the Heart Division, they would both advance).

All leagues using this 8-team playoff option should take league-wide byes in weeks #13 and #14. For one thing, leagues using this playoff option and Scheduling Option #3 will need to wait until the end of week #13 for their regular 12-game fantasy season to be over. For another, a given NFL team might have a bye during week #13 or week #14. Even those leagues using Scheduling Option #1 or #2 would do best simply to postpone their first week of playoffs until week #15, when all 28 NFL teams will be back in action.

All eight teams are then seeded 1 through 8, with the team with the best record being #1 and so on. Seed #1 would play seed #8, seed #2 would play seed #7, seed #3 would play seed #6, and seed #4 would play seed #5 in the first round of the playoffs during week #15. Then the winners would advance to the semifinal round in week #16. Again, the four remaining teams would be seeded, this time 1 through 4. Seed #1 would play seed #4, and seed #2 would play seed #3. The winners would advance to the Fantasy Bowl in week #17. (For determining who should advance based on record, see Section IV, Playoffs.)

Key: 1. Read down for week #.
2. Read across top for team # and then down for opponents.
3. The asterisk (*) indicates a home game for the team heading the column.

SIXTEEN-TEAM LEAGUE

	SPADE				CLUB				DIAMOND				HEART			
Team #	1	2	3	4	5	6	7	8	9	10	11	12	13	14	15	16
Week #																
1	2*	1	4*	3	6*	5	8*	7	10*	9	12*	11	14*	13	16*	15
2	3	4*	1*	2	7	8*	5*	6	11	12*	9*	10	15	16*	13*	14
3	4*	3*	2	1	8	7*	6	5*	12	11*	10	9*	16	15*	14	13*
4	5	6*	8	7*	1*	2	4	3*	14*	16	13	15*	11*	9	12	10*
5	9*	10	11*	12	13*	14	15*	16	1	2*	3	4*	5	6*	7	8*
6	13	16*	15	14*	10	9*	11	12*	5*	6	7*	8	1*	4	3*	2
7	8*	7	6*	5	4*	3	2*	1	16*	15	14*	13	12*	11	10*	9
8	10	9*	12	11*	16	15*	14	13*	2	1*	4	3*	8	7*	6	5*
9	16*	14	13*	15	10	9*	12*	11	6	5*	8*	7	3	2*	4*	1
10	2	1*	4	3*	6	5*	8	7*	10	9*	12	11	14	13*	16	15*
11	3*	4	1	2*	7*	8	5	6*	11*	12	9	10*	15*	16	13	14*
12	4	3	2*	1*	8*	7	6*	5	12*	11	10*	9	16*	15	14*	13

	Scheduling Options #1 and #2	Scheduling Option #3
13	Bye or Playoffs	Complete Game #12
14	Bye or Playoffs	Bye
15	Playoffs	Playoffs
16	Playoffs	Playoffs
17	Fantasy Bowl	Fantasy Bowl

IV
PLAYOFFS & PAYOFFS

1. PLAYOFFS: WHO SHOULD ADVANCE

For each of the various preceding schedules, I included a suggested playoff structure. You may choose to follow these regular-season schedules and playoff structures, or you may decide to set up your own.

Whether you use the structure I suggest or one you have devised yourself, you are also going to need a tie-breaker system in cases of teams having identical win-loss records. Here is the tie-breaker system that I like:

1. Best win-loss record
2. Most points scored during the regular season

★★

> There is a reason for putting most points scored as a tie breaker before head-to-head competition. I feel any Fantasy Team could get lucky during the season and have a good game against a good team. The true test of a good Fantasy Team is how they fare throughout the entire season. This is better reflected by a comparison of the totals of points scored during the entire season.

★★

3. Head-to-head competition (most points vs. team tied with)
4. Best conference record
5. Coin flip

2. PLAYOFFS: DETERMINING THE HOME TEAM

In the event your league uses a sudden-death tie breaker, you will need a system to determine which will be the home team. Since the team with the better record should always be the home team, the same system used for determining who should advance to the playoffs would also apply nicely here. Remember the importance of the home team when using the sudden-death tie breaker. The team that is determined to be the home team will have the first shot at breaking the tie. Again, the system used to determine the home team in the playoffs is the same one used for determining who should advance as listed above.

3. LEAGUE PAYOFFS:

Our league has a small entry fee that is paid at the beginning of the year by each franchise. The purse that is collected is broken up by first paying the commissioner. (We let our commissioner play for free, which serves as payment for his duties or services. Therefore we don't actually take money out of the purse to pay him, but the purse is smaller because he has not contributed.) The remainder of the money is divided up to provide payment for the following:

1. First place—Fantasy Bowl winner
2. Second place—Fantasy Bowl runner-up
3. Third place—winner, third-place playoff
4. Fourth place—loser, third-place playoff
5. Trophies for top four teams
6. Stamps, photocopying, & miscellaneous. (Used by commissioner for issuing weekly results to franchise owners.)

V
THE DRAFT

Draft day may become the sports event of the year for most of you, but it can turn into a real headache for your commissioner if he's not properly prepared.

The following is a layout of how our draft is set up and run. Everything is set up for a 16-team league, but the process can easily be adapted to the number of teams you have in your league.

1. SETTING UP A DRAFT DAY
   One of the toughest jobs a commissioner faces is selecting a draft day. It is essential to find a day when all the franchises can be represented.

   In a small league, eight teams or fewer, it shouldn't be very difficult to find a time convenient for all eight team owners. In leagues of 10 or more, such as the one I'm involved with, select a date that is within two weeks of the National Football League regular-season opener. Then send out a notice more than a month in advance, to inform all the teams of the draft date.

2. TEAM REPRESENTATION
   With each team having a month's advance notice, there shouldn't be any reason why a team can't have a representative there to draft for the franchise, even if the owner can't be present.

   NOTE: After a year or two of having one of your fantasy franchise owners draft for both his team and another team that couldn't make it to the draft, you will begin to get many objections from the other franchise owners. Their beef is legitimate: How can an owner from one team put his heart into drafting for another team? It ruins the whole concept of the draft. So in our league, we follow these rules:

   A. No team is allowed to draft for another.
   B. Any team not represented at the draft must make its selections from the players remaining after the draft.

3. DRAFT ASSISTANT
   If a commissioner owns a franchise himself, he may want to seek an assistant for draft day, someone who can take care of logging picks as they are called off, and so on. This leaves the commissioner free to concentrate on his draft. I have done this the last four years, and it has worked out tremendously for both me and my assistant. In fact, my assistants have both thanked me for such a good time.

4. DETERMINING TEAM NUMBER AND DIVISIONS

Once each team is present, the draft can begin. The process for determining each franchise's team number for the purpose of scheduling and naming divisions is as follows:

    A. From a deck of cards select the Ace, Two, Three, and Four of each of the four suits, giving you 16 cards, one for each of the franchises.

    B. The 16 cards are shuffled and cut; each team takes one card to determine both its team number and the division it will be competing in.

    C. The 16 cards are interpreted as follows:

	Black Conference			**Red Conference**	
Spade	Ace of Spades	— Team #1	**Diamond**	Ace of Diamonds	— Team # 9
Division	Two of Spades	— Team #2	**Division**	Two of Diamonds	— Team #10
	Three of Spades	— Team #3		Three of Diamonds	— Team #11
	Four of Spades	— Team #4		Four of Diamonds	— Team #12
Club	Ace of Clubs	— Team #5	**Heart**	Ace of Hearts	— Team #13
Division	Two of Clubs	— Team #6	**Division**	Two of Hearts	— Team #14
	Three of Clubs	— Team #7		Three of Hearts	— Team #15
	Four of Clubs	— Team #8		Four of Hearts	— Team #16

5. 12 ROUNDS/7 STARTERS

After determining team number and division, we move on to the actual draft. In our league, we draft players in 12 rounds. In selecting these 12 players, we must remember that 7 of them will be used in our starting lineup, which consists of one quarterback, one tight end, two running backs, two wide receivers, and one kicker. The remaining five picks will be reserves and can be from any of the above-mentioned positions.

6. DRAFTING ORDER

We've found that we can best provide a fair draft and parity throughout the league by flopping the drafting order every other round. When determining the order of the draft, we first draw cards for the first round and then reverse that order for the second round.

This works out well, since the franchise that is lucky enough to get the #1 overall pick in the first round won't pick again until the 16th pick in the second round. Another way to look at this is that, if you have the misfortune of picking 16th in the first round, you will automatically be given the #1 pick in the second round, which ends up to be two picks in a row. This process has worked out well and keeps the drafting aspect pretty even. It also prevents someone who is lucky at picking cards from getting all the early picks in each of the rounds.

In determining the order of the draft, 16 cards are preselected from a whole deck. The cards used are the Ace through the Eight of Spades and the Ace through the Eight of Hearts. The 16 cards are shuffled, cut, and passed out. The order of the draft will be as follows:

Ace of Spades	—1st Pick	Ace of Hearts	—19th Pick
Two of Spades	—2nd Pick	Two of Hearts	—10th Pick
Three of Spades	—3rd Pick	Three of Hearts	—11th Pick
Four of Spades	—4th Pick	Four of Hearts	—12th Pick
Five of Spades	—5th Pick	Five of Hearts	—13th Pick
Six of Spades	6th Pick	Six of Hearts	—14th Pick
Seven of Spades	—7th Pick	Seven of Hearts	—15th Pick
Eight of Spades	—8th Pick	Eight of Hearts	—16th Pick

Remember, each even-numbered round is in the reverse order of the previous odd-numbered round. So if you grabbed the Four of Spades for your first-round pick, you would automatically draft 13th in the second round. This procedure will be repeated in rounds 3 and 4 and so on, with a new draw of cards every odd round until the 12 rounds are complete.

7. SPEEDING UP YOUR DRAFT

When drafting 192 players, as we do in our league, the process can sometimes become too long and drawn out. What we have developed is a quicker process for determining the order for all the rounds. Instead of drawing the cards every two rounds, we take six decks of cards which consist of the 16 predetermined cards (Ace through Eight of Spades and Hearts) and label them A through F. That means each group of 16 cards is labeled with a letter.

The six decks of cards are all shuffled, cut, and spread out on the table. Each franchise approaches the table and selects one card from each letter group. The following table shows the determination of drafting order for all of the rounds.

**Deck marked
with letter**

"A"—Rounds 1 and 2
"B"—Rounds 3 and 4
"C"—Rounds 5 and 6
"D"—Rounds 7 and 8
"E"—Rounds 9 and 10
"F"—Rounds 11 and 12

Samples:
Deck "A"

Ace of Spades	—	Draft 1st, 1st Round	—	16th, 2nd
Two of Spades	—	Draft 2nd, 1st Round	—	15th, 2nd
Ace of Hearts	—	Draft 9th, 1st Round	—	8th, 2nd

Deck "D"

Ace of Spades	—	Draft 1st, 7th Round	—	16th, 8th
Two of Spades	—	Draft 2nd, 7th Round	—	15th, 8th
Ace of Hearts	—	Draft 9th, 7th Round	—	8th, 8th

This process also allows some time for forming last-minute drafting strategies. After determining the drafting order for all the rounds, we take a 10-minute break to allow the teams to set up their picks, now that they know in what order they will draft.

8. TIME LIMIT

In many cases, such as in our league's draft of 192 players, the draft can last many, many hours. To prevent the draft from dragging on too long, we have established a limit on the time a team has to make each pick.

In the early rounds this should be no problem, since most of the better, more well-known players are being drafted. However, in the later rounds, selecting a player becomes more involved and may take longer.

The rules on the time limit for drafting players are as follows:

A. Two minutes allowed per pick.
B. If the time limit has been exceeded, the next team in line will then be able to pick. Following that choice, go back to the team that was skipped.
C. Four minutes are allowed if a team has two consecutive picks (such as when an owner has the last pick of an odd round and automatically has the first pick of the next round).
D. If a team exceeds the four-minute time limit for its consecutive picks, it must wait until after the next two teams are allowed picks before being allowed to make its selection(s).
E. A stopwatch should be used, and a warning given to the team that is selecting when there are 30 seconds to go.

NOTE: Below is a sample of the boards we use at our draft. They are about 2 feet by 3 feet in actual size, making it easy for everyone in the room to see. The draft assistant logs the draft picks as they are called off, making our draft run smoothly and giving it a more professional appearance.

1990
FANTASY FOOTBALL DRAFT

(ROUND #1)

Fantasy Team #	Player Drafted	Pro Team	Pos
1			
2			
3			
4			
5			
6			
7			
8			
9			
10			
11			
12			
13			
14			
15			
16			

VI
ROSTER CHANGES/TRANSACTIONS

Because the new 17-week NFL season may affect some transaction procedures, please refer to the suggestions for handling this change in the beginning of this chapter.

After the draft has been completed, you may find that you're not happy with all of the players you chose or, during the course of the season, one of your players may be sidelined because of injury or some other reason. In either of these events, you may choose to trade or pick up another player.

1. PICKUPS AND TRADES
   During the course of the season, you may elect to pick up or trade for another player. This can be done, keeping in mind that your roster may never exceed 12 players. For every player added to your roster, one must be dropped.

   A. Once a player is dropped by an FFL team, he becomes a free agent and is eligible to be picked up by any other franchise. He is, in effect, put on waivers.
   B. There are two types of roster changes that can be made. The first is actually labeled a *pickup*. This occurs when a team decides to pick up a player from the pool of players left unclaimed following the draft. Remember, for every additional player you pick up, you must also drop a player from your current roster to keep it at 12.
   C. Although there will be a limit of only one or two trades between teams, there is no limit to how many players can be picked up from the unclaimed pool.
   D. The other type of transaction is the *trade*. It's a move by one team in the league to trade a player to another team in the league. A limit of one or two of these exchanges or trades should be allowed per year. This prevents any two franchise owners who are close friends from trading between themselves exclusively in an attempt to build one super team between the two of them. In the event of a two-for-one trade, where one team offers two players in exchange for one better player, each team's roster must still end up with 12. This means that the team receiving the two players must drop an additional player besides the one they traded. The team giving up the two players and receiving only one must pick up another player from the unclaimed pool.
   E. Limit the number of transactions per franchise per trade night to *four*. For leagues using a phone-in method for transactions, this means that two transactions may be made in each of the two transaction hours allotted.

2. COMMISSIONER RESPONSIBILITIES
   A. To ease the commissioner's load, I suggest having your trade night the same night as you take lineups. This will then tie up only one night in league transactions.
   B. Set a time limit of two hours.

C. Keep good records to avoid the possibility of two teams picking up the same player.

D. I suggest the commissioner charge a small fee for each trade, for his time and the paperwork involved.

3. LEAGUE HANDLING OF PICKUPS AND TRADES (COMMISSIONER)

There are a number of ways to handle pickups and trades, based on how your league is handled by its commissioner. The first thing to determine is whether league transactions are going to be handled in person or by telephone. Here are some options:

A. Phone-In Leagues

OPTION #1: First come, first served
Efficient handling of the weekly phone call-in. Trades should be handled on a first-come, first-served basis. There may be many trade nights when the teams in your league are looking to pick up the same player. To prevent any hassles or showing of favoritism, state a time you will start taking calls. Take the phone off the hook five minutes before your declared starting time. Then at precisely, say, 6:00 PM, put the phone back on the hook and begin taking calls.

a. Each franchise may have only one caller trying to place the transaction order. (Some teams have only one owner while others have many.) If more than one owner from a franchise calls in within the same hour, the franchise goes to the bottom of the callback list, unless the transactions by the penalized team have already been accepted by the commissioner.

b. Set a limit of two trades per call or turn, so one team won't keep you on the phone for a long time. This will also give the other teams a chance at the desired players.

c. Offer no advice to teams calling in as to who you think they should pick up. If a team calls in looking for a player to fill a particular position, let the caller suggest who he wants and offer no help.

d. In the event that you as commissioner are looking for a player and want to be fair to both your league and yourself, you could handle it the way I do: If a player goes unclaimed for 10 minutes after the trading hour has started, the commissioner is allowed to pick up the player. Again, he, like the rest of the owners, can pick up no more than two players at a time. He cannot pick up another player until after 10 minutes into the second hour. In the event your league meets on transaction night the commissioner will draw a card like anyone else to determine his order of pickups.

OPTION #2: The worst goes first

This method allows the team with the worst record each week to have first chance at making its transactions.

a. In the weeks preceding the season, when transactions are allowed after the league's fantasy draft, the team with the worst record from the previous season will go first, then the team with the next worst record, and so on.

b. On a given transaction night the commissioner calls each franchise, starting with the one with the worst record. For teams with identical records, the tie breaker will be fewest points scored. If that's not enough, toss a coin.

c. Each franchise is responsible for giving the commissioner a telephone number where he will be able to reach someone for transactions during the season. If there will be no one at the number on a given night, the franchise is responsible for informing the commissioner prior to the transaction day and time and for leaving a new number where someone *can* be reached.

d. When a commissioner cannot reach a fantasy team:

   1. If a commissioner receives no answer at the given franchise number, it will be assumed that the franchise desires no transactions that evening and, after allowing 15 rings, the commissioner may go on to the next team. If the team involved calls later in the hour to make their transactions, they will go to the end of the list.

   2. If a commissioner gets a busy signal, he must continue to call that team for 5 minutes. If the commissioner fails to reach a team, he goes on to the next team. If the skipped team calls in and wants to make transactions, it must go to the end of the list.

★★★

   3. If a commissioner reaches a telephone recorder, he should leave a message with the time of the call. If the team calls back in and wants to make transactions, it must go to the end of the list.

★★★

e. Three transactions per night

   (One the first hour, up to two the second hour, for a total of three.)

   Any team that was bypassed in the first hour's transactions because of no answer or a busy signal and that also failed to contact the commissioner forfeits one of its allowed transactions for the evening. With a maximum of three transactions per transaction night, the first hour's selection would be forfeited.

★★★

The reason for allowing only one transaction the first hour is so that each team has a shot at obtaining at least one significant player. If the commissioner allowed two trades in the first hour, by the time the owners choosing later got their chance, very few desirable players would be left.

★★★

f. Second-hour transactions
1. Only those teams that expressed interest in making second-hour transactions when called during the first hour will be called back by the commissioner during the second hour. They should be called back in the same sequence as the first hour.
2. Any team that did not talk to the commissioner during the first hour but that does so during the second hour goes to the end of the list, behind those that did express interest during the first hour in making second-hour transactions when contacted by the commissioner. They will be called in the sequence they called in, if more than one team calls in.

g. Transaction-Position Trading

★★★

Two teams may desire to change or trade their weekly transaction-position numbers. This may come as part of a trade condition. The two teams can be allowed to trade their transaction positions on the condition that both teams *must* make a first hour-transaction. This would hopefully prevent any two teams in cahoots from just passing their favorable positions to each other. So both teams *have to* make this first-hour transaction. The commissioner must be assured that this condition has been met before the transaction-position trading is allowed.

★★★

B. Weekly Get-Together Leagues

OPTION #1: The worst goes first
For those leagues that meet weekly, an easy and fair way to handle transactions is the worst-goes-first option as defined in Option #2 for phone-in leagues. The team with the worst record gets to make its selections first, and so on. If two teams have identical records, then the tie breakers would be, first, least points scored, and then a coin toss.

OPTION #2: Cut the cards
Use a deck of cards to determine who goes first, and then second, and so on.

OPTION #3: Player bidding

Another option used in many fantasy leagues for player transactions is *player bidding*. Fantasy teams pick up players from the unclaimed-player pool by bidding for them.

a. Fantasy teams use the trade night to bid on players. If only one team bids on a player, then obviously they acquire the player. If more than one team bids on a player, then the player goes to the team with the highest bid.

 Example: Let's say a player goes undrafted but gets hot, so a number of fantasy teams in the league are interested in him. Team A bids $3.00. Team B bids $2.00. Team C bids $5.00. Team C, the highest bidder, gets the player.

b. In the event of two or more teams making the same highest bid, the commissioner will advise each of this at the end of the evening and let each make another bid, with the highest bidder getting the player. (NOTE: If three teams bid on a player, but only two have identical high bids, only the two high bidders are allowed to rebid at the end of the evening.)

c. Because it is not known until the end of the evening which teams get which players, the fantasy franchise acquiring the player may not use him as part of its team that week. However that franchise must announce which player from its team is being released, so the rest of the league is notified who is going back in the player pool.

d. Do not allow the commissioner, if he is also a franchise owner, the advantage of knowing what the other teams are bidding. The commissioner must give his bid to another league member at the outset of the evening. In the event the commissioner wants to bid on a player also wanted by the franchise owner whom he normally calls with his bid, he would just place his bid with a different owner that week.

OPTION #4: No-trade leagues

For leagues in which the commissioner elects not to get involved in handling trades, you may decide to increase the number of rounds for your league draft. Instead of drafting 12 rounds, you could increase your draft to 15 rounds. This would give each team a chance to stock enough players at each position to survive the year, thus eliminating the need for trades.

4. TRANSACTION DEADLINE

A transaction deadline day that will fall during the season should be established before the season starts. One suggestion would be to have the deadline one week after the halfway point of the season. From that day on, the 12 players who make up a franchise roster must finish the season with that team.

There are a number of ways to help a fantasy team that suffers player injuries after the trade deadline and therefore cannot field a full team. Your league has two options. One deals with a player on injured reserve, and the other simply allows every franchise to obtain more players after the trade deadline, to avoid not having each position covered in the event of an injury. (I prefer the second option.)

OPTION #1: Injured-reserve and cut-player options

a. Injured-reserve option:
   1. The only exception to the transaction deadline would be the case of a player being injured after this date. In many instances, this would leave a team without a player at a particular position.
   2. Any FFL team that suffers an injury after the transaction deadline has an option. If that player goes on the NFL injured reserve (which puts him out for at least four weeks), that franchise may replace him with another player from the unclaimed-player pool. The new player must play the same position as the player released. The injured player, once released from his permanent team after the trade deadline, is out for the year. He may not be picked up by any other team.

   Proof that a player is out should be obtained from a current, reliable source of sports information, such as *USA Today, The Sporting News,* or your local newspaper.

NOTE: Unless your league specifically votes otherwise, this rule applies only to players who go on injured reserve. Fantasy players lost because of trades, waivers, or being cut do not fall under this rule. Example: If a fantasy player is cut by an NFL team, his fantasy team is still stuck with him unless your league adopts the cut-player option described later in this section.

NOTE: If you have a good player and you elect to replace him using this rule, he is lost to you for the season. However, this may be a necessary loss. You really don't have the luxury of an injured reserve in your fantasy league. You can take an injured player out of the *starting* lineup, but even then he takes up bench space that could be occupied by a healthy player. You just have to decide for yourself whether your good-but-injured player is so valuable that you can afford to have him sit, useless, on your bench for at least four weeks.

NOTE: Commissioners should require that any FFL team using this rule to pick up a player on injured reserve send in a copy of some statement that verifies that their player is out. This is proof in case any questions or protests from other teams arise later.

b. Cut-player option:
   Because some franchise owners have been frustrated by being stuck with players cut from NFL teams after the trade deadline, I have included the following option, on which your league can vote.

If a fantasy team possesses a player cut, waived, or released after your league's trade deadline, that player may be replaced under the following provisions:

1. The player being released by the fantasy team must be replaced by a player from the same position.
2. The player being released by the fantasy team, like a player released because of being put on injured reserve, cannot be picked up by any other team and is released from the player pool.
3. The fantasy team releasing the player must do so the same week as the player is released. Here are some rules for this release:
   a. If your trade night is Thursday night and the NFL player has been released during the seven days including or preceding your trade day, he must be transacted that night. However, the player's release by his NFL team and the date of that release must be provable on trade night. A clipping from a reliable daily publication is sufficient proof.
   b. If the NFL transaction is not provable on trade night—if someone heard that it had occurred earlier that day, for example, but cannot yet offer proof—the fantasy team holding that player must conduct its transaction the next trade night, the next week.
   c. If the transaction by the fantasy team isn't done in the proper week, that fantasy team is stuck with the player.
4. This rule does NOT apply to NFL players TRADED to another NFL team after your trade deadline. However, it does apply to players cut, waived, or released by an NFL team even if they are picked up by another NFL team that same week.

OPTION #2: Roster-expansion draft

Another alternative for your league is allowing for roster expansion after the trade deadline. You could do this instead of, or in addition to, Option #1.

Because players suffer minor injuries that wouldn't necessitate their going on the four-week injured reserve, many fantasy teams find themselves short a player or two in any given week. To help eliminate this problem, the 12-player limit should be expanded to 14 following the trade deadline, allowing each franchise two more spots on their roster. This will keep all positions filled despite weekly injuries that may occur. The rules for expanding to 14 players after the trade deadline are as follows:

a. Player eligibility
   1. The players drafted for the roster-expansion draft may come only from the unclaimed-player pool.
   2. Any player dropped by a franchise after the trade deadline does not go into the unclaimed-player pool for another team to pick up and may not be used in the playoff player-addition draft.

b. Transaction procedures
1. *Leagues that physically meet to make roster-expansion selections.* In leagues where all the franchise owners are able to get together for the roster expansion, the selecting should start with the team with the worst record and work its way through to the team with the best record.

The team with the worst record selects one player, and the rest of the teams continue until each franchise has selected its 13th player. Then, starting over again, the team with the worst record selects its 14th player and so on until each franchise has 14 members. The 14-player roster is now permanent. (If two teams have identical records, then the team that has scored the fewest points shall be designated the "worst" and should select first. If two teams have identical records and identical points, then a coin toss should determine their draft order.)

NOTE: If a team does not have a representative at the roster expansion draft, it must select its two additional players after all of the other teams are done.

2. *Leagues that use the phone for expansion selections.* I suggest using a method similar to that used during the year by your league. The drafting should be done in two one-hour periods.

The first hour would take care of player #13 on the roster, and the second hour would be for player #14.

NOTE:
1. If a fantasy team is not reached by the commissioner and then fails to call in to take a player during the first hour, it forfeits its right to fill one of its roster-expansion spots.
2. If a fantasy team is not reached by the commissioner and fails to call in at all to take a player during the two-hour roster-expansion draft, that team forfeits its right for the remainder of the year to *one* of the two players it could have chosen during the roster-expansion draft. That team may, however, select one player during any of the remaining regular-season weeks to add to its roster.
3. A fantasy team electing to draft one player during the first hour of the expansion draft and electing not to pick a second player during the draft's second hour is also eligible to pick up a second selection during any of the remaining regular-season weeks. A fantasy team that does not participate in the first hour of the expansion draft forfeits its right to expand its roster by two players. Such a team may expand by only one and would end up with a maximum of 13 players rather than 14.
4. The order of selecting roster-expansion players following the roster-expansion draft date will follow the transaction procedures used by your league during the season.

OPTION # 3: Playoff player-addition draft

To further insure fantasy franchises against finding themselves short a player at playoff time, I suggest incorporating a playoff player-addition draft. This would expand each playoff team's roster by one player, giving them a possible total of 15.

  a. The player can be from any position.
  b. The player must be selected from the unclaimed-player pool as it stood prior to the player-transaction deadline. No player dropped by one fantasy franchise after the player-transaction deadline may be selected in this draft.
  c. The playoff player-addition draft will take place on the trade night prior to the fantasy playoffs.
  d. A team not participating in the player-addition draft on that evening forfeits, for the remainder of the playoffs, its right to add a player to its roster.
  e. Selections in the playoff player-addition draft will follow the transaction procedures used by your league during the season.

NOTE: Transactions made in the roster-expansion draft and the playoff player-addition draft should carry the normal transaction fees to be paid to the commissioner.

VII
LINEUPS

Because the new expanded 17-week NFL season may affect some of the handling procedures for transactions, please refer to the suggestions in the beginning of this chapter to see how to handle this change.

The commissioner should set up a night and a period of time (for example, 6:00 to 8:00 PM) when he is free and can take everyone's lineups. To make it easier on the commissioner, lineup submissions can be scheduled for the same night as trades are taken. The commissioner would then be involved only one night. The following can be used as a commissioner's guide for taking lineups:

1. COMMISSIONER FAVORITISM
   Commissioners, make sure to have your franchise owners prepared when they call you. Each one should be able to call you, read off his lineup, and get off the phone. Don't let them call you and ask your opinion on who they should start or which NFL teams play which. I've run into this on plenty of occasions and it's really frustrating, especially if it's a good friend doing it to me. Besides taking up a lot of my time, it puts me in an awkward position. I don't feel it is ethical for a league commissioner to show any favoritism and guide a team's choice of whom to start. The easiest way to remedy this kind of problem is to make sure at the draft that each team understands: No lineup will be logged in the books unless the team calling it in is ready to give the full lineup without guidance from the commissioner.

2. LINEUP NIGHT
   The day selected for taking lineups should be later in the week, allowing every team in the league a chance to check on its players, via the newspaper or television, for injuries or other late-breaking news that would change its strategy for the game.

3. FANTASY WEEKS THAT START EARLY
   In the event you elect to take lineups on Thursday nights, for instance, and there is a National Football League game scheduled for that night, your lineup and trade night should automatically be changed to Wednesday. This would prevent anybody calling in his lineup after the Thursday night game had started.

   It's important that all lineups be in prior to the first game played that week. Even your FFL teams that don't have any players participating in these games still must have their lineups in on the same night as the teams that do have players involved. This gives every team the same amount of time to check the media for injury or other pertinent news. Once the kickoff from the first National Football League game of the week occurs, all FFL games for that week have officially begun.

4. RIDING THE SAME LINEUP

If a team fails to call the commissioner and give him its lineup, its previous week's lineup will automatically be used.

5. OPTIONS

A. One Lineup Change.

Here is an option I use in our league. After your original starting lineup is called in, each FFL team is allowed one lineup change. This must be done prior to the first National Football League game that week. If your original lineup is called in on Thursday and the first National Football League game for that week is played on Sunday, your commissioner can set up a period of time (like between 11:00 AM and 12:00 noon on Sunday) when each team would have a chance to call in its one lineup change. This allows every team a chance to check Sunday morning's paper for any late-breaking news. By Sunday morning, a player's playing status should be pretty well determined. The opponent should then be notified of the lineup change prior to the game.

In the event you replace one of your starters by using this one lineup change, the replaced player would then automatically take the spot of the reserve in your league.

NOTE: Again the commissioner should charge a small fee for his time and paperwork.

B. Sudden-Death Tie Breaker.

Commissioners, don't forget to write in every team's reserve players for use in the sudden-death tie breaker. (See Section IX, "Variations on Fantasy Football; Sudden-Death Tie Breaker," for details.)

VIII
SELECTING A SCORING METHOD

After finding the right person to head your league as commissioner, your next step in beginning your league is to establish which method of scoring your league will use. In the following pages, I describe the three methods of scoring that are the most commonly used. I have also included a few variations used by different leagues. You may want to expand on the rules a little yourself. After reading through the following rules for the different methods, select the one you feel will give your league the most enjoyment. Before we consider the three methods individually, let's look at the general rules that apply to all of them.

NOTE: Before your regular season begins, you should establish which particular sports-reporting source you are going to use for your game results. This should be done because of possible discrepancies in scoring, or missing stats. Among your options, of course, are your local newspaper, *USA Today, The Sporting News* (which will be received a week later), and so on. Select one for your league's official results, but in case of a discrepancy, have two other backups for help in deciding the correct scoring.

NUMBER OF PLAYERS

    A. At the fantasy draft each franchise will draft 12 players.
    B. Of the 12 NFL players selected on draft day, seven will be used in your starting lineup and the other five will be reserves.
    C. Of the starting seven players, the following positions will make up the starting lineup:

    *STANDARD OPTION (used by most leagues):
                1 Quarterback
                2 Running Backs
                2 Wide Receivers
                1 Tight End
                1 Kicker

    *FLEX OPTION: Because of the many varieties of formations being used today, like the two-tight-end offense or the "h-back" (see below), our league uses the Flex Option in an attempt to simplify differentiating between a player being qualified as a wide receiver, tight end, or h-back. We suggest that leagues go to three receivers, with no limitations on how many are wide receivers, tight ends, or h-backs.

Here is the FLEX OPTION:

> 1 Quarterback
> 2 Running Backs
> 3 Receivers
> 1 Place Kicker

(The position of h-back, a recent phenomenon in the NFL, is used to designate what most would consider a blocking tight end. Usually this player lines up in the backfield and goes in motion either to block or run a pass pattern. If you do not use the Flex Option, h-backs would most likely fall into the tight-end category).

D. On some occasions, you may find players who are able to play a few positions or who change positions during the course of the year. You may find a need to set up some sort of rule to clarify what position that player must be used in.

A good example of this would be Earl Cooper of the San Francisco 49ers. In 1982, Cooper was a running back, but when San Francisco acquired Wendell Tyler from the Rams in the off-season, Cooper was given a shot at tight end. In our league, the team that drafted him picked him as a running back, but during the course of the 1983 season switched him to tight end.

Another example is Jim Jensen of the Miami Dolphins. Jensen can be listed at a variety of different positions, including quarterback, wide receiver, and tight end. It should be determined prior to the season at which position your league will accept him.

The rule we have established for clarification of position is as follows:

1. Choose one respected sports magazine to use as your league's book. The position listed in this book is the position the player must be drafted for.
2. If during the course of the year the player switches positions, a team may change his position with the following provisions:
   a. The fantasy owner must provide evidence to the commissioner that his player has played that position for at least two consecutive weeks.
   b. If that fantasy team owner is the commissioner, two other team owners of the league must approve the switch.
   c. One publication you could use for this rule is *Pro Football Weekly,* which lists the players by position each week.
3. If the team that's playing against an opponent who has a player in this situation has a protest, the protest must be lodged prior to the start of their game. Once the game has started, no protest may be made. All commissioner decisions should be fair and are final.

THE BASIC SCORING METHOD

The Basic Scoring Method is the most commonly used scoring method. It is the tabulation of actual scoring done in NFL games by various NFL players. Let's take a look at how this is done.

1. SCORING TABULATION BY POSITION
   The following are the seven starting positions, broken down by the number of points tallied for each score.

   A. Quarterback
      1. Three points are awarded for each touchdown pass thrown.
      2. Six points are awarded for each touchdown scored rushing.
      3. Six points are awarded for each touchdown scored receiving a pass (in the instance where the quarterback becomes a pass receiver in a play).
   B. Running Backs, Wide Receivers, Tight Ends
      1. Six points are awarded for each touchdown scored, either by running or catching a pass.
      2. Three points are awarded for each touchdown pass thrown (such as in a halfback option).
   C. Kickers
      1. Three points are awarded for each field goal.
      2. One point is awarded for each extra point.

2. ADDITIONAL SCORING POSSIBILITIES
   A. If a running back or wide receiver doubles as a punt or kickoff returner and scores a touchdown on a runback, the six points awarded for a touchdown apply.
   B. If any player recovers a fumble in the end zone for a touchdown, the six points for a touchdown are awarded.
   C. If a player (such as a quarterback) who holds for extra points scores by running in or receiving a pass that results in a successful extra point, the player is awarded one point. (If an extra-point try is successful on a play involving a pass from one player to another, only the player actually scoring the extra point is awarded the one point. This is a very infrequent occurrence, but it may happen).
   D. If a kicker on a botched extra point either runs or receives a pass to complete a successful extra point, he is awarded one point.

3. SAMPLE SCORING FOR A FANTASY FOOTBALL GAME
   To better explain the scoring process of the Basic Scoring Method, let's look at two fictitious fantasy teams. You will be team #1 and I will be team #2.

   First, let's put together a scorecard listing our starting lineups. (See Detail A.)

Detail A

TEAM #1		TEAM #2	
QB	Majkowski (GB)	QB	Aikman (DALL)
RB	Settle (ATL)	RB	Bell (LARm)
RB	Harmon (BUF)	RB	Johnston (DALL)
WR	Quick (PHIL)	WR	McKinnon (CHI)
WR	Kemp (GB)	WR	Irvin (DALL)
TE	D. Johnson (LARm)	TE	Boso (CHI)
K	McFadden (ATL) ____	K	Zendejas (DALL) ____

As commissioner of a league, I have found the easiest way to tally scores is to use the following key:

A. Quarterbacks, Running Backs, Wide Receivers, and Tight Ends
   1. For each rushing or pass-receiving touchdown, a T is marked to the right of the player's team initials on the scorecard. (Remember, six points are tallied for each.)
   2. For each touchdown pass thrown, a P is marked in the same area. (Remember, three points are tallied for each.)

B. Kickers
   1. For each field goal, an F is marked, again next to a player's team initials. (Remember, three points are tallied for each.)
   2. For each extra point, an X is marked in the same area. (Remember, one point is awarded for each.)

Taking some sample box scores from actual NFL games, let's fill in our scorecard.

Looking first at your team (team #1), we will start with your quarterback, Don Majkowski of the Green Bay Packers. Using the following box score from the Packers-Bears game (see Detail B), we find that Majkowski threw two touchdown passes, one to Kemp and one to West. The box score shows him rushing for one touchdown. In our scorecard we would put one T for the rushing touchdown and two Ps for the two touchdown passes.

Detail B

BEARS 23, PACKERS 21

Green Bay   7 7 0 7-21
Chicago   7 0 7 9-23
   Chi-McKinnon 35 pass from
Tomczak (Butler kick)
   GB-Majkowski 1 run (Jacke
kick)
   GB-Kemp 31 pass from
Majkowski (Jacke kick)
   Chi-Morris 22 pass from
Tomczak (Butler kick)
   Chi-Tomczak 6 run (kick failed)
   GB-West 5 pass from
Majkowski (Jacke kick)
   Chi-FG Butler 22
   A-35,908

His score would then add up to 12 points, 6 points for the one rushing touchdown and 6 points for the two touchdown passes thrown (3 points each). Now our scorecard would look like this. (See Detail C.)

Detail C

	TEAM #1			TEAM #2	
QB	Majkowski (GB) TPP	12	QB	Aikman (DALL)	
RB	Settle (ATL)		RB	Bell (LARm)	
RB	Harmon (BUF)		RB	Johnston (DALL)	
WR	Quick (PHIL)		WR	McKinnon (CHI)	
WR	Kemp (GB)		WR	Irvin (DALL)	
TE	D. Johnson (LARm)		TE	Boso (CHI)	
K	McFadden (ATL)	──	K	Zendejas (DALL)	──

Using the following box scores, (Detail D), let's fill in the rest of our scorecard to determine a winner.

CARDINALS 31, EAGLES 7

Philadelphia	0 0 0 7- 7
Phoenix	7 7 10 7-31

Phoe-Mitchell 12 run (Del Greco kick)

Phoe-Green 10 pass from Lomax (Del Greco kick)

Phoe-FG Del Greco

Phoe-Ferrell 1 run (Del Greco kick)

Phoe-Awalt 29 pass from Lomax (Del Greco kick)

Phil-Carter 20 pass from Cunningham (Ruzek kick)

A-21,902

RAMS 24, COWBOYS 17

LA Rams	7 0 7 10-24
Dallas	0 7 3 7-17

FIRST QUARTER

LA-D. Johnson 13 pass from Everett (Lansford kick), 3:26

SECOND QUARTER

Dal-Edwards 14 pass from Aikman (Zendejas kick), 14:43

THIRD QUARTER

Dal-FG Zendejas 41, 3:00

LA-Ellard 16 pass from Everett (Lansford kick), 7:37

FOURTH QUARTER

LA-R. Brown 8 pass from Everett (Lansford kick), 1:06

LA-FG Lansford 20, 8:00

Dal-Folsom 2 pass from Aikman (Zendejas kick), 12:57

A-43,521

FALCONS 31, BILLS 14

Buffalo	0 7 0 7-14
Atlanta	3 14 7 7-31

Atl-FG McFadden 40

Atl-Heller 7 pass from Miller (McFadden kick)

Atl-Settle 10 run (McFadden kick)

Buf-Reed 13 pass from Kelly (Norwood kick)

Atl-Settle 1 run (McFadden kick)

Atl-Settle 6 pass from Miller (McFadden kick)

Buf-Lofton 28 pass from Kelly (Norwood kick)

A-31,015

BEARS 23, PACKERS 21

Green Bay	7 7 0 7-21
Chicago	7 0 7 9-23

Chi-McKinnon 35 pass from Tomczak (Butler kick)

GB-Majkowski 1 run (Jacke kick)

GB-Kemp 31 pass from Majkowski (Jacke kick)

Chi-Morris 22 pass from McMahon (Butler kick)

Chi-Tomczak 6 run (kick failed)

GB-West 5 pass from Majkowski (Jacke kick)

Chi-FG Butler 22

A-35,908

Continuing with team #1, next we evaluate John Settle of the Atlanta Falcons. Looking at the Atlanta-Buffalo game, we find that Settle ran for two touchdowns and caught a touchdown pass. In his slot on the scorecard, we would mark three Ts and give him 18 points.

Next is the other running back, Ronnie Harmon of the Buffalo Bills. Again, we would look at the Atlanta-Buffalo box score, and this time we find that Harmon failed to score. So this one is easy; just put a big zero in his results column.

Move on now to your first wide receiver, Mike Quick of the Philadelphia Eagles. Looking at the Philadelphia-Phoenix game, we find that Quick also failed to score, so again we mark a zero in the results column.

Your other wide receiver is Perry Kemp of the Green Bay Packers. This time your luck prevails as we see Kemp scored on a touchdown pass from your quarterback, Don Majkowski. Mark a T and give him six points.

Now check out Damone Johnson, the tight end of the Los Angeles Rams. Johnson scored on a touchdown pass from Jim Everett, so give him a T and six points.

Last would be Paul McFadden, kicker for the Atlanta Falcons. McFadden was successful on one field-goal attempt and four extra-point tries. Give him one F and four Xs, resulting in seven points.

Now let's take a look at my team, team #2, starting with my quarterback, Troy Aikman of the Dallas Cowboys. Looking at the Rams-Cowboys game, we can see that Aikman threw one touchdown to Steve Folsom and one to Kelvin Edwards. Give him two Ps and six points.

Next is Greg Bell of the Los Angeles Rams. Looking again at the Rams-Cowboys game, we find Bell did not score. Mark a zero in his slot.

In the Dallas-Los Angeles box score, we find that my other running back, Daryl Johnston, also failed to score, so mark zero in his slot.

Dennis McKinnon of the Chicago Bears scored once on a touchdown reception against Green Bay. Give him a T and six points.

Michael Irvin of the Dallas Cowboys failed to score in their game with the Rams. Give Irvin a big zero in his slot.

My tight end, Cap Boso of the Chicago Bears, was another one of my players who failed to score. Mark a zero in his space on the scorecard.

Lastly, my kicker, Luis Zendejas of the Cowboys, booted one field goal and had two extra points. Give him one F for the field goal and two Xs for the two extra points, totaling five points.

Now our final scorecard should look something like this. (See Detail E.)

Detail E

TEAM #1				TEAM #2	
QB	Majkowski (GB) TPP	12	QB	Aikman (DALL) PP	6
RB	Settle (ATL) TTT	18	RB	Bell (LARm)	0
RB	Harmon (BUF)	0	RB	Johnston (DALL)	0
WR	Quick (PHIL)	0	WR	McKinnon (CHI) T	6
WR	Kemp (GB) T	6	WR	Irvin (DALL)	0
TE	D. Johnson (LARm) T	6	TE	Boso (CHI)	0
K	McFadden (ATL) FXXX	7	K	Zendejas (DALL) FXX	5
		49			**17**

Congratulations on your first Fantasy Football victory!

What follows are samples of how one league's weekly score sheets may look after the conclusion of its fantasy games.

Basic Scoring Method Samples

FFL Box Scores

Tm# 3 — S & M Boys VS. Tm# 1 — Deciding Factor

S & M Boys		Pts	Deciding Factor		Pts
QB	(Phoe.) PP Lomax	6	QB	(Seat.) PP Krieg	6
RB	(T.B.) T Wilder	6	RB	(Mia.) T Smith	6
RB	(Ind.) Bentley	0	RB	(Phoe.) Mitchell	0
WR	(Dall.) Martin	0	WR	(S.F.) TT Rice	12
WR	(Ind.) Brooks	0	WR	(Seat.) Blades	6
TE	(L.A.Rm) Holohan	0	TE	(N.Y.J.) Shuler	0
K	(N.Y.G.) FXX Allegre	5	K	(Pitt.) FFXX Anderson	8
Reserves			**Reserves**		
1	(Cle.) Langhorne		1	(G.B.) Woodside	
2	(N.E.) Stephens		2	(N.O.) Martin	
3	(Phoe.) Green		3	(Pitt.) Worley	
4	(K.C.) Hayes		4	(S.D.) Early	
5	(Wash.) Clark		5	(S.D.) Bernstine	
		17			**38**

Tm# 2 — Lodi's Big Daddys VS. Tm# 4 — Mike's Marauders

Lodi's Big Daddys		Pts	Mike's Marauders		Pts
QB	(T.B.) P Testaverde	3	QB	(K.C.) De Berg	0
RB	(S.F.) TT Craig	12	RB	(Mia.) S. Smith	0
RB	(Den.) T Humphrey	6	RB	(Minn.) T Anderson	6
WR	(L.A.Rd.) T Gault	6	WR	(Seat.) Largent	0
WR	(Den.) Nattiel	0	WR	(Minn.) Jones	0
TE	(Cin.) Holman	0	TE	(Mia.) Edmunds	0
K	(Det.) XX Murray	2	K	(Atl.) FXX McFadden	5
Reserves			**Reserves**		
1	(Det.) Sanders		1	(S.D.) Anderson	
2	(N.Y.J.) Hector		2	(Minn.) Carter	
3	(Pitt.) Hoge		3	(Det.) Mandley	
4	(L.A.Rd.) Beuerlein		4	(Phoe.) Awalt	
5	(L.A.Rm.) D. Johnson		5	(Pitt.) Blackledge	
		29			**11**

Tm# 7 — Mediterranean Meatballs VS. Tm# 5 — Treanor's Electric Co

Mediterranean Meatballs		Pts	Treanor's Electric Co		Pts
QB	(L.A.Rd.) P Schroeder	3	QB	(L.A.Rm.) P Everett	3
RB	(Wash.) J. Morris	0	RB	(Ind.) Dickerson	12
RB	(Minn.) Walker	0	RB	(N.Y.J.) McNeil	0
WR	(L.A.Rd.) Gault	0	WR	(Mia.) Duper	0
WR	(N.Y.J.) Walker	0	WR	(Phil.) Quick	6
TE	(Minn.) T Jordan	6	TE	(N.Y.G.) Bavaro	6
K	(Cle.) XXXX M. Bahr	4	K	(S.D.) C. Bahr	2
Reserves			**Reserves**		
1	(N.O.) Fourcade		1	(Det.) Peete	
2	(T.B.) Hall		2	(T.B.) B. Hill	
3	(Buf.) Reed		3	(L.A.Rm.) Bell	
4	(L.A.Rm.) Delpino		4	(S.F.) Rathman	
5	(Dall.) Johnston		5	(K.C.) S. Paige	
		13			**29**

Tm# 6 — Armchair Sleepers VS. Tm# 8 — J.M.D. Warriors

Armchair Sleepers		Pts	J.M.D. Warriors		Pts
QB	(S.F.) PP Montana	6	QB	(N.Y.G.) PP Simms	6
RB	(Wash.) Byner	0	RB	(N.Y.G.) Rouson	0
RB	(Dall.) Palmer	0	RB	(L.A.Rd.) B. Jackson	0
WR	(L.A.Rm.) Anderson	0	WR	(Den.) V. Johnson	0
WR	(L.A.Rd.) Fernandez	6	WR	(N.E.) C. Jones	0
TE	(Cle.) Newsome	0	TE	(G.B.) T West	6
K	(Minn.) FXX Karlis	5	K	(S.F.) FFXXXXX Cofer	11
Reserves			**Reserves**		
1	(Den.) Elway		1	(G.B.) Sharpe	
2	(T.B.) Carrier		2	(Phil.) K. Jackson	
3	(Cle.) Mack		3	(N.Y.G.) Carthon	
4	(Phoe.) J.T. Smith		4	(N.Y.J.) Ryan	
5	(N.Y.J.) Toon		5	(Seat.) J.L. Williams	
		17			**23**

FFL STANDINGS

(Black Conference) Spade Division	Team #	Won	Lost	Tie	Points	Points Agst
Deciding Factor	1	7	4	0	314	234
Lodi's Big Daddys	2	6	5	0	241	227
S & M Boys	3	5	6	0	237	283
Mike's Marauders	4	2	9	0	205	317

Club Division	Team #	Won	Lost	Tie	Points	Points Agst
Mediterranean Meatballs	7	8	3	0	283	244
Treanor's Elec. Co.	5	7	4	0	274	247
Armchair Sleepers	6	5	6	0	231	245
J.M.D. Warriors	8	3	8	0	248	287

(Red Conference) Diamond Division	Team #	Won	Lost	Tie	Points	Points Agst
Costra Nostra	10	8	3	0	220	187
D.C. Express	11	7	4	0	285	236
F-Troop	12	5	6	0	186	224
Boyer's Spoilers	9	4	7	0	197	294

Heart Division	Team #	Won	Lost	Tie	Points	Points Agst
French Connection	13	10	1	0	329	164
Farrell's Untouchables	16	4	7	0	237	242
P.D. Destroyers	14	4	7	0	204	250
The Jayhawks	15	3	8	0	286	296

THIS WEEK'S SCORES:

Team #	3 (17)	Team #	2 (29)
Team #	1 (38)	Team #	4 (11)
Team #	5 (29)	Team #	8 (23)
Team #	7 (13)	Team #	6 (17)
Team #	11 (30)	Team #10	(18)
Team #	9 (9)	Team #12	(5)
Team #	13 (28)	Team #14	(16)
Team #	15 (14)	Team #16	(8)

THIS WEEK'S TRANSACTIONS:

Tm#		Dropped/Tm-Pos	Acquired/Tm-Pos
1	5	Byars Phil RB	Bell LARm RB
2	7	Lewis Minn. WR	Reed Buf. WR
3	16	T. Johnson Det WR	Stradford Mia RB
4	12	Beach Ind. TE	Egu NE RB
5	13	Cox LARm WR	Kemp GB WR
6	—		
7	—		
8	—		
9	—		
10	—		

THE PERFORMANCE POINT METHOD

The Performance Point Method is a tabulation of scoring based on a player's game performance, not including touchdowns. This method includes each player's yardage performances. It differs from the Basic Scoring Method in that less luck is involved in winning. In the Basic Scoring Method a player may rush for 120 yards in a game, but every time his team gets close to the goal line, someone else is called on to score the touchdown, leaving the player who rushed for 120 yards unrewarded for his performance. The Performance Point Method of scoring, however, looks only at a player's yardage performance and, although the final scores are not typical football scores as in the Basic Method, it is an interesting way to play the game of Fantasy Football. Let's take a look at this method of scoring.

1. SCORING TABULATION BY POSITION
   The following is the scoring breakdown by each position:
   A. Quarterbacks, Running Backs, Wide Receivers, Tight Ends, Kickers
      1. These players are awarded one point for every 20 yards passing.
      2. These players are awarded one point for every 10 yards rushing.
      3. These players are awarded one point for every 10 yards pass receiving.
      4. No players will have points deducted for having negative yardage in a game. That is, if a player has two rushes that account for minus 12 yards, he is not penalized one point.
      5. You must tabulate the passing, rushing, and pass-receiving scores separately. For instance, if a quarterback passes for 300 yards and rushes for 29 yards, you cannot add the yardage together. You would just award him 15 points for his passing yardage and then 2 more points for his rushing yardage, giving him 17 total points.

      This also applies to the rushing and pass-receiving yardage of a running back or wide receiver. If, for example, a running back rushes 97 yards and catches passes for 24 pass-receiving yards, you can't add the yardage together in awarding him points. Again, you just take his 97 rushing yards and award him nine points and then take his 24 pass-receiving yards and award him two more points. This would give him a total of 11 points.

Passing Yardage

0— 19 yards	0 points
20— 39 yards	1 point
40— 59 yards	2 points
60— 79 yards	3 points
80— 99 yards	4 points
100—119 yards	5 points
120—139 yards	6 points
140—159 yards	7 points
160—179 yards	8 points
180—199 yards	9 points
200—219 yards	10 points

And so on

Rushing Yardage

0— 9 yards	0 points
10— 19 yards	1 point
20— 29 yards	2 points
30— 39 yards	3 points
40— 49 yards	4 points
50— 59 yards	5 points
60— 69 yards	6 points
70— 79 yards	7 points
80— 89 yards	8 points
90— 99 yards	9 points
100—109 yards	10 points

And so on

Pass-Receiving Yardage

0— 9 yards	0 points
10— 19 yards	1 point
20— 29 yards	2 points
30— 39 yards	3 points
40— 49 yards	4 points
50— 59 yards	5 points
60— 69 yards	6 points
70— 79 yards	7 points
80— 89 yards	8 points
90— 99 yards	9 points
100—109 yards	10 points

And so on

B. Kickers

   Points awarded are the same as in the Basic Scoring Method, except when a kicker for some reason would carry the ball and pick up yardage.

   1. Three points are awarded for each field goal.
   2. One point is awarded for each extra point.
   3. If a kicker rushes for yardage on a blocked kick, for example, he is awarded rushing points for the amount of yardage gained. Or if he completes a pass, he again is awarded the passing points for the yardage gained.

2. SAMPLE SCORING FOR A FANTASY FOOTBALL GAME

The following key will help you in logging each player's scoring results:

A. Quarterbacks, Running Backs, Wide Receivers, Tight Ends

   1. For passing yardage, mark a P followed by a comma, and then the number of points associated with that player's passing results. Then put parentheses around that group. For example, (P,14) would show that a player threw for between 280 and 299 yards. He receives 1 point for every 20 yards, giving him 14 passing points.
   2. For rushing yardage, mark an R, again followed by a comma, and then the number of points associated with that player's rushing results. Then put parentheses around that group. For example, (R,9) would show that the player rushed for between 90 and 99 yards. He received one point for every 10 yards, giving him nine rushing points.
   3. For pass-receiving yardage, mark a P with a small r, followed by a comma and the number of points associated with that player's pass-receiving results. Then put parentheses around that group. The notation (Pr,6) would show that the player had caught passes resulting in between 60 and 69 yards. He received one point for every 10 yards, giving him six pass-receiving points.

B. Kickers

   1. For each field goal, mark an F (three points for each).
   2. For each extra point, mark an X (one point for each).
   3. If a kicker is involved in any play where he may have passed for more than 20 yards or rushed or caught a pass amounting to more than 10 yards, the appropriate number of points previously explained applies.

To explain better and demonstrate the scoring process of the Performance Point Method, we will again set up two fictitious fantasy teams. Use the following lineups in Detail F and the box scores shown in Detail G to figure out the score between team #5 and team #6.

Detail F

TEAM #5		TEAM #6	
QB	Schroeder (LARd)	QB	Krieg (SEAT)
RB	Sanders (DET)	RB	Spencer (SD)
RB	Hoge (PITT)	RB	Allen (LARd)
WR	Fernandez (LARd)	WR	Morgan (NE)
WR	Largent (SEAT)	WR	R. Johnson (DET)
TE	Sievers (NE)	TE	Newsome (CLE)
K	Jaeger (LARd)	K	Murray (DET)

Detail G

LIONS 23, BUCS 20

Tampa Bay	7 6 0 7-20
Detroit	8 10 3 10-23

TB-Hall 4 pass from Testaverde (Igwebuike kick)
Det-Sanders 3 run (Murray kick)
Det-FG Murray 34
TB-Wilder 29 pass from Testaverde (kick failed)
Det-FG Murray 36
Det-FG Murray 38
Det-R. Johnson 6 pass from Peete (Murray kick)
TB-B. Hill 29 pass from Testaverde (Igwebuike kick)
A-54,133
INDIVIDUAL STATISTICS
RUSHING—Tampa Bay, Wilder 23-44, Tate 11-63. Detroit, Sanders 15-56, Peete 2-20.
PASSING—Tampa Bay, Testaverde 28-42-1-373. Detroit, Peete 19-25-0-180,
RECEIVING—Tampa Bay, Wilder 8-136, Carrier 8-67, B. Hill 5-82, Hall 3-49, Tate 4-39, Detroit, Sanders 5-81 R. Johnson 4-46, Clark 2-21
MISSED FIELD GOALS— Tampa Bay, Igwebuike 29. Detroit, Murray 55.

RAIDERS 30, CHARGERS 14

San Diego	7 0 7 0-14
LA Raiders	7 6 3 14-30

SD-Miller 40 pass from Tolliver (Bahr kick)
LA-Allen 8 run (Jaeger kick)
LA-FG Jaeger 21
LA-FG Jaeger 32
LA-FG Jaeger 28
SD-Spencer 2 run (Bahr kick)
LA-Fernandez 4 pass from Schroeder (Jaeger kick)
LA-Allen 5 run (Jaeger kick)
A-57, 325
INDIVIDUAL STATISTICS
RUSHING—San Diego, Spencer 18-78, Butts 3-5. Los Angeles, Allen 16-72, B. Jackson 11-36, Fernandez 1-20
PASSING—San Diego, Tolliver 20-36-1-236. Los Angeles, Schroeder 21-30-1-332.
RECEIVING—San Diego, Spencer 5-43, Butts 5-40, Early 3-41, Miller 7-112, Los Angeles, Gault 8-134, Fernandez 6-93, Allen 5-49, Dyal 3-54.
MISSED FIELD GOALS— None.

BROWNS 30, STEELERS 17

| Pittsburgh | 3 7 0 7-17 |
| Cleveland | 9 14 7 0-30 |

Pit-FG Anderson 34
Cle-Langhorne 64 pass from
Kosar (kick failed)
Cle-FG Bahr 30
Cle-Tennell 3 pass from Kosar
(Bahr kick)
Pit-Brister 3 run (Anderson kick)
Cle-Brennan 4 pass from
Kosar (Bahr kick)
Cle-Tennell 1 pass from Kosar
(Bahr kick)
Pit-Hoge 2 pass from
Brister (Anderson kick)
A-72,313
INDIVIDUAL STATISTICS
RUSHING—Pittsburgh, 6-40,
Worley 6-40, Brister 4-29,
Cleveland, Metcalf 12-66, Mack 15-43, Kosar
2-(minus 2).
PASSING—Pittsburgh, Brister
14-33-2-202.
Cleveland, Kosar 14-22-0-199.
RECEIVING—Pittsburgh, Lipps 5-66,
Hoge 1-9, D. Hill 4-96.
Cleveland, Newsome 4-30, Brennan
3-45, Langhorne 1-64, Slaughter 2-4,
Metcalf 1-33, Mack 2-16.

SEAHAWKS 24, PATRIOTS 6

| New England | 0 6 0 0 - 6 |
| Seattle | 3 7 7 7-24 |

Sea-FG N. Johnson 29
Sea-Largent 46 pass from
Krieg (N. Johnson kick)
NE-Sievers 33 pass from Wilson
(kick failed)
Sea-Williams 16 pass from
Krieg (N. Johnson kick)
Sea-Krieg 2 run (N. Johnson kick)
A-59,688
INDIVIDUAL STATISTICS
RUSHING—New England, Stephens
12-48, Perryman 3-10,
Wilson 2-4. Seattle, Warner 26-116,
Williams 3-14, Krieg 2-11.
PASSING—New England, Wilson
10-22-1-104, Grogan 6-14-1-72.
Seattle, Krieg 13-21-0-230.
RECEIVING—New England, Morgan
4-37, C. Jones 4-36, Sievers 3-52,
Stephens 2-14, Fryar 1-10.
Seattle, Largent 7-133, Blades 2-62,
Williams 2-23, R. Morris 1-3.
MISSED FIELD GOALS—
Seattle, N. Johnson 25.

Starting with team #5, let's take a look at quarterback Jay Schroeder of the Los Angeles Raiders. First, in looking at his passing stats, we find he completed 21 of 30 passes for 332 yards. In our scorecard, we would mark a P followed by a comma and then a 16, representing 1 point for every 20 yards he gained passing. Then we would look at both the rushing and pass-receiving stats to see if he had any additional points. As we can see, he didn't. Let's take a look at our scorecard with Schroeder's stats logged in. (See Detail H.)

Detail H

TEAM #5		TEAM #6	
QB	Schroeder (LARd) (P,16)	QB	Krieg (SEAT)
RB	Sanders (DET)	RB	Spencer (SD)
RB	Hoge (PITT)	RB	Allen (LARd)
WR	Fernandez (LARd)	WR	Morgan (NE)
WR	Largent (SEAT)	WR	R. Johnson (DET)
TE	Sievers (NE)	TE	Newsome (CLE)
K	Jaeger (LARd)	K	Murray (DET)

Continuing with team #5, we look at Barry Sanders, running back of the Detroit Lions. Of course, with a running back we first look at the rushing and pass-receiving stats for his point total, but don't forget to look at the passing stats in the event he may have thrown an option pass. We find Sanders had 15 carries for 56 yards and 5 receptions for 81 yards. In his slot on the scorecard we would mark (R,5) for his rushing stats and (Pr,8) for his pass-receiving yardage, totaling 13 points.

Then move on to Merril Hoge of the Pittsburgh Steelers. We find Hoge rushing six times for 40 yards, and catching one pass for 9 yards. In his slot we would mark only (R,4), representing his rushing yardage, because his nine yards of pass-receiving yardage is not enough to qualify him for any pass-receiving points. His total points therefore would be only four.

Mervyn Fernandez of the Los Angeles Raiders is next. Looking at the pass-receiving stats first, we find he caught six passes for 93 yards, shown as (Pr,9) but he also carried the ball once for 20 yards, shown as (R,2). This would give him 11 points for his performance.

Now let's look at Steve Largent of the Seattle Seahawks. Largent appears only in the pass-receiving stats, where we see he caught 7 passes for 133 yards, shown as (Pr,13), totaling 13 points.

On to Eric Sievers, tight end of the New England Patriots. Again, Sievers appears only in the pass-receiving stats, where we find he caught three passes for 52 yards, shown as (Pr,5), totaling five points.

Team #5's kicker is Jeff Jaeger of the Los Angeles Raiders. Just to make sure, we check the passing, rushing, and pass-receiving stats and find he gained no yardage. Now, looking at the scoring stats, we find he kicked three field goals and three extra points, shown as FFFXXX, totaling 12 points.

Now let's go on to team #6. First we will look at the quarterback, Dave Krieg of the Seattle Seahawks. Looking first at his passing stats, we find he was 13 of 21 for 230 yards, shown as (P,11). We also find under the rushing stats that he had two rushes for 11 yards, shown as (R,1). Combining the two, we would give him 12 total points.

Move on to Tim Spencer of the San Diego Chargers. In the rushing stats, we find he had 18 rushes for 78 yards, shown as (R,7). In the pass-receiving stats, we find he had five catches for 43 yards, shown as (Pr,4). Again, combining the two, we would total 11 points.

Next would be Marcus Allen of the Los Angeles Raiders. Looking at the rushing stats, we find he rushed 16 times for 72 yards, shown as (R,7), and under the receiving stats, we find he caught five passes for 49 yards, shown as (Pr,4), giving him a total of 11 points.

On to Stanley Morgan, wide receiver for the New England Patriots. Morgan has only pass-receiving yardage, four catches for 37 yards, shown as (Pr,3), totaling three points.

Richard Johnson of the Detroit Lions is next. Johnson also has only pass-receiving yardage, with four receptions for 46 yards, shown as (Pr,4), totaling four points.

Now we will look at the tight end, Ozzie Newsome of the Cleveland Browns. Again, we find Newsome has only pass-receiving yardage, with four catches for 30 yards, shown as (Pr,3), totaling three points.

Lastly, the kicker is Eddie Murray of the Detroit Lions. Murray has no yardage stats, so we just have to tally his three field goals and two extra points, shown as FFFXX, totaling 11 points.

Let's check to see how our final scorecard will look. (See Detail I.)

Detail I

	TEAM #5			TEAM #6	
QB	Schroeder (LARd) (P,16)	16	QB	Krieg (SEAT) (P,11) (R,1)	12
RB	Sanders (DET) (R,5) (Pr,8)	13	RB	Spencer (SD) (R,7) (Pr,4)	11
RB	Hoge (PITT) (R,4)	4	RB	Allen (LARd) (R,7) (Pr,4)	11
WR	Fernandez (LARd) (Pr,9) (R,2)	11	WR	Morgan (NE) (Pr,3)	3
WR	Largent (SEAT) (Pr,13)	13	WR	R. Johnson (DET) (Pr,4)	4
TE	Sievers (NE) (Pr,5)	5	TE	Newsome (CLE) (Pr,3)	3
K	Jaeger (LARd) FFFXXX	12	K	Murray (DET) FFFXX	11
		74			55

We can see by this final score that typical football scores are rare, but the Performance Point Method can be a very interesting way to play the game.

What follows are samples of how one league's weekly score sheets may look after the completion of its fantasy games.

Performance Point Method Samples

FFL BOX SCORES

Tm# 3 — S & M Boys VS. Tm# 1 — Deciding Factor

Pos	S & M Boys (team)	Pts		Pos	Deciding Factor (team)	Pts
QB	Lomax (Phoe.) P,19	19		QB	Krieg (Seat.) P,7	7
RB	Wilder (T.B.) R,9	9		RB	Smith (Mia.)	0
RB	Bentley (Ind.) R,1	1		RB	Mitchell (Phoe.)	0
WR	Martin (Dall.) Pr,3	3		WR	Rice (S.F.) Pr,10	10
WR	Brooks (Ind.) Pr,1	1		WR	Blades (Seat.) Pr,6	6
TE	Holohan (L.A.Rm.)	0		TE	Shuler (N.Y.J.) Pr,5	5
K	Allegre (N.Y.G.) FXX	5		K	Anderson (Pitt.) FFXX	8
Reserves				**Reserves**		
1	Langhorne (Cle.)			1	Woodside (G.B.)	
2	Stephens (N.E.)			2	Martin (N.O.)	
3	Green (Phoe.)			3	Worley (Pitt.)	
4	Hayes (K.C.)			4	Early (S.D.)	
5	Clark (Wash.)			5	Bernstine (S.D.)	
		38				**36**

Tm# 2 — Lodi's Big Daddys VS. Tm# 4 — Mike's Marauders

Pos	Lodi's Big Daddys (team)	Pts		Pos	Mike's Marauders (team)	Pts
QB	Testaverde (T.B.) P,11	11		QB	De Berg (K.C.)	0
RB	Craig (S.F.) R,4 Pr,4	8		RB	S Smith (Mia.)	0
RB	Humphrey (Den.) R,3 Pr,1	4		RB	Anderson (Minn.) Pr,2 R,2	4
WR	Gault (L.A.Rd.) Pr,11	11		WR	Largent (Seat.)	0
WR	Nattiel (Den.) Pr,5	5		WR	Jones (Minn.) Pr,4	4
TE	Holman (Cin.) Pr,3	3		TE	Edmunds (Mia.) Pr,2	2
K	Murray (Det.) XX	2		K	McFadden (Atl.) FXX	5
Reserves				**Reserves**		
1	Sanders (Det.)			1	Anderson (S.D.)	
2	Hector (N.Y.J.)			2	Carter (Minn.)	
3	Hoge (Pitt.)			3	Mandley (Det.)	
4	Beuerlein (L.A.Rd.)			4	Awalt (Phoe.)	
5	D. Johnson (L.A.Rd.)			5	Blackledge (Pitt.)	
		44				**15**

Tm# 7 — Mediterranean Meatballs VS. Tm# 5 — Treanor's Electric Co

Pos	Mediterranean Meatballs (team)	Pts		Pos	Treanor's Electric Co (team)	Pts
QB	Schroeder (L.A.Rd.) P,8	8		QB	Everett (L.A.Rm.) P,8	8
RB	J. Morris (Wash.)	0		RB	Dickerson (Ind.) R,14	14
RB	Walker (Minn.)	0		RB	McNeil (N.Y.J.)	0
WR	Gault (L.A.Rd.) Pr,1	1		WR	Duper (Mia.) Pr,2	2
WR	Walker (N.Y.J.) Pr,2	2		WR	Quick (Phil.) Pr,2	2
TE	Jordan (Minn.) Pr,1	1		TE	Bavaro (N.Y.G.) Pr,4	4
K	M. Bahr (Cle.) XXXX	4		K	C. Bahr (S.D.) XX	2
Reserves				**Reserves**		
1	Fourcade (N.O.)			1	Peete (Det.)	
2	Hall (T.B.)			2	B. Hill (T.B.)	
3	Reed (Buf.)			3	Bell (L.A.Rm.)	
4	Delpino (L.A.Rm.)			4	Rathman (S.F.)	
5	Johnston (Dall.)			5	S. Paige (K.C.)	
		16				**32**

Tm# 6 — Armchair Sleepers VS. Tm# 8 — J.M.D. Warriors

Pos	Armchair Sleepers (team)	Pts		Pos	J.M.D. Warriors (team)	Pts
QB	Montana (S.F.) P,13	13		QB	Simms (N.Y.G.) P,9	9
RB	Byner (Wash.)	0		RB	Rouson (N.Y.G.) R,4	4
RB	Palmer (Dall.) R,14	14		RB	B. Jackson (L.A.Rd.) R,6	6
WR	Anderson (L.A.Rm.) Pr,1	1		WR	V. Johnson (Den.) Pr,3	3
WR	Fernandez (L.A.Rd.) Pr,7	7		WR	C. Jones (N.E.) Pr,1	1
TE	Newsome (Cle.) Pr,5	5		TE	West (G.B.) Pr,4	4
K	Karlis (Minn.) FXX	5		K	Cofer (S.F.) FFXXXXX	11
Reserves				**Reserves**		
1	Elway (Den.)			1	Sharpe (G.B.)	
2	Carrier (T.B.)			2	K. Jackson (Phil.)	
3	Mack (Cle.)			3	Carthon (N.Y.G.)	
4	J.T. Smith (Phoe.)			4	Ryan (N.Y.J.)	
5	Toon (N.Y.J.)			5	J.L. Williams (Seat.)	
		45				**38**

FFL STANDINGS

(Black Conference)

Spade Division	Team #	Won	Lost	Tie	Points	Points Agst
Deciding Factor	1	7	4	0	432	381
Lodi's Big Daddys	2	6	5	0	421	394
S & M Boys	3	5	6	0	373	391
Mike's Marauders	4	2	9	0	307	455

Club Division	Team #	Won	Lost	Tie	Points	Points Agst
Mediterranean Meatballs	7	8	3	0	402	356
Treanor's Elec. Co.	5	7	4	0	388	344
Armchair Sleepers	6	5	6	0	351	365
J.M.D. Warriors	8	3	8	0	310	372

(Red Conference)

Diamond Division	Team #	Won	Lost	Tie	Points	Points Agst
Costra Nostra	10	8	3	0	397	336
D.C. Express	11	7	4	0	346	302
F-Troop	12	5	6	0	323	316
Boyer's Spoilers	9	4	7	0	297	345

Heart Division	Team #	Won	Lost	Tie	Points	Points Agst
French Connection	13	10	1	0	469	317
The Jayhawks	15	4	7	0	398	403
Farrell's Untouchables	16	4	7	0	367	367
P.D. Destroyers	14	3	8	0	343	377

THIS WEEK'S SCORES:

Team # 3 (38)	Team # 2 (44)
Team # 1 (36)	Team # 4 (15)
Team # 7 (16)	Team # 6 (45)
Team # 5 (32)	Team # 8 (38)
Team # 11 (45)	Team # 10 (37)
Team # 9 (44)	Team # 12 (30)
Team # 15 (48)	Team # 14 (42)
Team # 13 (52)	Team # 16 (29)

THIS WEEK'S TRANSACTIONS:

Tm#	Dropped/Tm-Pos	Acquired/Tm-Pos
1	5 Byars Phil RB	Bell LARm RB
2	7 Lewis Minn. WR	Reed Buf. WR
3	16 T. Johnson Det WR	Stradford Mia RB
4	12 Beach Ind. TE	Egu NE TE
5	13 Cox LARm WR	Kemp GB WR
6		
7		
8		
9		
10		

THE DISTANCE SCORING METHOD

The Distance Scoring Method is a tabulation of scoring that uses the yardage covered in a touchdown-scoring play to determine the number of points awarded to the player who scored. This method rewards the "big play" players, those who score on long, exciting plays, as compared to the big fullback who scores on one-yard plunges. Let's take a look at our third method of scoring.

1. SCORING TABULATION BY POSITION

    A. Quarterbacks, Running Backs, Wide Receivers, Tight Ends, Kickers

        1. The following points are awarded for touchdowns scored by either rushing or pass receiving:

Distance of TD scored	Points Awarded
1 — 9 yards	2 points
10 — 19 yards	4 points
20 — 29 yards	6 points
30 — 39 yards	8 points
40 — 49 yards	10 points
50 — 59 yards	12 points
60 — 69 yards	14 points
70 — 79 yards	16 points
80 — 89 yards	18 points
90 — 99 yards	20 points

        2. The following points are awarded for touchdown passes thrown:

Distance of TD Pass Thrown	Points Awarded
1 — 9 yards	1 point
10 — 19 yards	2 points
20 — 29 yards	3 points
30 — 39 yards	4 points
40 — 49 yards	5 points
50 — 59 yards	6 points
60 — 69 yards	7 points
70 — 79 yards	8 points
80 — 89 yards	9 points
90 — 99 yards	10 points

B. Kickers

    1. The following points are awarded for each field goal:

Distance of Field Goal	Points Awarded
1 — 9 yards	1 point
10 — 19 yards	2 points
20 — 29 yards	3 points
30 — 39 yards	4 points
40 — 49 yards	5 points
50 — 59 yards	6 points
60 — 69 yards	7 points
70 yards & over	10 points

    2. A kicker is awarded one point for each extra point.

2. SAMPLE SCORING FOR A FANTASY FOOTBALL GAME

The following key will help in logging each player's scoring results.

In the area on the scorecard following the player's team name, use the following guidelines:

A. Include with All Players

    1. For a touchdown scored by means of rushing or pass receiving, mark a T followed by a comma, then the associated number of points for the distance of the touchdown scored, and lastly surround the group with parentheses. For example, (T,8) would indicate a touchdown scored from between 30 and 39 yards out.

    2. For a touchdown pass thrown, mark a P followed by a comma, then the appropriate number of points for the distance of the touchdown pass thrown, and lastly surround the group with parentheses. For example, (P,5) would indicate a touchdown pass thrown from between 40 and 49 yards out.

B. Kickers

    1. For field goals, mark an F followed by a comma, then the associated number of points for the distance of the field goal, and lastly surround the group with parentheses. For example, (F,4) would indicate a field goal from between 30 and 39 yards out.

    2. For each successful extra point, mark an X (one point for each). As we did with both the Basic Scoring Method and the Performance Point Method, we will again set up two fictitious fantasy teams to demonstrate further the Distance Scoring Method. We will use the lineups shown in Detail J and the box scores shown in Detail K.

Detail J

TEAM #7		TEAM #8	
QB	Montana (SF)	QB	Tomczak (CHI)
RB	Craig (SF)	RB	Mitchell (PHOE)
RB	Byars (PHIL)	RB	N. Anderson (CHI)
WR	Martin (DALL)	WR	B. Hill (TB)
WR	Sharpe (GB)	WR	Green (PHOE)
TE	Awalt (PHOE)	TE	Jones (SF)
K	Cofer (SF)	K	Ruzek (PHIL)

Detail K

BEARS 23, PACKERS 21

Green Bay	7 7 0 7-21
Chicago	7 0 7 9-23

Chi-McKinnon 35 pass from Tomczak (Butler kick)
GB-Majkowski 1 run (Jacke kick)
GB-Kemp 31 pass from Majkowski (Jacke kick)
Chi-Morris 22 pass from Tomczak (Butler kick)
Chi-Tomczak 6 run (kick failed)
GB-West 5 pass from Majkowski (Jacke kick)
Chi-FG Butler 22
A-35,908

CARDINALS 31, EAGLES 7

Philadelphia	0 0 0 7- 7
Phoenix	7 7 10 7-31

Phoe-Mitchell 12 run (Del Greco kick)
Phoe-Green 10 pass from Lomax (Del Greco kick)
Phoe-FG Del Greco 28
Phoe-Ferrell 1 run (Del Greco kick)
Phoe-Awalt 29 pass from Lomax (Del Greco kick)
Phil-Carter 20 pass from Cunningham (Ruzek kick)
A-21,902

Detail K (continued)

LIONS 23, BUCS 20

Tampa Bay	7	6	0	7-20
Detroit	8	10	3	10-23

TB-Hall 4 pass from Testaverde
(Igwebuike kick)
  Det-Sanders 3 run (Murray kick)
  Det-FG Murray 34
  TB-Wilder 29 pass from Testaverde
(kick failed)
  Det-FG Murray 36
  Det-FG Murray 38
  Det-R. Johnson 6 pass from Peete
(Murray kick)
  TB-B. Hill 29 pass from Testaverde
(Igwebuike kick)
A-54,133

RAIDERS 30, CHARGERS 14

San Diego	7	0	7	0-14
LA Raiders	7	6	3	14-30

SD-Miller 40 pass from Tolliver
(Bahr kick)
  LA-Allen 8 run (Jaeger kick)
  LA-FG Jaeger 21
  LA-FG Jaeger 32
  LA-FG Jaeger 28
  SD-Spencer 2 run
(Bahr kick)
  LA-Fernandez 4 pass from Schroeder
(Jaeger kick)
  LA-Allen 5 run (Jaeger kick)
  A-57,325

49ers 42, COWBOYS 17

Dallas	3	7	0	7-17
San Francisco	21	0	7	14-42

SF-Craig 6 pass from Montana
(Cofer kick), 2:30
  SF-Taylor 56 punt return
(Cofer kick), 6:37
  Dal-FG Zendejas 47, 10:58
  SF-Rice 77 pass from Montana
(Cofer kick), 11:23
  Dal-Aikman 1 run (Zendejas kick) 6:49
  SF-Jones 18 pass from Montana
(Cofer kick), 4:40
  Dal-Martin 13 pass from Aikman
(Zendejas kick), :17
  SF-Wright 48 interception return
(Cofer kick), 4:32
SF-Craig 16 pass from Montana
(Cofer kick), 8:31
A-59,002

Beginning with team #7, we will start with the quarterback, Joe Montana of the San Francisco 49ers. Looking at the box scores from Detail K, we find that in the 49ers-Cowboys game, Montana threw four touchdown passes. The first, from six yards, is shown as (P,1). The next, from 77 yards, is shown as (P,8). The third, from 18 yards, is shown as (P,2). The last, from 16 yards, is shown as (P,2). Combining all 4 gives him 13 total points. Let's check how this would look in our scorecard. (See Detail L.)

Detail L

TEAM #7		TEAM #8	
QB	Montana (SF) (P,1) (P,8) 13	QB	Tomczak (CHI)
	(P,2) (P,2)		
RB	Craig (SF)	RB	Mitchell (PHOE)
RB	Byars (PHIL)	RB	N. Anderson (CHI)
WR	Martin (DALL)	WR	B. Hill (TB)
WR	Sharpe (GB)	WR	Green (PHOE)
TE	Awalt (PHOE)	TE	Jones (SF)
K	Cofer (SF)	K	Ruzek (PHIL)

Now let's fill in the rest of the scorecard, following the previously mentioned key.

Next for team #7 is Roger Craig, running back for the San Francisco 49ers. Looking at the box scores, we find Craig caught two touchdown passes; the first, from 6 yards, is shown as (T,2), and the other, from 16 yards, is shown as (T,4). This totals six points.

Let's move on to Keith Byars of the Philadelphia Eagles. Taking a good look at the Philadelphia-Phoenix game, we find that Byars failed to score, giving him zero points.

Okay, how about Kelvin Martin of the Dallas Cowboys? Martin did catch a Troy Aikman touchdown pass from 13 yards out, shown as (T,4), totaling four points.

Sterling Sharpe of the Green Bay Packers is the other wide receiver. Looking at the Green Bay-Chicago game, we find that Sharpe failed to score, so mark his slot with a big zero.

The tight end is Robert Awalt of the Phoenix Cardinals. In the Phoenix-Philadelphia box score, we can see Awalt scored on a 29-yard pass reception shown as (T,6), totaling six points.

Team #7's kicker is Mike Cofer of the San Francisco 49ers. In the 49ers-Cowboys box score, we find Cofer was successful on all six extra-point attempts, shown as XXXXXX, totaling six points.

Now let's look at team #8, starting with the quarterback, Mike Tomczak of the Chicago Bears. In the Chicago-Green Bay box score, we find Tomczak first threw a touchdown pass to Dennis McKinnon from 35 yards out, shown as (P,4), then threw another touchdown pass to Ron Morris from 22 yards out, shown as (P,3), and finally ran in a touchdown from 6 yards out, shown as (T,2). These all combine to make a total of nine points.

Next is Stump Mitchell of the Phoenix Cardinals. Glancing at the Phoenix-Philadelphia box score, we find Mitchell running in a 12-yard touchdown run, shown as (T,4) totaling four points.

The other running back for team #8 is Neal Anderson of the Chicago Bears. Anderson failed to score in the Chicago-Green Bay game and thus ends up with a zero in his point-results column.

Let's move on to Bruce Hill of the Tampa Bay Buccaneers. Hill, a wide receiver, scored on a 29-yard touchdown pass, shown as (T,6), to total six points.

Checking the other wide receiver, Roy Green of the Phoenix Cardinals, we find Green caught a 10-yard touchdown pass in the Philadelphia-Phoenix game, shown as (T,4), giving him four points.

Team #8's tight end is Brent Jones of the San Francisco 49ers. In studying the 49ers-Cowboys game, we find Jones was the recipient of one of the four touchdown passes thrown by Joe Montana. The 18-yard touchdown reception by Jones is shown as (T,4), giving him four points.

Last we evaluate the kicker, Roger Ruzek of the Philadelphia Eagles. Looking at the Philadelphia-Phoenix game, we find Ruzek was only able to account for one extra point and had no field goals. This would be shown as an X, totaling one point.

Let's take a look at how our final scorecard would appear. (See Detail M.)

Detail M

	TEAM #7			TEAM #8	
QB	Montana (SF) (P,1)(P,8) (P,2) (P,2)	13	QB	Tomczak (CHI) (P,4) (P,3) (T,2)	9
RB	Craig (SF) (T,2) T,4)	6	RB	Mitchell (PHOE) (T,4)	4
RB	Byars (PHIL)	0	RB	N. Anderson (CHI)	0
WR	Martin (DALL) (T,4)	4	WR	B. Hill (TB) (T,6)	6
WR	Sharpe (GB)	0	WR	Green (PHOE) (T,4)	4
TE	Awalt (PHOE) (T,6)	6	TE	Jones (SF) (T,4)	4
K	Cofer (SF) XXXXXX	6	K	Ruzek (PHIL) X	1
		35			28

What follows are samples of how one league's weekly score sheets may look after the completion of its fantasy games.

Distance Scoring Method Samples

FFL BOX SCORES

Tm# 3 — S & M Boys VS. Tm# 1 — Deciding Factor

Pos	S & M Boys			Pts		Pos	Deciding Factor			Pts
QB	Lomax (Phoe.)	P,1	P,2	3		QB	Krieg (Seat.)	P,1	P,3	4
RB	Wilder (T.B.)	T,2		2		RB	Smith (Mia.)	T,2		2
RB	Bentley (Ind.)			0		RB	Mitchell (Phoe.)			0
WR	Martin (Dall.)			0		WR	Rice (S.F.)	T,14	T,2	16
WR	Brooks (Ind.)			0		WR	Blades (Seat.)	T,6		6
TE	Holohan (L.A.Rm.)			0		TE	Shuler (N.Y.J.)			0
K	Allegre (N.Y.G.)	XXF,5		7		K	Anderson (Pitt.)	XXF,3	F,3	8
Reserves						**Reserves**				
1	Langhorne (Cle.)					1	Woodside (G.B.)			
2	Stephens (N.E.)					2	Martin (N.O.)			
3	Green (Phoe.)					3	Worley (Pitt.)			
4	Hayes (K.C.)					4	Early (S.D.)			
5	Clark (Wash.)					5	Bernstine (S.D.)			
				12						**36**

Tm# 2 — Lodi's Big Daddys VS. Tm# 4 — Mike's Marauders

Pos	Lodi's Big Daddys			Pts		Pos	Mike's Marauders			Pts
QB	Testaverde (T.B.)	P,2		2		QB	De Berg (K.C.)			0
RB	Craig (S.F.)			0		RB	S. Smith (Mia.)			0
RB	Humphrey (Den.)	T,2		2		RB	Anderson (Minn.)	T,6		6
WR	Gault (L.A.Rd.)	T,14		14		WR	Largent (Seat.)			0
WR	Nattiel (Den.)			0		WR	Jones (Minn.)			0
TE	Holman (Cin.)			0		TE	Edmunds (Mia.)			0
K	Murray (Det.)	XX		2		K	McFadden (Atl.)	XXF,3		5
Reserves						**Reserves**				
1	Sanders (Det.)					1	Anderson (S.D.)			
2	Hector (N.Y.J.)					2	Carter (Minn.)			
3	Hoge (Pitt.)					3	Mandley (Det.)			
4	Beuerlein (L.A.Rd.)					4	Awalt (Phoe.)			
5	D. Johnson (L.A.Rm.)					5	Blackledge (Pitt.)			
				20						**11**

Tm# 7 — Mediterranean Meatballs VS. Tm# 5 — Treanor's Electric Co

Pos	Mediterranean Meatballs			Pts		Pos	Treanor's Electric Co			Pts
QB	Schroeder (L.A.Rd.)	P,1		1		QB	Everett (L.A.Rm.)	P,7		7
RB	J. Morris (Wash.)			0		RB	Dickerson (Ind.)	T,2	T,2	4
RB	Walker (Minn.)			0		RB	McNeil (N.Y.J.)			0
WR	Gault (L.A.Rd.)			0		WR	Duper (Mia.)			0
WR	Walker (N.Y.J.)			0		WR	Quick (Phil.)	T,4		4
TE	Jordan (Minn.)	T,4		4		TE	Bavaro (N.Y.G.)	T,6		6
K	M. Bahr (Cle.)	XXXX		4		K	C. Bahr (S.D.)	XX		2
Reserves						**Reserves**				
1	Fourcade (N.O.)					1	Peete (Det.)			
2	Hall (T.B.)					2	B. Hill (T.B.)			
3	Reed (Buf.)					3	Bell (L.A.Rm.)			
4	Delpino (L.A.Rm.)					4	Rathman (S.F.)			
5	Johnston (Dall.)					5	S. Paige (K.C.)			
				9						**23**

Tm# 6 — Armchair Sleepers VS. Tm# 8 — J.M.D. Warriors

Pos	Armchair Sleepers			Pts		Pos	J.M.D. Warriors			Pts
QB	Montana (S.F.)	P,1	P,7	8		QB	Simms (N.Y.G.)	P,3	P,2	5
RB	Byner (Wash.)			0		RB	Rouson (N.Y.G.)			0
RB	Palmer (Dall.)			0		RB	B. Jackson (L.A.Rd.)			0
WR	Anderson (L.A.Rm.)			0		WR	V. Johnson (Den.)			0
WR	Fernandez (L.A.Rd.)	T,2		2		WR	C. Jones (N.E.)			0
TE	Newsome (Cle.)			0		TE	West (G.B.)	T,2		2
K	Karlis (Minn.)	XXF,4		6		K	Cofer (S.F.)	XXXXXF,3	F,5	13
Reserves						**Reserves**				
1	Elway (Den.)					1	Sharpe (G.B.)			
2	Carrier (T.B.)					2	K. Jackson (Phil.)			
3	Mack (Cle.)					3	Carthon (N.Y.G.)			
4	J. T. Smith (Phoe.)					4	Ryan (N.Y.J.)			
5	Toon (N.Y.J.)					5	J. L. Williams (Seat.)			
				16						**20**

FFL STANDINGS

(Black Conference) Spade Division	Team #	Won	Lost	Tie	Points	Points Agst
Deciding Factor	1	7	4	0	444	357
Lodi's Big Daddys	2	6	5	0	404	398
S & M Boys	3	5	6	0	377	374
Mike's Marauders	4	2	9	0	302	419

Club Division	Team #	Won	Lost	Tie	Points	Points Agst
Mediterranean Meatballs	7	8	3	0	396	342
Treanor's Elec. Co.	5	7	4	0	382	322
Armchair Sleepers	6	5	6	0	368	358
J.M.D. Warriors	8	3	8	0	333	372

(Red Conference) Diamond Division	Team #	Won	Lost	Tie	Points	Points Agst
Costra Nostra	10	8	3	0	387	309
D.C. Express	11	7	4	0	316	287
F-Troop	12	5	6	0	366	322
Boyer's Spoilers	9	4	7	0	342	353

Heart Division	Team #	Won	Lost	Tie	Points	Points Agst
French Connection	13	10	1	0	453	329
The Jayhawks	15	4	7	0	427	404
Farrell's Untouchables	16	4	7	0	339	345
P.D. Destroyers	14	3	8	0	326	356

THIS WEEK'S SCORES:

Team # 3 (12)	Team # 2 (20)
Team # 1 (36)	Team # 4 (11)
Team # 7 (9)	Team # 8 (20)
Team # 5 (23)	Team # 6 (16)
Team # 11 (40)	Team # 10 (12)
Team # 9 (12)	Team # 12 (7)
Team # 15 (22)	Team # 14 (16)
Team # 13 (23)	Team # 16 (8)

THIS WEEK'S TRANSACTIONS:

	Tm#	Dropped/Tm-Pos	Acquired/Tm-Pos
1	5	Byars Phil RB	Bell LARm RB
2	7	Lewis Minn. WR	Reed Buf. WR
3	16	T. Johnson Det WR	Stradford Mia RB
4	12	Beach Ind. TE	Egu NE RB
5	13	Cox LARm WR	Kemp GB WR
6			
7			
8			
9			
10			

IX
VARIATIONS ON FANTASY FOOTBALL

Up to this point, I have explained the scoring for the three most commonly used methods. Now I want to show you a few variations that some leagues use.

1. DRAFT AN NFL COACH
   Some leagues draft an NFL coach who serves as an eighth man in their lineup. If the coach of the NFL team wins his game, the fantasy team is awarded three points. Let's say you had drafted John Robinson of the Los Angeles Rams, and the Rams beat the Cowboys. Three points would have been awarded and your scorecard would have looked like this, with a W marked after Robinson's team initials to signify the win. (See Detail N.)

Detail N

	TEAM #5	
QB	Majkowski (GB) TPP	12
RB	Settle (ATL) TTT	18
RB	Harmon (BUF)	0
WR	Quick (PHIL)	0
WR	Sharpe (GB) T	6
TE	D. Johnson (LARm) T	6
K	Davis (ATL) FXXX	7
C	Robinson (LARm) W	3
		52

2. DRAFT AN NFL DEFENSE OR SPECIALTY TEAM
   In another league, team defense is used as an eighth player. That is, every franchise in the fantasy league would draft a team defense. If any member of the defensive team scores a touchdown, either by way of interception or fumble recovery, 6 points are awarded. If a team scores by means of a safety, two points are awarded.

   Let's say that you drafted the San Francisco 49ers to be your team defense. Looking at the box score in Detail O for the 49ers-Cowboys game, we find that Eric Wright of the 49ers intercepted a pass for a touchdown. This would give your team six additional points.

You will notice that Ronnie Lott ran back a punt for a touchdown. Although he is a member of the defensive team, the touchdown would not count because it was scored while he was playing on a specialty team. Only a defensive touchdown scored by a member of a defensive team by means of an interception or fumble recovery will be counted.

Detail O

49ERS 42, COWBOYS 17

Dallas   3 7 0   7-17
San Francisco   21 0 7 14-42
    SF-Craig 6 pass from Montana
(Cofer kick), 2:30
    SF-Lott 56 punt return
(Cofer kick), 6:37
    Dal-FG Zendejas 47, 10:58
    SF-Rice 77 pass from Montana
(Cofer kick), 11:23
    Dal-Aikman 1 run (Zendejas kick) 6:49
    SF-Jones 18 pass from Montana
(Cofer kick), 4:40
    Dal-Martin 13 pass from Aikman
(Zendejas kick), :17
    SF-Wright 48 interception return
(Cofer kick), 4:32
SF-Craig 16 pass from Montana
(Cofer kick), 8:31
A–59,002

Again, let's take a look at our scorecard. (See Detail P.)

Detail P

TEAM #1

QB	Majkowski (GB) TPP	12
RB	Settle (ATL) TTT	18
RB	Harmon (BUF)	0
WR	Quick (PHIL) T	0
WR	Sharpe (GB) T	6
TE	D. Johnson (LARm) T	6
K	Davis (ATL) FXXX	7
TD	49ers T	6
		55

3. TIE BREAKERS

Because the new 17-week NFL season may affect some handling procedures for transactions, please refer to the suggestions in the beginning of this chapter to see how to handle this change.

OPTION #1: Sudden-death Tie Breaker (for leagues using the Basic Scoring Method or Distance Scoring Method)
Here is where your reserves come in. In our league we have seven starters and five reserves. When it is time to call in lineups, not only do we list our seven starters, but we would also list our five reserves. This listing of our reserves would be used in the event of a tie after regulation play. If a tie exists, we would go through the reserves to break the tie. The *first* team scoring any additional points would be the winner.

The home team (as predetermined on the league schedule) is granted the first opportunity to break the tie. If the home team's first reserve scores, the game is over, using whatever number of points he scored to determine the final score. If he failed to score, we would go to the visitors' first reserve to see if he scored. If he did, his team would win the game. If both of the teams' first reserves failed to score, we would continue on to the second overtime period. Again, go to the home team's player first. If he scores, the game is over. If not, go to the visitors' second player. This would continue until the tie is finally broken or until all the reserves are used. If none of the reserves from either team can break the deadlock, then the game will be declared a tie.

★★★

Formerly, a tie could be broken by any player scoring at least one point. So most fantasy teams carried an additional kicker, which made it very easy to score, since most kickers score at least one extra point. Since a kicker in the NFL cannot kick an extra point to break a tie, why should it be allowed in Fantasy Football? Now a tie can be broken by any scoring player—except a kicker, unless he kicks a *field goal*. If he kicks seven extra points and no field goals, the tie is not broken. So, a tie may be broken in sudden death by:
1) Any player scoring a touchdown
2) Any player (usually a quarterback) throwing a touchdown pass
3) A kicker kicking a field goal (extra points cannot break a tie)
The points accumulated will be used in the standings, except that only a kicker's *field goals* would be counted.

★★★

To show how this tie breaker works, let's take a look at a game between team #3 and team #4 (see Detail Q). First we are going to assume that the score, after tallying each of the teams' starters, ended up knotted 17-17. To break the tie, we would first go to team #3, which was the predetermined home team, to see if their first reserve scored. Team #3's first reserve player is Keith Byars of the Phildelphia Eagles. Looking at the box score for the Phoenix-Philadelphia game (see Detail R), we find that Byars failed to score.

Next we jump to team #4's first reserve, who is Neil Lomax of the Phoenix Cardinals. In checking the same box score, we find that Lomax threw two touchdown passes. Lomax is credited with 6 points (three points for each touchdown pass), and thus breaks the tie. Now the final score would read team #4, 23, and team #3, 17. There is no need to continue with the rest of the reserves, once the tie is broken. Let's take a look at our final scorecard. (See Detail Q.)

Detail Q

TEAM #3		TEAM #4	
QB	6	QB	3
RB	0	RB	6
RB	0	RB	0
WR	6	WR	0
WR	0	WR	6
TE	0	TE	0
K	5	K	2
	17		17

	Reserves			Reserves	
1	Byars (PHIL)	0	1	Lomax (PHOE) PP	6
2	Anderson (MINN)		2	Quick (PHIL)	
3	Early (SD)		3	Fernandez (LARd)	
4	Mitchell (PHOE)		4	Rozier (HOUS)	
5	Taylor (SF)		5	Muster (CHI)	
		17			23

Detail R

CARDINALS 31, EAGLES 7

Philadelphia	0 0 0 7 - 7
Phoenix	7 7 10 7 -31

Phoe-Mitchell 12 run (Del Greco kick)
Phoe-Green 10 pass from Lomax
(Del Greco kick)
Phoe-FG Del Greco
Phoe-Ferrell 1 run (Del Greco kick)
Phoe-Awalt 29 pass from Lomax
(Del Greco kick)
Phil-Carter 20 pass from
Cunningham (Ruzek kick)
A-21,902

★★★

OPTION #2: Reserves Tie Breaker (for leagues using the Performance Point Scoring Method)

Because in the Performance Point Scoring Method almost every player is assured of scoring some points, a different tie-breaking method, other than sudden-death, should be used. An effective and fair method for breaking a tie is the Reserves Tie-Breaking Method, where the team whose reserves score the most points wins. If the score remains tied after adding all the reserve players from each team, then revert to sudden death to break the tie, taking the home team's first reserve first, and so on. If the score remains tied, the game then becomes a tie. This prevents any home team with a kicker as first reserve getting an automatic win. The points totaled from this tie breaker do *not* count for either team in the Points Scored column of the league standings. (See Detail S.)

★★★

Detail S

TEAM #3		TEAM #4	
QB	6	QB	3
RB	0	RB	6
RB	0	RB	0
WR	6	WR	0
WR	0	WR	6
TE	0	TE	0
K	5	K	2
	17		17

	Reserves			Reserves	
1	Byars (PHIL)	0	1	Lomax (PHOE) PP	6
2	Anderson (MINN) X	6	2	Quick (PHIL) X	6
3	Early (SD)	0	3	Fernandez (LARd)	0
4	Mitchell (PHOE) XX	12	4	Rozier (HOUS) X	6
5	Taylor (SF) X	6	5	Muster (CHI)	0
		24			18

Because team #3's reserves accounted for 24 points, compared to 18 points for team #4, team #3 is the victor. The final score remains 17-17, and team #3 gets the win. Each team receives 17 points in the standings. Remember, the additional points accumulated by the reserves are *not* added to the game's final score or the teams' yearly point totals. Reserves can accumulate a lot of points and final scores can wind up in the 70s or 80s in a tie breaker. It would be unfair to use those large totals in the league standings. This is especially true if your league's #1 tie breaker in the win-loss column is most points scored, which is true in many leagues.

4. LIFE-LONG FRANCHISES

We have found many fantasy leagues in which the teams from the previous season draft only incoming rookies. This method of playing has many positive and negative sides. On the positive side, it provides ownership like the real thing; you must build on your team each year. If you have a good young team, you may enjoy success for a number of years.

On the other hand, if you have a poor team you may not enjoy waiting for years until your rookies pan out and your franchise finally realizes success. Also, being a little biased, I don't think your fantasy draft would be as enjoyable. In our league the draft is the social event of the year. Being able to start fresh and have a shot at picking a Fantasy Bowl team is truly exciting.

5. PLAYER AUCTIONING

Another option that is used is to hold a player "auction" rather than a player draft. This is done by each franchise buying into the league for a set number of dollars. These dollars are then used to buy or payroll their teams. Let's take this by steps:

A. An order for choosing which player is to be auctioned is determined. This can be done by a draw of cards or by letting the team with the worst record from the previous year select the first player, and so on.
B. Once a player is up for auction, the bidding begins and goes around the room. For the sake of discussion, we'll establish that this league's entry fee is $100.00 per franchise. The bidding for the player on the auction block begins at $1.00. The bidding goes around the room in clockwise order, with each team having a chance to increase the bid or pass completely.
C. There is no ceiling on the player bids.
D. The bidding for players continues until each team has acquired 12 players.
E. The total cost of the 12 players must not exceed $100.00, or whatever the entry fee is.

SAMPLE OF AUCTION DRAFTING:

ROUND #1

Player Auctioned			Team #	Price
1 Woods	CIN	RB	6	$27
2 Dickerson	IND	RB	1	$31
3 Bell	LARm	RB	14	$24
4 N. Anderson	CHI	RB	2	$22
5 Warner	SEAT	RB	11	$20
6 McNeil	NYJ	RB	13	$21
7 Mitchell	PHOE	RB	5	$22
8 Humphrey	DEN	RB	7	$24
9 Sanders	DET	RB	3	$22
10 Green	PHOE	WR	16	$25
11 Marino	MIA	QB	4	$26
12 Settle	ATL	RB	9	$21
13 Esiason	CIN	QB	8	$22
14 Quick	PHIL	WR	10	$18
15 Duper	MIA	WR	15	$19
16 Montana	SF	QB	12	$22

ROUND #2

Player Auctioned			Team #	Price
1 Blades	SEAT	WR	10	$17
2 Stephens	NE	RB	8	$14
3 Clayton	MIA	WR	7	$18
4 Simms	NYG	QB	2	$15
5 G. Anderson	SD	RB	15	$18
6 Schroeder	LARd	QB	4	$20
7 Smith	MIA	RB	12	$17
8 Craig	SF	RB	4	$14
9 Tate	TB	RB	3	$16
10 Sharpe	GB	RB	13	$12
11 Rathman	SF	RB	16	$13
12 Reed	BUF	WR	1	$14
13 E. Brown	CIN	RB	6	$13
14 Hector	NYJ	RB	11	$15
15 Brooks	CIN	WR	9	$18
16 Jackson	LARd	TE	5	$19

6. PLAYOFF REDRAFT

Another twist used by some people is to redraft for their league's playoffs. The teams that make the fantasy league's playoffs will draft from the NFL playoff teams the week immediately following the end of the NFL regular season. (Four fantasy teams is a good number to have for playoff teams, keeping in mind that only 10 NFL teams advance to the playoffs, which greatly decreases the number of players from which to choose.) This twist obviously carries with it many strategies. First, the four teams that advance do not meet in head-to-head competition; rather, the winner is determined by most points accumulated by the fantasy team through the entire round of NFL playoffs. With this variation, not only do you want the better players, but you also must keep in mind that valuable players are those from teams you feel will make it beyond the first round, so that they will play in more games and have more chances to score points for you.

Here is a more detailed description of how this is done:

A. Redraft:

<u>16 Players</u>

2 quarterbacks
4 running backs
4 wide receivers
2 tight ends
2 kickers
2 team defenses

B. Player Protection:

Any fantasy team can protect up to three of its regular-season players for the playoffs.

C. Drafting Order:

After the protected players are determined by each fantasy team, a group of four player cards can be used to determine drafting order, with every round being in the reverse order of the previous round.

D. Scoring:

Quarterbacks:

3 points (TD/pass thrown)
6 points (TD/rushing)

Running Backs, Wide Receivers, & Tight Ends:

3 points (TD/pass thrown on a halfback option)
6 points (TD/rushing or receiving)
6 points (TD/rushing or receiving)

Kickers:

3 points (field goal)
1 point (extra point)

Team Defense:

6 points (interception or fumble-recovery score)
2 points (safety)
1 point (interception)
1 point (fumble recovery)

All NFL players' performances are counted until their teams are eliminated from the playoffs. The fantasy team amassing the most points through the NFL playoffs, including the Super Bowl, is declared the league's winner.

7. WEEKLY OFFICE POOLS

Some week your office may find it fun to throw in a couple of bucks and draft a fantasy team. My research found this to be very popular. Get 4 or even 10 or more football followers each to draft a team for a given weekend's slate of games. To keep it simple and fun, we suggest the following as a guide:

A. Each team selects 7 players
   - 1 Quarterback
   - 2 Running Backs
   - 3 Receivers (can be wide receivers or tight ends)
   - 1 Kicker

B. Use our Basic Scoring Method for scoring points awarded:

Quarterbacks	3 points (TD/pass thrown)
	6 points (TD/rushing)
Running Backs and Receivers	3 points (TD/pass thrown)
	6 points (TD/rushing or receiving)
Kicker	3 points (field goal)
	1 point (extra point)

C. Payoffs
   - Up to 6 teams
     - 1st Place - 75% of pot
     - 2nd Place - 25% of pot
   - 6 teams and up
     - 1st Place - 50% of pot
     - 2nd Place - 25% of pot
     - 3rd Place - 15% of pot
     - Commissioner - 10% of pot

Winners are determined by the total number of points amassed by the seven players selected by the fantasy team.

1990 NFL SCHEDULE

Because of the byes in this year's NFL schedule, we have done something a little different. To assist you in tracking which number game a particular team is playing, the game number for each team is in parentheses next to each team's name (before the first name in each pair, after the second).

WEEK # 1

(Sunday, Sept. 9)

(1) MINNESOTA at KANSAS CITY (1)
(1) PHOENIX at WASHINGTON (1)
(1) LA RAMS at GREEN BAY (1)
(1) SEATTLE at CHICAGO (1)
(1) TAMPA BAY at DETROIT (1)
(1) DENVER at LA RAIDERS (1)
(1) HOUSTON at ATLANTA (1)
(1) INDIANAPOLIS at BUFFALO (1)
(1) NY JETS at CINCINNATI (1)
(1) MIAMI at NEW ENGLAND (1)
(1) PITTSBURGH at CLEVELAND (1)
(1) SAN DIEGO at DALLAS (1)
(1) PHILADELPHIA at NY GIANTS (1)

(Monday, Sept. 10)

(1) SAN FRANCISCO at NEW ORLEANS (1)

WEEK #2

(Sunday, Sept. 16)

(2) ATLANTA at DETROIT (2)
(2) BUFFALO at MIAMI (2)
(2) CHICAGO at GREEN BAY (2)
(2) CINCINNATI at SAN DIEGO (2)
(2) CLEVELAND at NY JETS (2)
(2) NEW ENGLAND at INDIANAPOLIS (2)
(2) LA RAMS at TAMPA BAY (2)
(2) PHOENIX at PHILADELPHIA (2)
(2) NEW ORLEANS at MINNESOTA (2)
(2) NY GIANTS at DALLAS (2)
(2) LA RAIDERS at SEATTLE (2)
(2) WASHINGTON at SAN FRANCISCO (2)
(2) HOUSTON at PITTSBURGH (2)

(Monday, Sept. 17)

(2) KANSAS CITY at DENVER (2)

WEEK #3

(Sunday, Sept. 23)

(3) DALLAS at WASHINGTON (3)
(3) INDIANAPOLIS at HOUSTON (3)
(3) KANSAS CITY at GREEN BAY (3)
(3) MIAMI at NY GIANTS (3)
(3) MINNESOTA at CHICAGO (3)
(3) NEW ENGLAND at CINCINNATI (3)
(3) PHOENIX at NEW ORLEANS (3)
(3) SAN DIEGO at CLEVELAND (3)
(3) ATLANTA at SAN FRANCISCO (3)
(3) PHILADELPHIA at LA RAMS (3)
(3) PITTSBURGH at LA RAIDERS (3)
(3) SEATTLE at DENVER (3)
(3) DETROIT at TAMPA BAY (3)

(Monday, Sept. 24)

(3) BUFFALO at NY JETS (3)

WEEK #4

(Sunday, Sept. 30)

(4) DALLAS at NY GIANTS (4)
(4) DENVER at BUFFALO (4)
(4) GREEN BAY at DETROIT (4)
(4) INDIANAPOLIS at PHILADELPHIA (4)
(4) MIAMI at PITTSBURGH (4)
(4) TAMPA BAY at MINNESOTA (4)
(4) CHICAGO at LA RAIDERS (4)
(4) CLEVELAND at KANSAS CITY (4)
(4) HOUSTON at SAN DIEGO (4)
(4) NY JETS at NEW ENGLAND (4)
(4) WASHINGTON at PHOENIX (4)

(Monday, Oct. 1)

(4) CINCINNATI at SEATTLE (4)

WEEK #5

(Sunday, Oct. 7)

(5) DETROIT at MINNESOTA (5)
(5) KANSAS CITY at INDIANAPOLIS (5)
(4) NEW ORLEANS at ATLANTA (4)
(5) NY JETS at MIAMI (5)
(5) SAN DIEGO at PITTSBURGH (5)
(4) SAN FRANCISCO at HOUSTON (5)
(5) SEATTLE at NEW ENGLAND (5)
(5) TAMPA BAY at DALLAS (5)
(5) CINCINNATI at LA RAMS (4)
(5) GREEN BAY at CHICAGO (5)
(5) LA RAIDERS at BUFFALO (5)

(Monday, Oct. 8)

(5) CLEVELAND at DENVER (5)

WEEK #6

(Sunday, Oct. 14)

(6) CLEVELAND at NEW ORLEANS (5)
(6) DETROIT at KANSAS CITY (6)
(6) GREEN BAY at TAMPA BAY (6)
(6) HOUSTON at CINCINNATI (6)
(6) SAN DIEGO at NY JETS (6)
(5) SAN FRANCISCO at ATLANTA (5)
(6) DALLAS at PHOENIX (5)
(5) NY GIANTS at WASHINGTON (5)
(6) PITTSBURGH at DENVER (6)
(6) SEATTLE at LA RAIDERS (6)
(5) LA RAMS at CHICAGO (6)

(Monday, Oct. 15)

(6) MINNESOTA at PHILADELPHIA (5)

WEEK #7

(Thursday, Oct. 18)

(6) NEW ENGLAND at MIAMI (6)

(Sunday, Oct. 21)

(7) DALLAS at TAMPA BAY (7)
(7) DENVER at INDIANAPOLIS (6)
(6) NEW ORLEANS at HOUSTON (7)
(7) NY JETS at BUFFALO (6)
(6) PHILADELPHIA at WASHINGTON (6)
(6) ATLANTA at LA RAMS (6)
(7) KANSAS CITY at SEATTLE (7)
(6) PHOENIX at NY GIANTS (6)
(7) PITTSBURGH at SAN FRANCISCO (6)
(7) LA RAIDERS at SAN DIEGO (7)

(Monday, Oct. 22)

(7) CINCINNATI at CLEVELAND (7)

WEEK #8

(Sunday, Oct. 28)

(7) BUFFALO at NEW ENGLAND (7)
(7) DETROIT at NEW ORLEANS (7)
(7) MIAMI at INDIANAPOLIS (7)
(7) MINNESOTA vs GREEN BAY (Milw) (7)
(8) NY JETS at HOUSTON (8)
(7) PHILADELPHIA at DALLAS (8)
(7) CHICAGO at PHOENIX (7)
(8) CLEVELAND at SAN FRANCISCO (7)
(8) TAMPA BAY at SAN DIEGO (8)
(7) WASHINGTON at NY GIANTS (7)
(8) CINCINNATI at ATLANTA (7)

(Monday, Oct. 29)

(7) LA RAMS at PITTSBURGH (8)

WEEK #9

(Sunday, Nov. 4)

(8) ATLANTA at PITTSBURGH (9)
(8) BUFFALO at CLEVELAND (9)
(9) DALLAS at NY JETS (9)
(8) NEW ENGLAND at PHILADELPHIA (8)
(8) NEW ORLEANS at CINCINNATI (9)
(8) PHOENIX at MIAMI (8)
(8) LA RAIDERS at KANSAS CITY (8)
(8) SAN FRANCISCO at GREEN BAY (8)
(8) WASHINGTON at DETROIT (8)
(8) CHICAGO at TAMPA BAY (9)
(9) HOUSTON at LA RAMS (8)
(9) SAN DIEGO at SEATTLE (8)
(8) DENVER at MINNESOTA (8)

(Monday, Nov. 5)

(8) NY GIANTS at INDIANAPOLIS (8)

WEEK #10

(Sunday, Nov. 11)

(9) ATLANTA at CHICAGO (9)
(9) INDIANAPOLIS at NEW ENGLAND (9)
(9) MIAMI at NY JETS (10)
(9) MINNESOTA at DETROIT (9)
(9) PHOENIX at BUFFALO (9)
(9) SEATTLE at KANSAS CITY (9)
(10) TAMPA BAY at NEW ORLEANS (9)
(9) DENVER at SAN DIEGO (10)
(9) GREEN BAY at LA RAIDERS (9)
(9) NY GIANTS at LA RAMS (9)
(9) SAN FRANCISCO at DALLAS (10)

(Monday, Nov. 12)

(9) WASHINGTON at PHILADELPHIA (9)

WEEK #11

(Sunday, Nov. 18)

(10) DETROIT at NY GIANTS (10)
(10) HOUSTON at CLEVELAND (10)
(10) NEW ENGLAND at BUFFALO (10)
(10) NEW ORLEANS at WASHINGTON (10)
(10) PHILADELPHIA at ATLANTA (10)
(11) SAN DIEGO at KANSAS CITY (10)
(10) CHICAGO at DENVER (10)
(11) DALLAS at LA RAMS (10)
(10) GREEN BAY at PHOENIX (10)
(10) MINNESOTA at SEATTLE (10)
(11) NY JETS at INDIANAPOLIS (10)
(11) TAMPA BAY at SAN FRANCISCO (10)
(10) PITTSBURGH at CINCINNATI (10)

(Monday, Nov. 19)

(10) LA RAIDERS at MIAMI (10)

WEEK #12

(Thursday, Nov 22)

(11) DENVER at DETROIT (11)
(11) WASHINGTON at DALLAS (12)

(Sunday, Nov. 25)

(11) ATLANTA at NEW ORLEANS (11)
(11) CHICAGO at MINNESOTA (11)
(11) INDIANAPOLIS at CINCINNATI (11)
(11) MIAMI at CLEVELAND (11)
(11) NY GIANTS at PHILADELPHIA (11)
(12) TAMPA BAY vs GREEN BAY (Milw) (11)
(11) KANSAS CITY at LA RAIDERS (11)
(11) LA RAMS at SAN FRANCISCO (11)
(11) NEW ENGLAND at PHOENIX (11)
(11) PITTSBURGH at NY JETS (12)
(11) SEATTLE at SAN DIEGO (12)

(Monday, Nov. 26)

(11) BUFFALO at HOUSTON (11)

WEEK #13

(Sunday, Dec. 2)

(12) ATLANTA at TAMPA BAY (13)
(12) CINCINNATI at PITTSBURGH (12)
(12) DETROIT at CHICAGO (12)
(12) KANSAS CITY at NEW ENGLAND (12)
(12) LA RAMS at CLEVELAND (12)
(12) MIAMI at WASHINGTON (12)
(12) PHILADELPHIA at BUFFALO (12)
(12) HOUSTON at SEATTLE (12)
(12) INDIANAPOLIS at PHOENIX (12)
(12) LA RAIDERS at DENVER (12)
(12) NEW ORLEANS at DALLAS (13)
(13) NY JETS at SAN DIEGO (13)
(12) GREEN BAY at MINNESOTA (12)

(Monday, Dec. 3)

(12) NY GIANTS at SAN FRANCISCO (12)

WEEK #14

(Sunday, Dec. 9)

(13) BUFFALO at INDIANAPOLIS (13)
(13) CLEVELAND at HOUSTON (13)
(13) MINNESOTA at NY GIANTS (13)
(13) NEW ENGLAND at PITTSBURGH (13)
(13) PHOENIX at ATLANTA (13)
(13) SAN FRANCISCO at CINCINNATI (13)
(13) SEATTLE vs GREEN BAY (Milw) (13)
(13) CHICAGO at WASHINGTON (13)
(13) DENVER at KANSAS CITY (13)
(13) NEW ORLEANS at LA RAMS (13)
(13) PHILADELPHIA at MIAMI (13)

(Monday, Dec. 10)

(13) LA RAIDERS at DETROIT (13)

WEEK #15

(Saturday, Dec. 15)

(14) BUFFALO at NY GIANTS (14)
(14) WASHINGTON at NEW ENGLAND (14)

(Sunday, Dec. 16)

(14) ATLANTA at CLEVELAND (14)
(14) GREEN BAY at PHILADELPHIA (14)
(14) HOUSTON at KANSAS CITY (14)
(14) INDIANAPOLIS at NY JETS (14)
(14) MINNESOTA at TAMPA BAY (14)
(14) PHOENIX at DALLAS (14)
(14) PITTSBURGH at NEW ORLEANS (14)
(14) SEATTLE at MIAMI (14)
(14) CINCINNATI at LA RAIDERS (14)
(14) SAN DIEGO at DENVER (14)
(14) CHICAGO at DETROIT (14)

(Monday, Dec. 17)

(14) SAN FRANCISCO at LA RAMS (14)

WEEK #16

(Saturday, Dec 22)

(15) DETROIT at GREEN BAY (15)
(15) LA RAIDERS at MINNESOTA (15)
(15) WASHINGTON at INDIANAPOLIS (15)

(Sunday, Dec. 23)

(15) CINCINNATI at HOUSTON (15)
(15) CLEVELAND at PITTSBURGH (15)
(15) DALLAS at PHILADELPHIA (15)
(15) MIAMI at BUFFALO (15)
(15) NEW ENGLAND at NY JETS (15)
(15) LA RAMS at ATLANTA (15)
(15) TAMPA BAY at CHICAGO (15)
(15) KANSAS CITY at SAN DIEGO (15)
(15) NEW ORLEANS at SAN FRANCISCO (15)
(15) NY GIANTS at PHOENIX (15)
(15) DENVER at SEATTLE (15)

WEEK #17

(Saturday, Dec. 29)

(16) KANSAS CITY at CHICAGO (16)
(16) PHILADELPHIA at PHOENIX (16)

(Sunday, Dec. 30)

(16) BUFFALO at WASHINGTON (16)
(16) CLEVELAND at CINCINNATI (16)
(16) DALLAS at ATLANTA (16)
(16) INDIANAPOLIS at MIAMI (16)
(16) NY GIANTS at NEW ENGLAND (16)
(16) SAN FRANCISCO at MINNESOTA (16)
(16) DETROIT at SEATTLE (16)
(16) GREEN BAY at DENVER (16)
(16) NY JETS at TAMPA BAY (16)
(16) SAN DIEGO at LA RAIDERS (16)
(16) PITTSBURGH at HOUSTON (16)

(Monday, Dec. 31)

(16) LA RAMS at NEW ORLEANS (16)

KEEPING IN TOUCH

First, I would like to thank the many of you who wrote to us in 1989. We really appreciate your ideas, rule suggestions, and comments. They certainly help in each year's book and newsletter productions.

I sure hope you continue to take the time to write. Please send your letters to:

The Author
Fantasy Sports, Inc.
674 E. 6th Street
St. Paul, MN 55106